genshiken げんしけん
SECOND SEASON

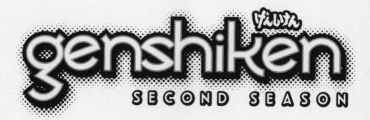

1

Shimoku Kio

Translated and adapted by
Stephen Paul

Lettered by
Aaron Alexovich

KC
KODANSHA COMICS

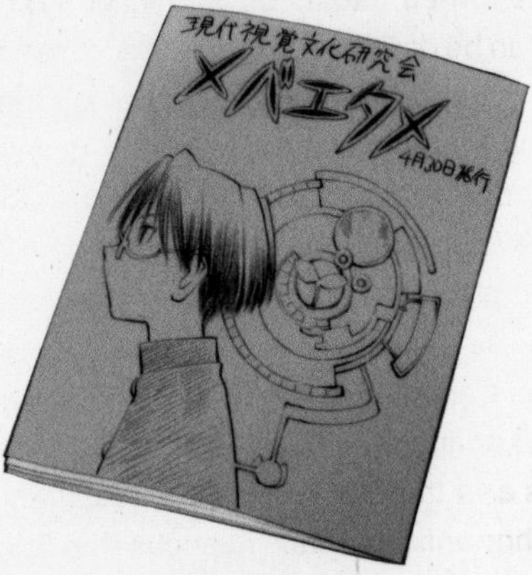
現代視覚文化研究会
4月30日発行

SOCIETY FOR THE STUDY OF
MODERN VISUAL CULTURE

MEBAETAME
APRIL 30TH

Honorifics Explained

Throughout the Kodansha Comics books, you will find Japanese honorifics left intact in the translations. For those not familiar with how the Japanese use honorifics and, more important, how they differ from American honorifics, we present this brief overview.

Politeness has always been a critical facet of Japanese culture. Ever since the feudal era, when Japan was a highly stratified society, use of honorifics—which can be defined as polite speech that indicates relationship or status—has played an essential role in the Japanese language. When addressing someone in Japanese, an honorific usually takes the form of a suffix attached to one's name (example: "Asuna-san"), is used as a title at the end of one's name, or appears in place of the name itself (example: "Negi-sensei," or simply "Sensei!").

Honorifics can be expressions of respect or endearment. In the context of manga and anime, honorifics give insight into the nature of the relationship between characters. Many English translations leave out these important honorifics and therefore distort the feel of the original Japanese. Because Japanese honorifics contain nuances that English honorifics lack, it is our policy at Kodansha Comics not to translate them. Here, instead, is a guide to some of the honorifics you may encounter in Kodansha Comics.

-san: This is the most common honorific and is equivalent to Mr., Miss, Ms., or Mrs. It is the all-purpose honorific and can be used in any situation where politeness is required.

-sama: This is one level higher than "-san" and is used to confer great respect.

-dono: This comes from the word "tono," which means "lord." It is an even higher level than "-sama" and confers utmost respect.

-kun: This suffix is used at the end of boys' names to express familiarity or endearment. It is also sometimes used by men among friends, or when addressing someone younger or of a lower station.

-chan: This is used to express endearment, mostly toward girls. It is also used for little boys, pets, and even among lovers. It gives a sense of childish cuteness.

Bozu: This is an informal way to refer to a boy, similar to the English terms "kid" and "squirt."

Sempai/
Senpai: This title suggests that the addressee is one's senior in a group or organization. It is most often used in a school setting, where underclassmen refer to their upperclassmen as "sempai." It can also be used in the workplace, such as when a newer employee addresses an employee who has seniority in the company.

Kohai: This is the opposite of "sempai" and is used toward underclassmen in school or newcomers in the workplace. It connotes that the addressee is of a lower station.

Sensei: Literally meaning "one who has come before," this title is used for teachers, doctors, or masters of any profession or art.

-[blank]: This is usually forgotten in these lists, but it is perhaps the most significant difference between Japanese and English. The lack of honorific means that the speaker has permission to address the person in a very intimate way. Usually, only family, spouses, or very close friends have this kind of permission. Known as *yobisute*, it can be gratifying when someone who has earned the intimacy starts to call one by one's name without an honorific. But when that intimacy hasn't been earned, it can be very insulting.

げんしけん
genshiken
SECOND SEASON

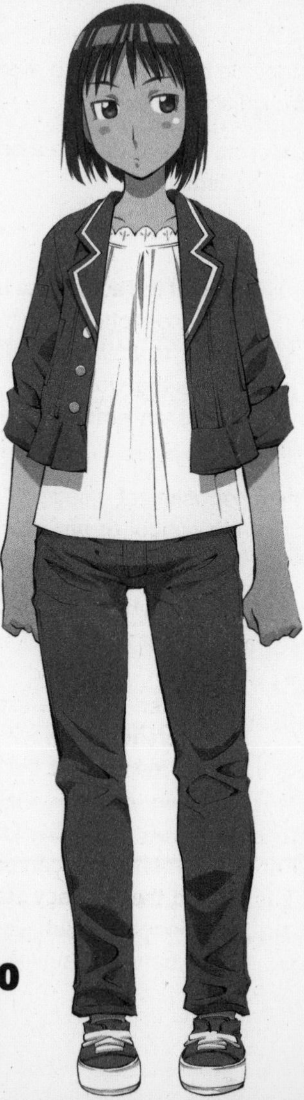

SHIMOKU KIO

genshiken
SECOND SEASON
Vol. 10
CONTENTS

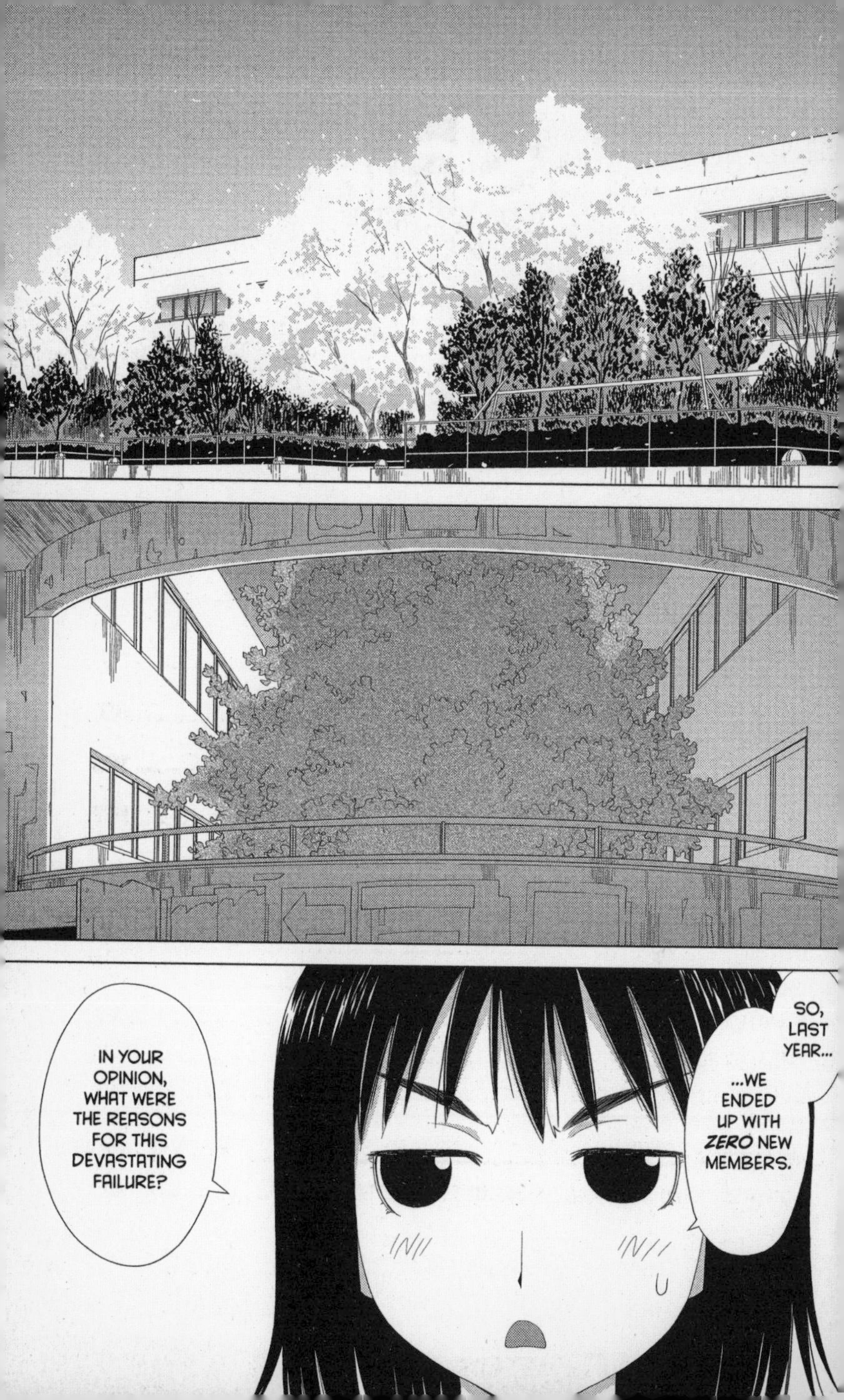
SO, LAST YEAR...
...WE ENDED UP WITH ZERO NEW MEMBERS.
IN YOUR OPINION, WHAT WERE THE REASONS FOR THIS DEVASTATING FAILURE?

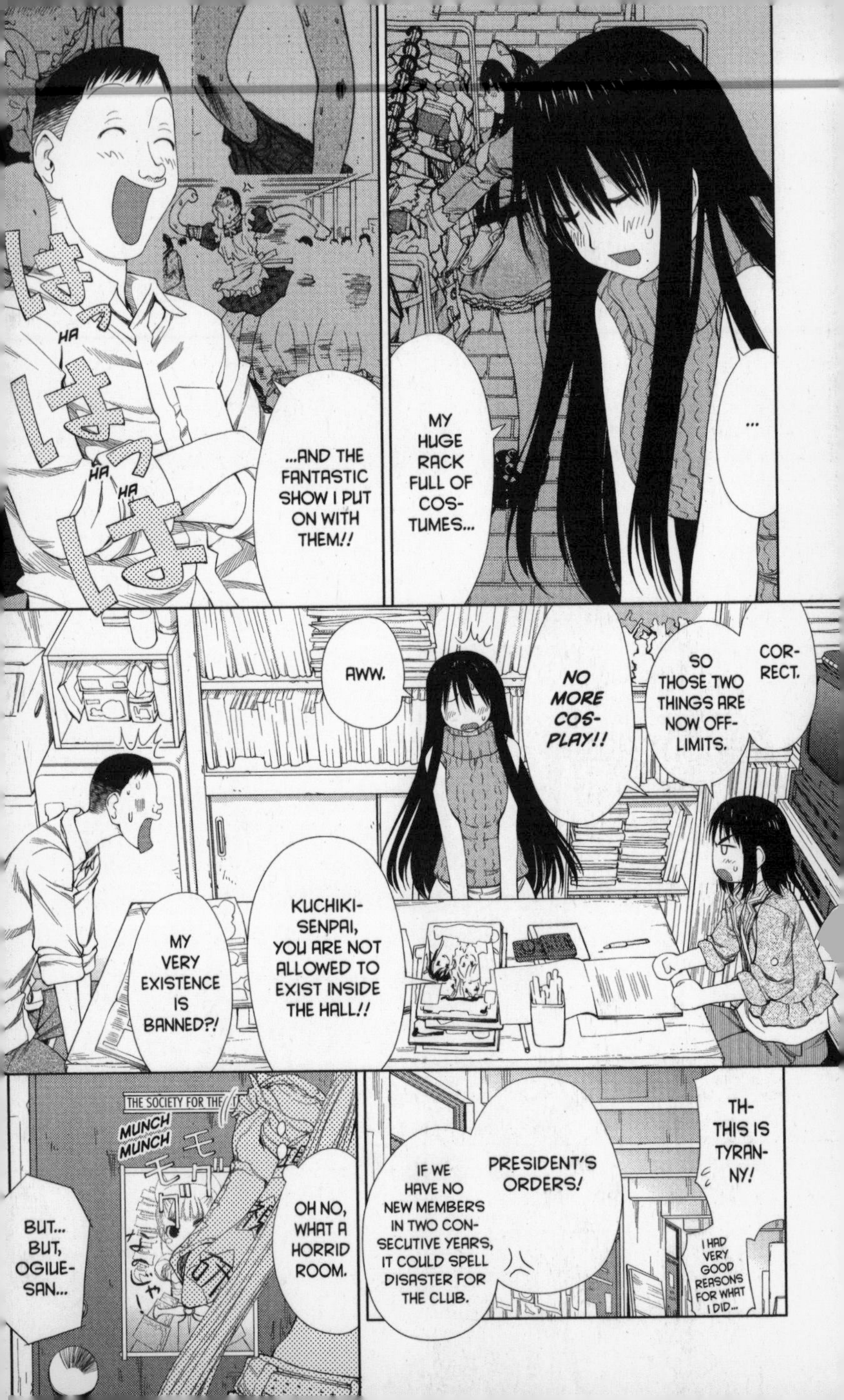
...
MY HUGE RACK FULL OF COS-TUMES...
...AND THE FANTASTIC SHOW I PUT ON WITH THEM!!
はっはっはっ
HA HA HA
COR-RECT.
SO THOSE TWO THINGS ARE NOW OFF-LIMITS.
NO MORE COS-PLAY!!
AWW.
KUCHIKI-SENPAI, YOU ARE NOT ALLOWED TO EXIST INSIDE THE HALL!!
MY VERY EXISTENCE IS BANNED?!
TH-THIS IS TYRAN-NY!
I HAD VERY GOOD REASONS FOR WHAT I DID...
PRESIDENT'S ORDERS!
IF WE HAVE NO NEW MEMBERS IN TWO CON-SECUTIVE YEARS, IT COULD SPELL DISASTER FOR THE CLUB.
OH NO, WHAT A HORRID ROOM.
THE SOCIETY FOR THE
MUNCH MUNCH
BUT... BUT, OGIUE-SAN...

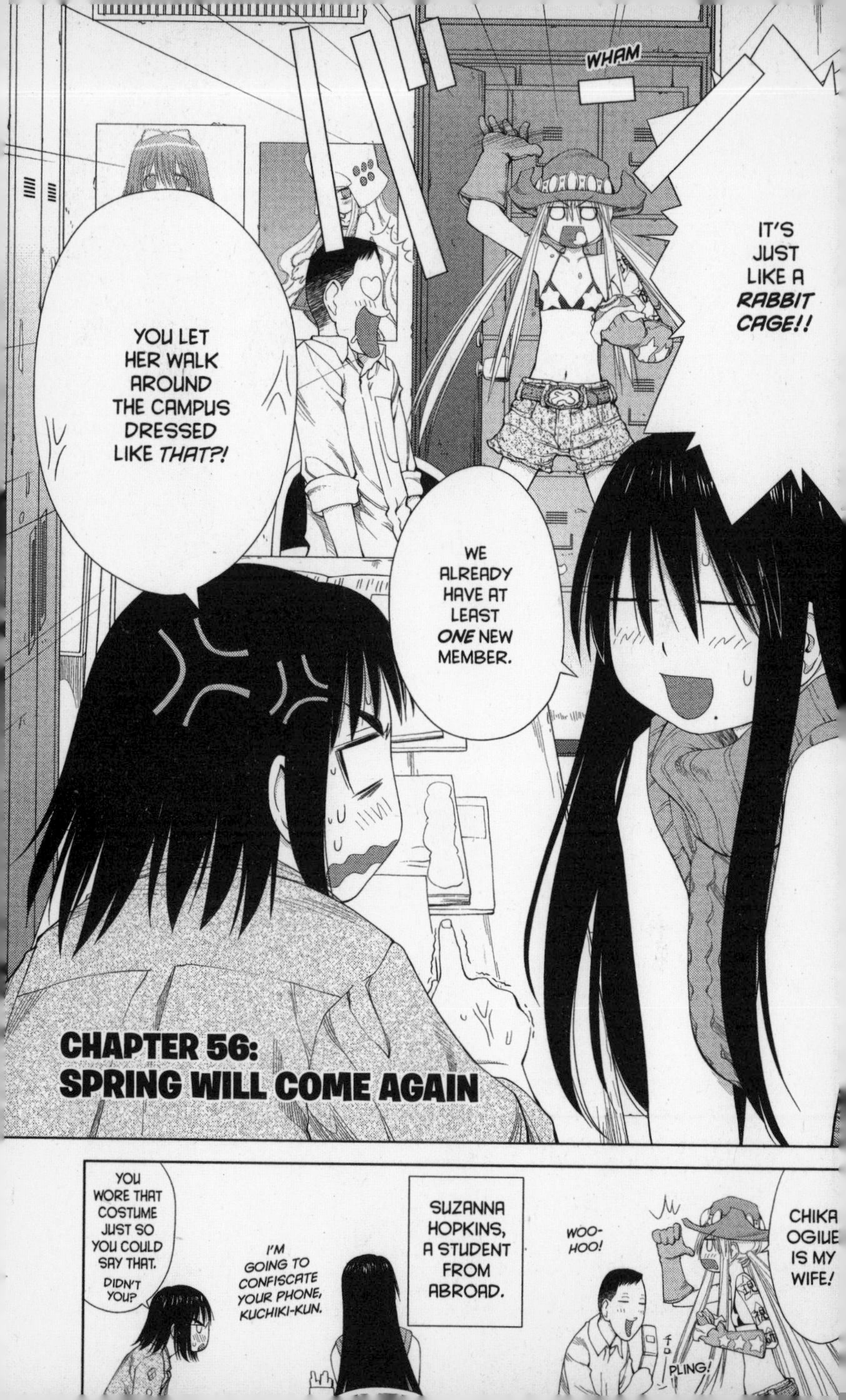
WHAM
IT'S JUST LIKE A RABBIT CAGE!!
WE ALREADY HAVE AT LEAST ONE NEW MEMBER.
YOU LET HER WALK AROUND THE CAMPUS DRESSED LIKE THAT?!
CHAPTER 56: SPRING WILL COME AGAIN
CHIKA OGIUE IS MY WIFE!
PLING!
WOO-HOO!
SUZANNA HOPKINS, A STUDENT FROM ABROAD.
I'M GOING TO CONFISCATE YOUR PHONE, KUCHIKI-KUN.
YOU WORE THAT COSTUME JUST SO YOU COULD SAY THAT.
DIDN'T YOU?

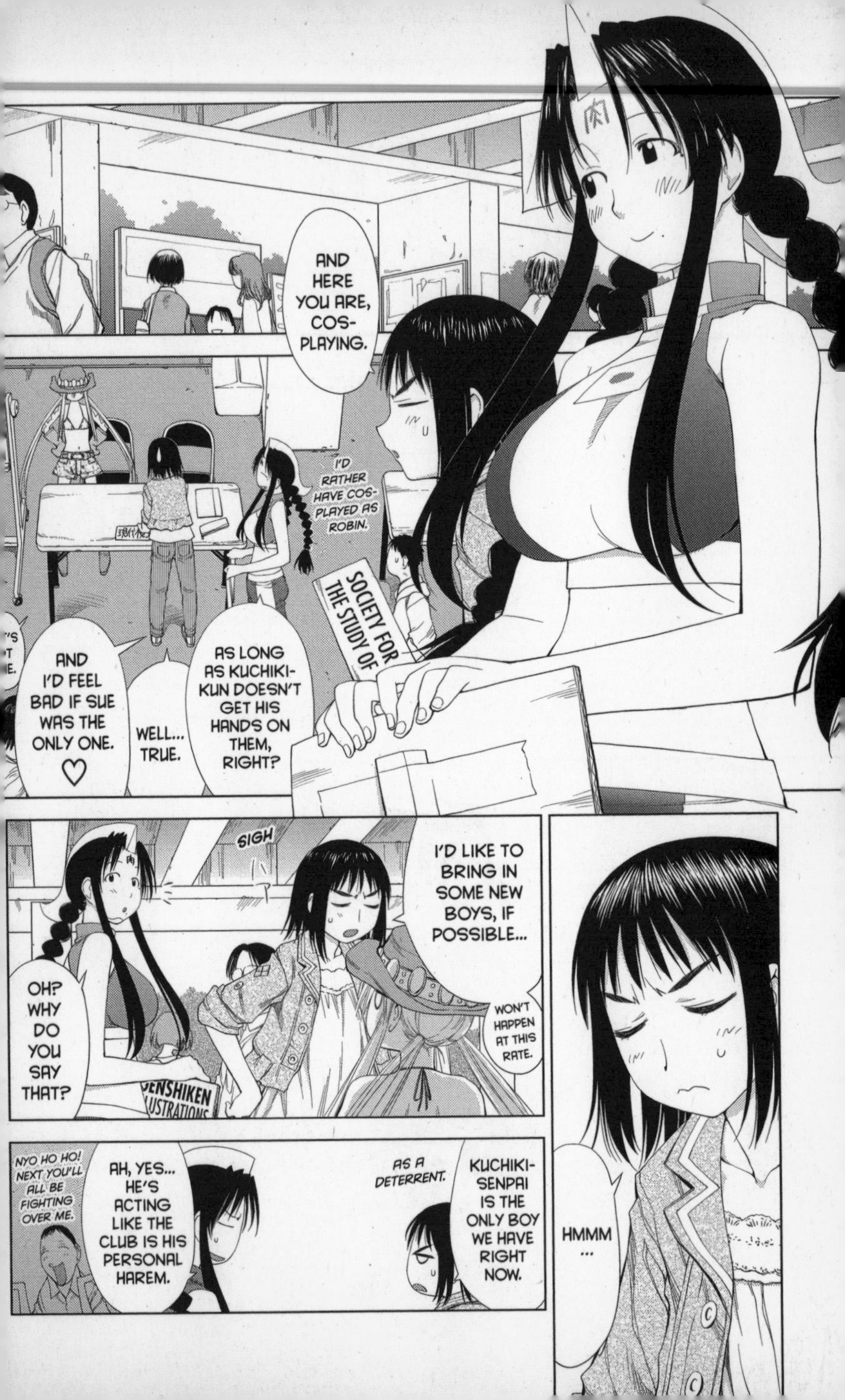
AND HERE YOU ARE, COS-PLAYING.
I'D RATHER HAVE COS-PLAYED AS ROBIN.
SOCIETY FOR THE STUDY OF
AS LONG AS KUCHIKI-KUN DOESN'T GET HIS HANDS ON THEM, RIGHT?
WELL... TRUE.
AND I'D FEEL BAD IF SUE WAS THE ONLY ONE. ♡
HMMM ...
SIGH
I'D LIKE TO BRING IN SOME NEW BOYS, IF POSSIBLE...
WON'T HAPPEN AT THIS RATE.
OH? WHY DO YOU SAY THAT?
KUCHIKI-SENPAI IS THE ONLY BOY WE HAVE RIGHT NOW.
AS A DETERRENT.
AH, YES... HE'S ACTING LIKE THE CLUB IS HIS PERSONAL HAREM.
NYO HO HO! NEXT YOU'LL ALL BE FIGHTING OVER ME.

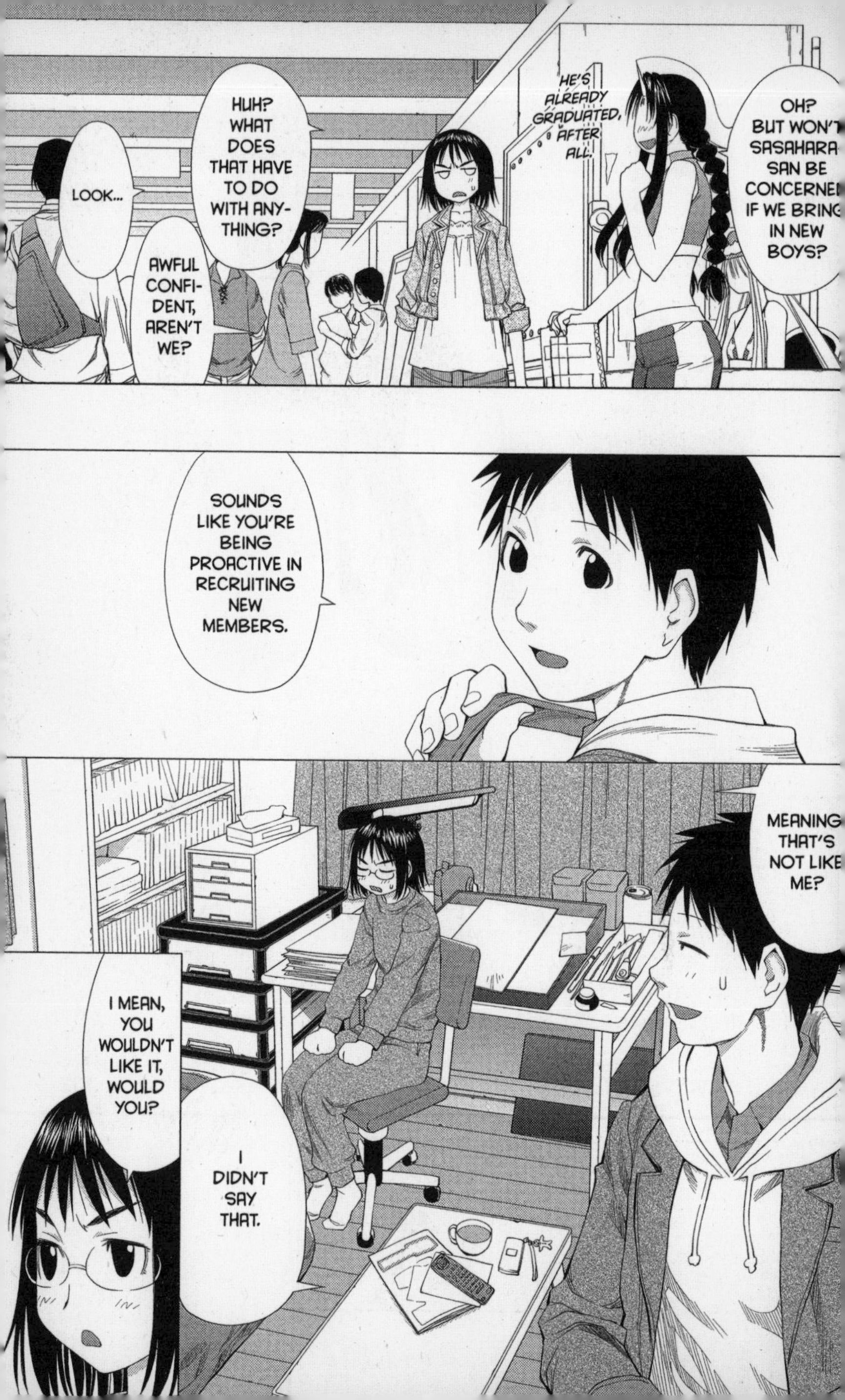
OH? BUT WON'T SASAHARA-SAN BE CONCERNE IF WE BRING IN NEW BOYS?
HE'S ALREADY GRADUATED, AFTER ALL.
HUH? WHAT DOES THAT HAVE TO DO WITH ANY-THING?
LOOK...
AWFUL CONFI-DENT, AREN'T WE?
SOUNDS LIKE YOU'RE BEING PROACTIVE IN RECRUITING NEW MEMBERS.
MEANING THAT'S NOT LIKE ME?
I MEAN, YOU WOULDN'T LIKE IT, WOULD YOU?
I DIDN'T SAY THAT.

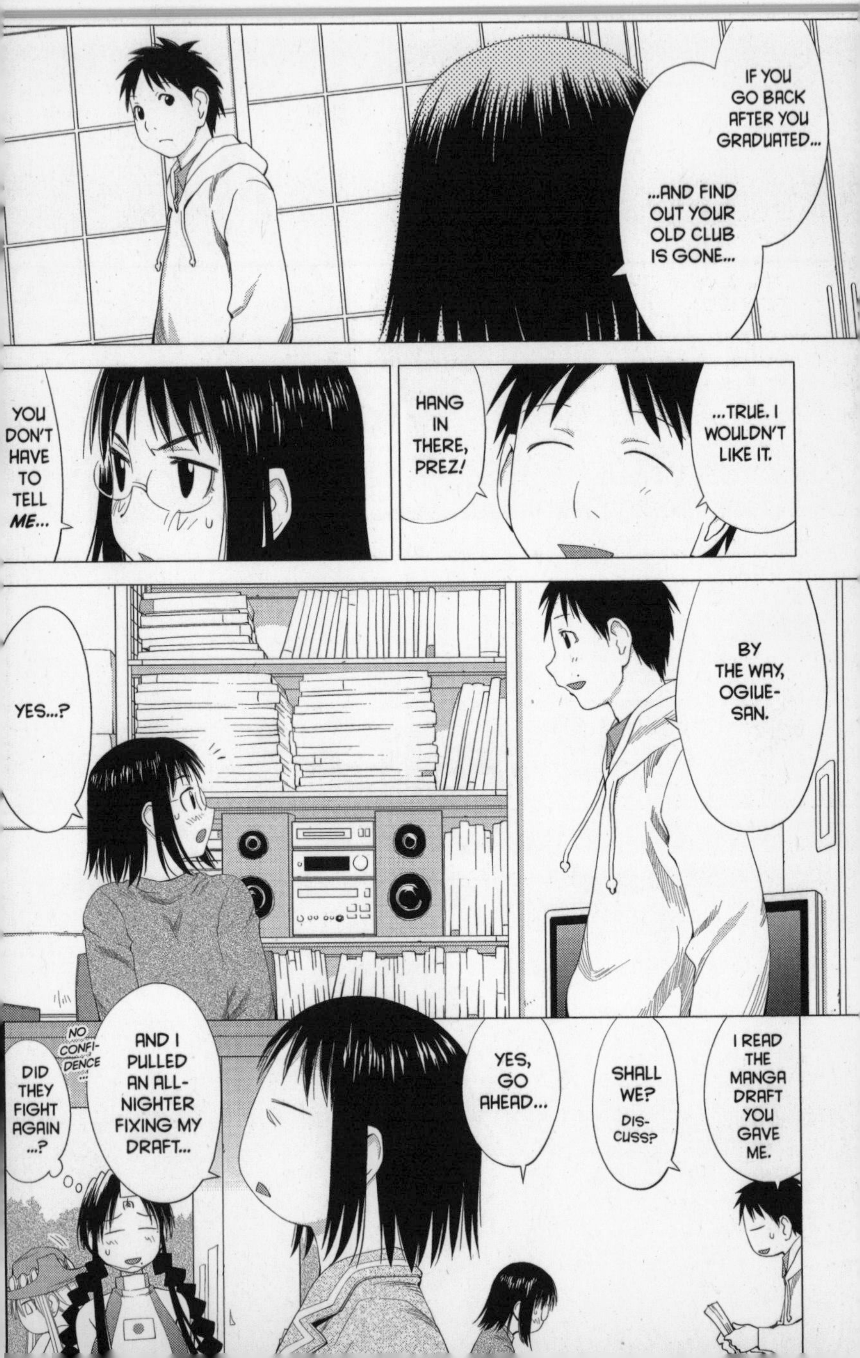
IF YOU GO BACK AFTER YOU GRADUATED...
...AND FIND OUT YOUR OLD CLUB IS GONE...
...TRUE. I WOULDN'T LIKE IT.
HANG IN THERE, PREZ!
YOU DON'T HAVE TO TELL ME...
BY THE WAY, OGIUE-SAN.
YES...?
I READ THE MANGA DRAFT YOU GAVE ME.
SHALL WE? DIS-CUSS?
YES, GO AHEAD...
AND I PULLED AN ALL-NIGHTER FIXING MY DRAFT...
NO CONFI-DENCE...
DID THEY FIGHT AGAIN...?

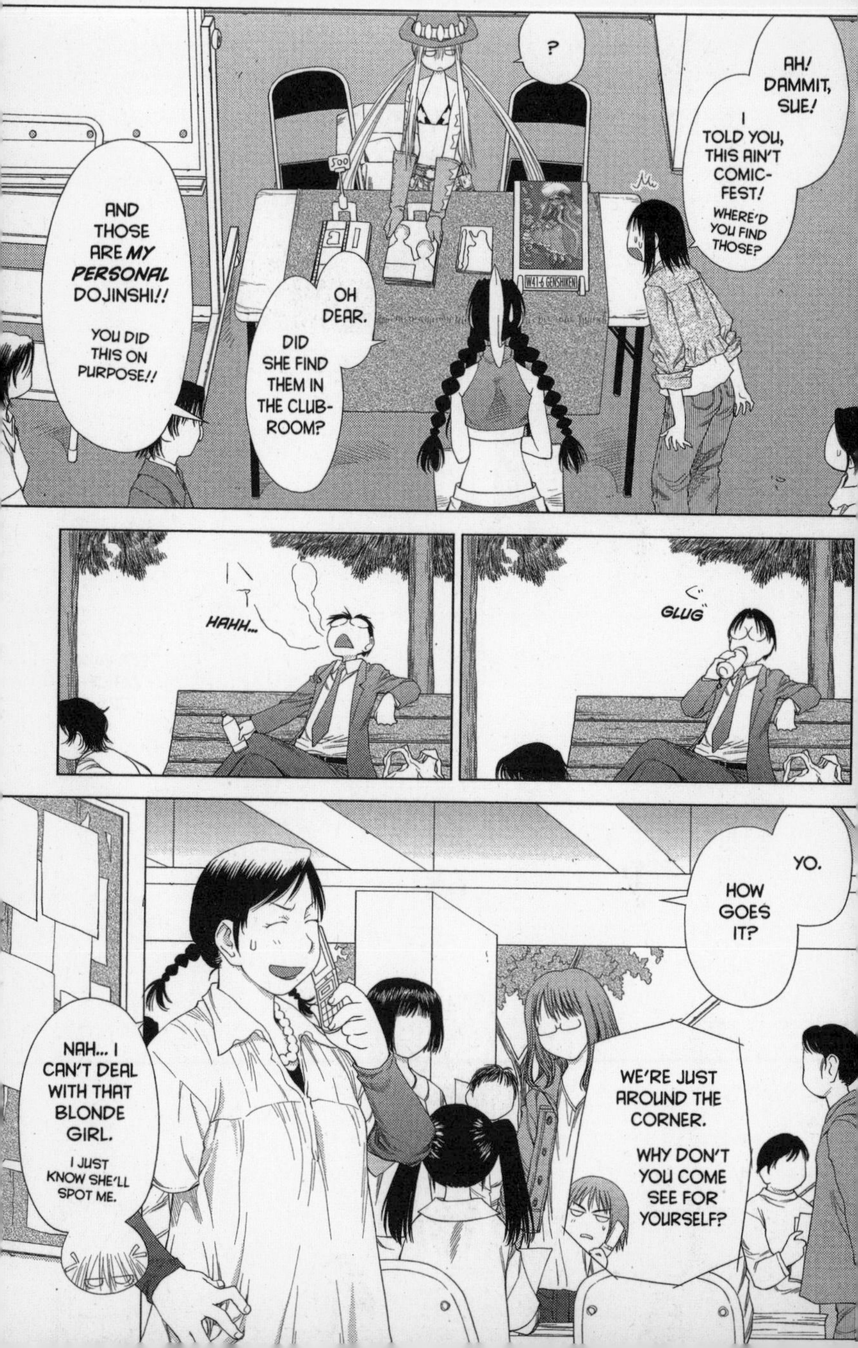
AH! DAMMIT, SUE! I TOLD YOU, THIS AIN'T COMIC-FEST!
WHERE'D YOU FIND THOSE?
?
AND THOSE ARE *MY PERSONAL* DOJINSHI!!
YOU DID THIS ON PURPOSE!!
OH DEAR.
DID SHE FIND THEM IN THE CLUB-ROOM?
500
W41-6 GENSHIKEN
GLUG
HAHH...
YO.
HOW GOES IT?
WE'RE JUST AROUND THE CORNER.
WHY DON'T YOU COME SEE FOR YOURSELF?
NAH... I CAN'T DEAL WITH THAT BLONDE GIRL.
I JUST KNOW SHE'LL SPOT ME.

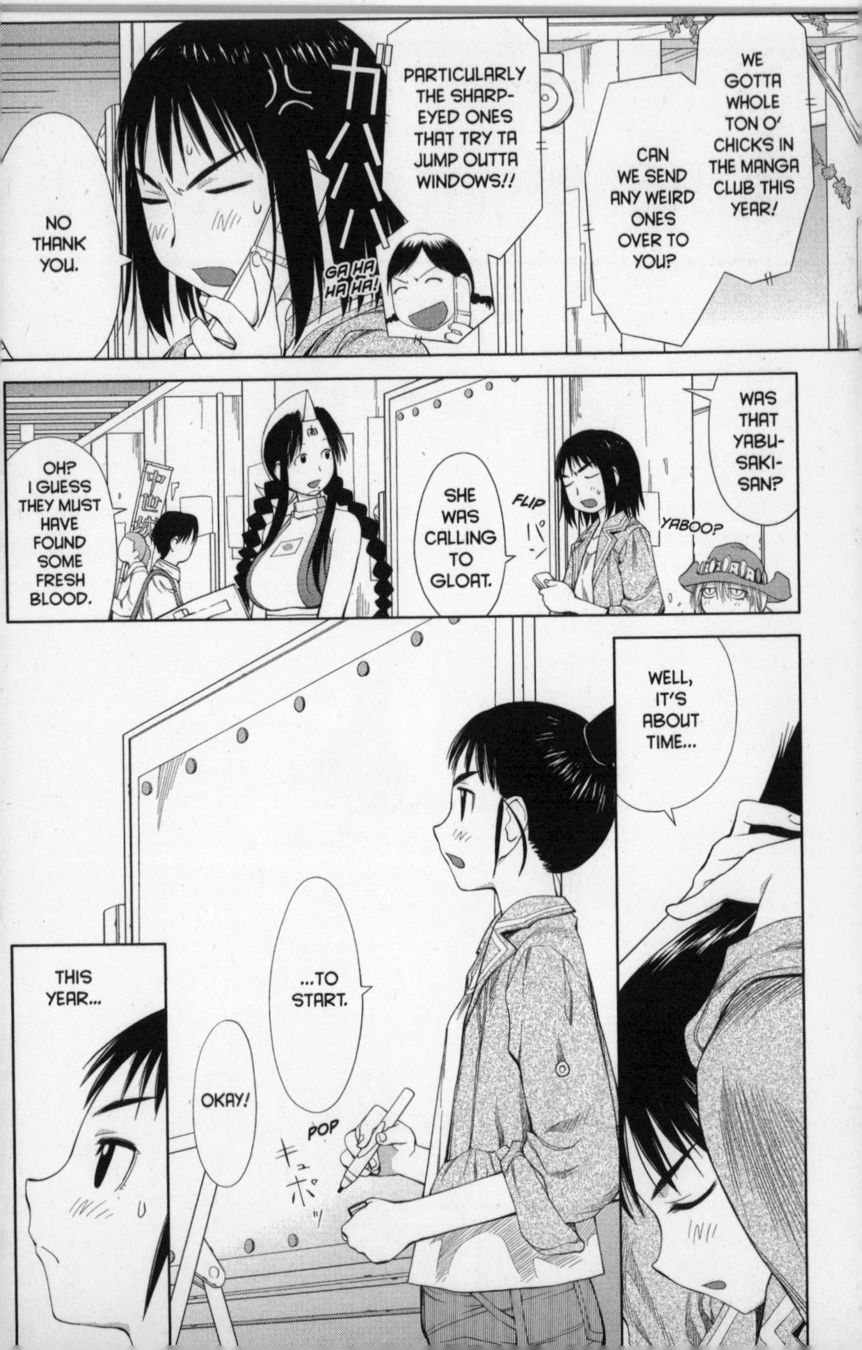
WE GOTTA WHOLE TON O' CHICKS IN THE MANGA CLUB THIS YEAR!
CAN WE SEND ANY WEIRD ONES OVER TO YOU?
PARTICULARLY THE SHARP-EYED ONES THAT TRY TA JUMP OUTTA WINDOWS!!
GA HA HA HA!
NO THANK YOU.
WAS THAT YABU-SAKI-SAN?
YABOO?
FLIP
SHE WAS CALLING TO GLOAT.
OH? I GUESS THEY MUST HAVE FOUND SOME FRESH BLOOD.
WELL, IT'S ABOUT TIME...
...TO START.
OKAY!
POP
THIS YEAR...

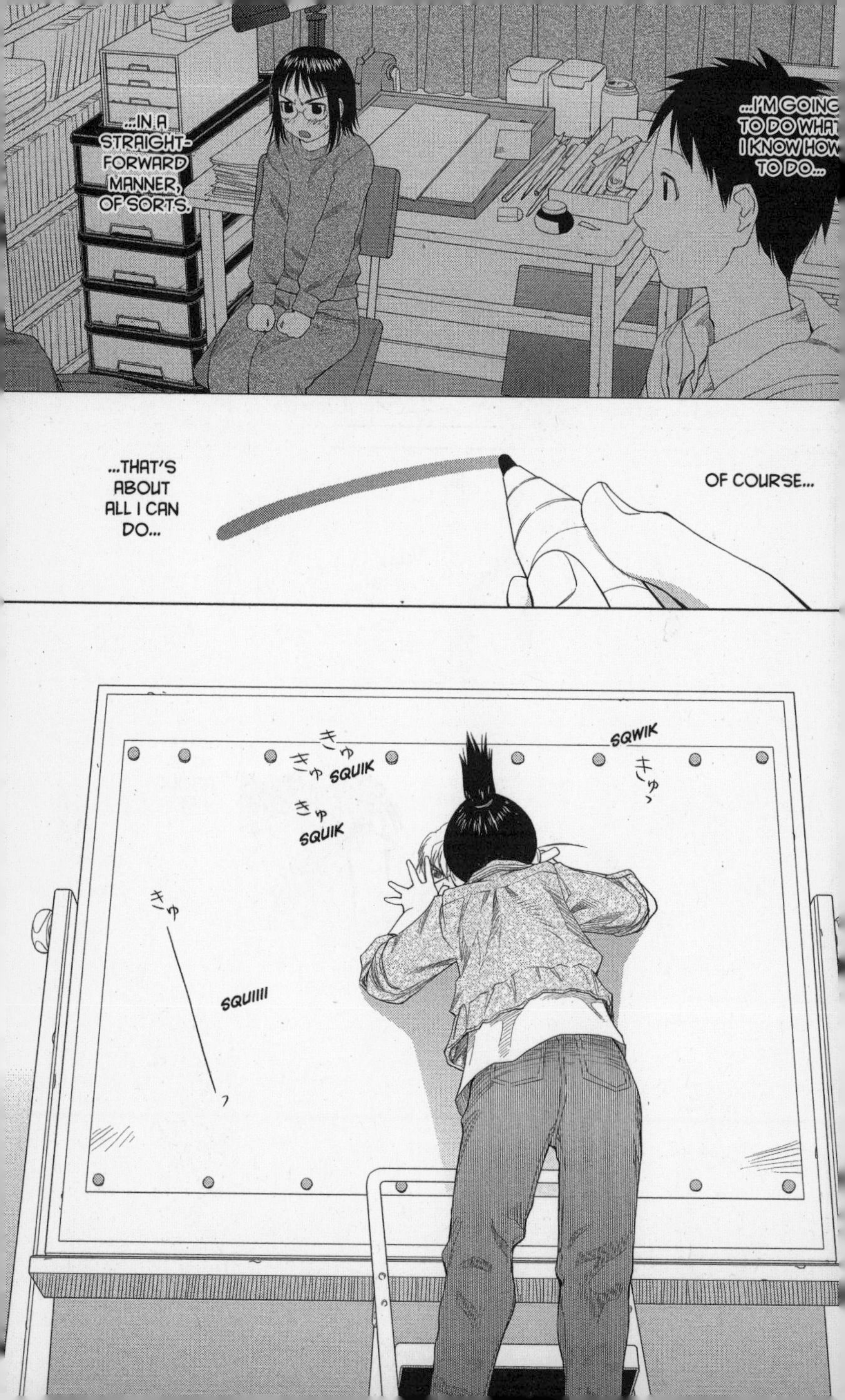
...I'M GOING TO DO WHAT I KNOW HOW TO DO...
...IN A STRAIGHT-FORWARD MANNER, OF SORTS.
OF COURSE...
...THAT'S ABOUT ALL I CAN DO...
SQWIK
きゅっ
きゅ
きゅ SQUIK
きゅ SQUIK
きゅ
SQUIIII

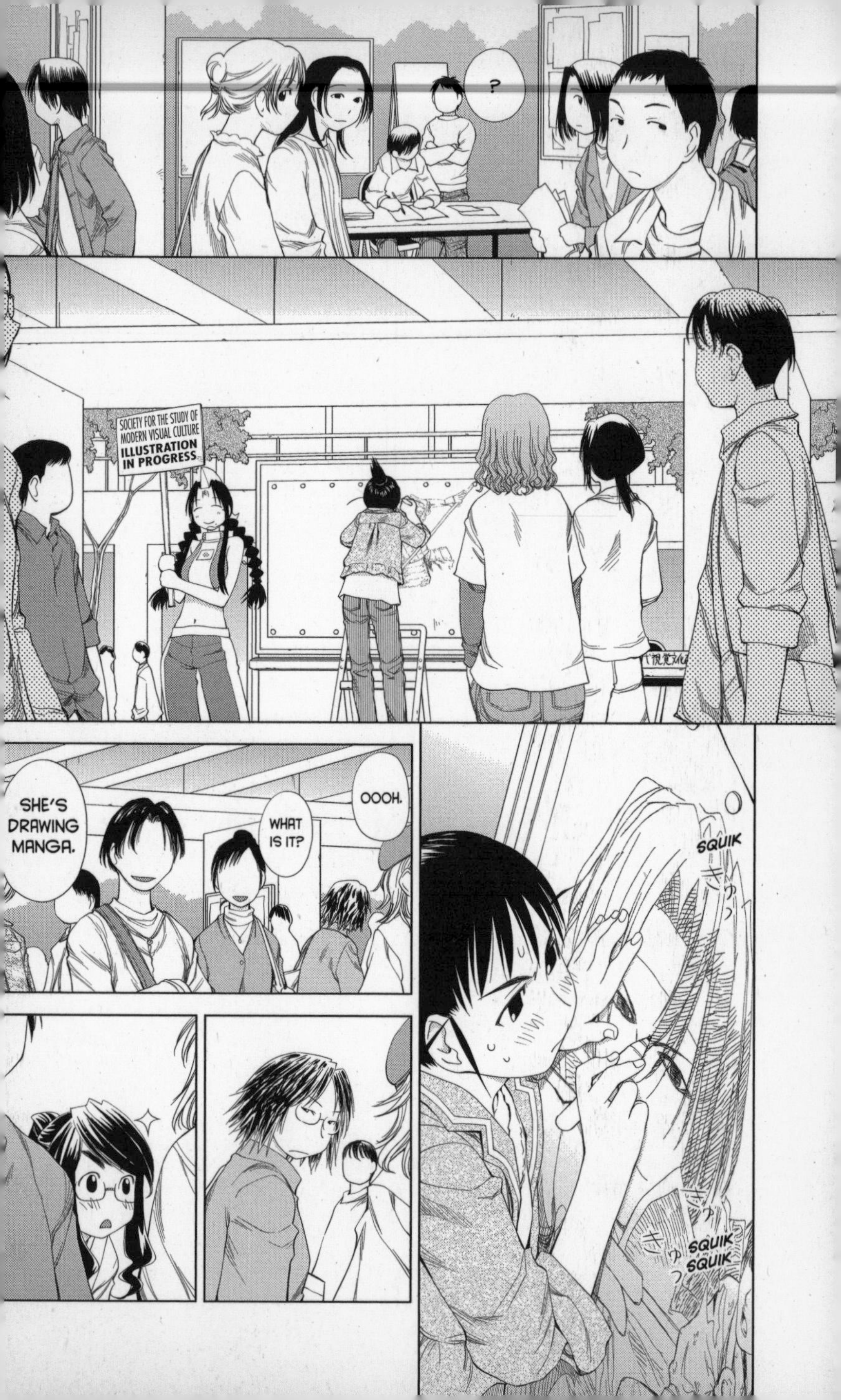
?
SOCIETY FOR THE STUDY OF MODERN VISUAL CULTURE
ILLUSTRATION IN PROGRESS
SQUIK
SQUIK SQUIK
OOOH.
WHAT IS IT?
SHE'S DRAWING MANGA.

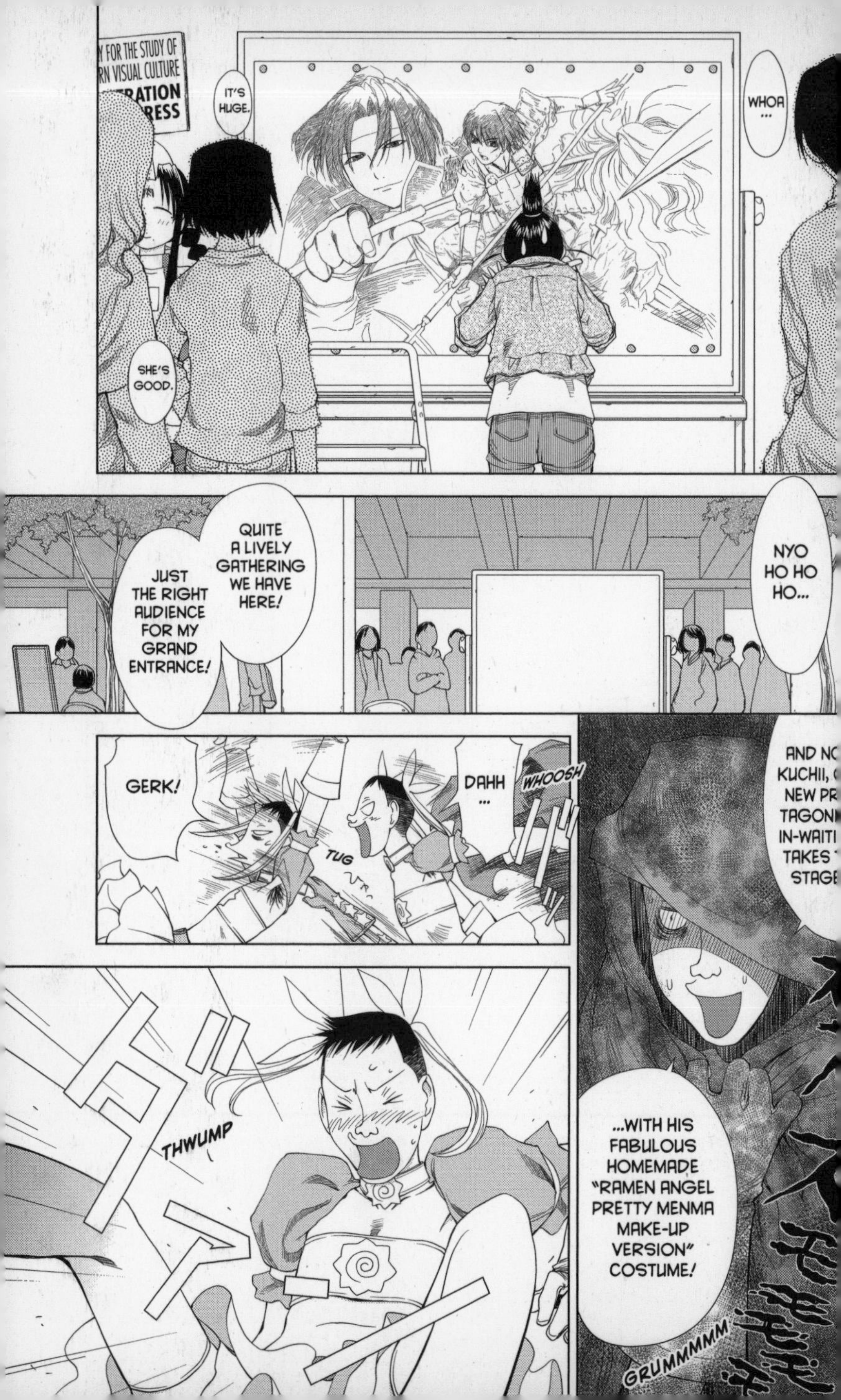
WHOA ...
FOR THE STUDY OF
VISUAL CULTURE
IT'S HUGE.
SHE'S GOOD.
NYO HO HO HO...
QUITE A LIVELY GATHERING WE HAVE HERE!
JUST THE RIGHT AUDIENCE FOR MY GRAND ENTRANCE!
AND NO
KUCHII,
NEW PR
TAGON
IN-WAITI
TAKES
STAGE
...WITH HIS FABULOUS HOMEMADE "RAMEN ANGEL PRETTY MENMA MAKE-UP VERSION" COSTUME!
GRUMMMMM
WHOOSH
DAHH ...
TUG
GERK!
THWUMP

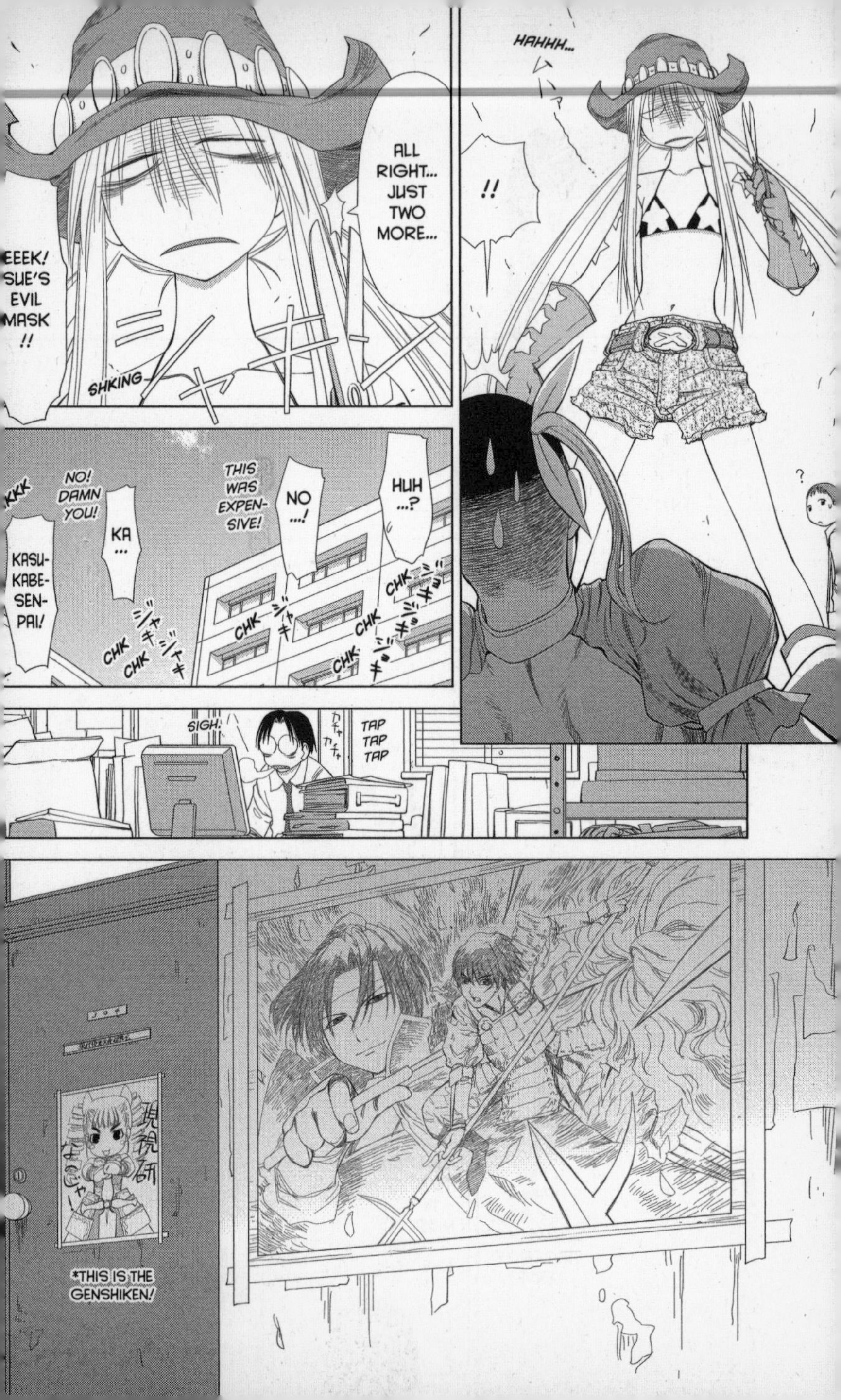
HAHHH...
!!
?
ALL RIGHT... JUST TWO MORE...
EEEK! SUE'S EVIL MASK!!
SHKING
HUH...?
NO...!
THIS WAS EXPENSIVE!
NO! DAMN YOU!
KA...
KASU-KABE-SEN-PAI!
KKK
CHK CHK CHK CHK
CHK CHK CHK
TAP TAP TAP
SIGH.
現視研
*THIS IS THE GENSHIKEN!

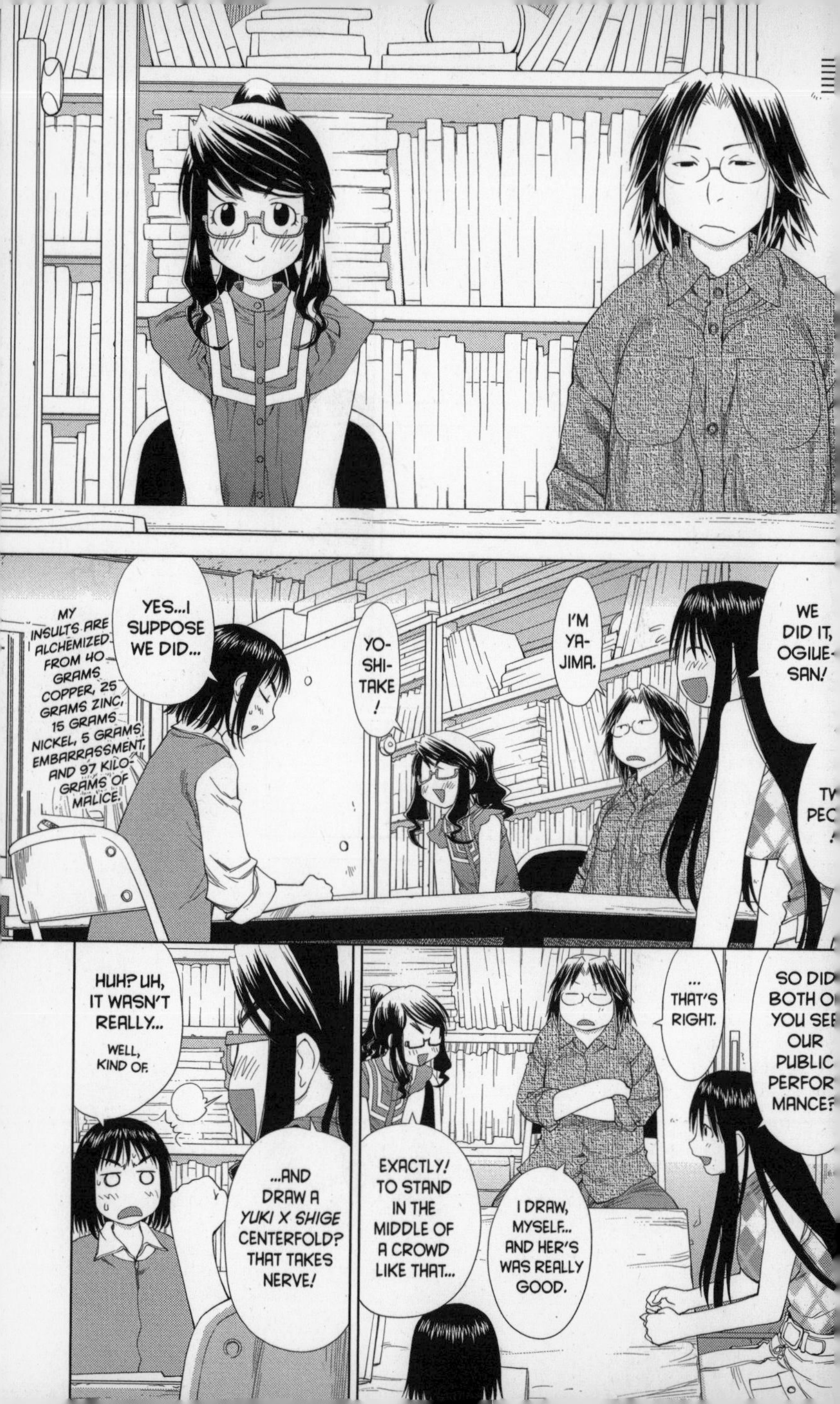
WE DID IT, OGIUE-SAN!
I'M YA-JIMA.
YO-SHI-TAKE!
YES...I SUPPOSE WE DID...
MY INSULTS ARE ALCHEMIZED FROM 40 GRAMS COPPER, 25 GRAMS ZINC, 15 GRAMS NICKEL, 5 GRAMS EMBARRASSMENT, AND 97 KILO-GRAMS OF MALICE.
SO DID BOTH O YOU SE OUR PUBLIC PERFORMANCE?
...THAT'S RIGHT.
I DRAW, MYSELF... AND HER'S WAS REALLY GOOD.
EXACTLY! TO STAND IN THE MIDDLE OF A CROWD LIKE THAT...
HUH? UH, IT WASN'T REALLY...
WELL, KIND OF.
...AND DRAW A *YUKI X SHIGE* CENTERFOLD? THAT TAKES NERVE!

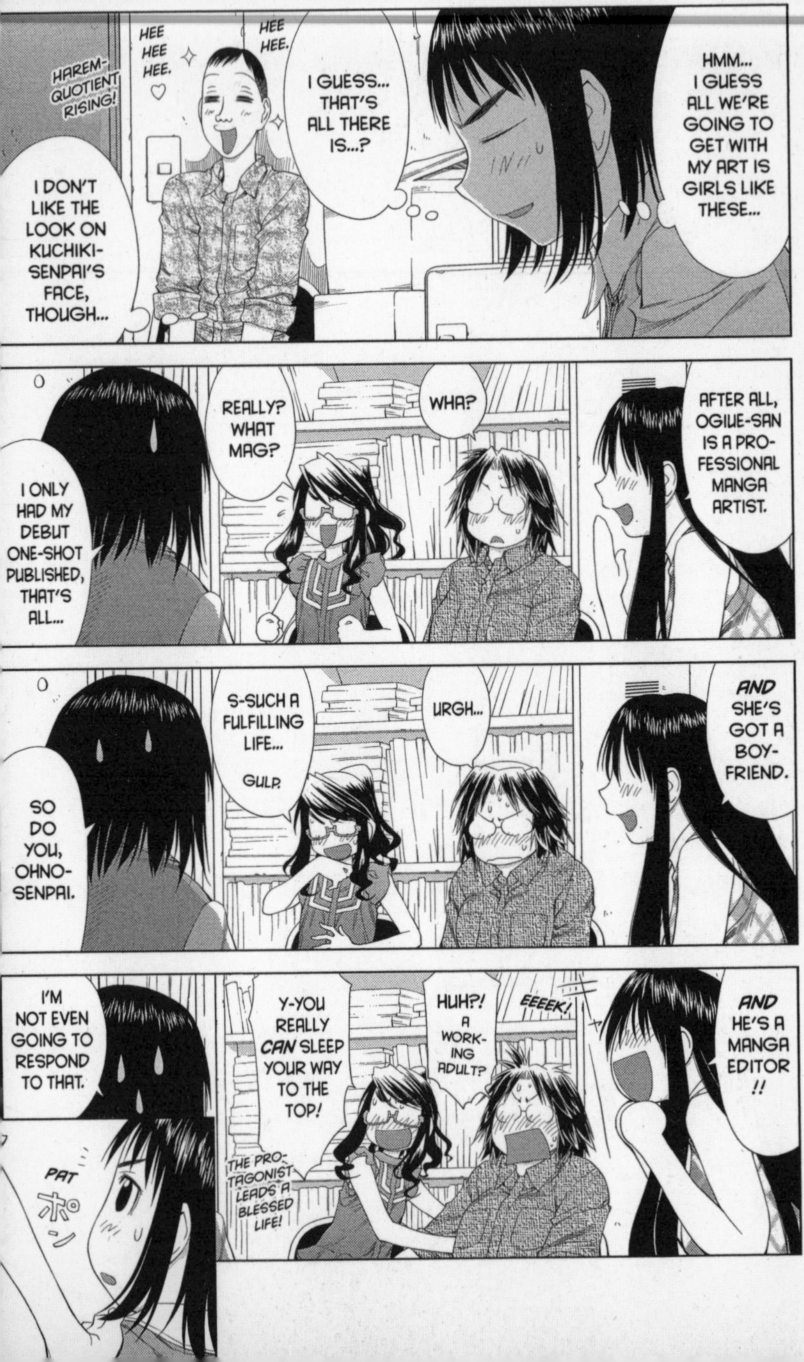
HMM... I GUESS ALL WE'RE GOING TO GET WITH MY ART IS GIRLS LIKE THESE...
I GUESS... THAT'S ALL THERE IS...?
HEE HEE.
HEE HEE HEE.
HAREM-QUOTIENT RISING!
I DON'T LIKE THE LOOK ON KUCHIKI-SENPAI'S FACE, THOUGH...
AFTER ALL, OGIUE-SAN IS A PRO-FESSIONAL MANGA ARTIST.
WHA?
REALLY? WHAT MAG?
I ONLY HAD MY DEBUT ONE-SHOT PUBLISHED, THAT'S ALL...
AND SHE'S GOT A BOY-FRIEND.
URGH...
S-SUCH A FULFILLING LIFE...
GULP.
SO DO YOU, OHNO-SENPAI.
AND HE'S A MANGA EDITOR !!
EEEEK!
HUH?! A WORKING ADULT?
Y-YOU REALLY CAN SLEEP YOUR WAY TO THE TOP!
THE PRO-TAGONIST LEADS A BLESSED LIFE!
I'M NOT EVEN GOING TO RESPOND TO THAT.
PAT
ポン

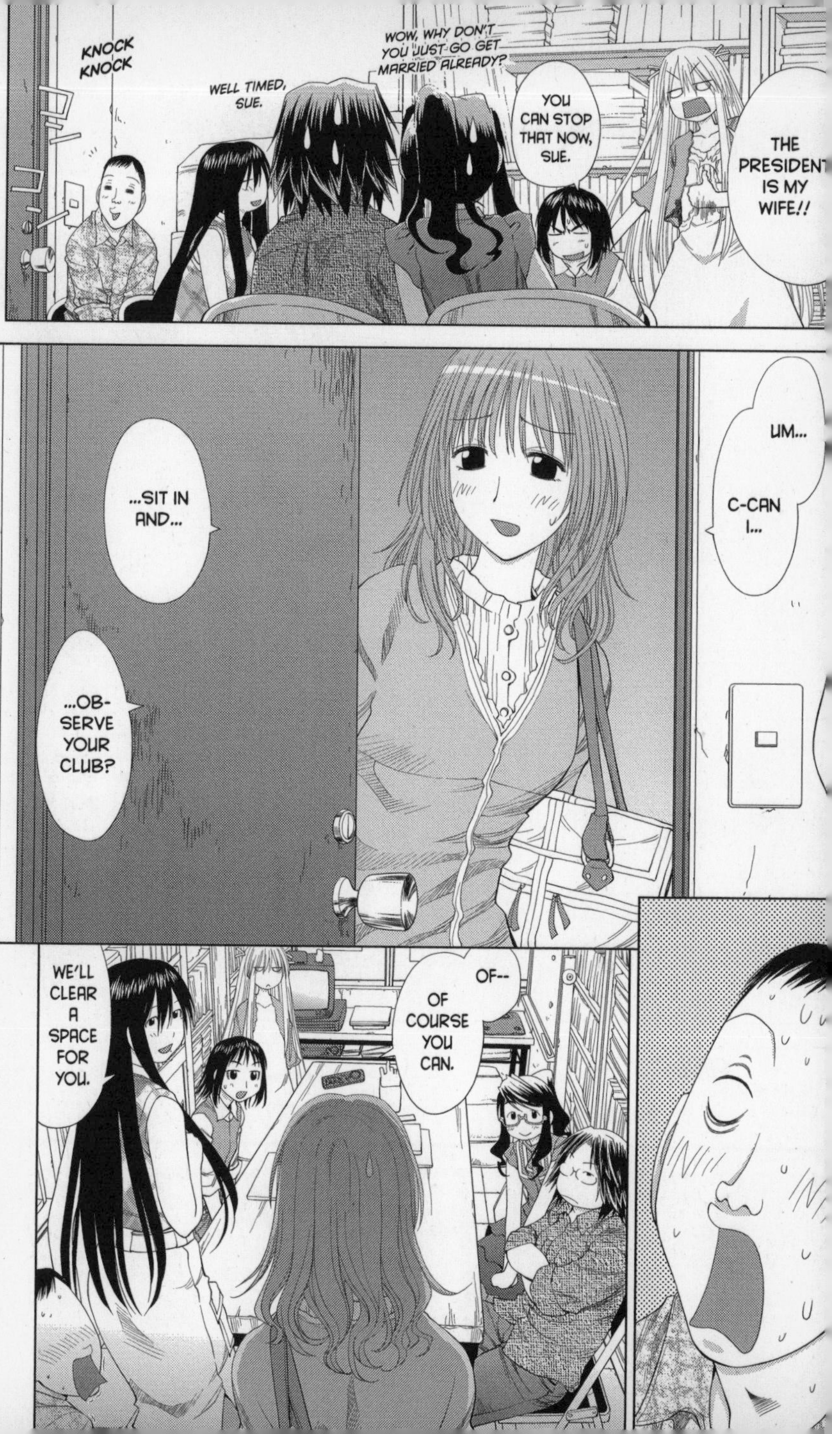
THE PRESIDENT IS MY WIFE!!
YOU CAN STOP THAT NOW, SUE.
WOW, WHY DON'T YOU JUST GO GET MARRIED ALREADY?
WELL TIMED, SUE.
KNOCK KNOCK
UM...
C-CAN I...
...SIT IN AND...
...OB-SERVE YOUR CLUB?
OF--
OF COURSE YOU CAN.
WE'LL CLEAR A SPACE FOR YOU.

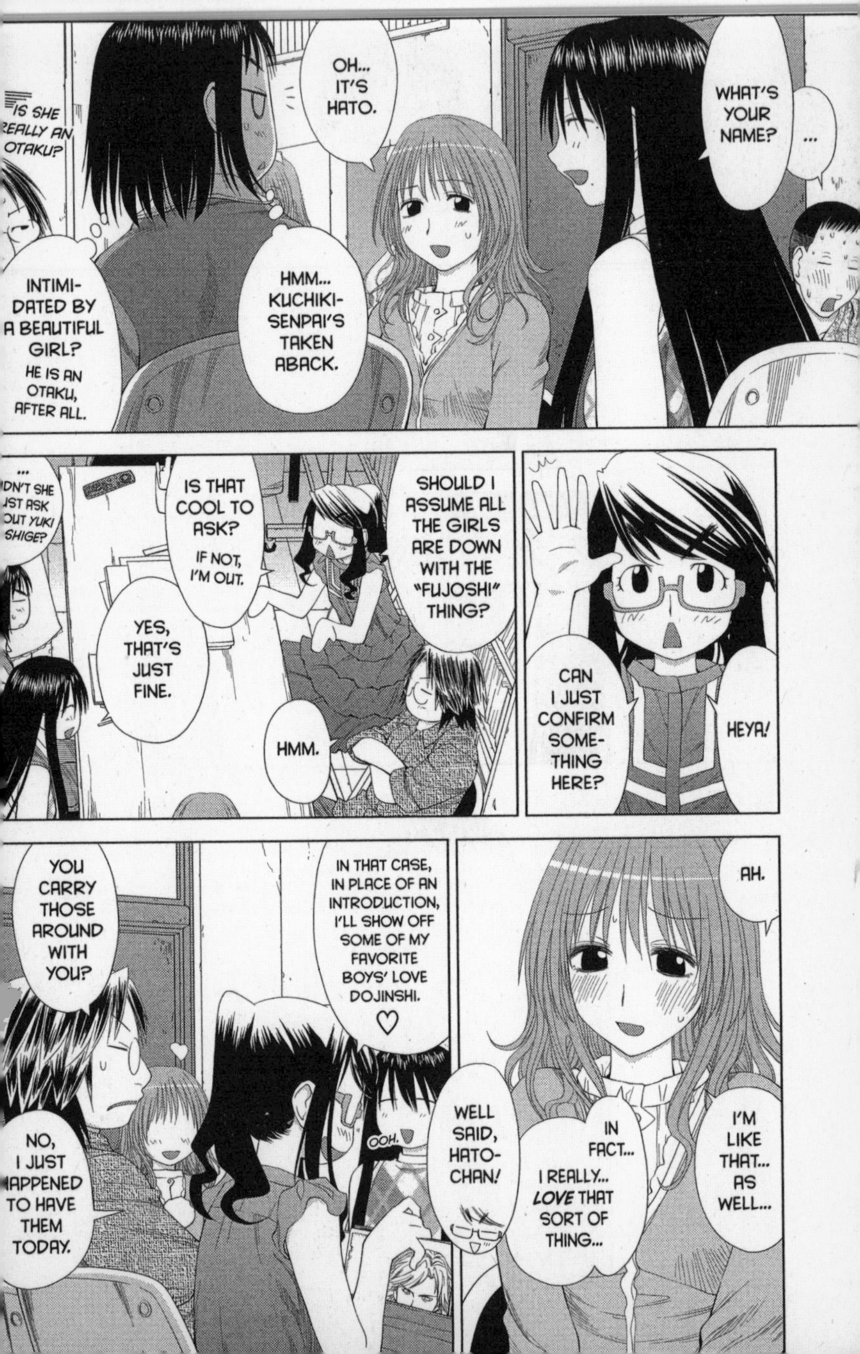
WHAT'S YOUR NAME?
...
OH... IT'S HATO.
HMM... KUCHIKI-SENPAI'S TAKEN ABACK.
IS SHE EALLY AN OTAKU?
INTIMI-DATED BY A BEAUTIFUL GIRL? HE IS AN OTAKU, AFTER ALL.
HEYA!
CAN I JUST CONFIRM SOME-THING HERE?
SHOULD I ASSUME ALL THE GIRLS ARE DOWN WITH THE "FUJOSHI" THING?
IS THAT COOL TO ASK? IF NOT, I'M OUT.
YES, THAT'S JUST FINE.
HMM.
... DN'T SHE JST ASK OUT YUKI SHIGE?
AH.
I'M LIKE THAT... AS WELL...
IN FACT... I REALLY... *LOVE* THAT SORT OF THING...
WELL SAID, HATO-CHAN!
OOH.
IN THAT CASE, IN PLACE OF AN INTRODUCTION, I'LL SHOW OFF SOME OF MY FAVORITE BOYS' LOVE DOJINSHI. ♡
YOU CARRY THOSE AROUND WITH YOU?
NO, I JUST APPENED TO HAVE THEM TODAY.

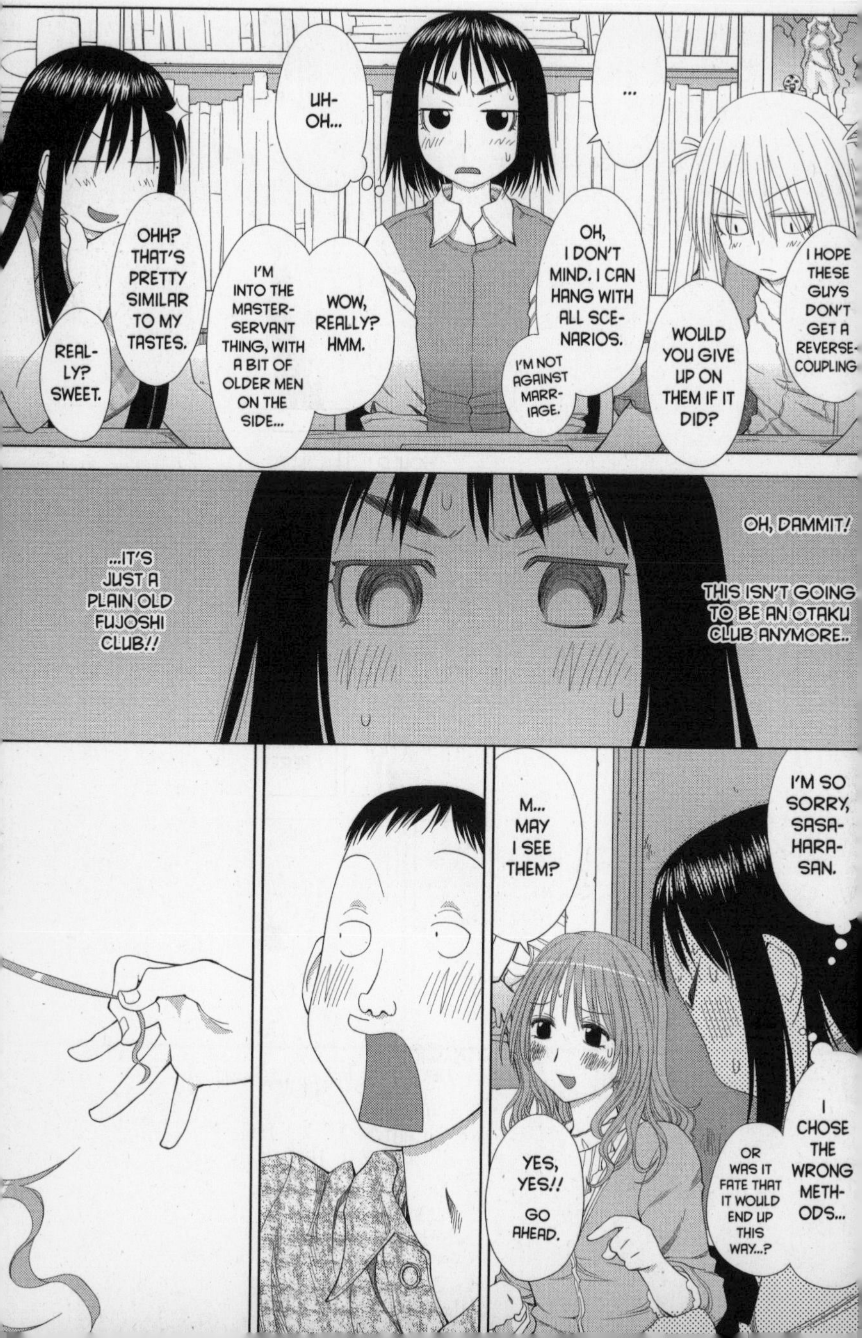
I HOPE THESE GUYS DON'T GET A REVERSE-COUPLING
...
WOULD YOU GIVE UP ON THEM IF IT DID?
OH, I DON'T MIND. I CAN HANG WITH ALL SCENARIOS.
I'M NOT AGAINST MARRIAGE.
UH-OH...
WOW, REALLY? HMM.
I'M INTO THE MASTER-SERVANT THING, WITH A BIT OF OLDER MEN ON THE SIDE...
OHH? THAT'S PRETTY SIMILAR TO MY TASTES.
REALLY? SWEET.
OH, DAMMIT!
THIS ISN'T GOING TO BE AN OTAKU CLUB ANYMORE..
...IT'S JUST A PLAIN OLD FUJOSHI CLUB!!
I'M SO SORRY, SASAHARA-SAN.
M... MAY I SEE THEM?
I CHOSE THE WRONG METHODS...
OR WAS IT FATE THAT IT WOULD END UP THIS WAY...?
YES, YES!! GO AHEAD.

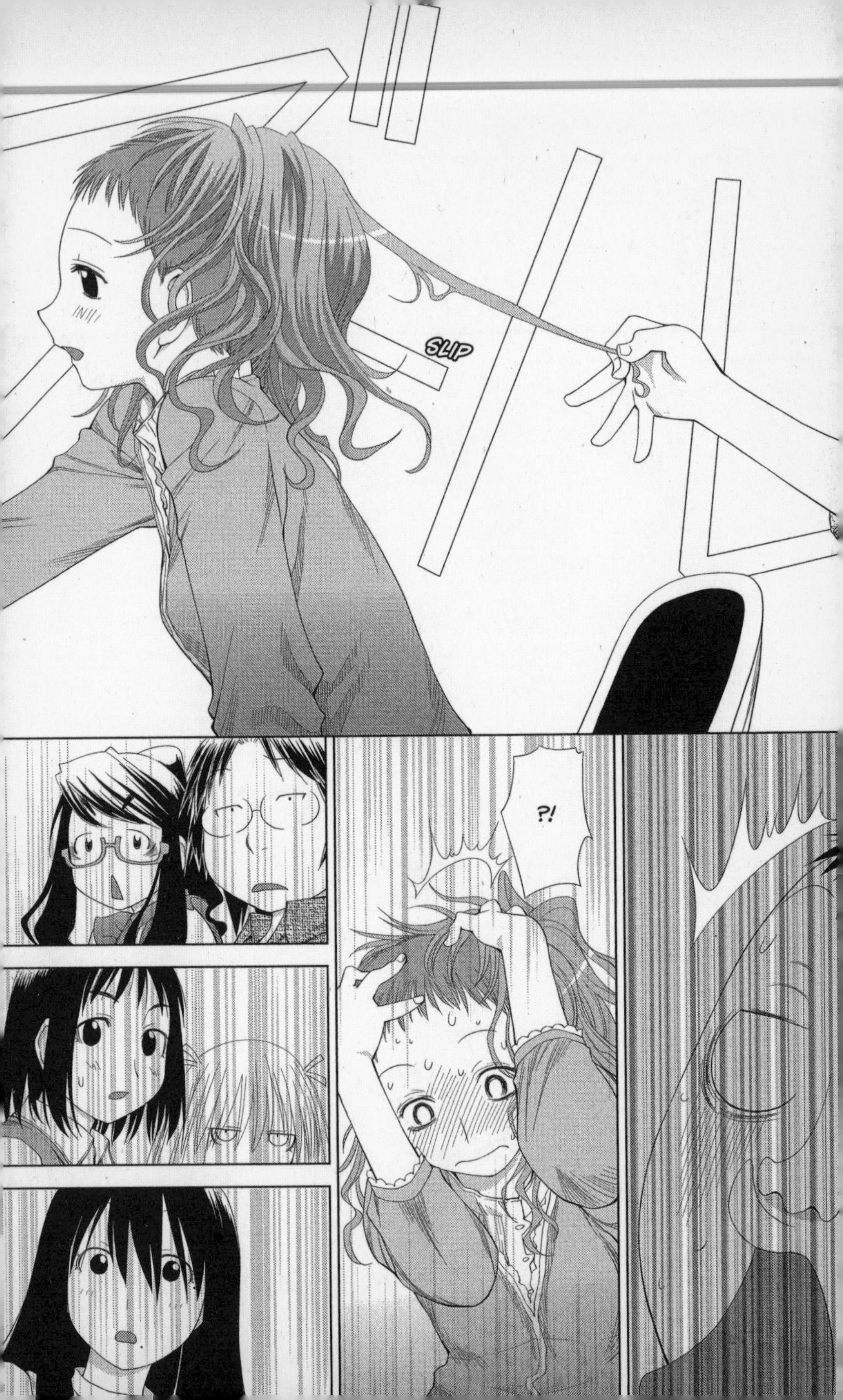
SLIP
?!

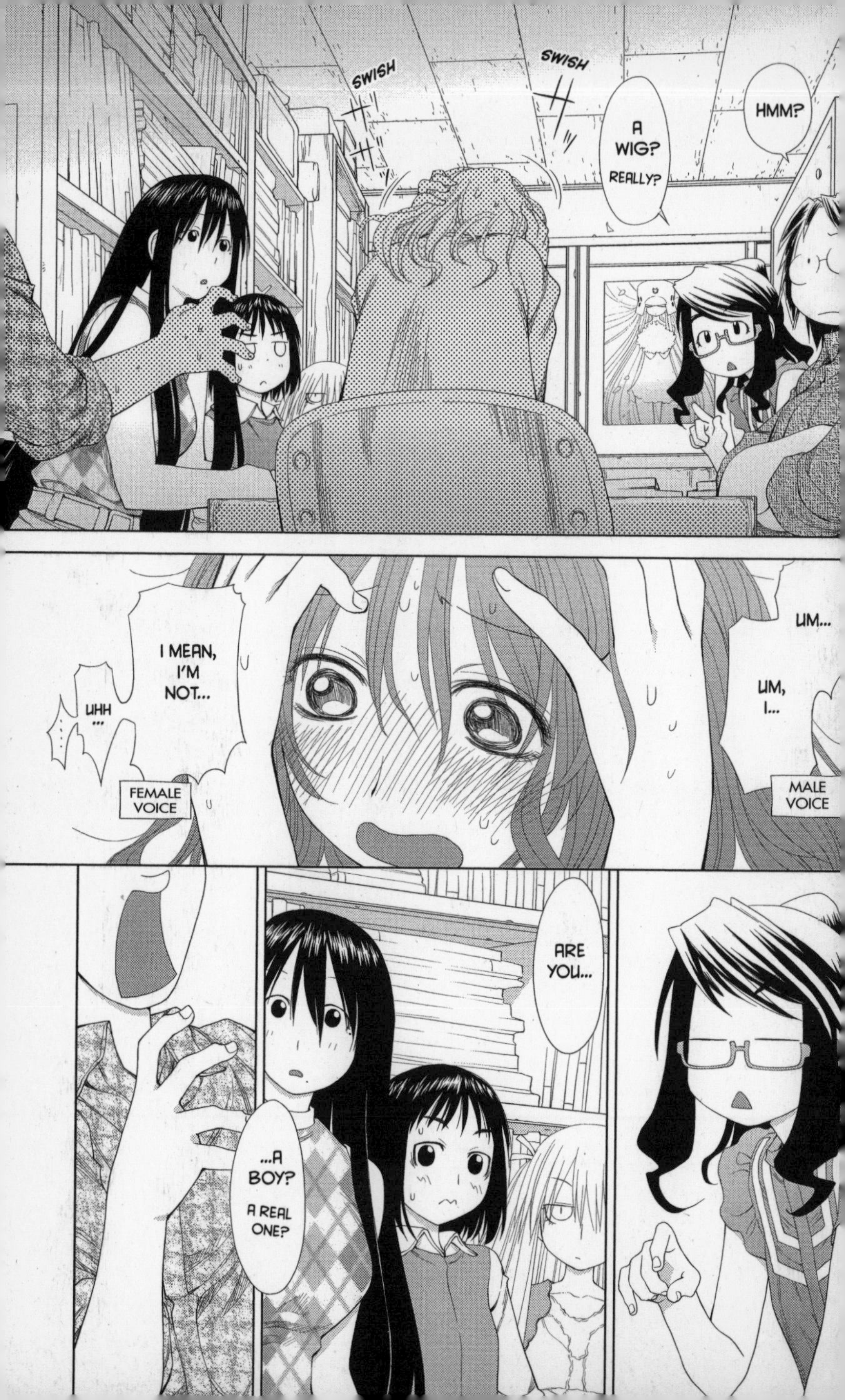
HMM?
A WIG? REALLY?
SWISH
SWISH
UM...
UM, I...
MALE VOICE
I MEAN, I'M NOT...
UHH...
FEMALE VOICE
ARE YOU...
...A BOY? A REAL ONE?

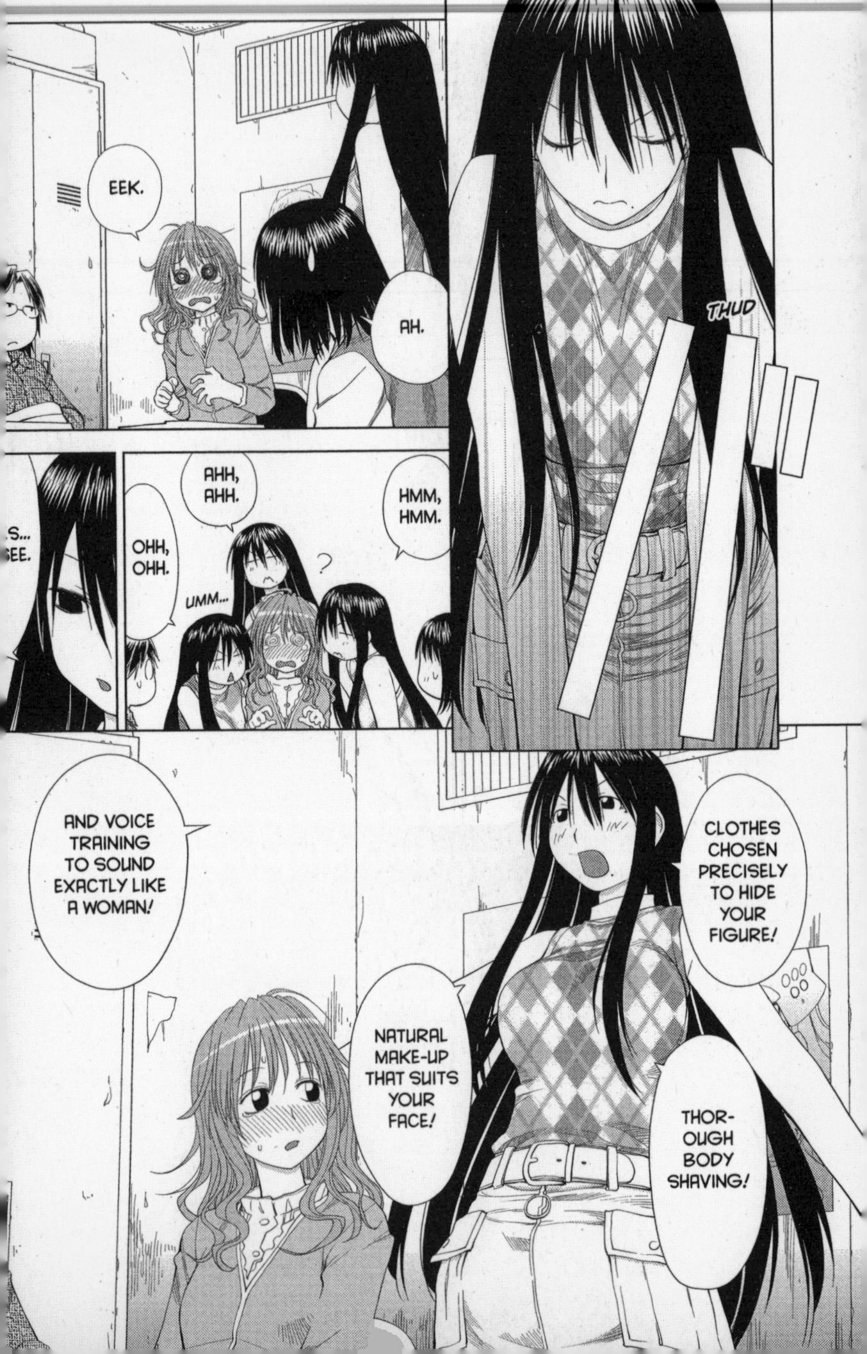
THUD
AH.
EEK.
HMM, HMM.
AHH, AHH.
OHH, OHH.
UMM...
S...
SEE.
CLOTHES CHOSEN PRECISELY TO HIDE YOUR FIGURE!
THOR-OUGH BODY SHAVING!
NATURAL MAKE-UP THAT SUITS YOUR FACE!
AND VOICE TRAINING TO SOUND EXACTLY LIKE A WOMAN!

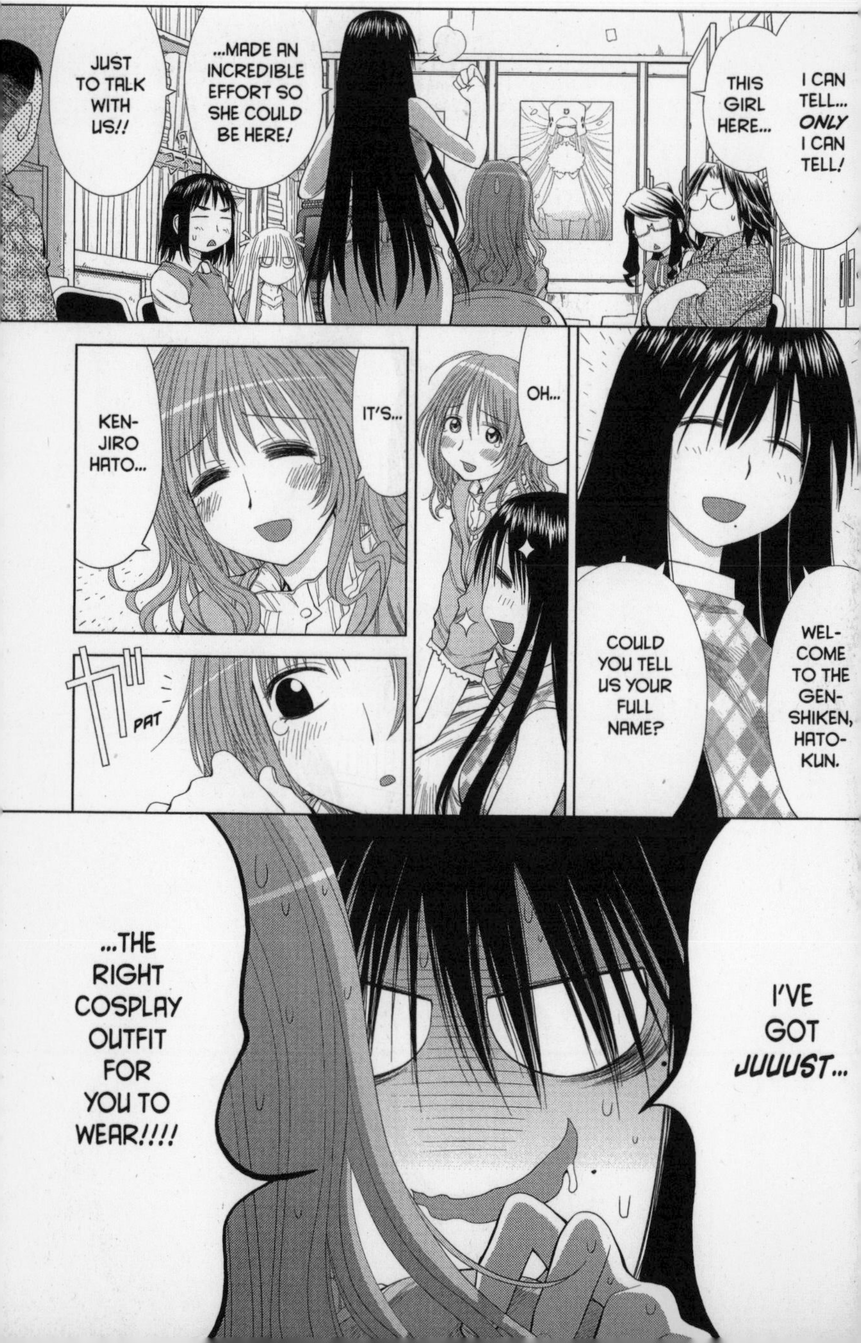
I CAN TELL... *ONLY* I CAN TELL!
THIS GIRL HERE...
...MADE AN INCREDIBLE EFFORT SO SHE COULD BE HERE!
JUST TO TALK WITH US!!
WEL-COME TO THE GEN-SHIKEN, HATO-KUN.
COULD YOU TELL US YOUR FULL NAME?
OH...
IT'S...
KEN-JIRO HATO...
PAT
I'VE GOT *JUUUST*...
...THE RIGHT COSPLAY OUTFIT FOR YOU TO WEAR!!!!

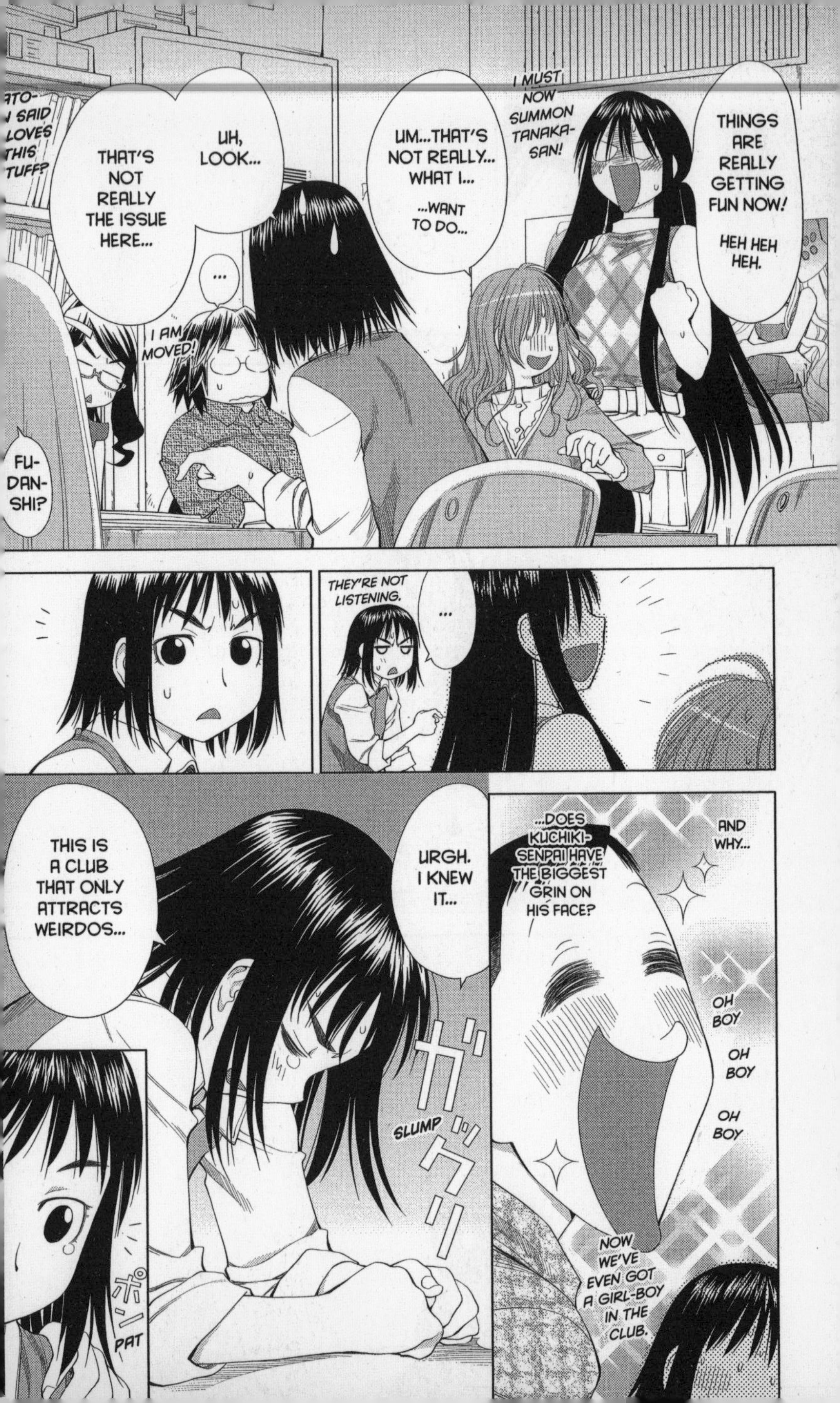
THINGS ARE REALLY GETTING FUN NOW! HEH HEH HEH.
I MUST NOW SUMMON TANAKA-SAN!
UM...THAT'S NOT REALLY... WHAT I...
...WANT TO DO...
UH, LOOK...
THAT'S NOT REALLY THE ISSUE HERE...
...
I AM MOVED!
ATO- N SAID LOVES THIS TUFF?
FU-DAN-SHI?
THEY'RE NOT LISTENING.
...
AND WHY...
...DOES KUCHIKI-SENPAI HAVE THE BIGGEST GRIN ON HIS FACE?
OH BOY
OH BOY
OH BOY
NOW WE'VE EVEN GOT A GIRL-BOY IN THE CLUB.
URGH. I KNEW IT...
THIS IS A CLUB THAT ONLY ATTRACTS WEIRDOS...
ガックリ
SLUMP
ポン
PAT

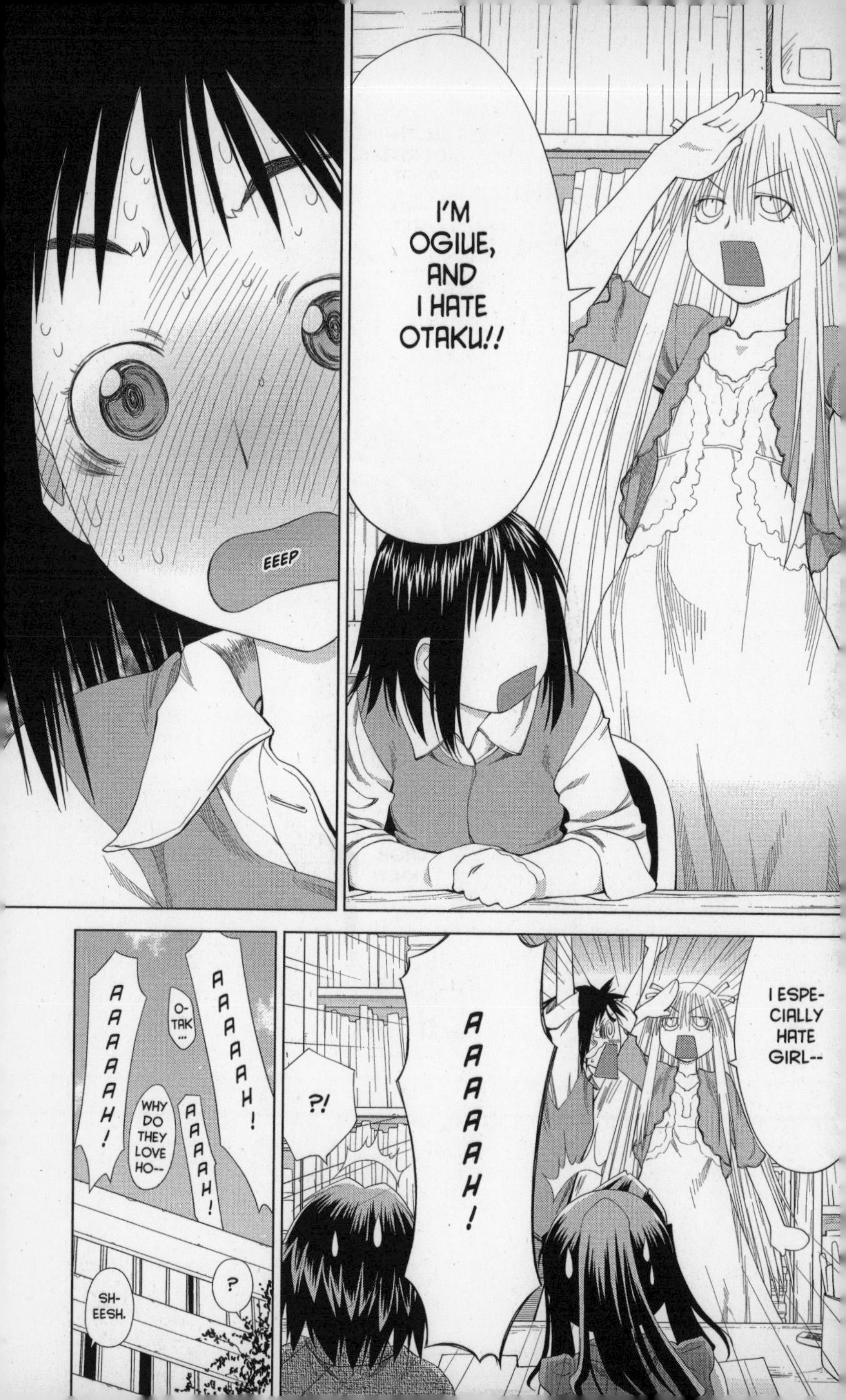
I'M OGIUE, AND I HATE OTAKU!!
EEEP
I ESPE-CIALLY HATE GIRL--
AAAAAH!
?!
AAAAAH!
O-TAK...
AAAAAH!
AAAAH!
WHY DO THEY LOVE HO--
?
SH-EESH.

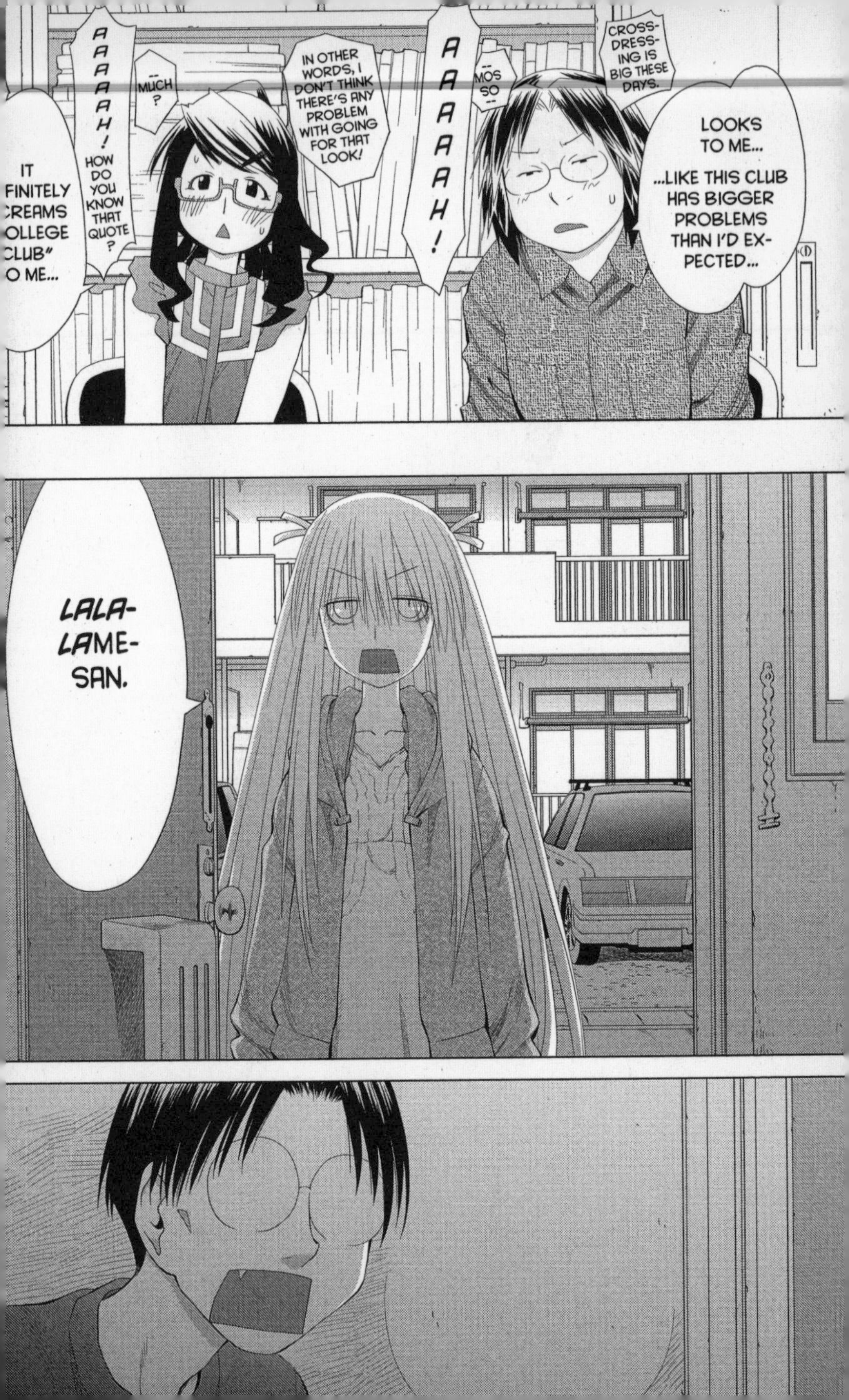
CROSS-DRESSING IS BIG THESE DAYS.
LOOKS TO ME... ...LIKE THIS CLUB HAS BIGGER PROBLEMS THAN I'D EXPECTED...
--MOS SO--
AAAAAAH!
IN OTHER WORDS, I DON'T THINK THERE'S ANY PROBLEM WITH GOING FOR THAT LOOK!
--MUCH?
AAAAAH! HOW DO YOU KNOW THAT QUOTE?
IT FINITELY CREAMS OLLEGE CLUB" O ME...
LALA-LAME-SAN.

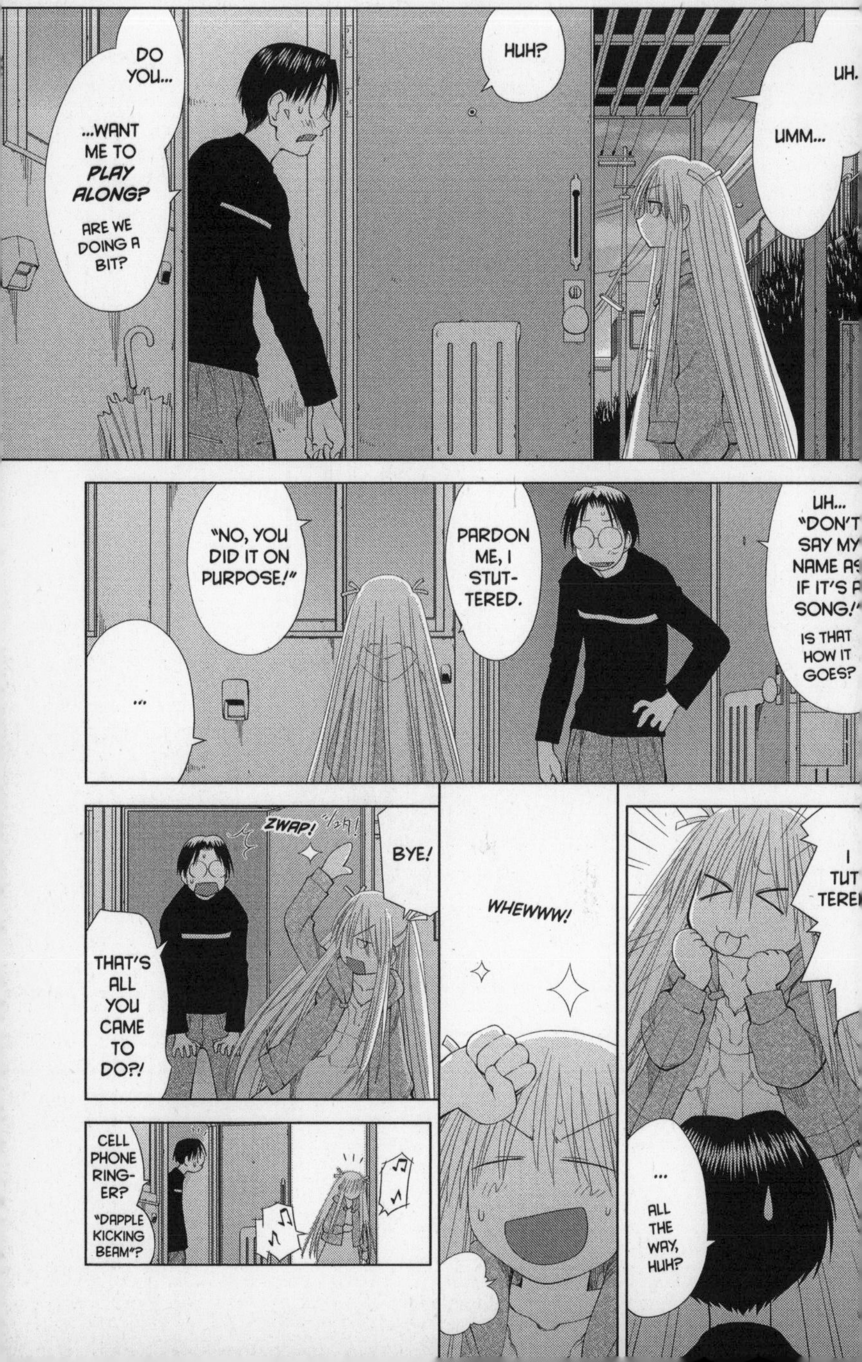
UH.
UMM...
HUH?
DO YOU...
...WANT ME TO *PLAY ALONG?*
ARE WE DOING A BIT?
UH... "DON'T SAY MY NAME AS IF IT'S A SONG!"
IS THAT HOW IT GOES?
PARDON ME, I STUT-TERED.
"NO, YOU DID IT ON PURPOSE!"
...
I TUT TERE
...
ALL THE WAY, HUH?
WHEWWW!
ZWAP!
BYE!
THAT'S ALL YOU CAME TO DO?!
CELL PHONE RINGER?
"DAPPLE KICKING BEAM"?

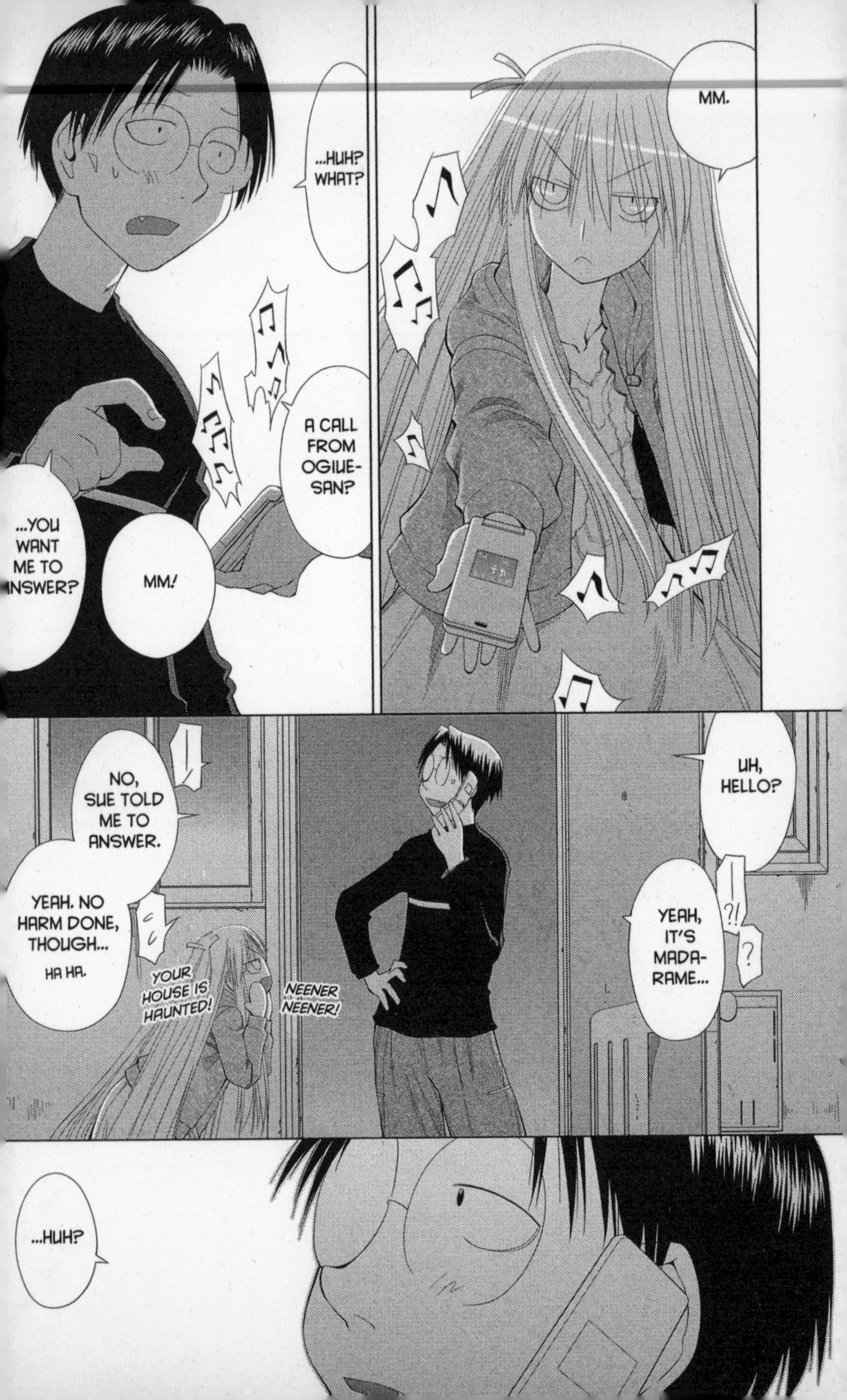
MM.
...HUH? WHAT?
A CALL FROM OGIUE-SAN?
...YOU WANT ME TO ANSWER?
MM!
UH, HELLO?
YEAH, IT'S MADA-RAME...
?!
?
NO, SUE TOLD ME TO ANSWER.
YEAH. NO HARM DONE, THOUGH...
HA HA.
NEENER NEENER!
YOUR HOUSE IS HAUNTED!
...HUH?

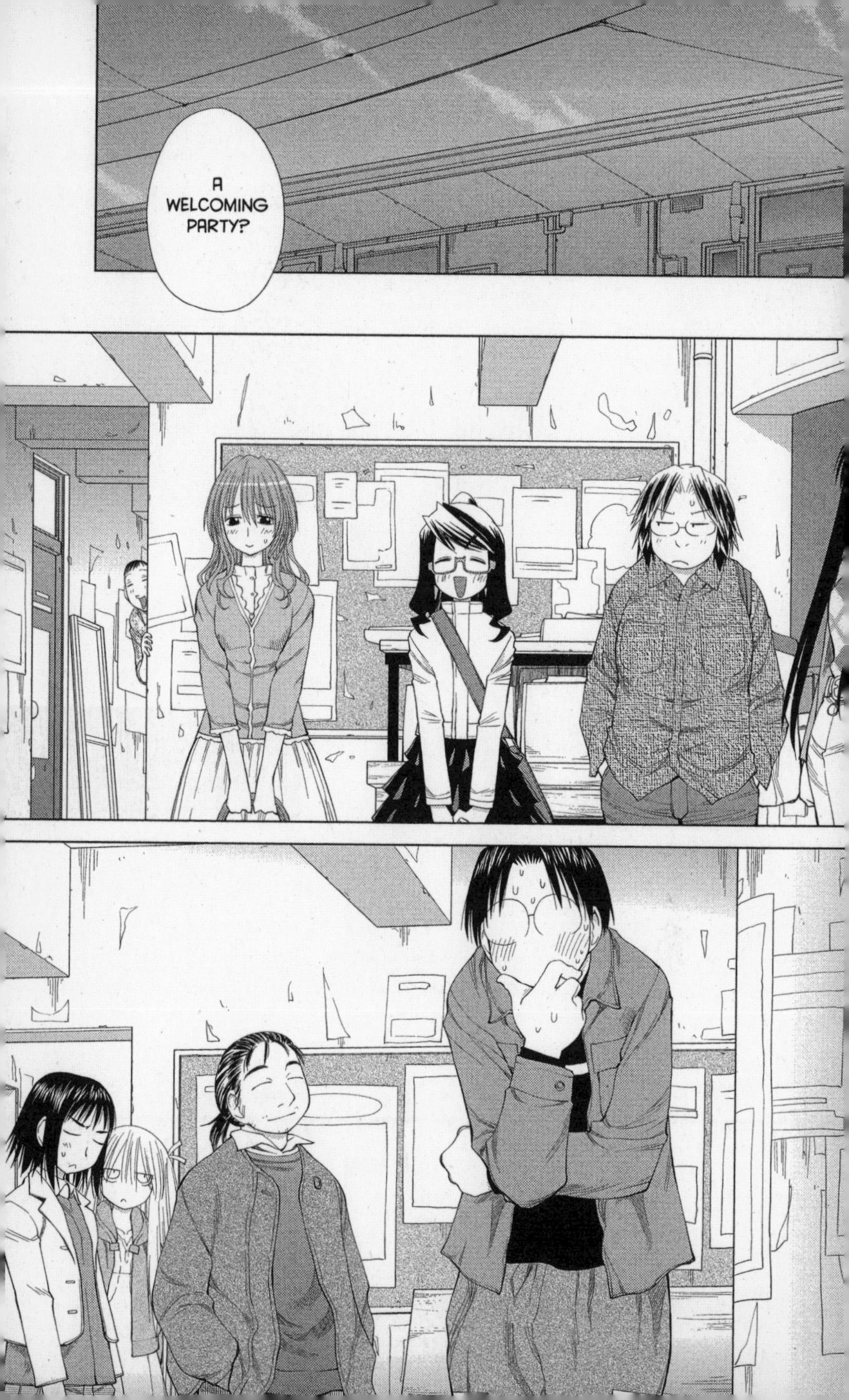
A WELCOMING PARTY?

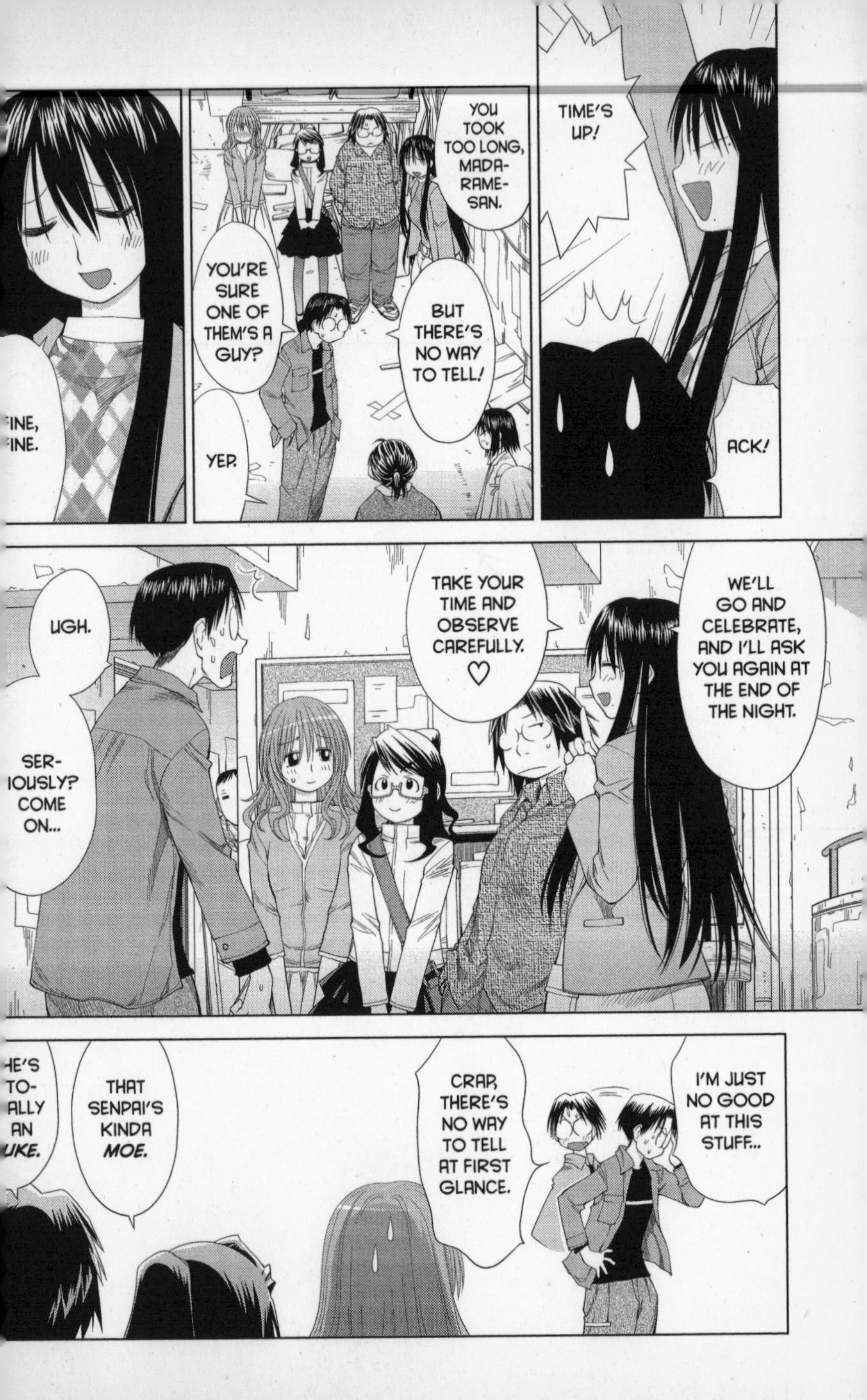
TIME'S UP!
ACK!
YOU TOOK TOO LONG, MADARAME-SAN.
BUT THERE'S NO WAY TO TELL!
YOU'RE SURE ONE OF THEM'S A GUY?
YEP.
FINE, FINE.
WE'LL GO AND CELEBRATE, AND I'LL ASK YOU AGAIN AT THE END OF THE NIGHT.
TAKE YOUR TIME AND OBSERVE CAREFULLY. ♡
UGH.
SER-IOUSLY? COME ON...
I'M JUST NO GOOD AT THIS STUFF...
CRAP, THERE'S NO WAY TO TELL AT FIRST GLANCE.
THAT SENPAI'S KINDA *MOE.*
HE'S TO-ALLY AN *UKE.*

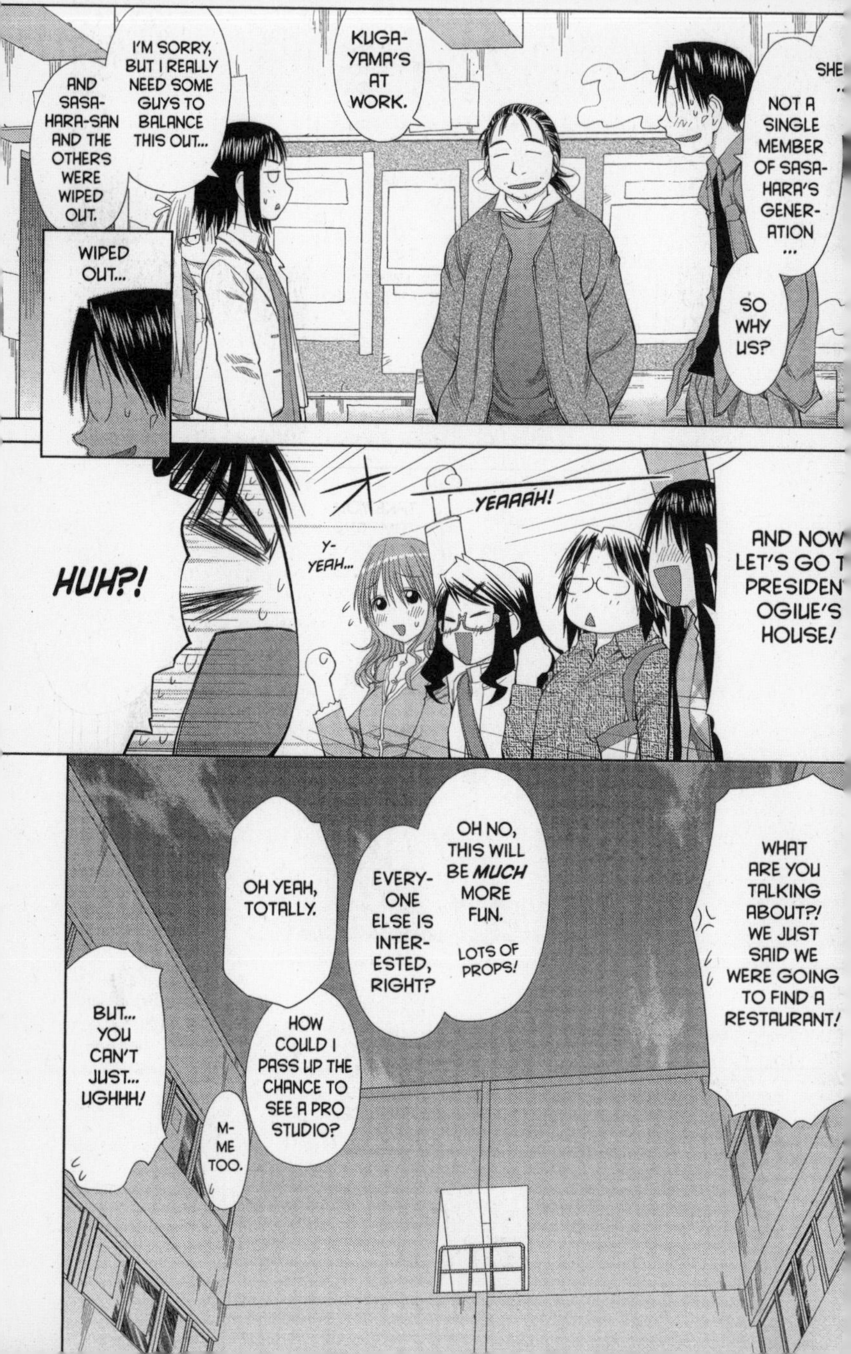

SHE
NOT A SINGLE MEMBER OF SASA-HARA'S GENER-ATION ...
SO WHY US?
KUGA-YAMA'S AT WORK.
I'M SORRY, BUT I REALLY NEED SOME GUYS TO BALANCE THIS OUT...
AND SASA-HARA-SAN AND THE OTHERS WERE WIPED OUT.
WIPED OUT...
AND NOW LET'S GO T PRESIDEN OGIUE'S HOUSE!
YEAAAH!
Y-YEAH...
HUH?!
WHAT ARE YOU TALKING ABOUT?! WE JUST SAID WE WERE GOING TO FIND A RESTAURANT!
OH NO, THIS WILL BE *MUCH* MORE FUN.
LOTS OF PROPS!
EVERY-ONE ELSE IS INTER-ESTED, RIGHT?
OH YEAH, TOTALLY.
HOW COULD I PASS UP THE CHANCE TO SEE A PRO STUDIO?
BUT... YOU CAN'T JUST... UGHHH!
M-ME TOO.

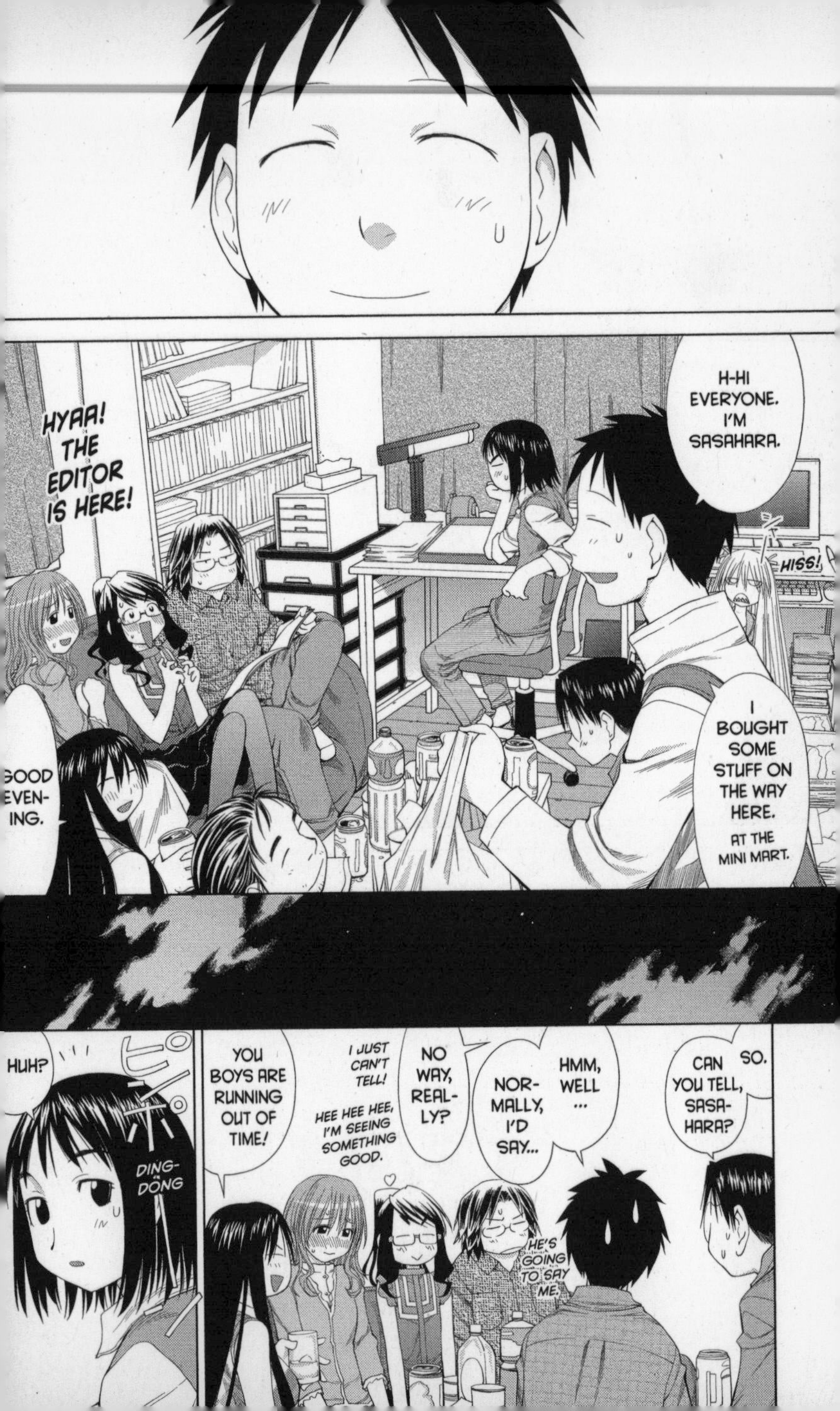
H-HI EVERYONE. I'M SASAHARA.
HISS!
I BOUGHT SOME STUFF ON THE WAY HERE.
AT THE MINI MART.
HYAA! THE EDITOR IS HERE!
GOOD EVEN-ING.
SO.
CAN YOU TELL, SASA-HARA?
HMM, WELL ...
NOR-MALLY, I'D SAY...
HE'S GOING TO SAY ME.
NO WAY, REAL-LY?
I JUST CAN'T TELL!
HEE HEE HEE, I'M SEEING SOMETHING GOOD.
YOU BOYS ARE RUNNING OUT OF TIME!
HUH?
DING-DONG

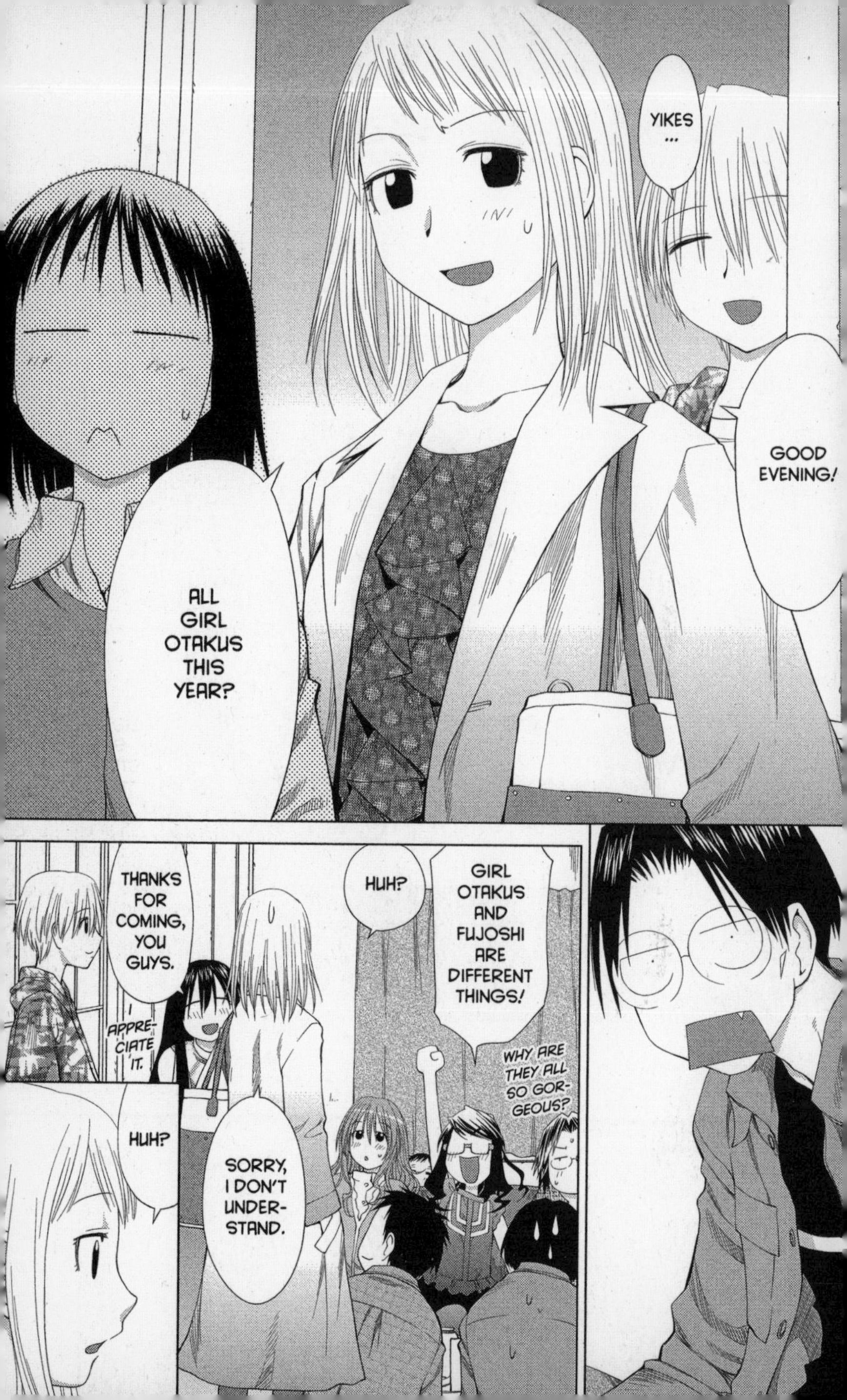
YIKES...
GOOD EVENING!
ALL GIRL OTAKUS THIS YEAR?
THANKS FOR COMING, YOU GUYS.
I APPRECIATE IT.
WHY ARE THEY ALL SO GORGEOUS?
GIRL OTAKUS AND FUJOSHI ARE DIFFERENT THINGS!
HUH?
HUH?
SORRY, I DON'T UNDERSTAND.

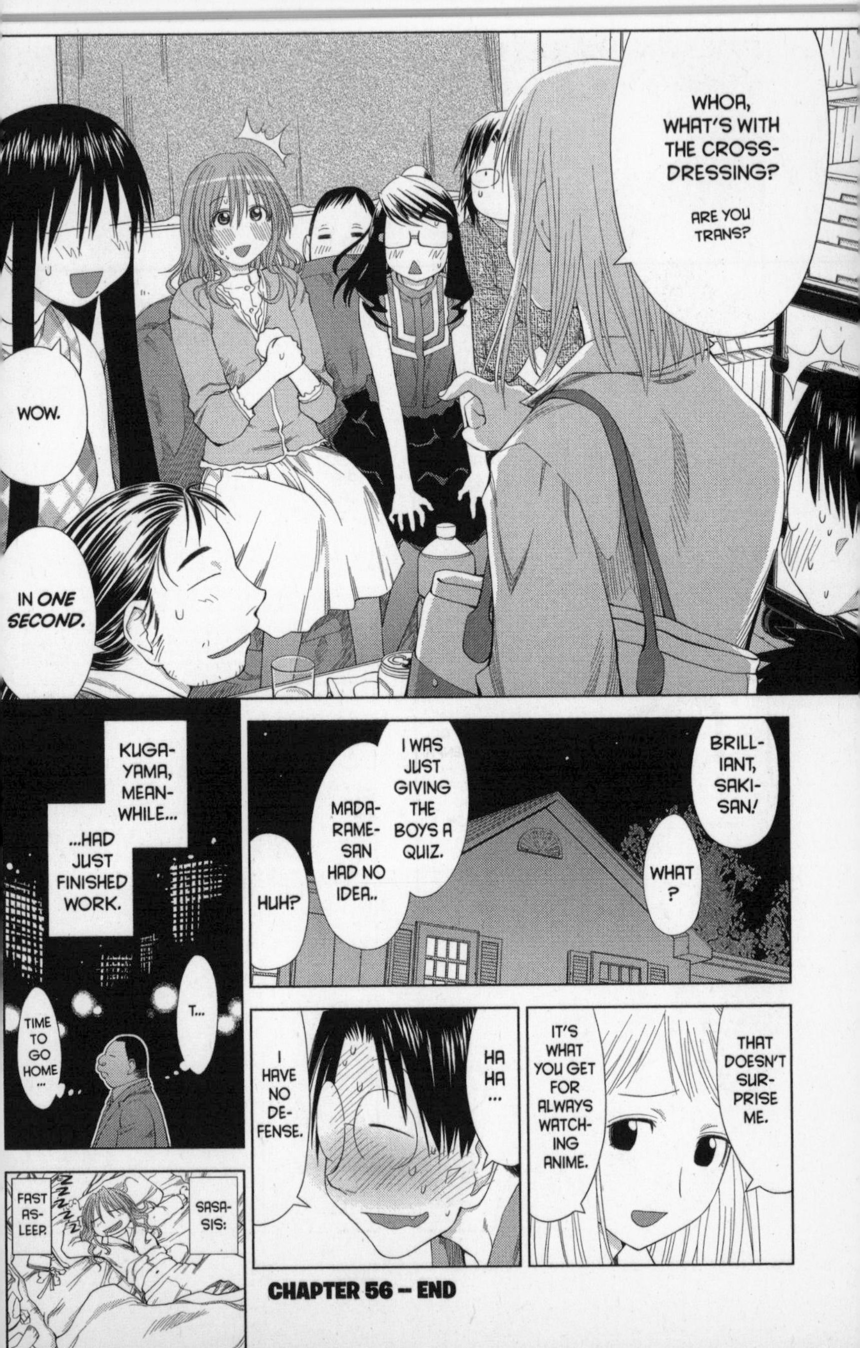
WHOA, WHAT'S WITH THE CROSS-DRESSING?
ARE YOU TRANS?
WOW.
IN *ONE SECOND.*
BRILLIANT, SAKI-SAN!
WHAT?
I WAS JUST GIVING THE BOYS A QUIZ.
MADARAME-SAN HAD NO IDEA..
HUH?
THAT DOESN'T SURPRISE ME.
IT'S WHAT YOU GET FOR ALWAYS WATCHING ANIME.
HA HA...
I HAVE NO DEFENSE.
KUGAYAMA, MEANWHILE...
...HAD JUST FINISHED WORK.
T...
TIME TO GO HOME...
SASA-SIS:
FAST ASLEEP.

CHAPTER 56 -- END

THE SHOCKING TRUTH

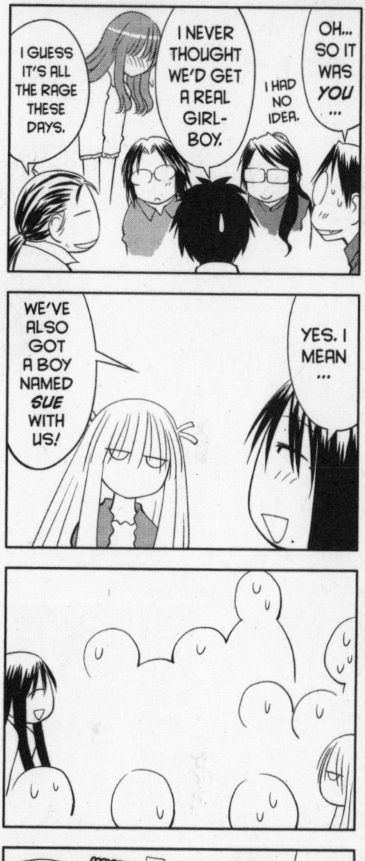
OH... SO IT WAS *YOU* ...
I HAD NO IDEA.
I NEVER THOUGHT WE'D GET A REAL GIRL-BOY.
I GUESS IT'S ALL THE RAGE THESE DAYS.
YES. I MEAN ...
WE'VE ALSO GOT A BOY NAMED *SUE* WITH US!
GUYS? I'M JUST KID-DING.
WHY ARE YOU ALL FROZEN?
WHEW
SMIRK
I WOULD HAVE BE-LIEVED IT...

WE ALWAYS FIGHT

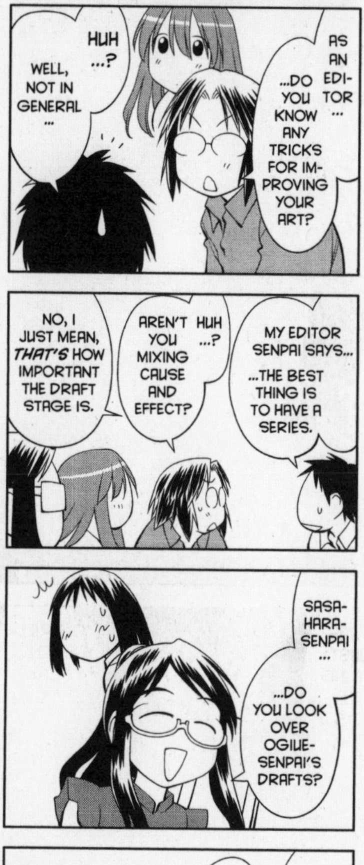
AS AN EDI-TOR ...
...DO YOU KNOW ANY TRICKS FOR IM-PROVING YOUR ART?
HUH ...?
WELL, NOT IN GENERAL ...
MY EDITOR SENPAI SAYS...
...THE BEST THING IS TO HAVE A SERIES.
HUH ...?
AREN'T YOU MIXING CAUSE AND EFFECT?
NO, I JUST MEAN, *THAT'S* HOW IMPORTANT THE DRAFT STAGE IS.
SASA-HARA-SENPAI ...
...DO YOU LOOK OVER OGIUE-SENPAI'S DRAFTS?
....
... HUH?

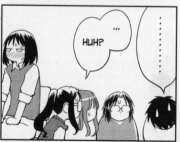

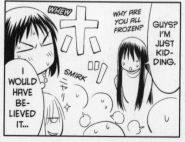

INHERITED TRADITIONS

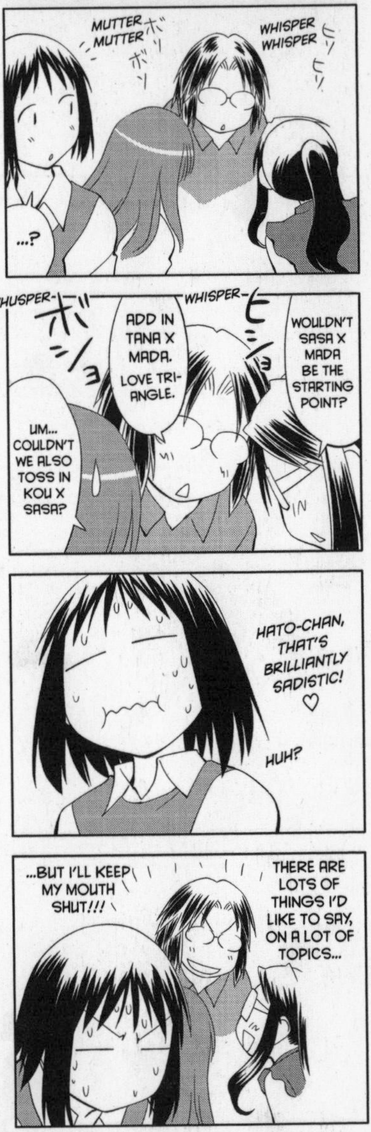
WHISPER WHISPER
ヒソヒソ
MUTTER MUTTER
ボソボソ
...?
WOULDN'T SASA X MADA BE THE STARTING POINT?
WHISPER-
ヒショ
ADD IN TANA X MADA. LOVE TRI-ANGLE.
WHUSPER-
ボショ
UM... COULDN'T WE ALSO TOSS IN KOU X SASA?
HATO-CHAN, THAT'S BRILLIANTLY SADISTIC! ♡
HUH?
THERE ARE LOTS OF THINGS I'D LIKE TO SAY, ON A LOT OF TOPICS...
...BUT I'LL KEEP MY MOUTH SHUT!!!

THE IMMOVABLE MOUNTAIN

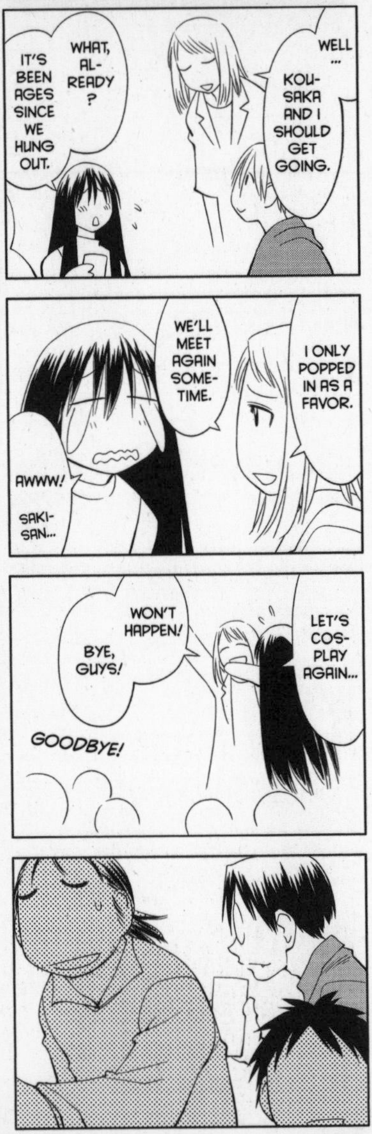
WELL ...
KOU-SAKA AND I SHOULD GET GOING.
WHAT, AL-READY?
IT'S BEEN AGES SINCE WE HUNG OUT.
I ONLY POPPED IN AS A FAVOR.
WE'LL MEET AGAIN SOME-TIME.
AWWW!
SAKI-SAN...
LET'S COS-PLAY AGAIN...
WON'T HAPPEN!
BYE, GUYS!
GOODBYE!

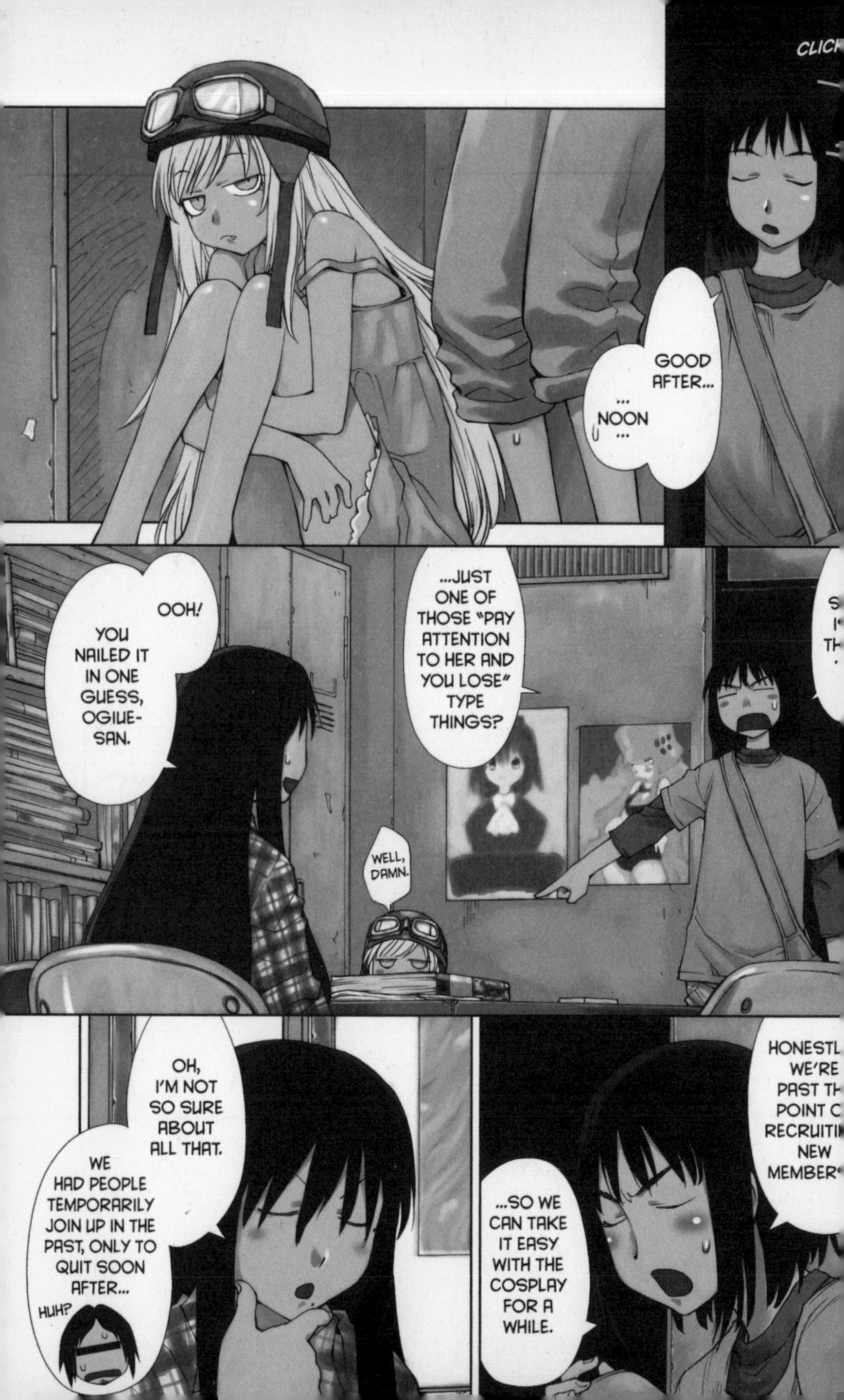
CLIC
GOOD AFTER...
... NOON ...
...JUST ONE OF THOSE "PAY ATTENTION TO HER AND YOU LOSE" TYPE THINGS?
OOH! YOU NAILED IT IN ONE GUESS, OGIUE-SAN.
WELL, DAMN.
HONESTL WE'RE PAST TH POINT O RECRUITI NEW MEMBER
...SO WE CAN TAKE IT EASY WITH THE COSPLAY FOR A WHILE.
OH, I'M NOT SO SURE ABOUT ALL THAT.
WE HAD PEOPLE TEMPORARILY JOIN UP IN THE PAST, ONLY TO QUIT SOON AFTER...
HUH?

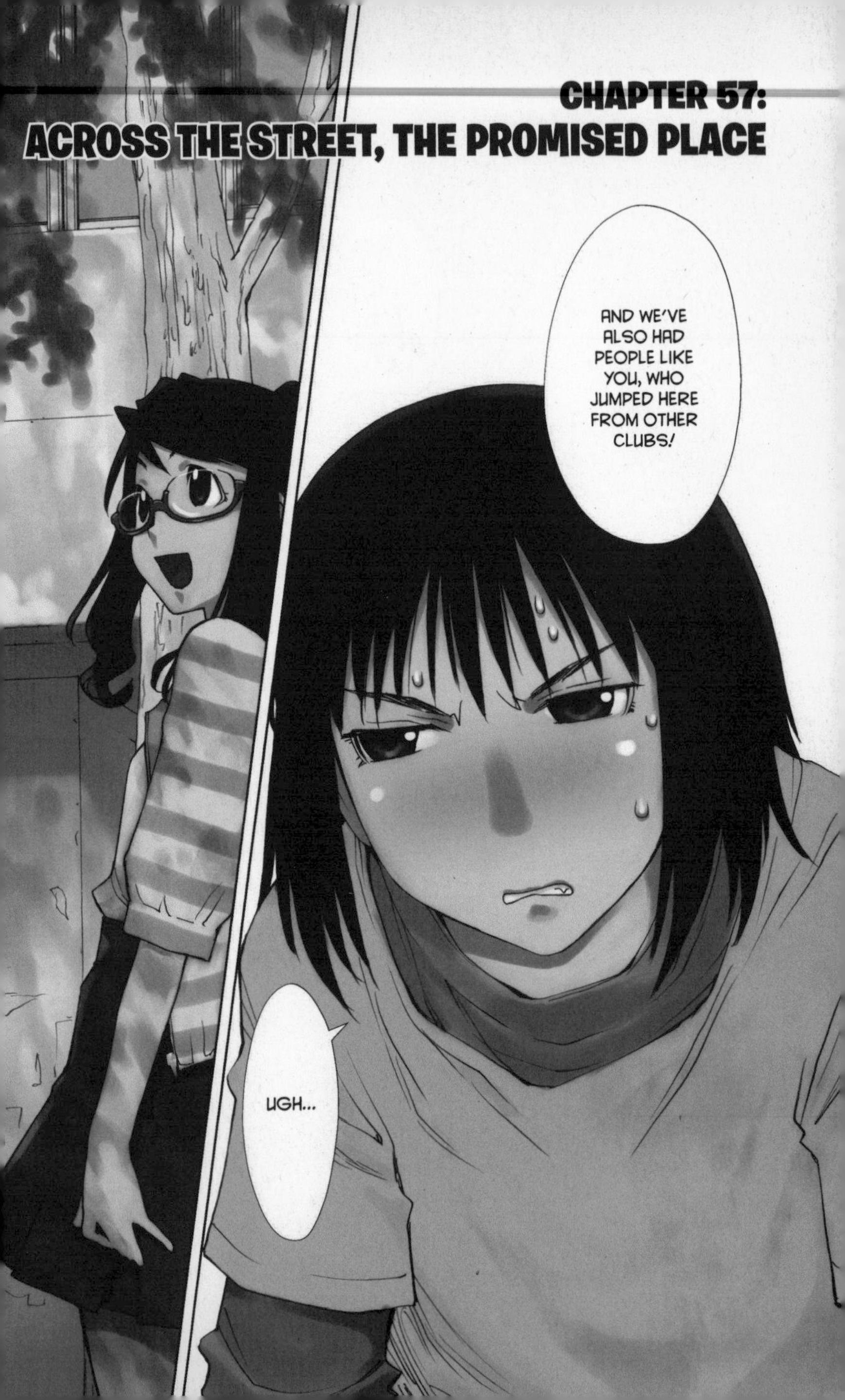
CHAPTER 57:
ACROSS THE STREET, THE PROMISED PLACE
AND WE'VE ALSO HAD PEOPLE LIKE YOU, WHO JUMPED HERE FROM OTHER CLUBS!
UGH...

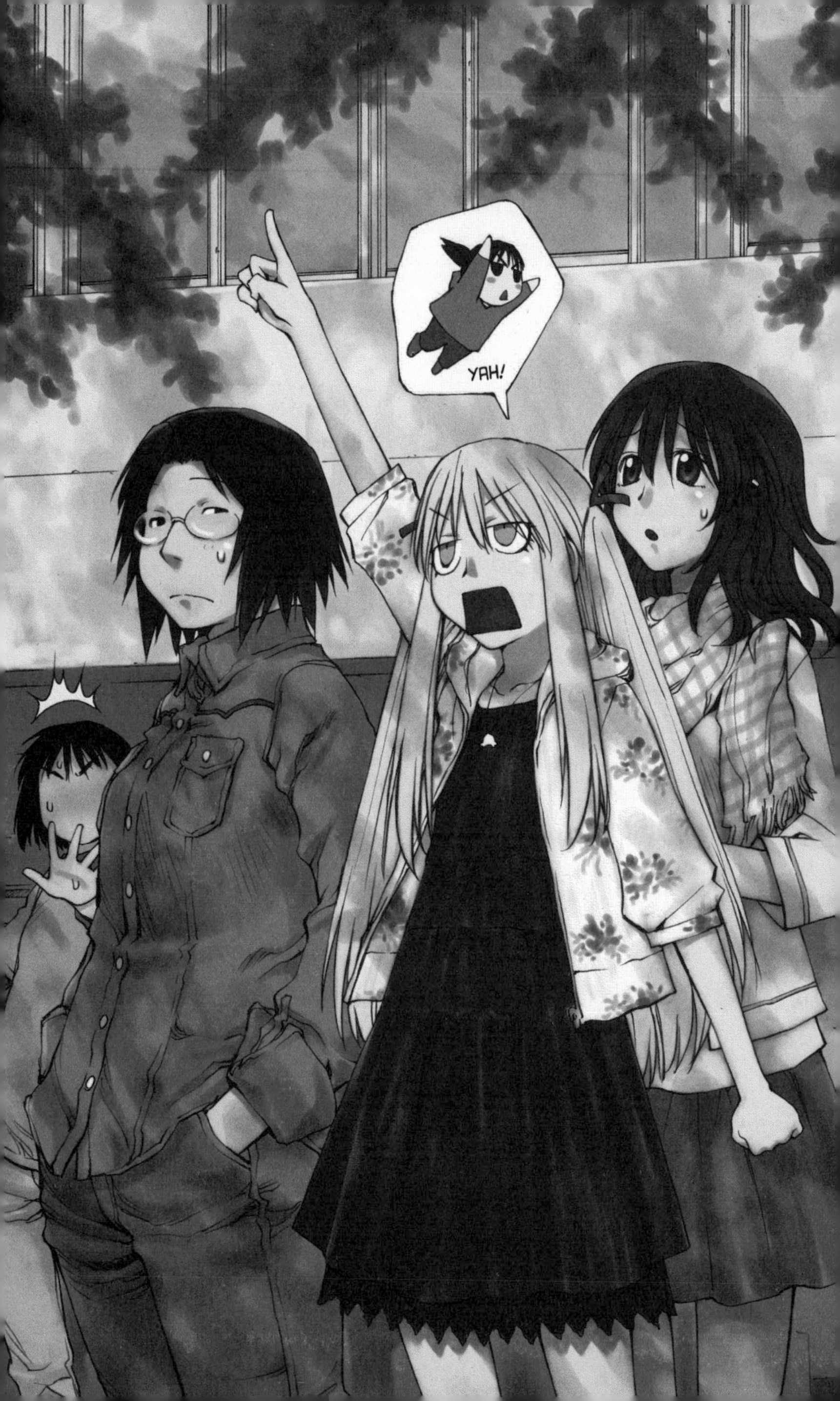
YAH!

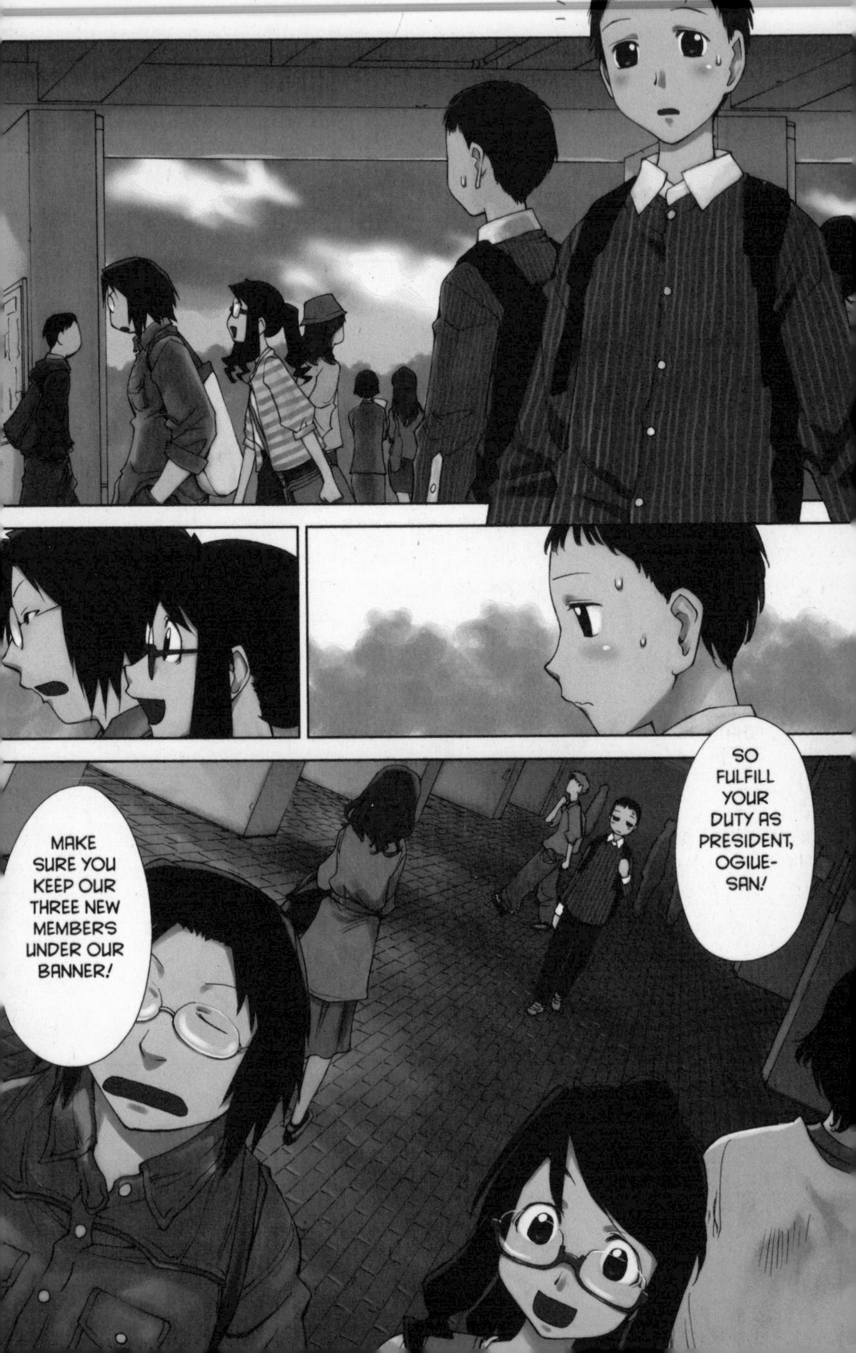
SO FULFILL YOUR DUTY AS PRESIDENT, OGIUE-SAN!
MAKE SURE YOU KEEP OUR THREE NEW MEMBERS UNDER OUR BANNER!

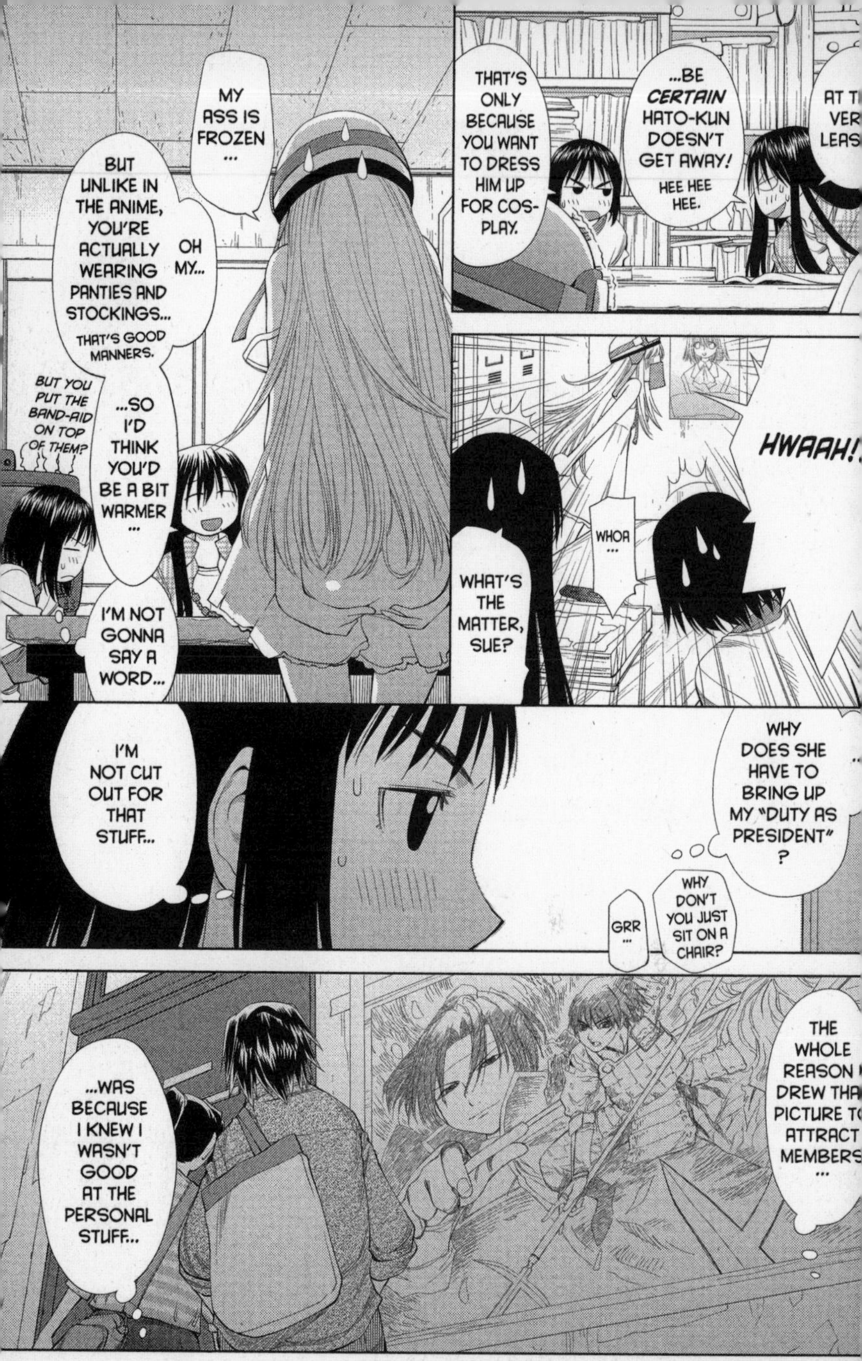

AT T VER LEAS
...BE *CERTAIN* HATO-KUN DOESN'T GET AWAY!
HEE HEE HEE.
THAT'S ONLY BECAUSE YOU WANT TO DRESS HIM UP FOR COS-PLAY.
HWAAH!
WHOA ...
WHAT'S THE MATTER, SUE?
MY ASS IS FROZEN ...
OH MY...
BUT UNLIKE IN THE ANIME, YOU'RE ACTUALLY WEARING PANTIES AND STOCKINGS...
THAT'S GOOD MANNERS.
...SO I'D THINK YOU'D BE A BIT WARMER ...
BUT YOU PUT THE BAND-AID ON TOP OF THEM?
I'M NOT GONNA SAY A WORD...
WHY DOES SHE HAVE TO BRING UP MY "DUTY AS PRESIDENT" ?
WHY DON'T YOU JUST SIT ON A CHAIR?
GRR ...
I'M NOT CUT OUT FOR THAT STUFF...
THE WHOLE REASON DREW THA PICTURE T ATTRACT MEMBERS ...
...WAS BECAUSE I KNEW I WASN'T GOOD AT THE PERSONAL STUFF...

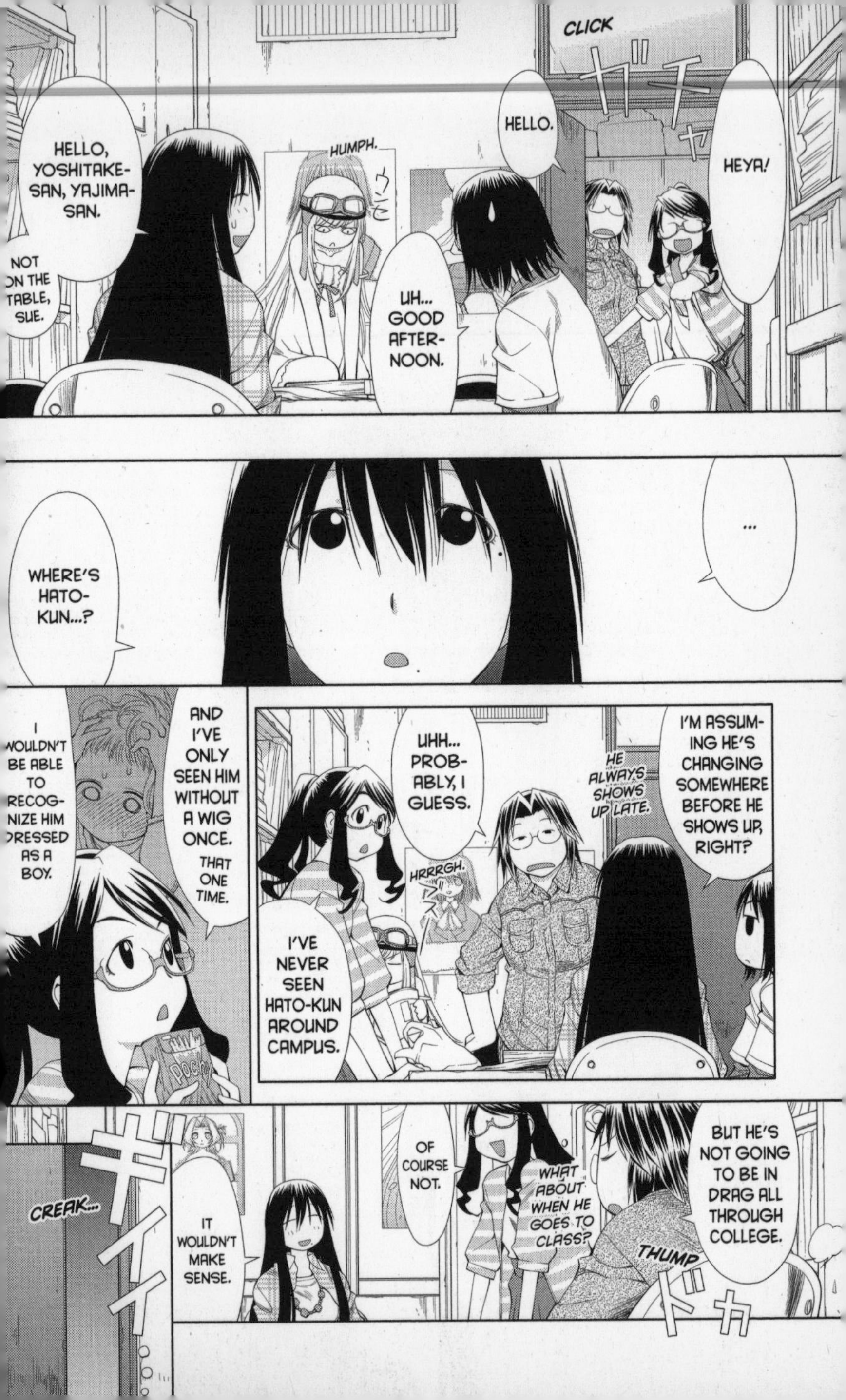
CLICK
HEYA!
HELLO.
UH... GOOD AFTERNOON.
HUMPH.
HELLO, YOSHITAKE-SAN, YAJIMA-SAN.
NOT ON THE TABLE, SUE.
...
WHERE'S HATO-KUN...?
I'M ASSUMING HE'S CHANGING SOMEWHERE BEFORE HE SHOWS UP, RIGHT?
HE ALWAYS SHOWS UP LATE.
UHH... PROBABLY, I GUESS.
HRRRGH.
I'VE NEVER SEEN HATO-KUN AROUND CAMPUS.
AND I'VE ONLY SEEN HIM WITHOUT A WIG ONCE.
THAT ONE TIME.
I WOULDN'T BE ABLE TO RECOGNIZE HIM DRESSED AS A BOY.
BUT HE'S NOT GOING TO BE IN DRAG ALL THROUGH COLLEGE.
THUMP
WHAT ABOUT WHEN HE GOES TO CLASS?
OF COURSE NOT.
IT WOULDN'T MAKE SENSE.
CREAK...

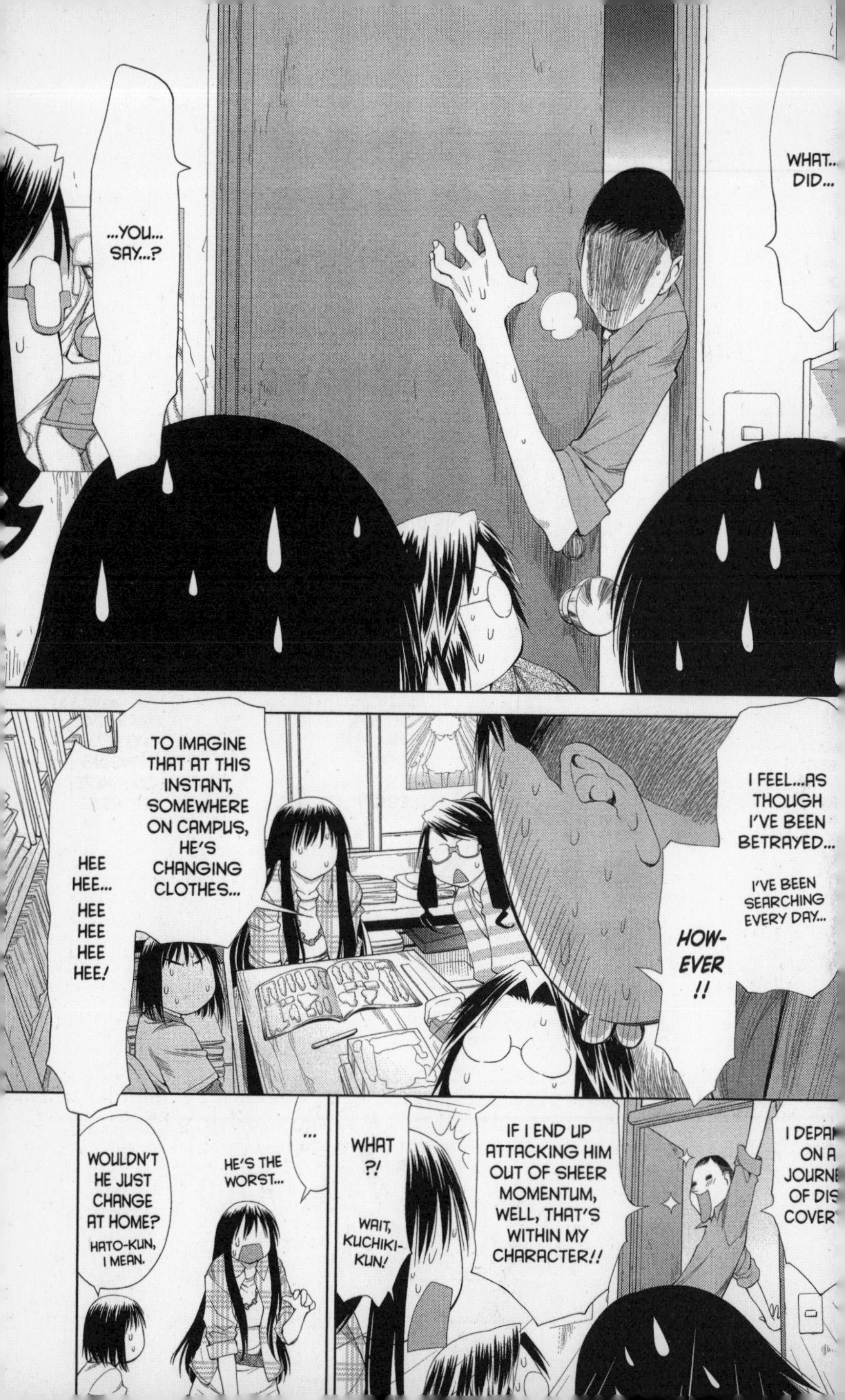

WHAT... DID...
...YOU... SAY...?
I FEEL...AS THOUGH I'VE BEEN BETRAYED...
I'VE BEEN SEARCHING EVERY DAY...
HOW-EVER!!
TO IMAGINE THAT AT THIS INSTANT, SOMEWHERE ON CAMPUS, HE'S CHANGING CLOTHES...
HEE HEE... HEE HEE HEE HEE!
I DEPAR ON A JOURNE OF DIS COVER
IF I END UP ATTACKING HIM OUT OF SHEER MOMENTUM, WELL, THAT'S WITHIN MY CHARACTER!!
WHAT ?!
WAIT, KUCHIKI-KUN!
...
HE'S THE WORST...
WOULDN'T HE JUST CHANGE AT HOME?
HATO-KUN, I MEAN.

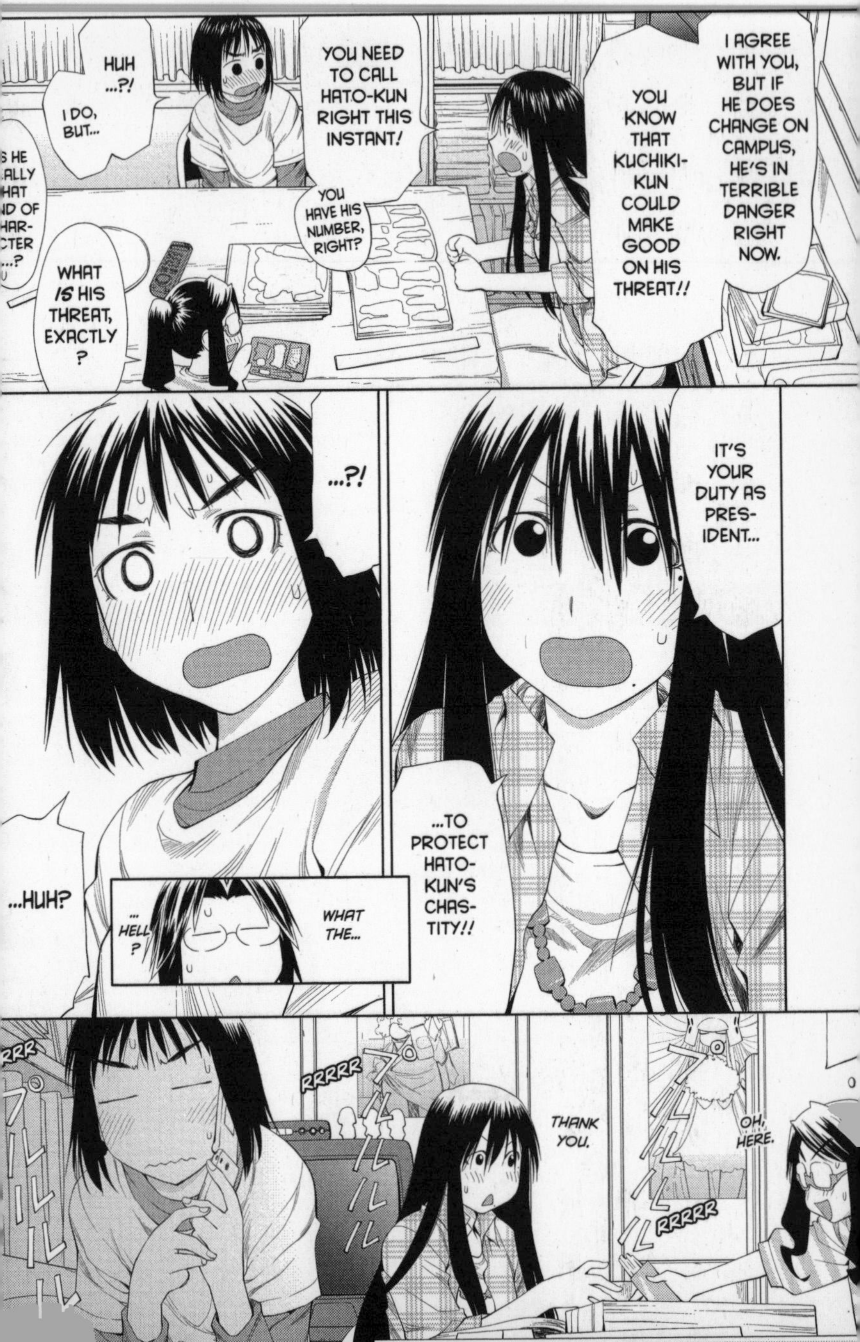
I AGREE WITH YOU, BUT IF HE DOES CHANGE ON CAMPUS, HE'S IN TERRIBLE DANGER RIGHT NOW.
YOU KNOW THAT KUCHIKI-KUN COULD MAKE GOOD ON HIS THREAT!!
YOU NEED TO CALL HATO-KUN RIGHT THIS INSTANT!
HUH ...?!
YOU HAVE HIS NUMBER, RIGHT?
I DO, BUT...
WHAT IS HIS THREAT, EXACTLY ?
IT'S YOUR DUTY AS PRES-IDENT...
...TO PROTECT HATO-KUN'S CHAS-TITY!!
...?!
...HUH?
WHAT THE...
...HELL ?
OH, HERE.
RRRRR
THANK YOU.
RRRRR
RRRR

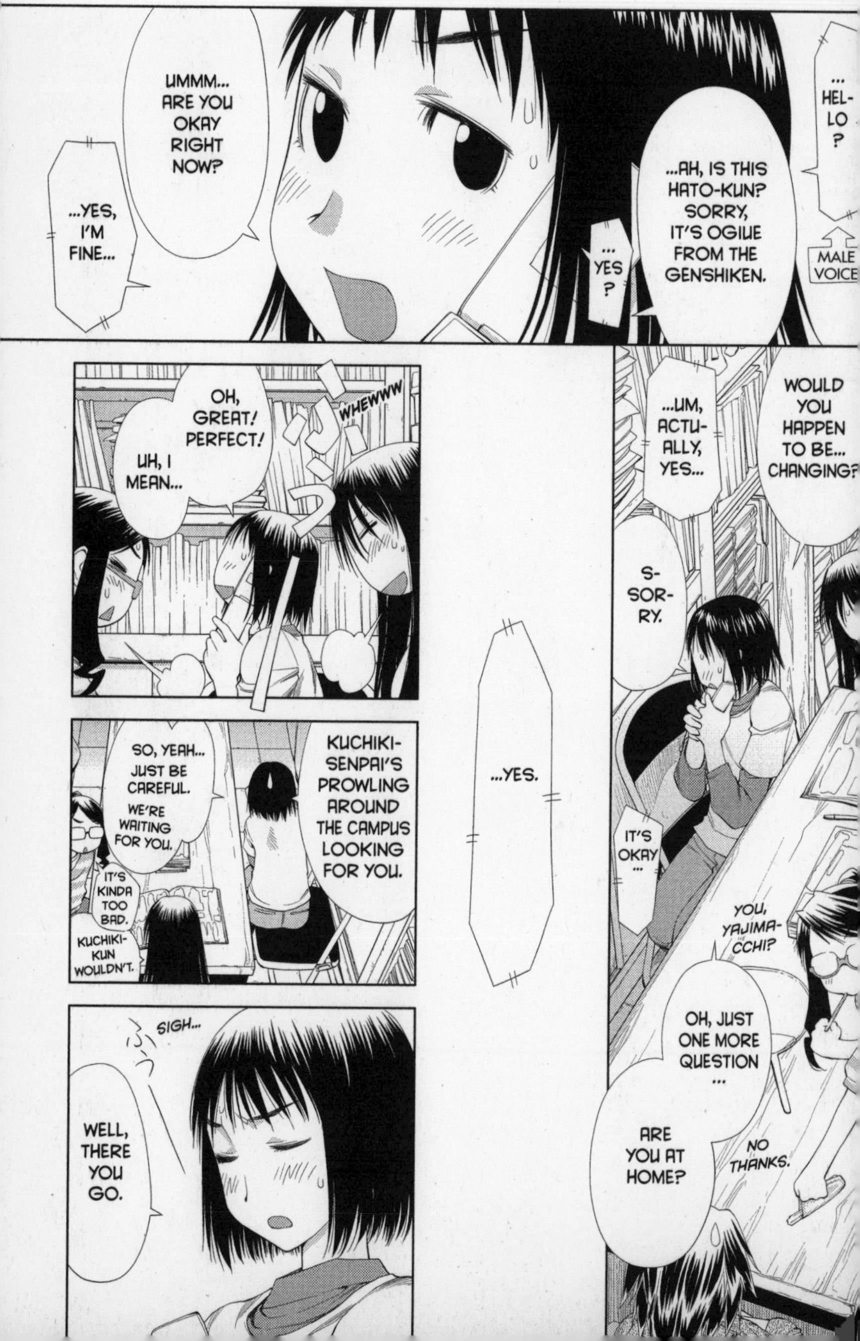
...HEL-LO?
MALE VOICE
...AH, IS THIS HATO-KUN? SORRY, IT'S OGIUE FROM THE GENSHIKEN.
...YES?
UMMM... ARE YOU OKAY RIGHT NOW?
...YES, I'M FINE...
WOULD YOU HAPPEN TO BE... CHANGING?
...UM, ACTU-ALLY, YES...
S-SOR-RY.
IT'S OKAY...
YOU, YAJIMA-CCHI?
OH, JUST ONE MORE QUESTION...
NO THANKS.
ARE YOU AT HOME?
...YES.
OH, GREAT! PERFECT!
WHEWWW
UH, I MEAN...
KUCHIKI-SENPAI'S PROWLING AROUND THE CAMPUS LOOKING FOR YOU.
SO, YEAH... JUST BE CAREFUL.
WE'RE WAITING FOR YOU.
IT'S KINDA TOO BAD.
KUCHIKI-KUN WOULDN'T.
SIGH...
WELL, THERE YOU GO.

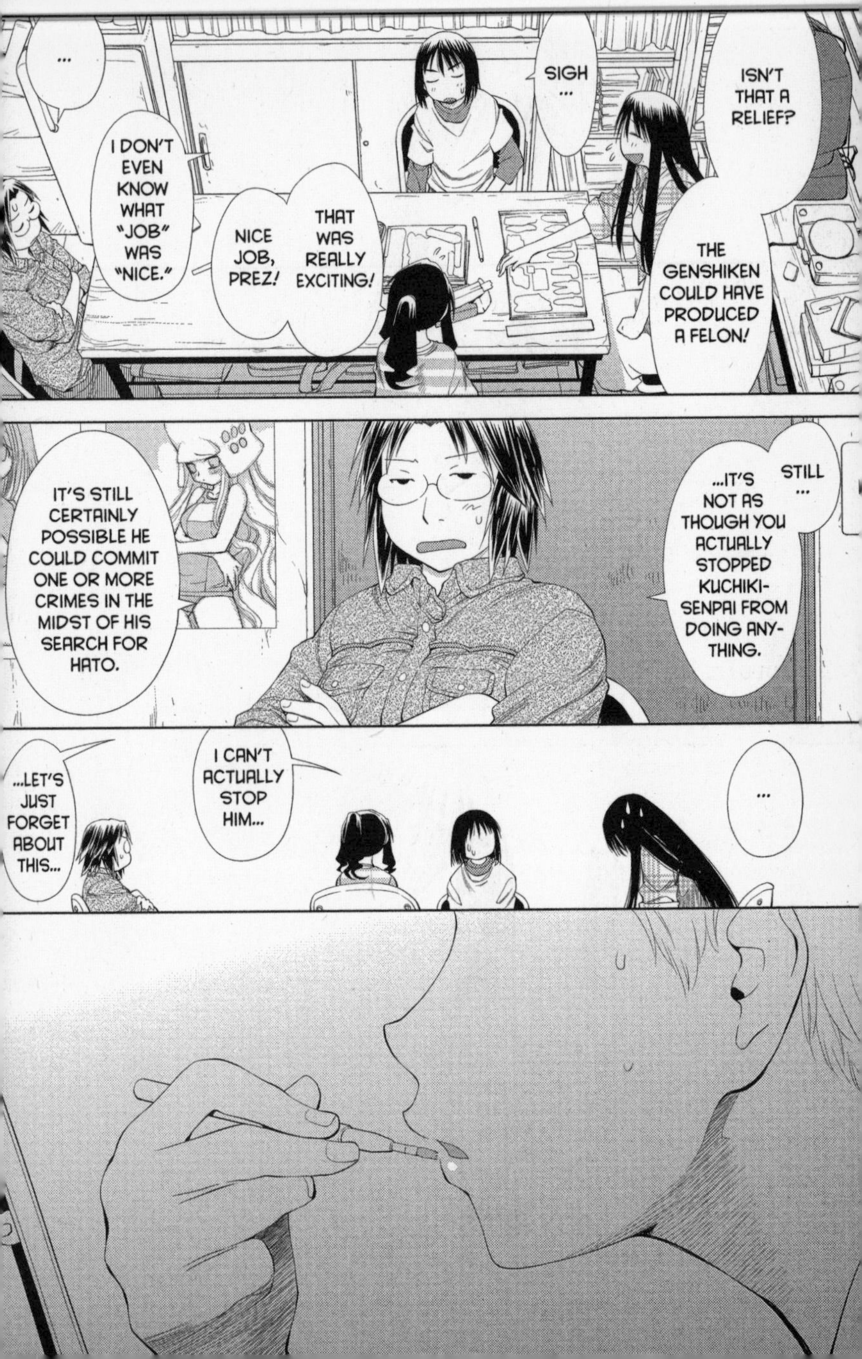
ISN'T THAT A RELIEF?
THE GENSHIKEN COULD HAVE PRODUCED A FELON!
SIGH ...
THAT WAS REALLY EXCITING!
NICE JOB, PREZ!
I DON'T EVEN KNOW WHAT "JOB" WAS "NICE."
...
STILL ...
...IT'S NOT AS THOUGH YOU ACTUALLY STOPPED KUCHIKI-SENPAI FROM DOING ANYTHING.
IT'S STILL CERTAINLY POSSIBLE HE COULD COMMIT ONE OR MORE CRIMES IN THE MIDST OF HIS SEARCH FOR HATO.
...
I CAN'T ACTUALLY STOP HIM...
...LET'S JUST FORGET ABOUT THIS...

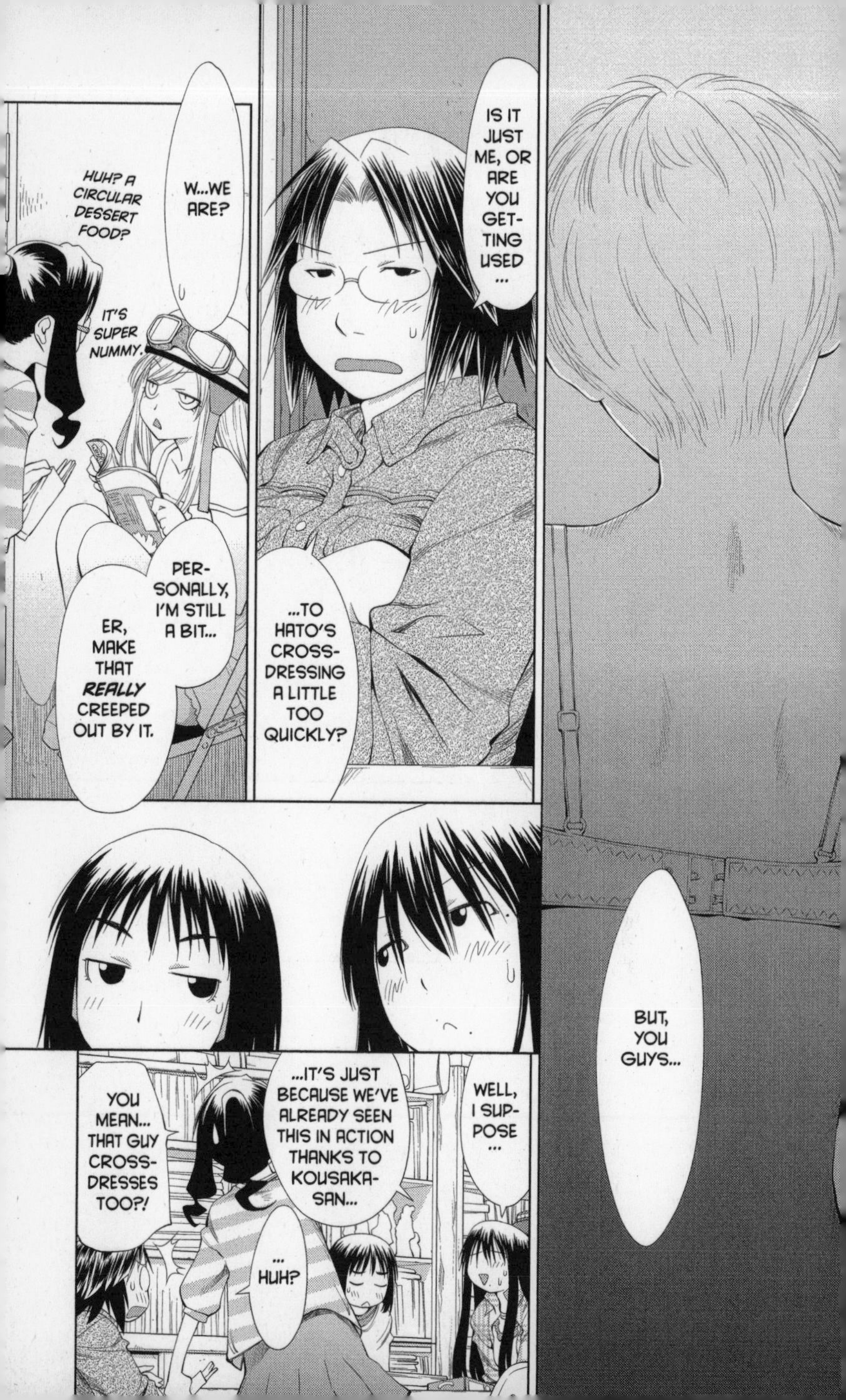
BUT, YOU GUYS...
IS IT JUST ME, OR ARE YOU GETTING USED...
...TO HATO'S CROSS-DRESSING A LITTLE TOO QUICKLY?
W...WE ARE?
HUH? A CIRCULAR DESSERT FOOD?
IT'S SUPER NUMMY.
PERSONALLY, I'M STILL A BIT...
ER, MAKE THAT *REALLY* CREEPED OUT BY IT.
WELL, I SUPPOSE...
...IT'S JUST BECAUSE WE'VE ALREADY SEEN THIS IN ACTION THANKS TO KOUSAKA-SAN...
YOU MEAN... THAT GUY CROSS-DRESSES TOO?!
... HUH?

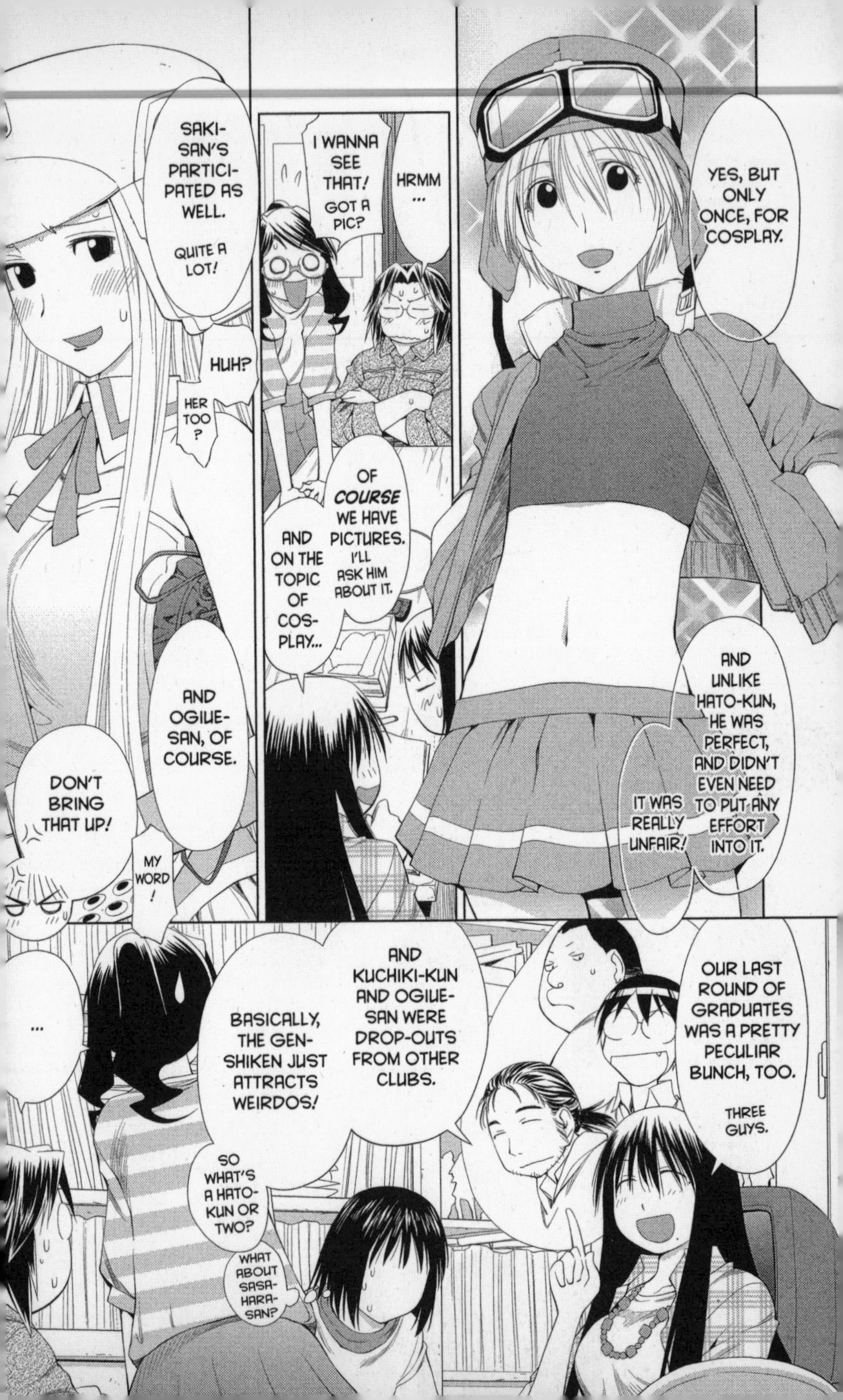
YES, BUT ONLY ONCE, FOR COSPLAY.
AND UNLIKE HATO-KUN, HE WAS PERFECT, AND DIDN'T EVEN NEED TO PUT ANY EFFORT INTO IT.
IT WAS REALLY UNFAIR!
HRMM ...
I WANNA SEE THAT!
GOT A PIC?
OF *COURSE* WE HAVE PICTURES.
I'LL ASK HIM ABOUT IT.
AND ON THE TOPIC OF COS-PLAY...
SAKI-SAN'S PARTICI-PATED AS WELL.
QUITE A LOT!
HUH?
HER TOO ?
AND OGIUE-SAN, OF COURSE.
DON'T BRING THAT UP!
MY WORD !
OUR LAST ROUND OF GRADUATES WAS A PRETTY PECULIAR BUNCH, TOO.
THREE GUYS.
AND KUCHIKI-KUN AND OGIUE-SAN WERE DROP-OUTS FROM OTHER CLUBS.
BASICALLY, THE GEN-SHIKEN JUST ATTRACTS WEIRDOS!
...
SO WHAT'S A HATO-KUN OR TWO?
WHAT ABOUT SASA-HARA-SAN?

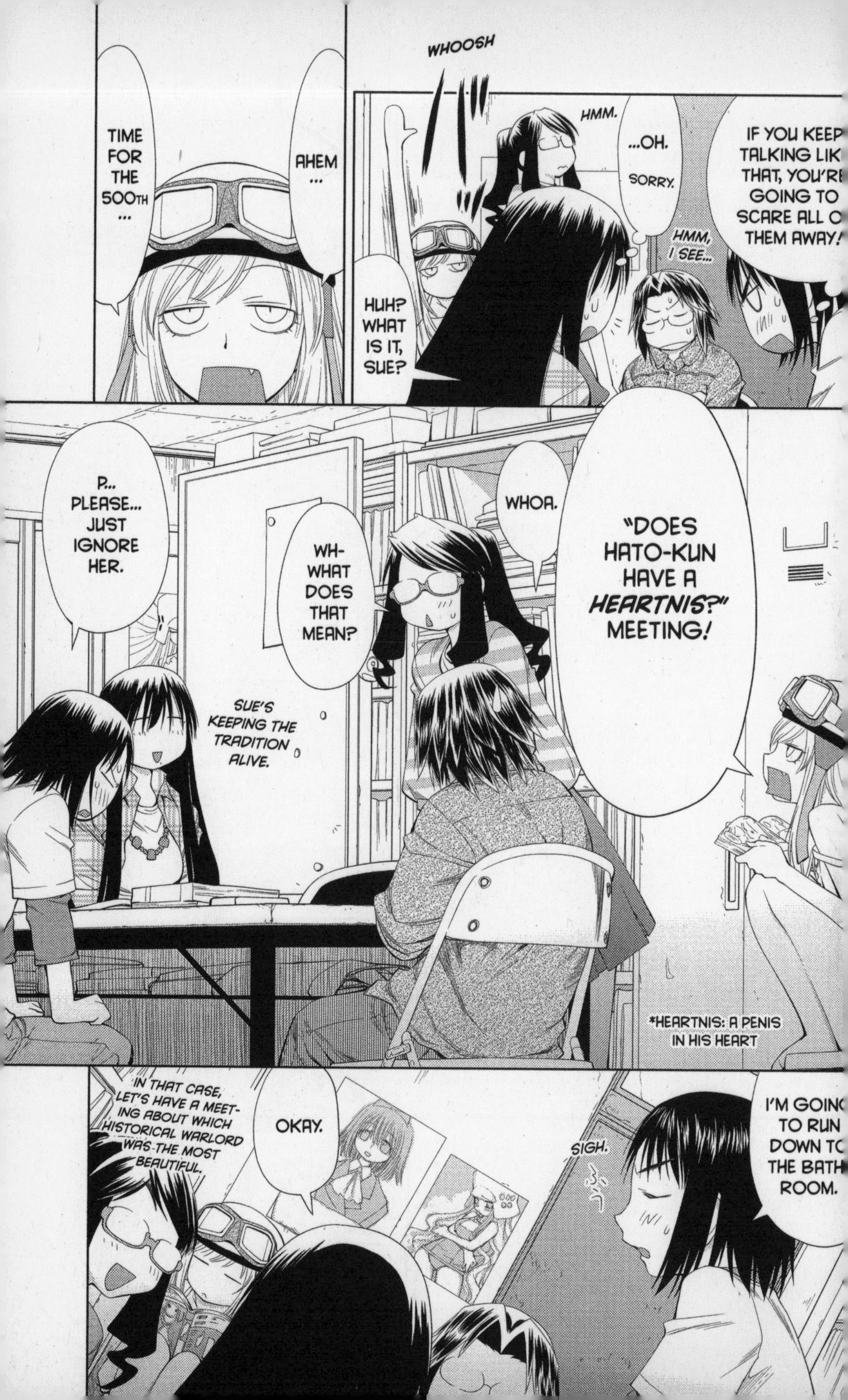
IF YOU KEEP TALKING LIK THAT, YOU'R GOING TO SCARE ALL O THEM AWAY!
HMM.
...OH.
SORRY.
HMM, I SEE...
WHOOSH
HUH? WHAT IS IT, SUE?
AHEM...
TIME FOR THE 500TH...
"DOES HATO-KUN HAVE A *HEARTNIS?*" MEETING!
WHOA.
WH-WHAT DOES THAT MEAN?
SUE'S KEEPING THE TRADITION ALIVE.
P... PLEASE... JUST IGNORE HER.
*HEARTNIS: A PENIS IN HIS HEART
I'M GOINC TO RUN DOWN TC THE BATH ROOM.
SIGH.
OKAY.
IN THAT CASE, LET'S HAVE A MEET-ING ABOUT WHICH HISTORICAL WARLORD WAS THE MOST BEAUTIFUL.

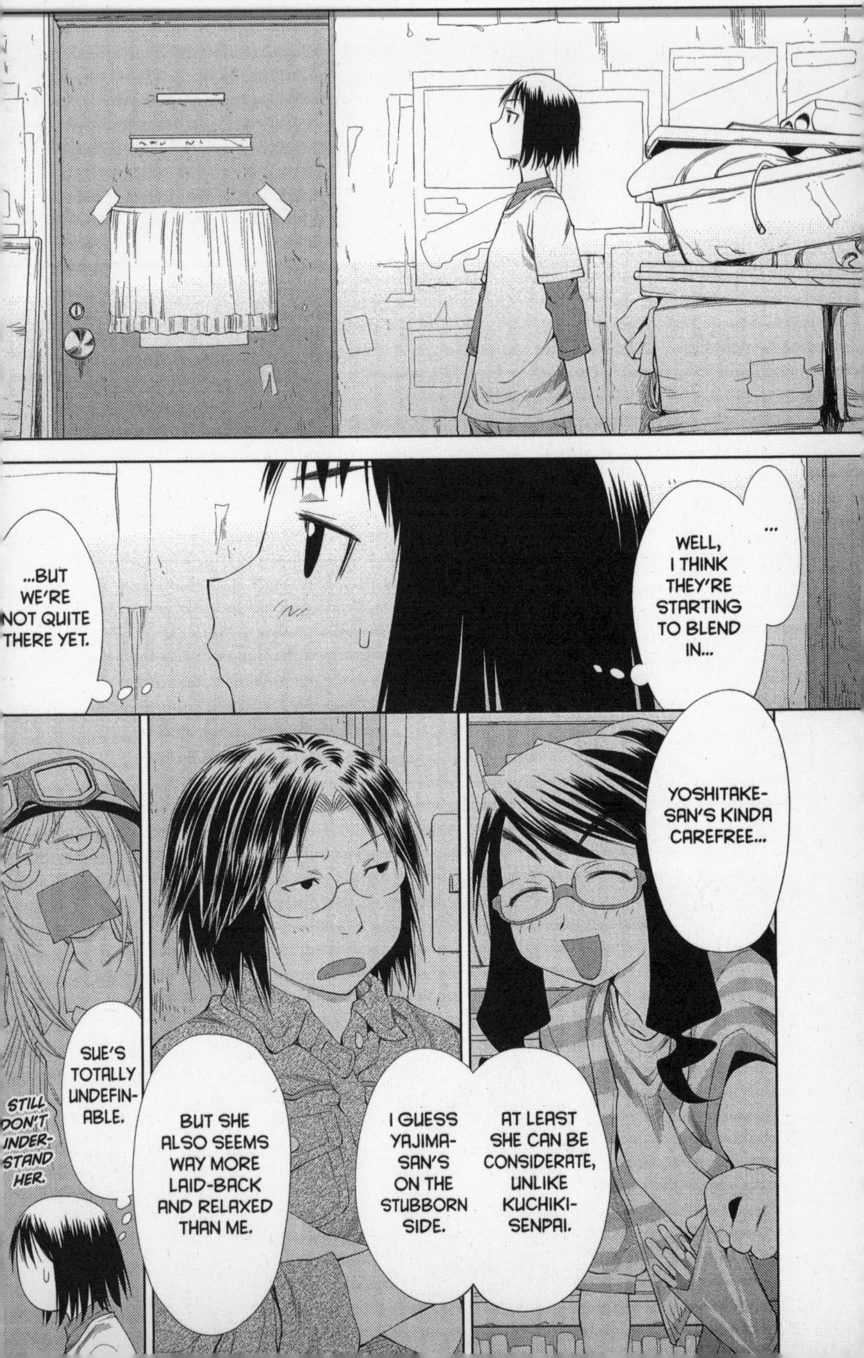
...
WELL, I THINK THEY'RE STARTING TO BLEND IN...
...BUT WE'RE NOT QUITE THERE YET.
YOSHITAKE-SAN'S KINDA CAREFREE...
AT LEAST SHE CAN BE CONSIDERATE, UNLIKE KUCHIKI-SENPAI.
I GUESS YAJIMA-SAN'S ON THE STUBBORN SIDE.
BUT SHE ALSO SEEMS WAY MORE LAID-BACK AND RELAXED THAN ME.
SUE'S TOTALLY UNDEFIN-ABLE.
STILL DON'T UNDER-STAND HER.

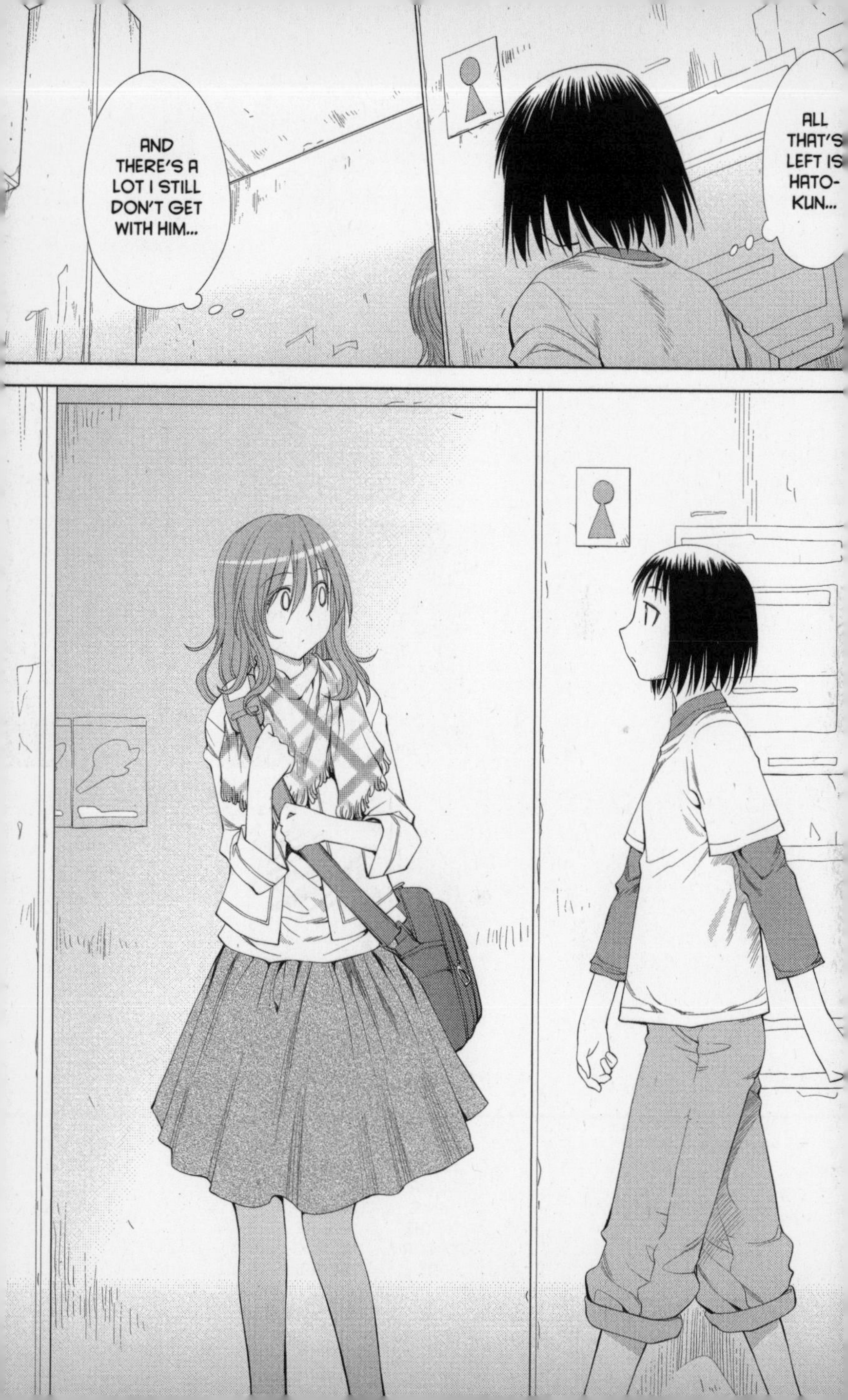
ALL THAT'S LEFT IS HATO-KUN...
AND THERE'S A LOT I STILL DON'T GET WITH HIM...

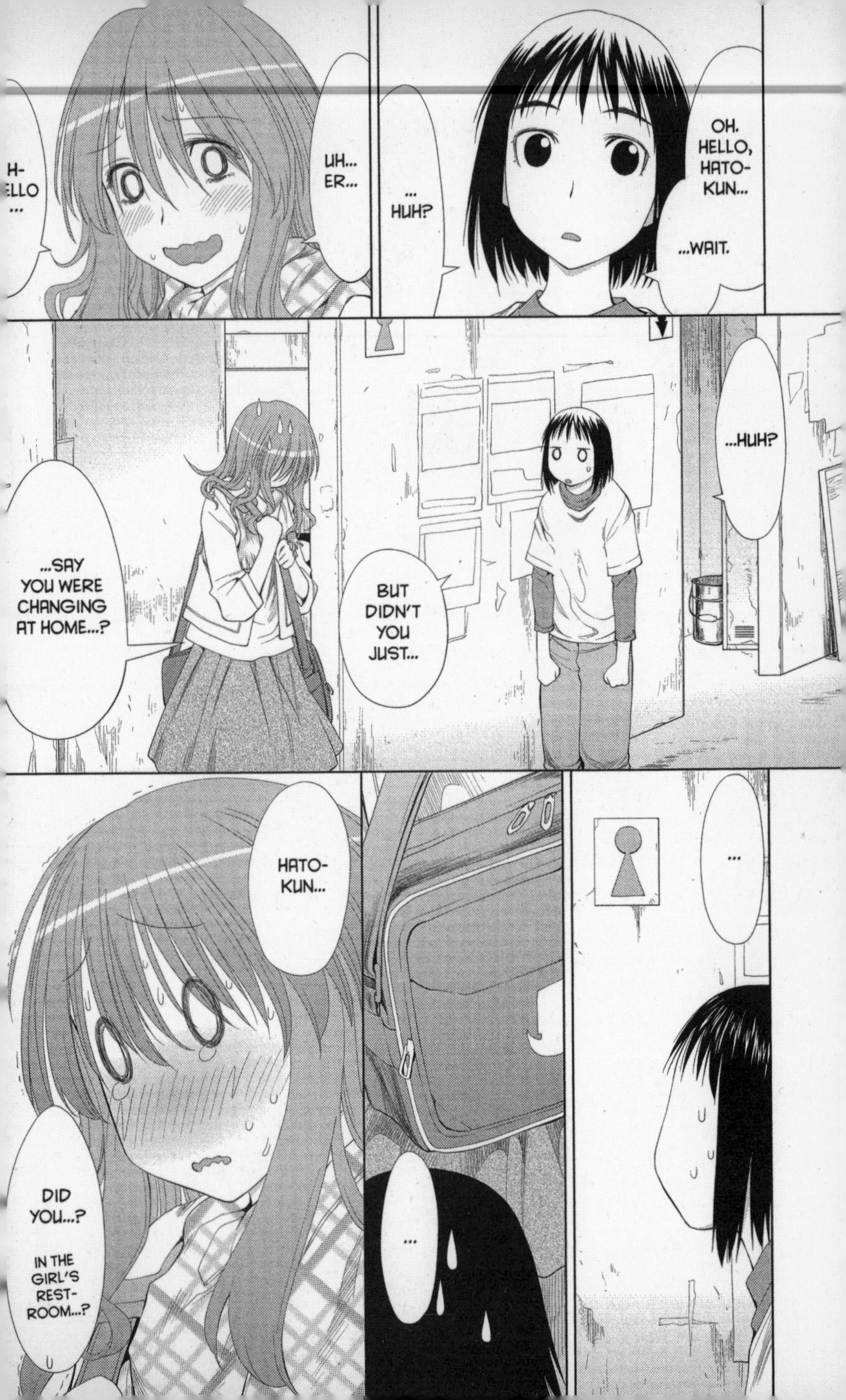
OH. HELLO, HATO-KUN...
...WAIT.
... HUH?
UH... ER...
H- ELLO ...
...HUH?
BUT DIDN'T YOU JUST...
...SAY YOU WERE CHANGING AT HOME...?
...
...
HATO-KUN...
DID YOU...?
IN THE GIRL'S REST-ROOM...?

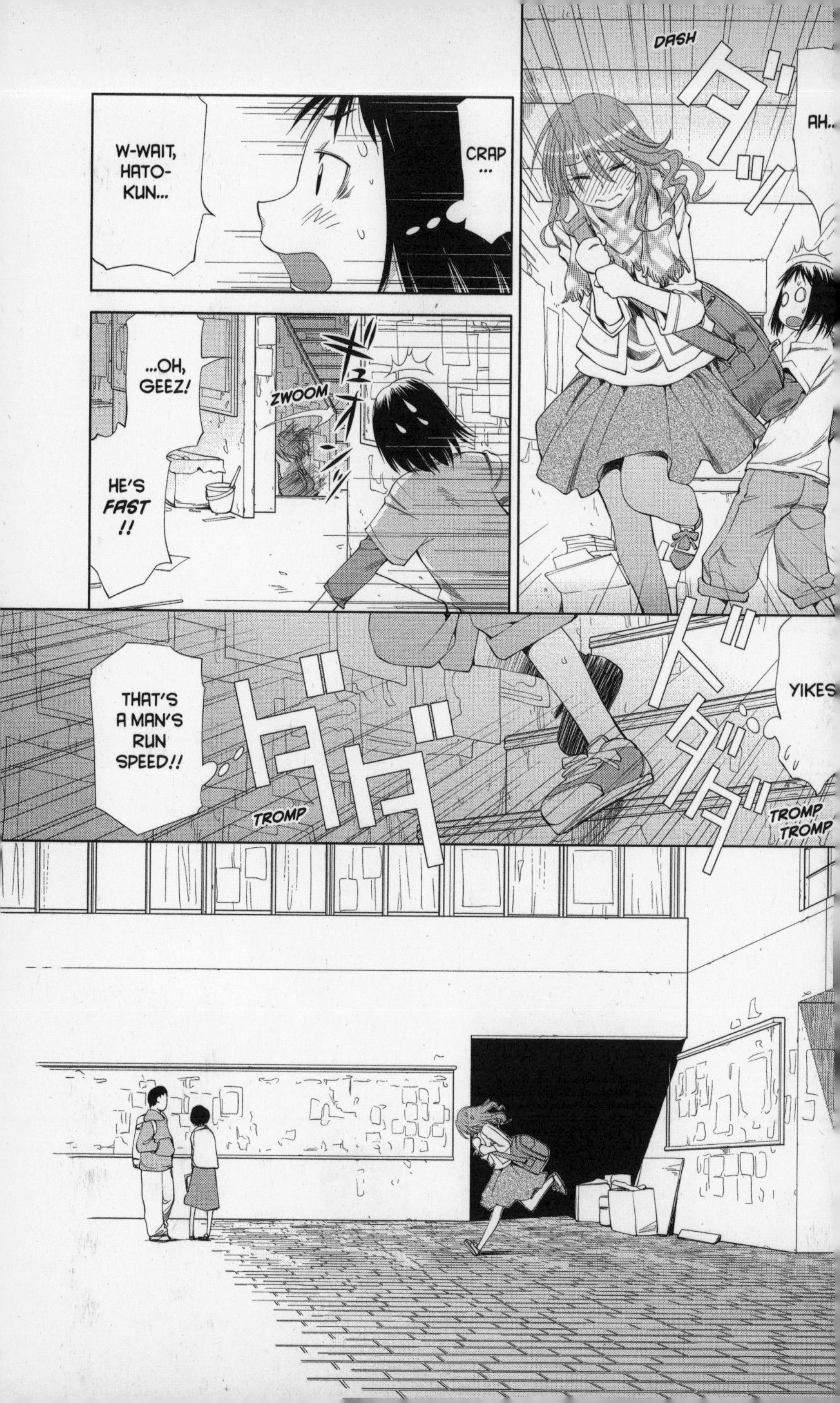
DASH
AH...
CRAP...
W-WAIT, HATO-KUN...
ZWOOM
...OH, GEEZ!
HE'S FAST!!
YIKES
TROMP TROMP
THAT'S A MAN'S RUN SPEED!!
TROMP

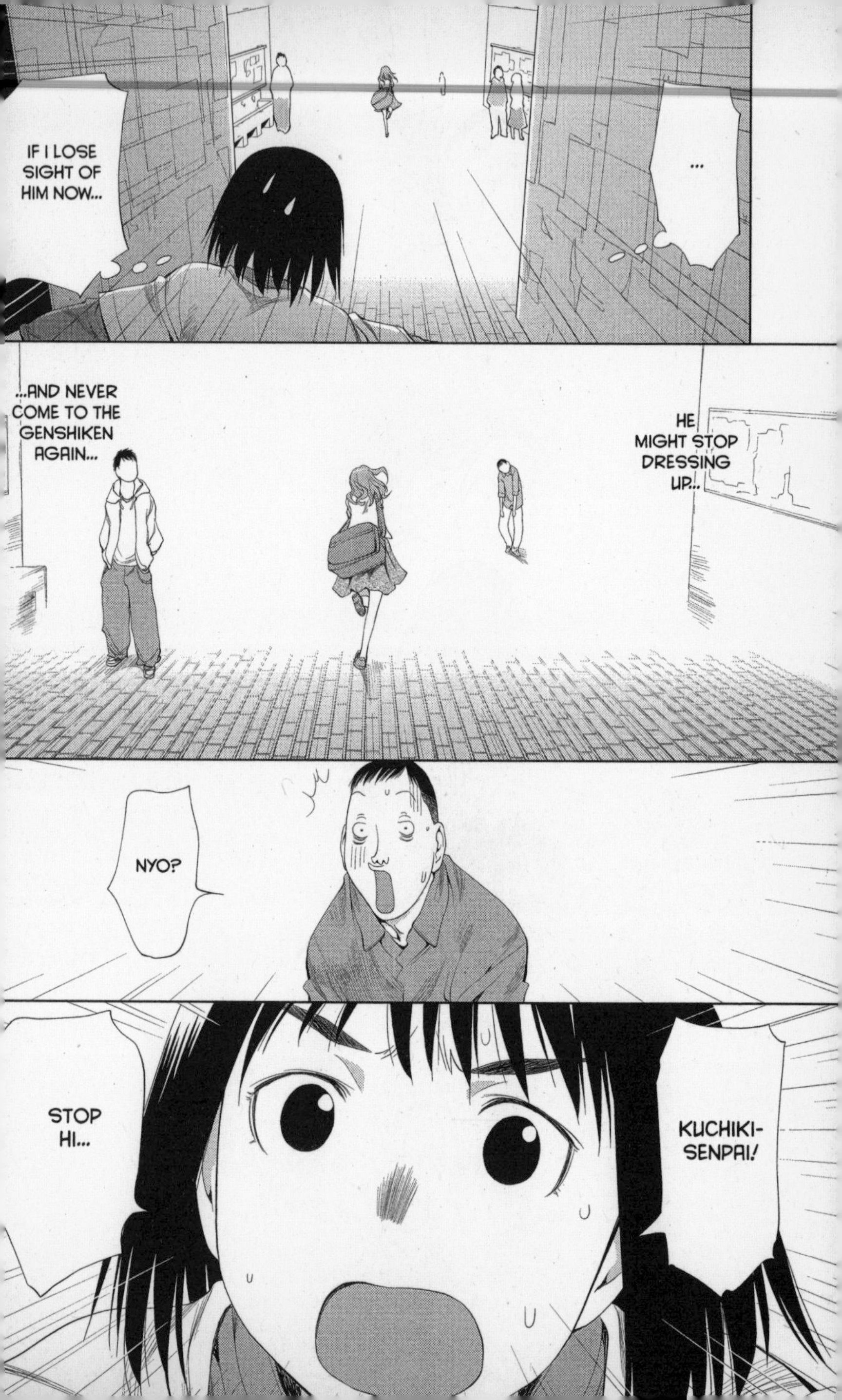
...
IF I LOSE SIGHT OF HIM NOW...
HE MIGHT STOP DRESSING UP...
...AND NEVER COME TO THE GENSHIKEN AGAIN...
NYO?
KUCHIKI-SENPAI!
STOP HI...

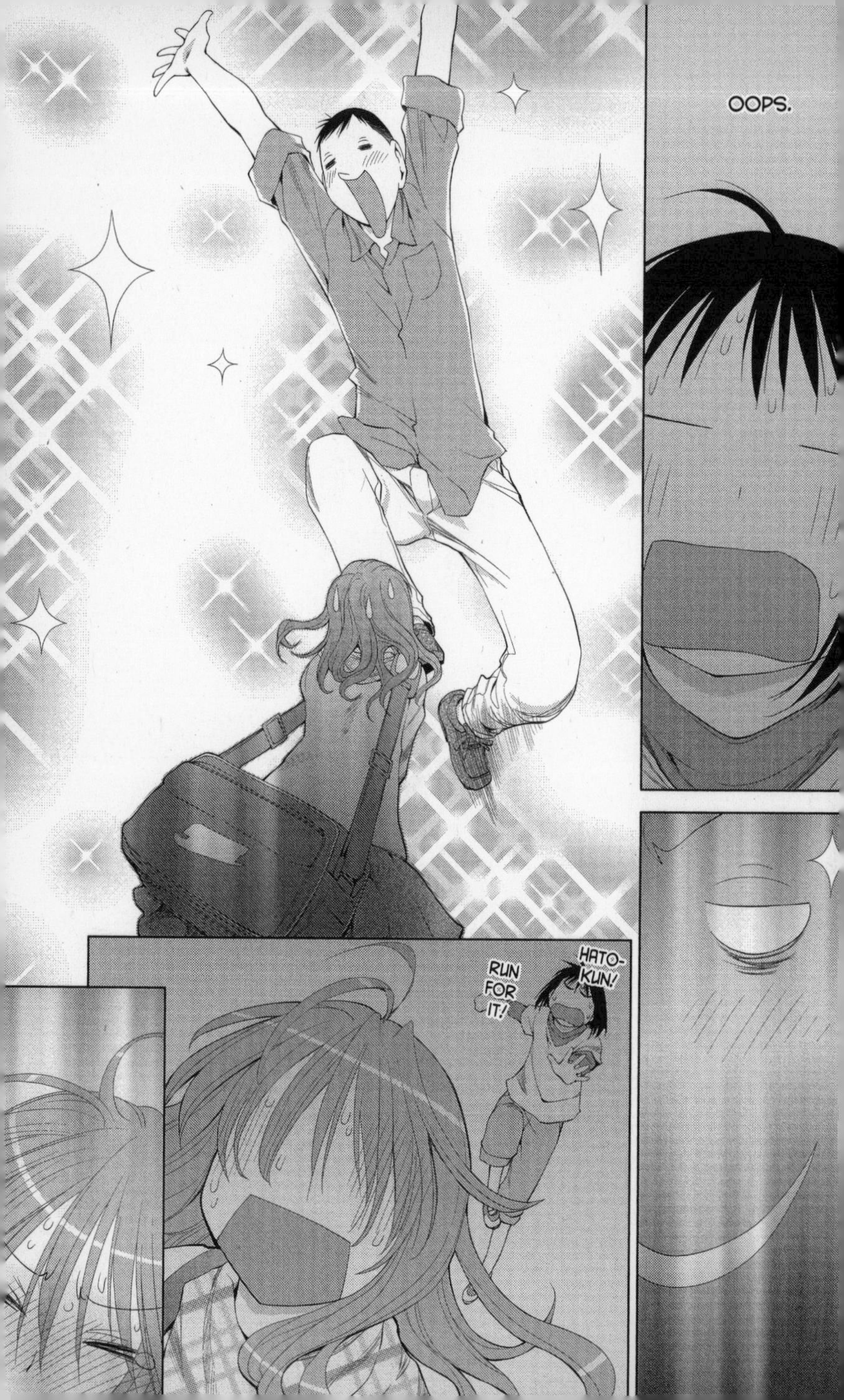
OOPS.
HATO-KUN!
RUN FOR IT!

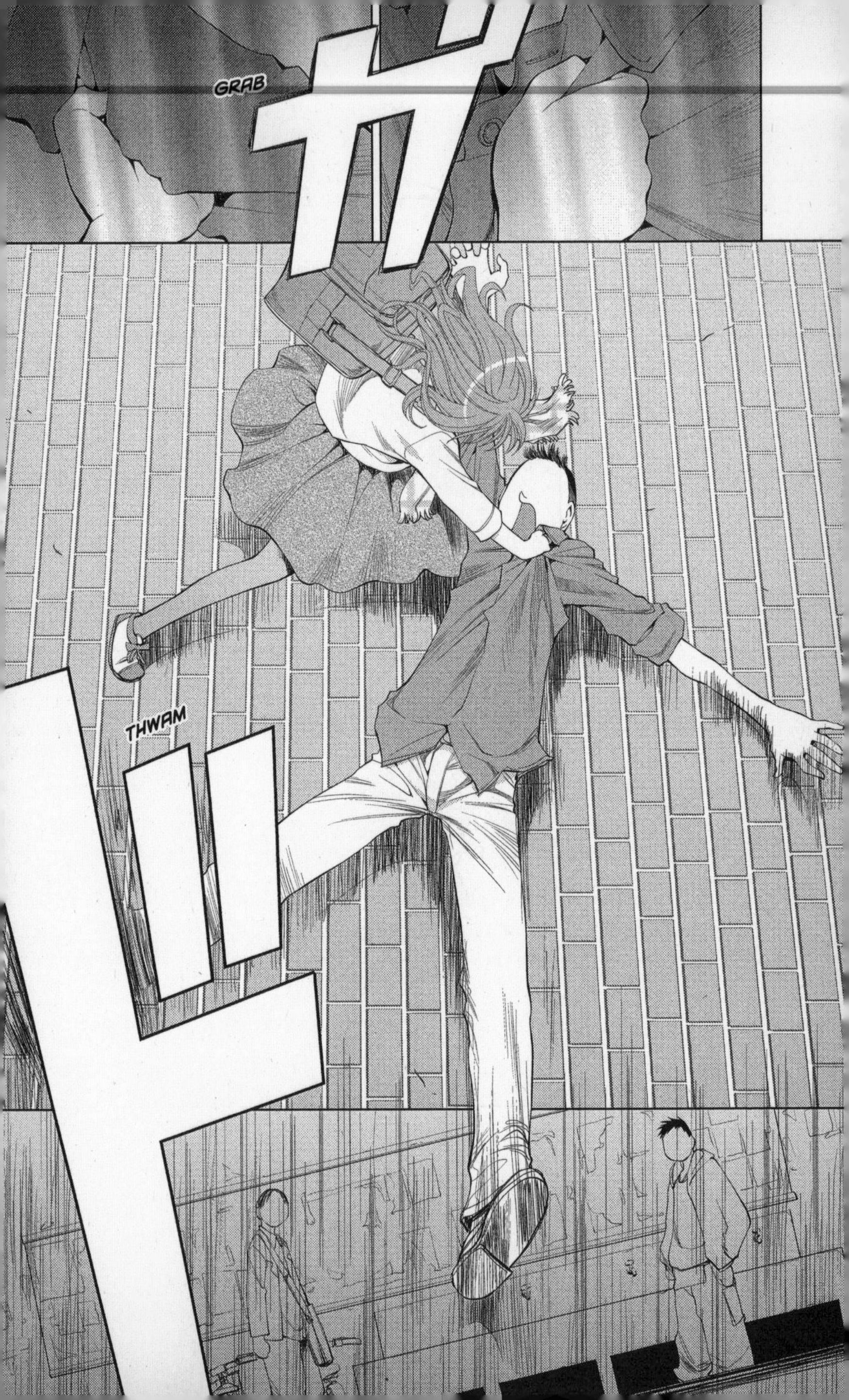
GRAB
THWAM

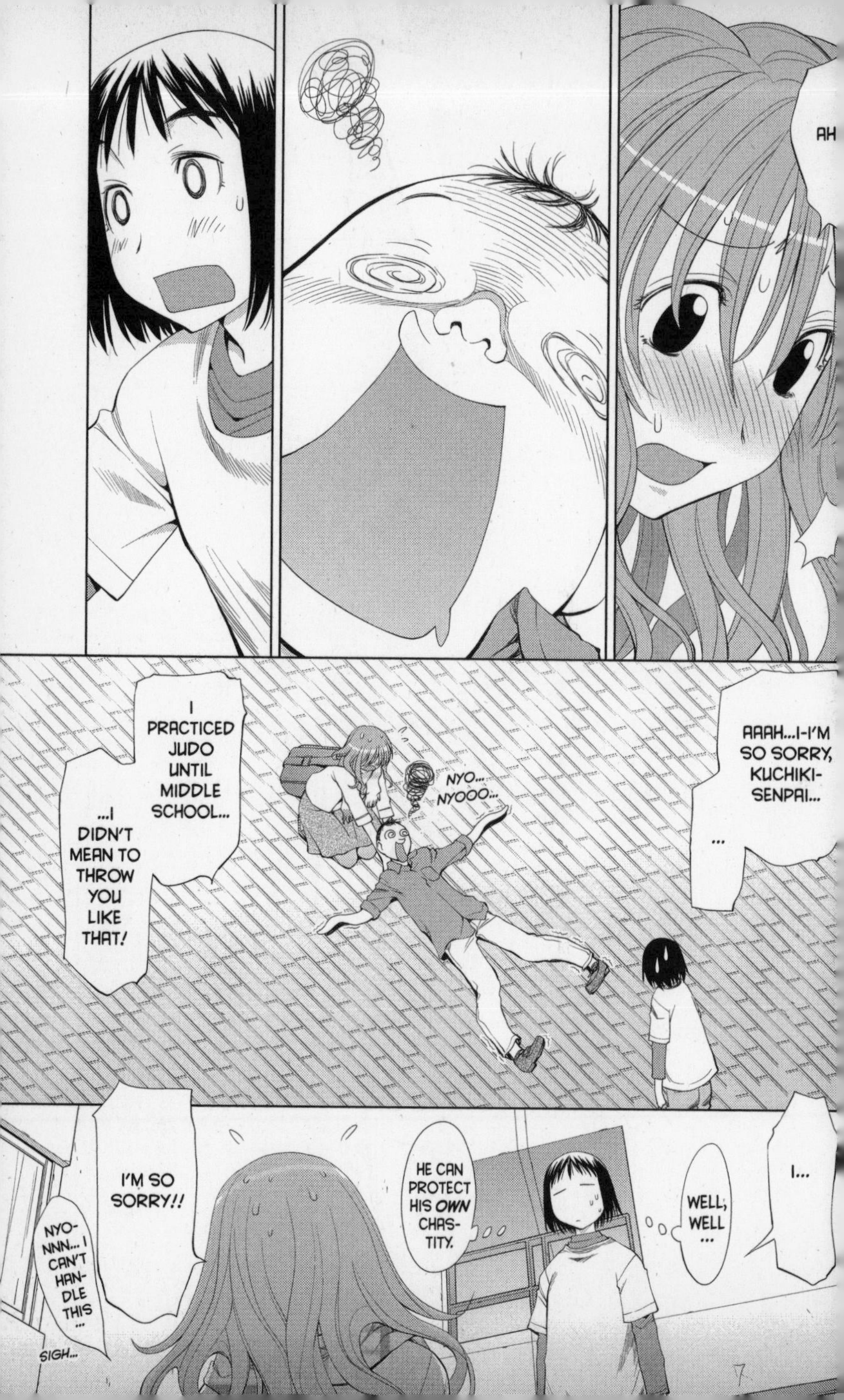
AH
AAAH...I-I'M SO SORRY, KUCHIKI-SENPAI...
...
NYO... NYOOO...
I PRACTICED JUDO UNTIL MIDDLE SCHOOL...
...I DIDN'T MEAN TO THROW YOU LIKE THAT!
I...
WELL, WELL ...
HE CAN PROTECT HIS *OWN* CHAS-TITY.
I'M SO SORRY!!
NYO-NNN... I CAN'T HAN-DLE THIS ...
SIGH...

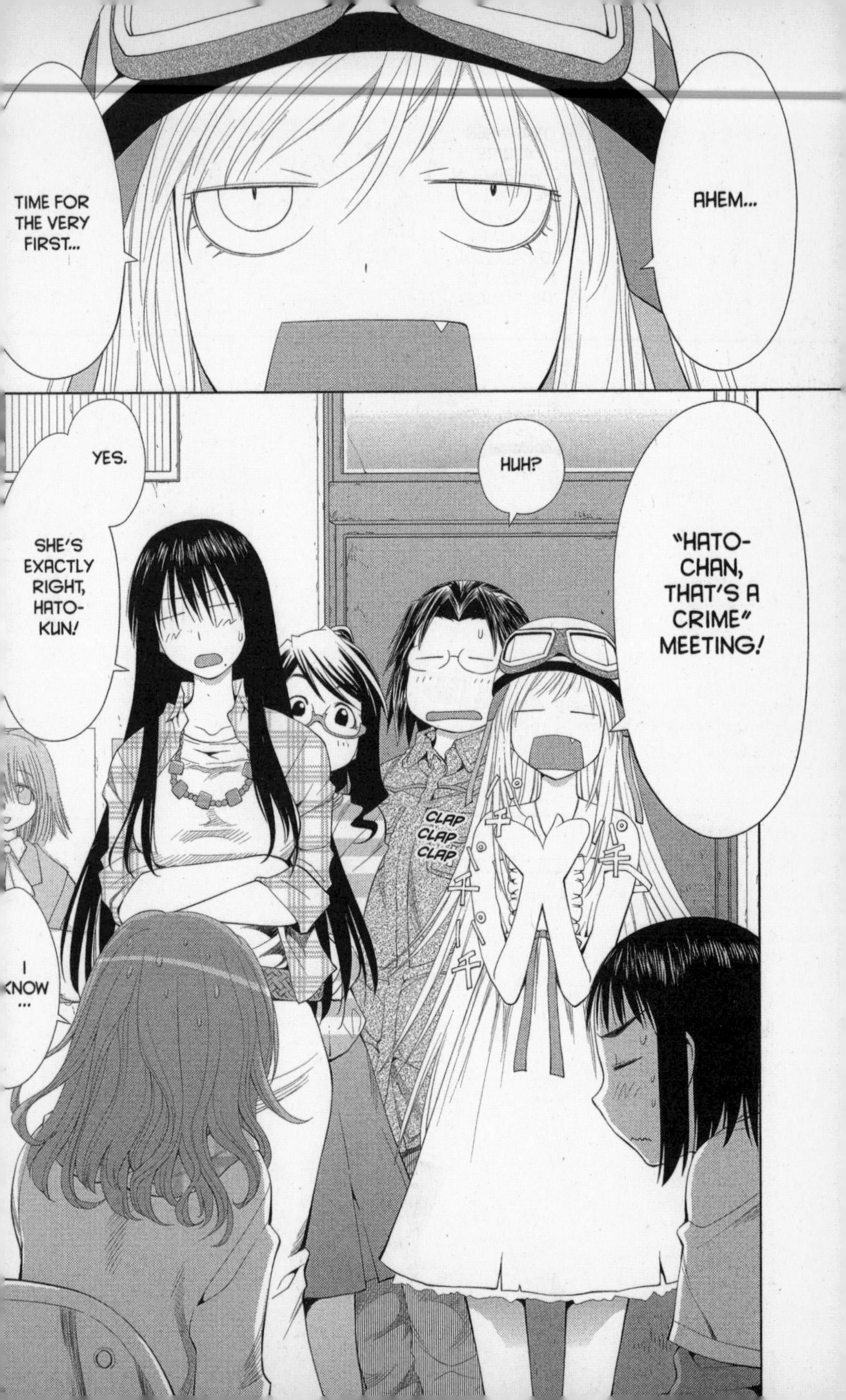
AHEM...
TIME FOR THE VERY FIRST...
"HATO-CHAN, THAT'S A CRIME" MEETING!
HUH?
YES.
SHE'S EXACTLY RIGHT, HATO-KUN!
CLAP CLAP CLAP
I KNOW ...

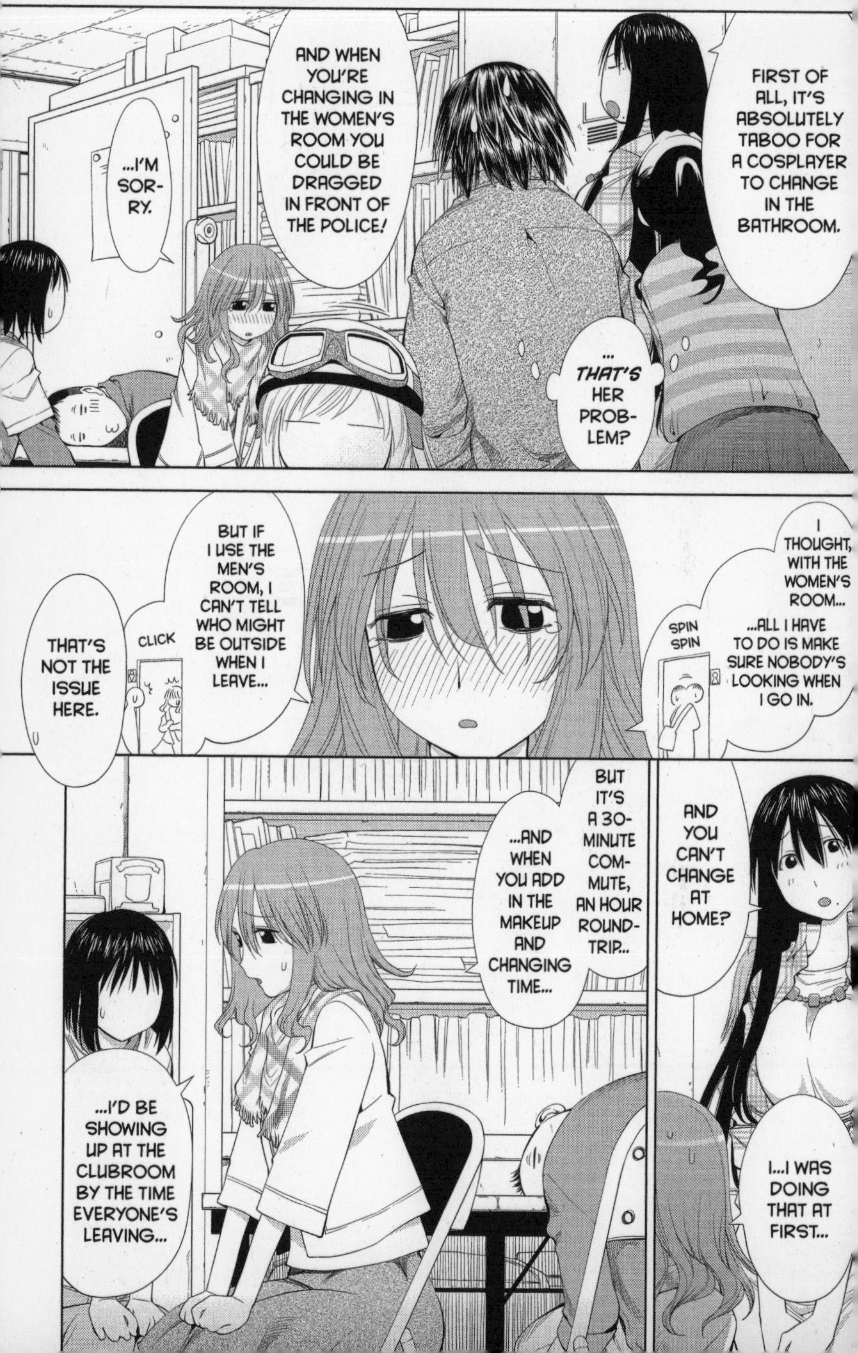
FIRST OF ALL, IT'S ABSOLUTELY TABOO FOR A COSPLAYER TO CHANGE IN THE BATHROOM.
AND WHEN YOU'RE CHANGING IN THE WOMEN'S ROOM YOU COULD BE DRAGGED IN FRONT OF THE POLICE!
...I'M SOR-RY.
...*THAT'S* HER PROB-LEM?
I THOUGHT, WITH THE WOMEN'S ROOM...
SPIN SPIN
...ALL I HAVE TO DO IS MAKE SURE NOBODY'S LOOKING WHEN I GO IN.
BUT IF I USE THE MEN'S ROOM, I CAN'T TELL WHO MIGHT BE OUTSIDE WHEN I LEAVE...
CLICK
THAT'S NOT THE ISSUE HERE.
AND YOU CAN'T CHANGE AT HOME?
I...I WAS DOING THAT AT FIRST...
BUT IT'S A 30-MINUTE COM-MUTE, AN HOUR ROUND-TRIP...
...AND WHEN YOU ADD IN THE MAKEUP AND CHANGING TIME...
...I'D BE SHOWING UP AT THE CLUBROOM BY THE TIME EVERYONE'S LEAVING...

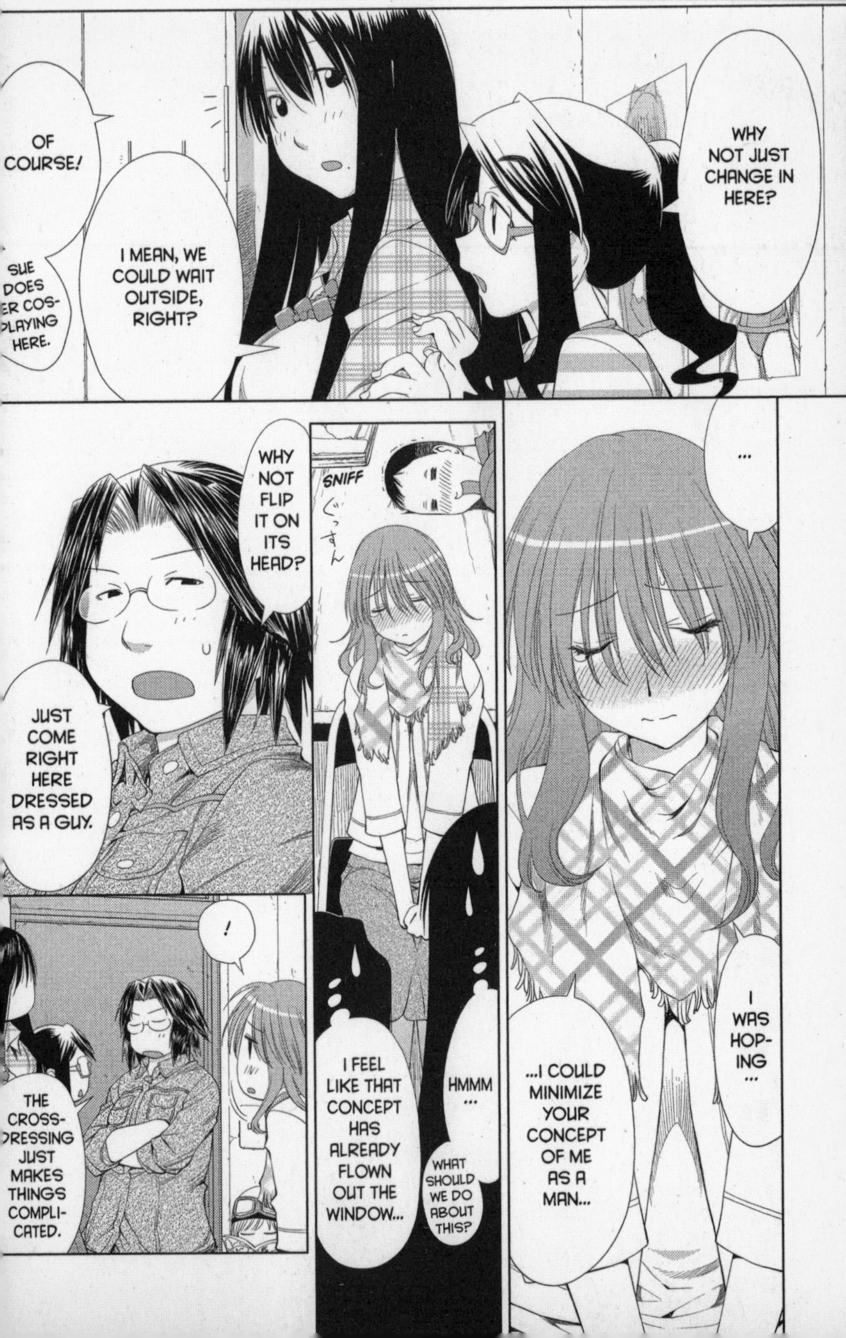
WHY NOT JUST CHANGE IN HERE?
I MEAN, WE COULD WAIT OUTSIDE, RIGHT?
OF COURSE!
SHE DOES ER COS-PLAYING HERE.
...
I WAS HOP-ING...
...I COULD MINIMIZE YOUR CONCEPT OF ME AS A MAN...
SNIFF
ぐっすん
HMMM...
WHAT SHOULD WE DO ABOUT THIS?
I FEEL LIKE THAT CONCEPT HAS ALREADY FLOWN OUT THE WINDOW...
WHY NOT FLIP IT ON ITS HEAD?
JUST COME RIGHT HERE DRESSED AS A GUY.
!
THE CROSS-DRESSING JUST MAKES THINGS COMPLI-CATED.

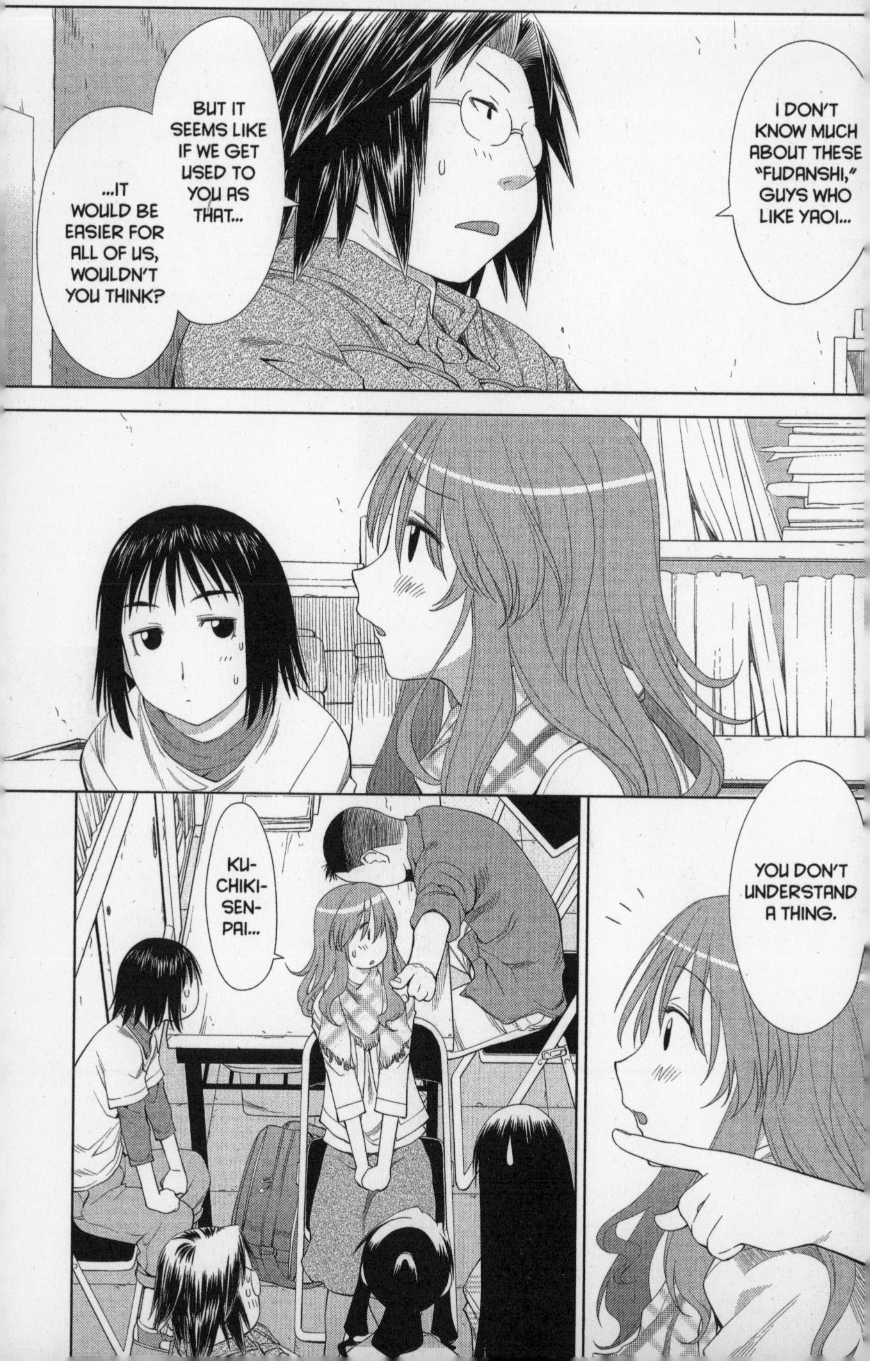
I DON'T KNOW MUCH ABOUT THESE "FUDANSHI," GUYS WHO LIKE YAOI...
BUT IT SEEMS LIKE IF WE GET USED TO YOU AS THAT...
...IT WOULD BE EASIER FOR ALL OF US, WOULDN'T YOU THINK?
YOU DON'T UNDERSTAND A THING.
KU-CHIKI-SEN-PAI...

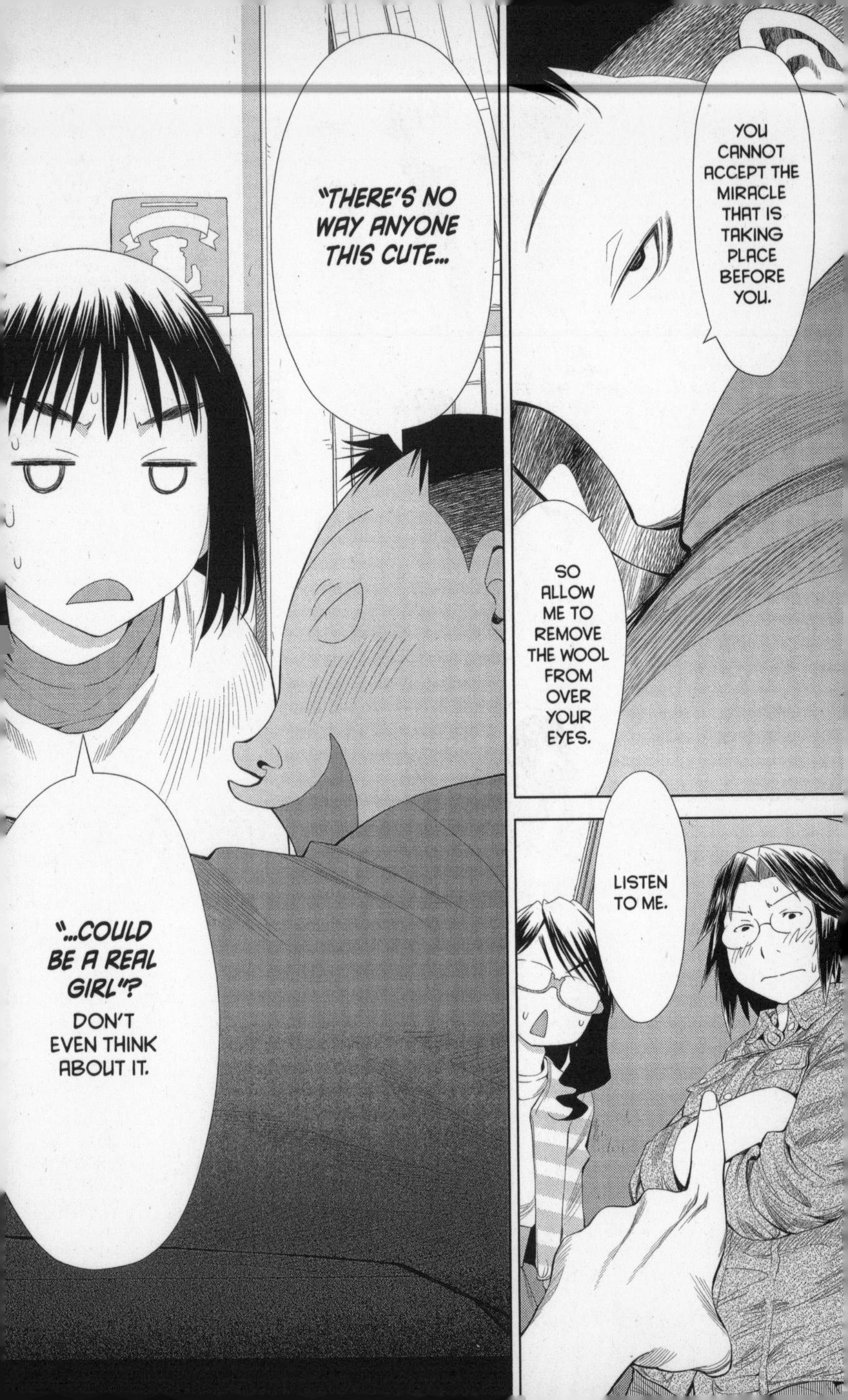
YOU CANNOT ACCEPT THE MIRACLE THAT IS TAKING PLACE BEFORE YOU.
SO ALLOW ME TO REMOVE THE WOOL FROM OVER YOUR EYES.
LISTEN TO ME.
"THERE'S NO WAY ANYONE THIS CUTE...
"...COULD BE A REAL GIRL"? DON'T EVEN THINK ABOUT IT.

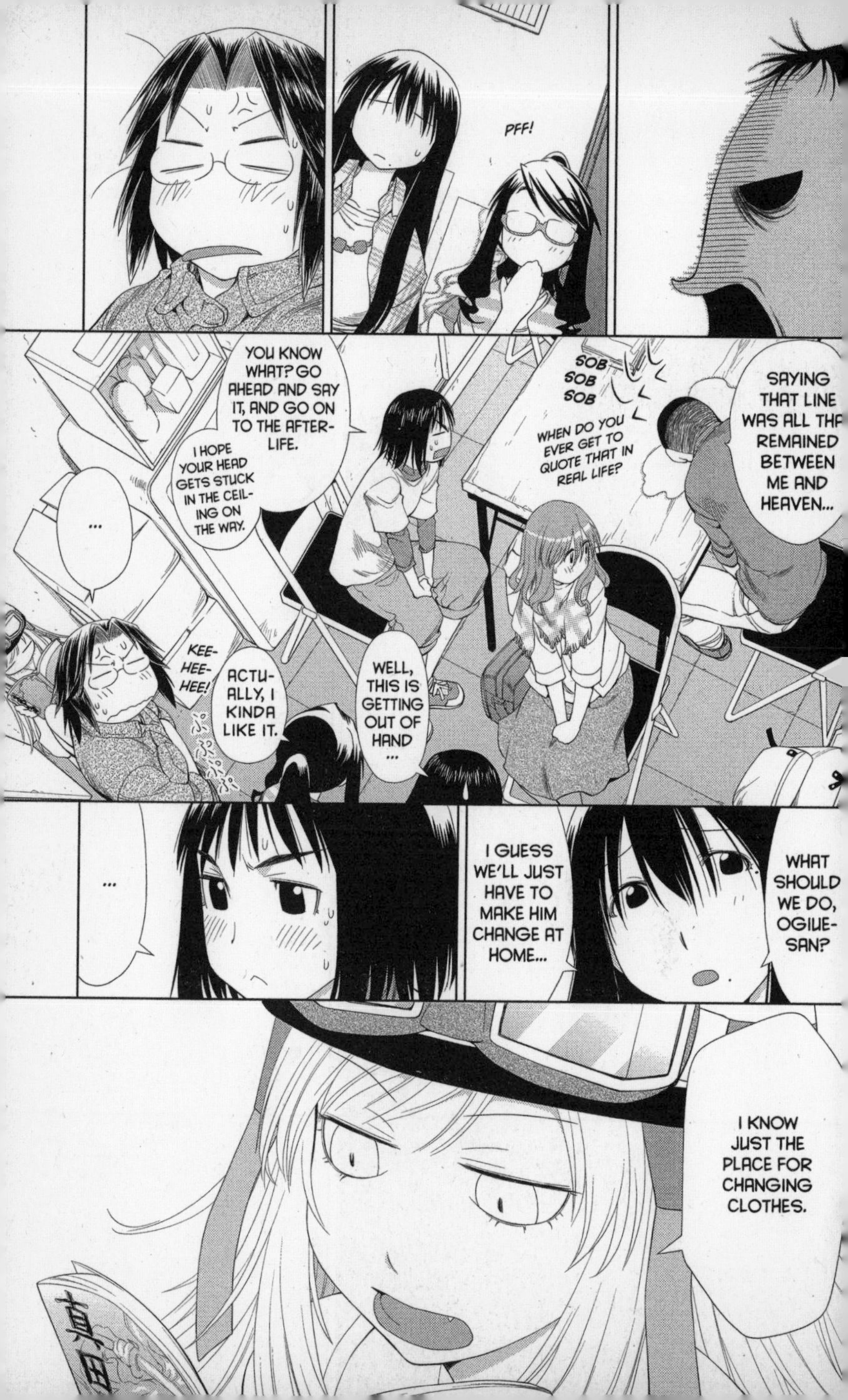
PFF!
SAYING THAT LINE WAS ALL THA REMAINED BETWEEN ME AND HEAVEN...
SOB SOB SOB
WHEN DO YOU EVER GET TO QUOTE THAT IN REAL LIFE?
YOU KNOW WHAT? GO AHEAD AND SAY IT, AND GO ON TO THE AFTER-LIFE.
I HOPE YOUR HEAD GETS STUCK IN THE CEIL-ING ON THE WAY.
...
WELL, THIS IS GETTING OUT OF HAND ...
ACTU-ALLY, I KINDA LIKE IT.
KEE-HEE-HEE!
WHAT SHOULD WE DO, OGIUE-SAN?
I GUESS WE'LL JUST HAVE TO MAKE HIM CHANGE AT HOME...
...
I KNOW JUST THE PLACE FOR CHANGING CLOTHES.

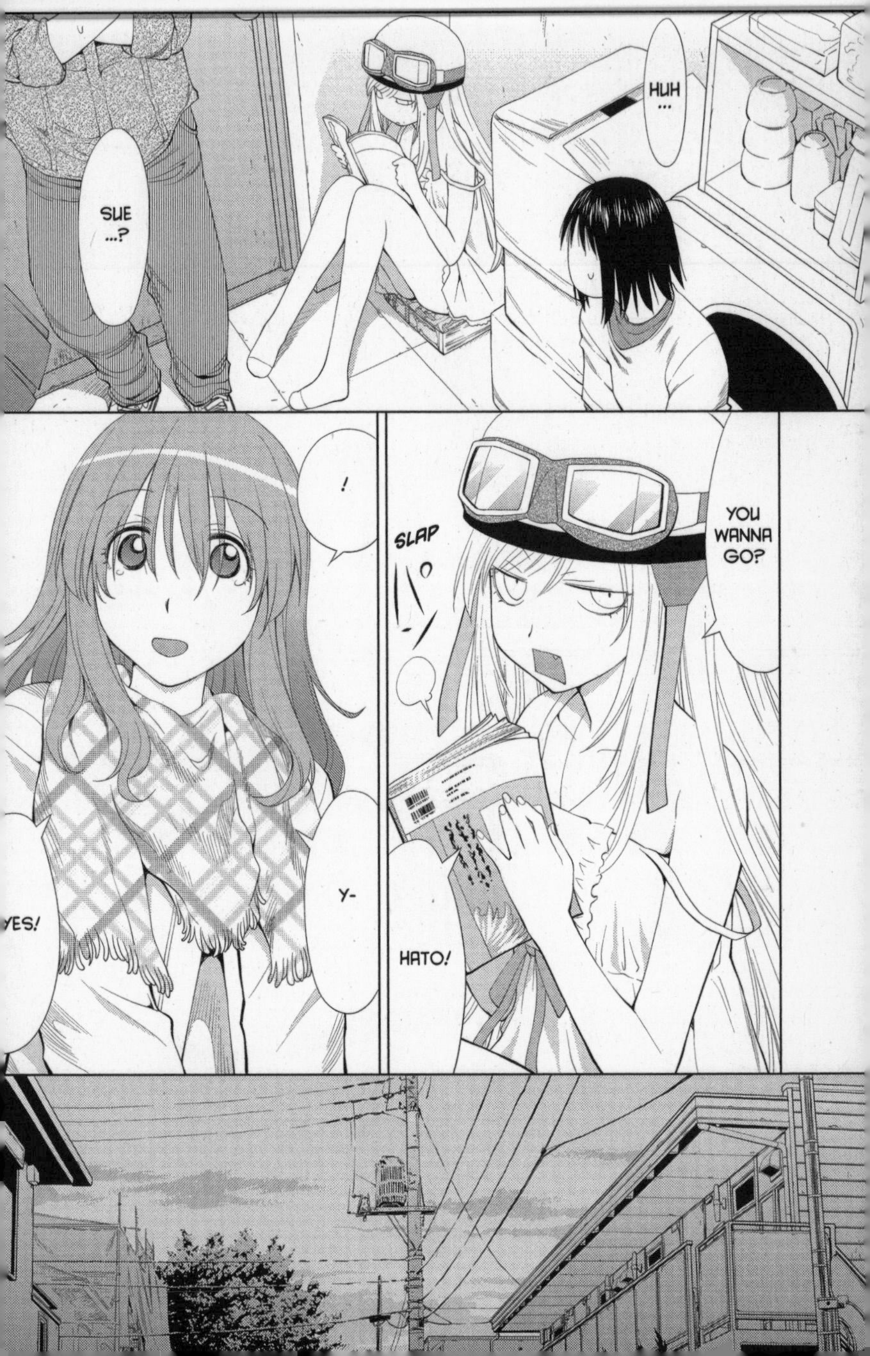
HUH ...
SUE ...?
YOU WANNA GO?
SLAP
HATO!
!
Y-
YES!

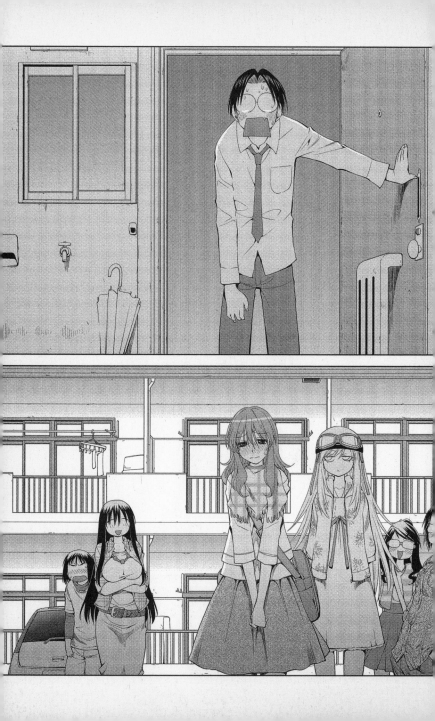

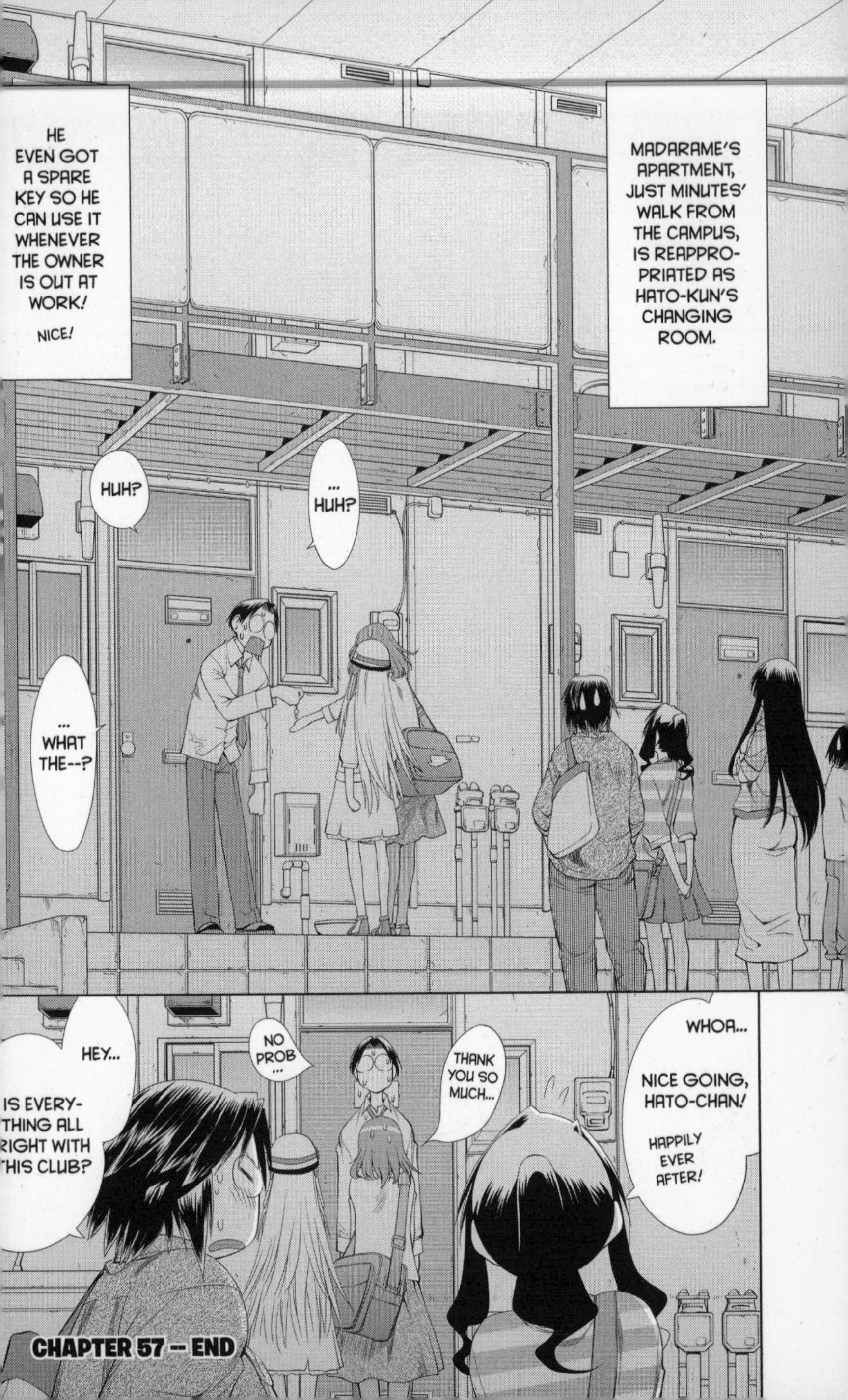
MADARAME'S APARTMENT, JUST MINUTES' WALK FROM THE CAMPUS, IS REAPPROPRIATED AS HATO-KUN'S CHANGING ROOM.
HE EVEN GOT A SPARE KEY SO HE CAN USE IT WHENEVER THE OWNER IS OUT AT WORK!
NICE!
... HUH?
HUH?
... WHAT THE--?
WHOA...
NICE GOING, HATO-CHAN!
HAPPILY EVER AFTER!
THANK YOU SO MUCH...
NO PROB ...
HEY...
IS EVERY-THING ALL RIGHT WITH THIS CLUB?
CHAPTER 57 -- END

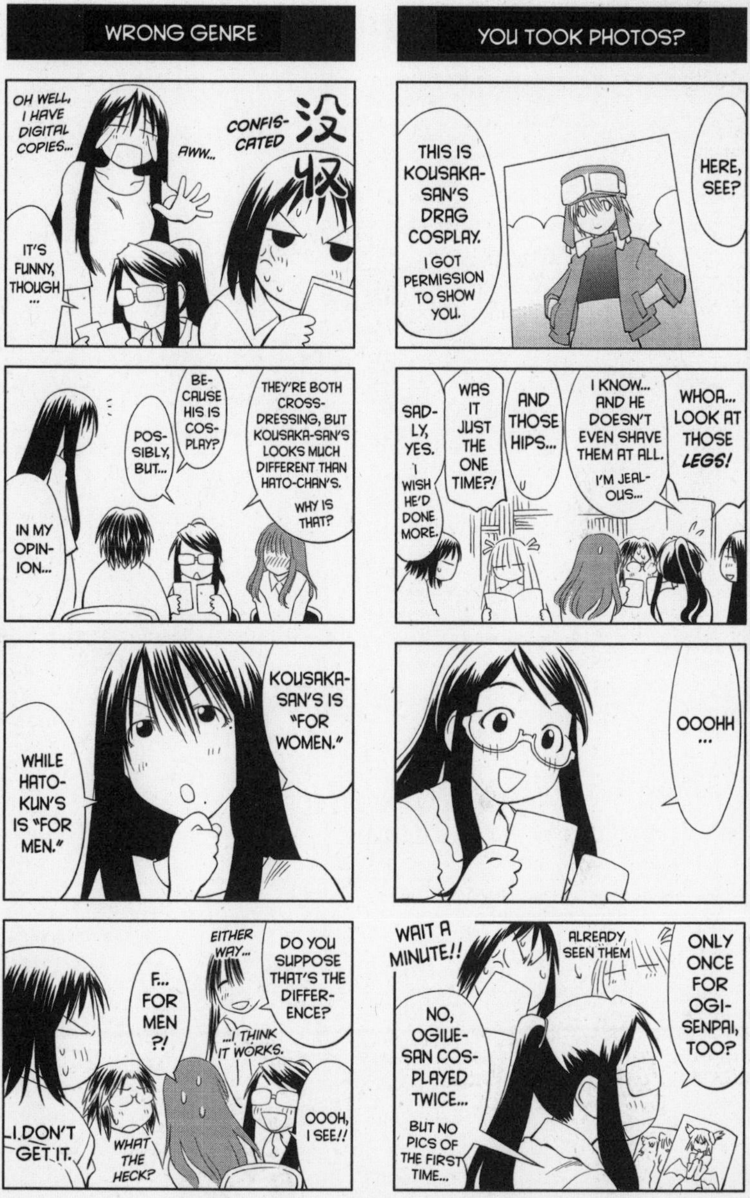
YOU TOOK PHOTOS?
HERE, SEE?
THIS IS KOUSAKA-SAN'S DRAG COSPLAY.
I GOT PERMISSION TO SHOW YOU.
WHOA... LOOK AT THOSE LEGS!
I KNOW... AND HE DOESN'T EVEN SHAVE THEM AT ALL.
I'M JEAL-OUS...
AND THOSE HIPS...
WAS IT JUST THE ONE TIME?!
SAD-LY, YES.
I WISH HE'D DONE MORE.
OOOHH ...
ONLY ONCE FOR OGI-SENPAI, TOO?
ALREADY SEEN THEM
WAIT A MINUTE!!
NO, OGIUE-SAN COS-PLAYED TWICE...
BUT NO PICS OF THE FIRST TIME...
WRONG GENRE
CONFIS-CATED
没収
AWW...
OH WELL, I HAVE DIGITAL COPIES...
IT'S FUNNY, THOUGH ...
THEY'RE BOTH CROSS-DRESSING, BUT KOUSAKA-SAN'S LOOKS MUCH DIFFERENT THAN HATO-CHAN'S.
WHY IS THAT?
BE-CAUSE HIS IS COS-PLAY?
POS-SIBLY, BUT...
IN MY OPIN-ION...
KOUSAKA-SAN'S IS "FOR WOMEN."
WHILE HATO-KUN'S IS "FOR MEN."
DO YOU SUPPOSE THAT'S THE DIFFER-ENCE?
EITHER WAY...
...I THINK IT WORKS.
F... FOR MEN?!
OOOH, I SEE!!
WHAT THE HECK?
I DON'T GET IT.

MOONSTRUCK

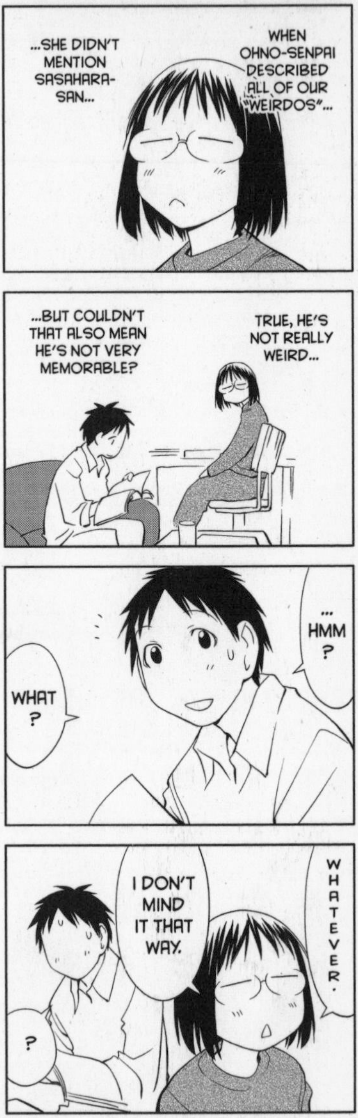
WHEN OHNO-SENPAI DESCRIBED ALL OF OUR "WEIRDOS"...
...SHE DIDN'T MENTION SASAHARA-SAN...
TRUE, HE'S NOT REALLY WEIRD...
...BUT COULDN'T THAT ALSO MEAN HE'S NOT VERY MEMORABLE?
... HMM?
WHAT?
WHATEVER.
I DON'T MIND IT THAT WAY.
?

WHAT DO I DO

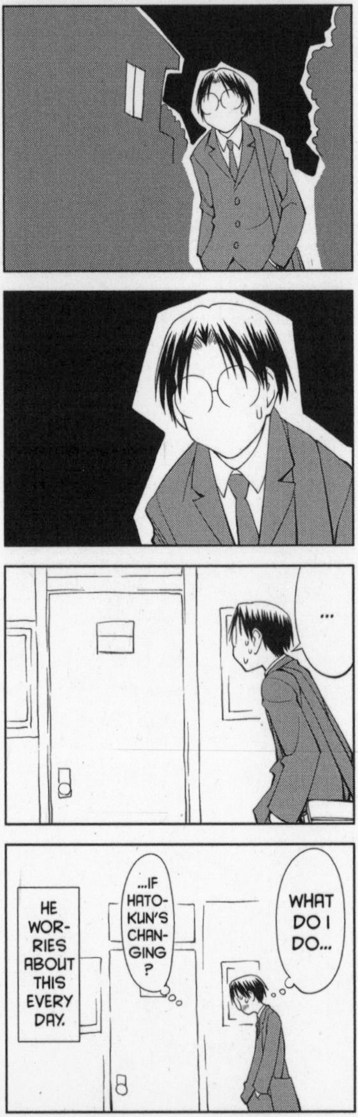
...
WHAT DO I DO...
...IF HATO-KUN'S CHANGING?
HE WORRIES ABOUT THIS EVERY DAY.

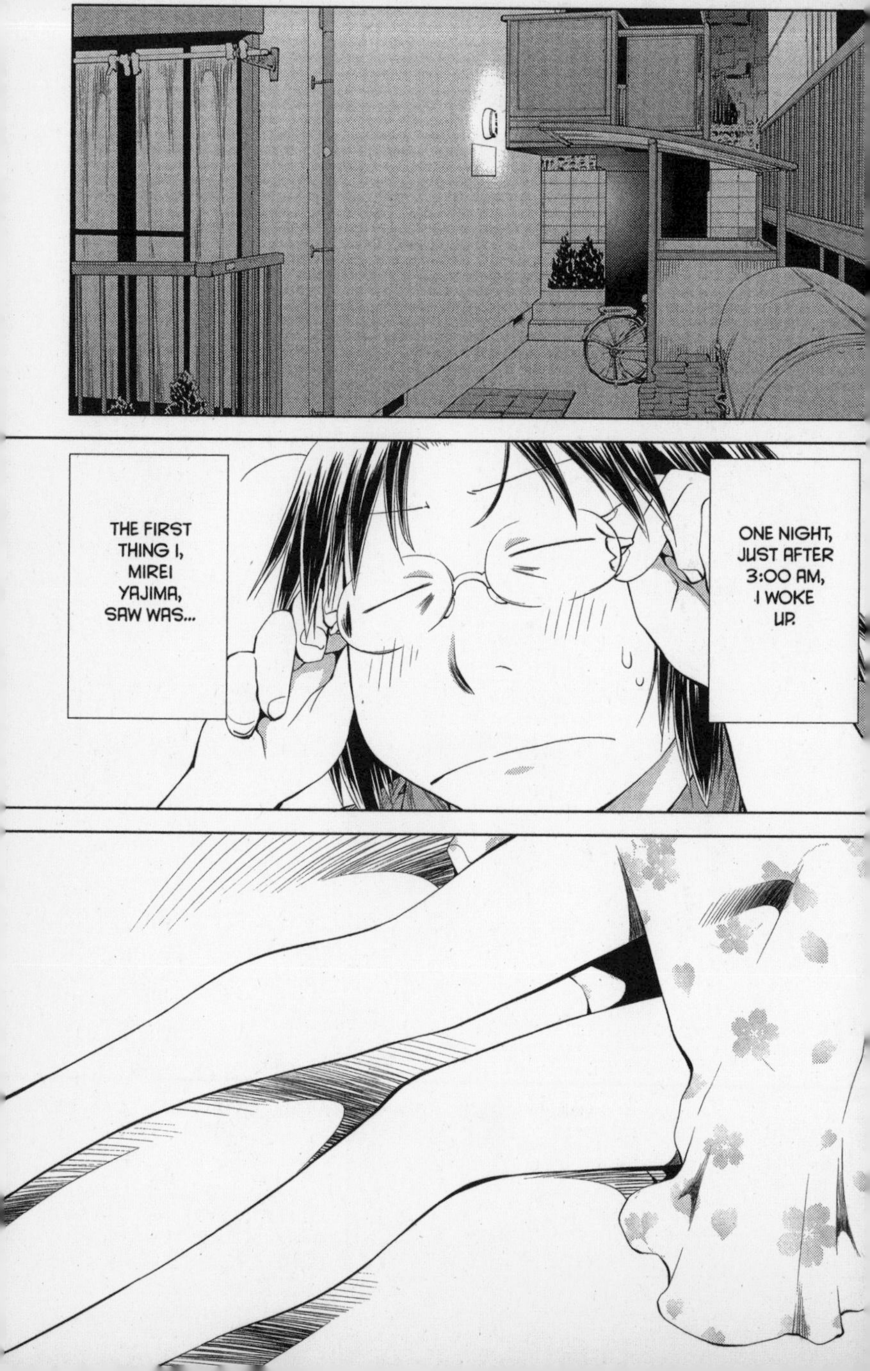
ONE NIGHT, JUST AFTER 3:00 AM, I WOKE UP.
THE FIRST THING I, MIREI YAJIMA, SAW WAS...

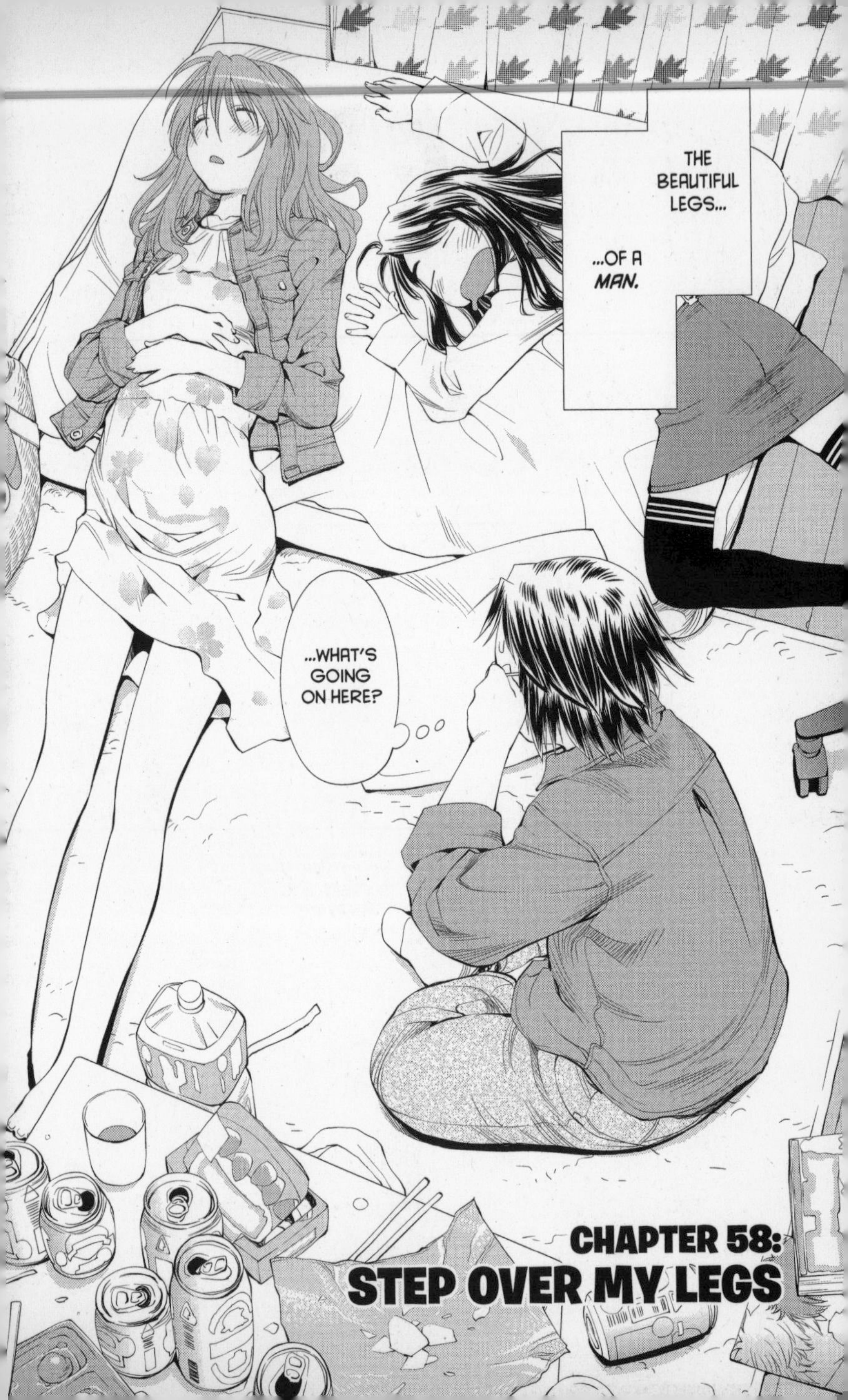
THE BEAUTIFUL LEGS...
...OF A *MAN.*
...WHAT'S GOING ON HERE?
CHAPTER 58:
STEP OVER MY LEGS

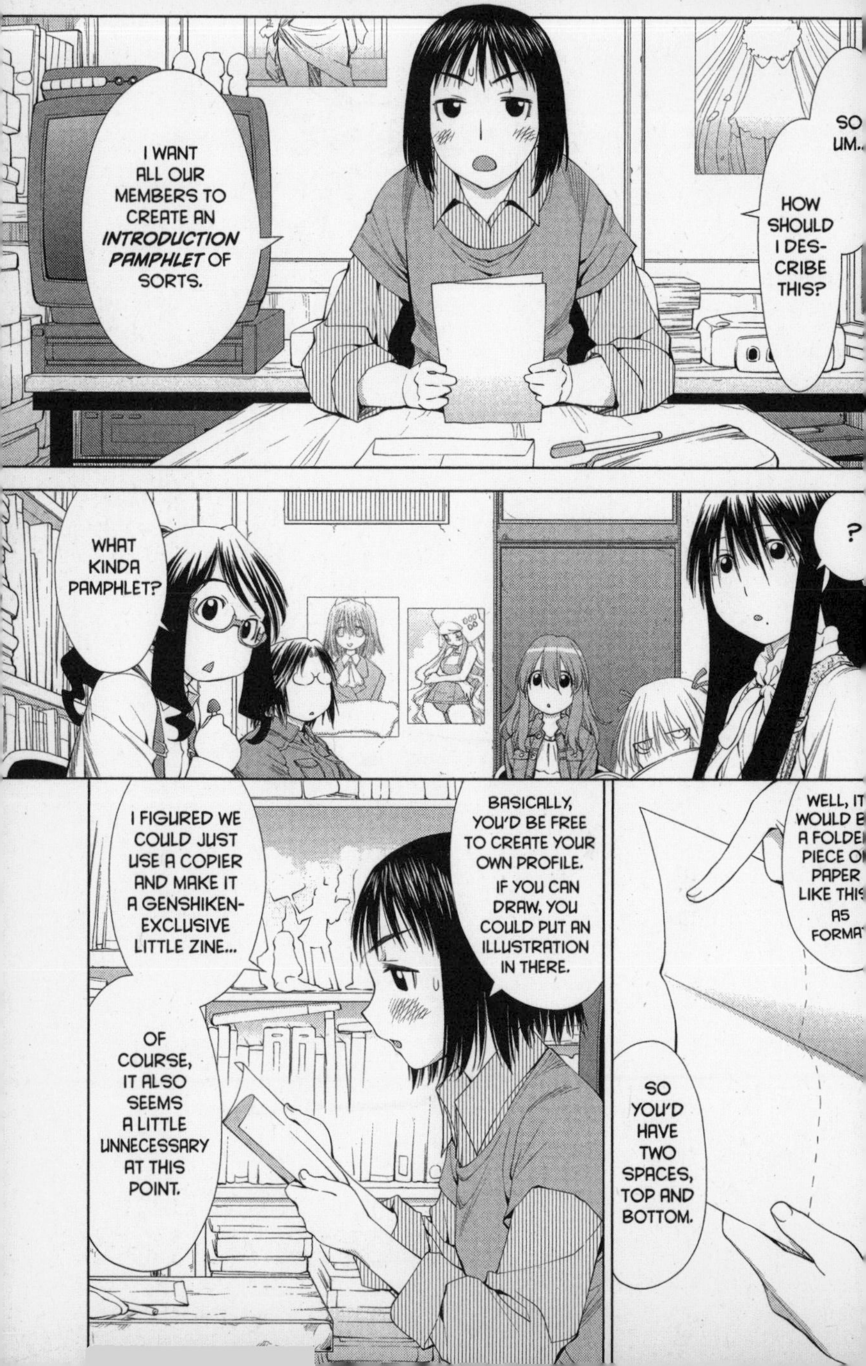
SO UM...
HOW SHOULD I DES-CRIBE THIS?
I WANT ALL OUR MEMBERS TO CREATE AN *INTRODUCTION PAMPHLET* OF SORTS.
?
WHAT KINDA PAMPHLET?
WELL, IT WOULD B A FOLDE PIECE O PAPER LIKE THIS AS FORMA
SO YOU'D HAVE TWO SPACES, TOP AND BOTTOM.
BASICALLY, YOU'D BE FREE TO CREATE YOUR OWN PROFILE.
IF YOU CAN DRAW, YOU COULD PUT AN ILLUSTRATION IN THERE.
I FIGURED WE COULD JUST USE A COPIER AND MAKE IT A GENSHIKEN-EXCLUSIVE LITTLE ZINE...
OF COURSE, IT ALSO SEEMS A LITTLE UNNECESSARY AT THIS POINT.

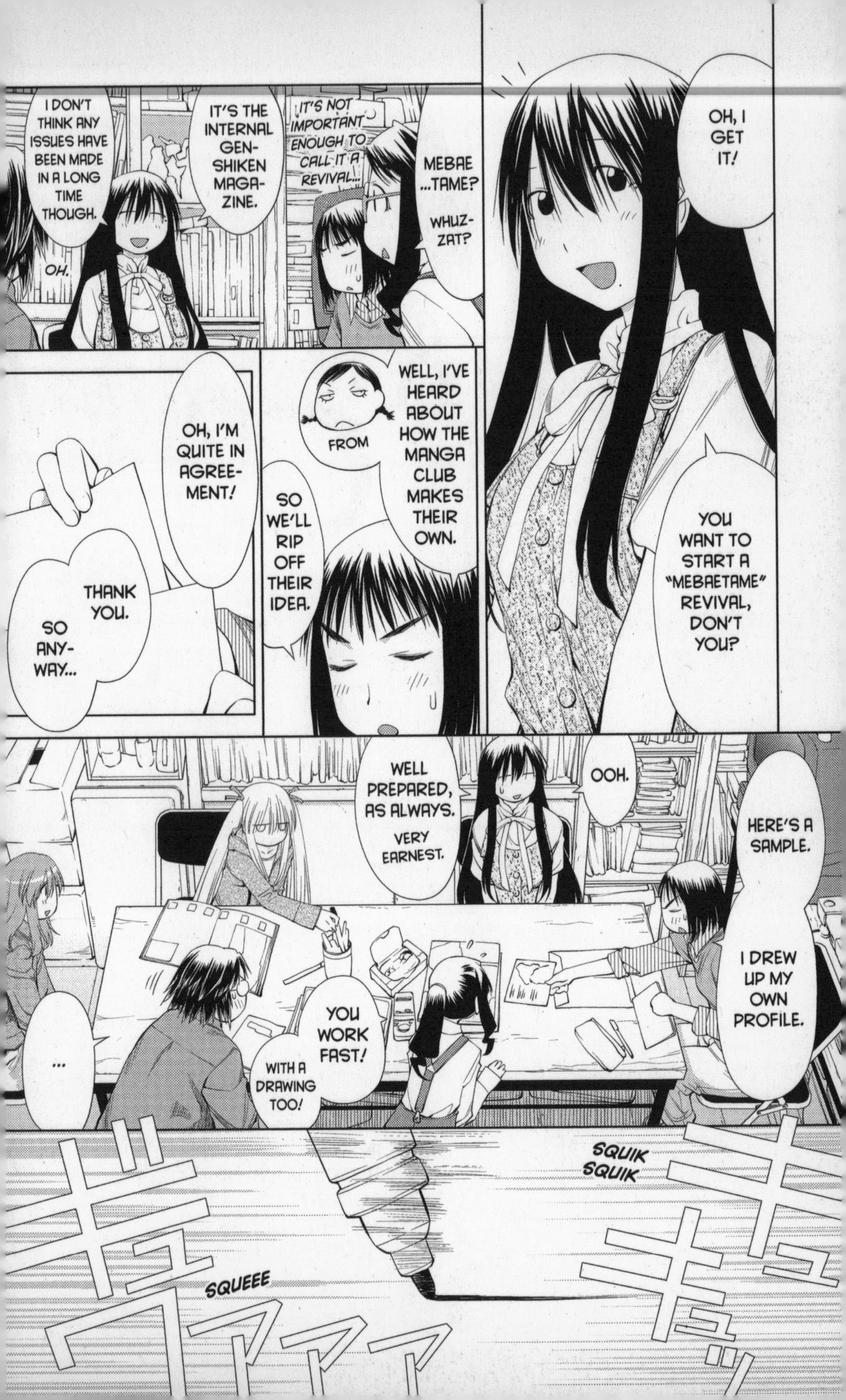
OH, I GET IT!
YOU WANT TO START A "MEBAETAME" REVIVAL, DON'T YOU?
MEBAE ...TAME?
WHUZ-ZAT?
IT'S NOT IMPORTANT ENOUGH TO CALL IT A REVIVAL...
IT'S THE INTERNAL GEN-SHIKEN MAGA-ZINE.
I DON'T THINK ANY ISSUES HAVE BEEN MADE IN A LONG TIME THOUGH.
OH.
WELL, I'VE HEARD ABOUT HOW THE MANGA CLUB MAKES THEIR OWN.
FROM
SO WE'LL RIP OFF THEIR IDEA.
OH, I'M QUITE IN AGREE-MENT!
THANK YOU.
SO ANY-WAY...
HERE'S A SAMPLE.
I DREW UP MY OWN PROFILE.
OOH.
WELL PREPARED, AS ALWAYS.
VERY EARNEST.
YOU WORK FAST!
WITH A DRAWING TOO!
...
SQUIK SQUIK
SQUEEE

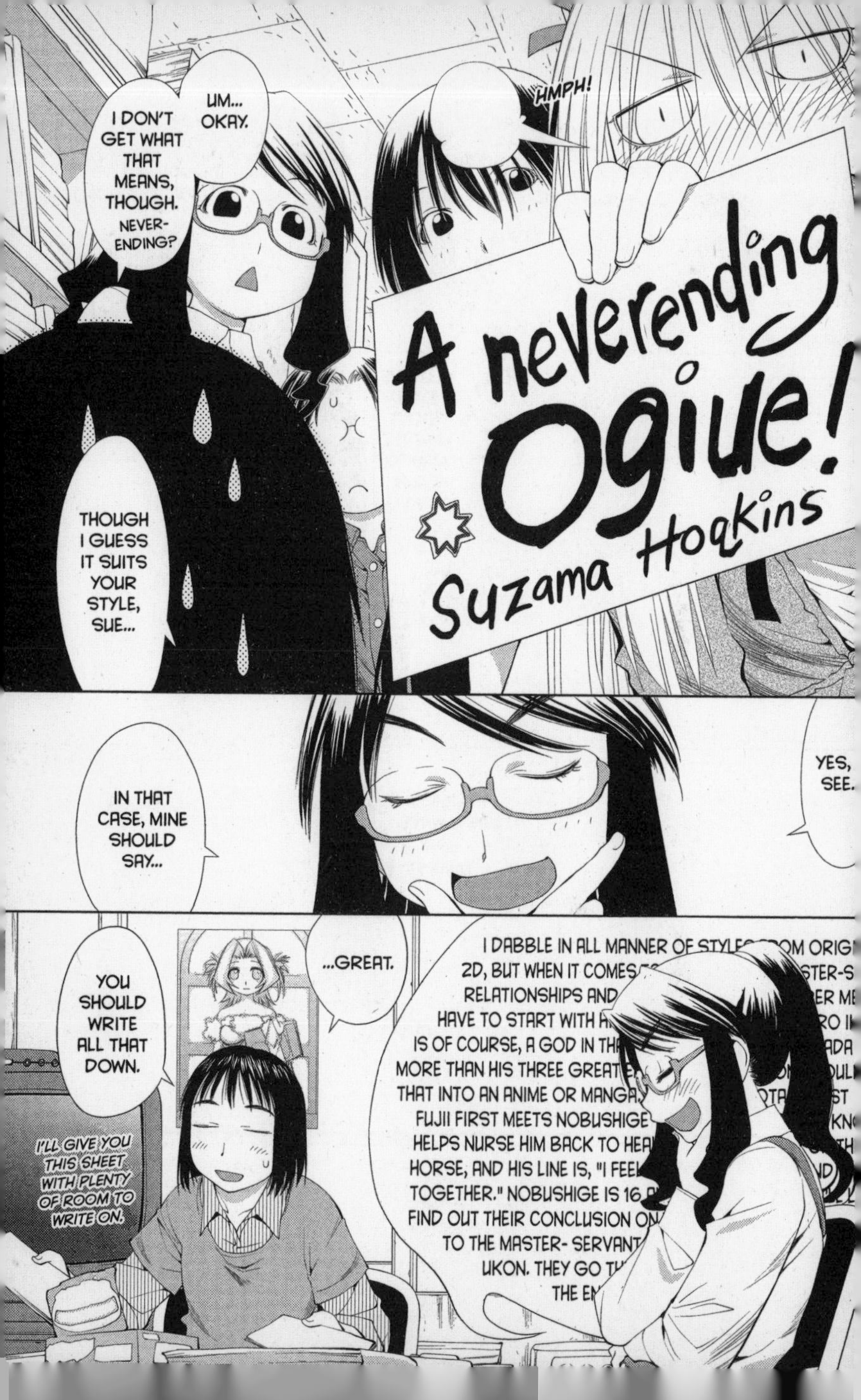
HMPH!
UM... OKAY.
I DON'T GET WHAT THAT MEANS, THOUGH. NEVER-ENDING?
A neverending Ogiue!
Suzama Hoqkins
THOUGH I GUESS IT SUITS YOUR STYLE, SUE...
YES, SEE.
IN THAT CASE, MINE SHOULD SAY...
I DABBLE IN ALL MANNER OF STYLES FROM ORIG
2D, BUT WHEN IT COMES
STER-S
RELATIONSHIPS AND
ER ME
HAVE TO START WITH
IS OF COURSE, A GOD IN TH
MORE THAN HIS THREE GREAT
THAT INTO AN ANIME OR MANGA
FUJII FIRST MEETS NOBUSHIGE
HELPS NURSE HIM BACK TO HEA
HORSE, AND HIS LINE IS, "I FEE
TOGETHER." NOBUSHIGE IS 16
FIND OUT THEIR CONCLUSION O
TO THE MASTER- SERVANT
UKON. THEY GO T
THE E
...GREAT.
YOU SHOULD WRITE ALL THAT DOWN.
I'LL GIVE YOU THIS SHEET WITH PLENTY OF ROOM TO WRITE ON.

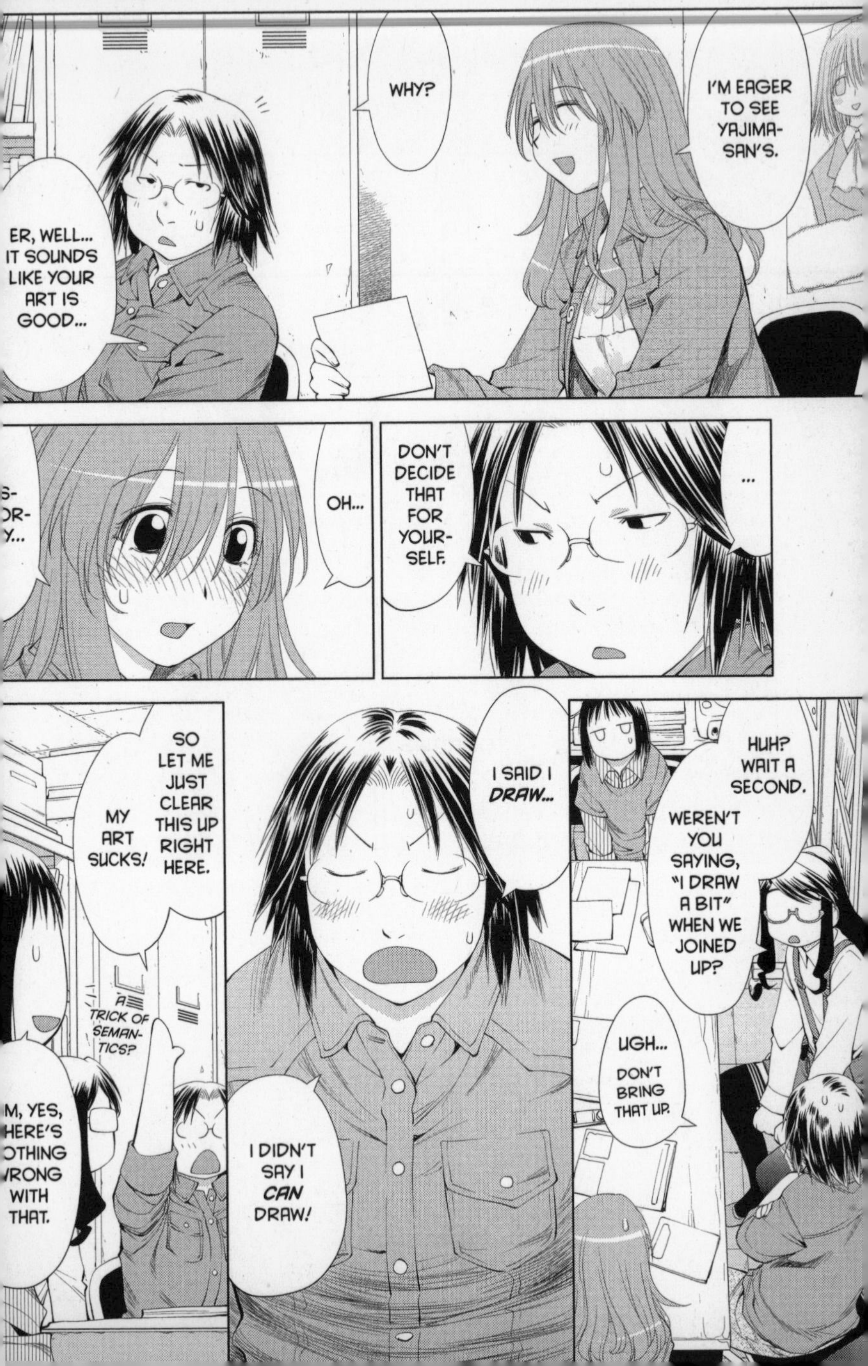
I'M EAGER TO SEE YAJIMA-SAN'S.
WHY?
ER, WELL... IT SOUNDS LIKE YOUR ART IS GOOD...
...
DON'T DECIDE THAT FOR YOURSELF.
OH...
S- OR- Y...
HUH? WAIT A SECOND.
WEREN'T YOU SAYING, "I DRAW A BIT" WHEN WE JOINED UP?
UGH... DON'T BRING THAT UP.
I SAID I *DRAW*...
I DIDN'T SAY I *CAN* DRAW!
SO LET ME JUST CLEAR THIS UP RIGHT HERE.
MY ART SUCKS!
A TRICK OF SEMANTICS?
M, YES, HERE'S OTHING VRONG WITH THAT.

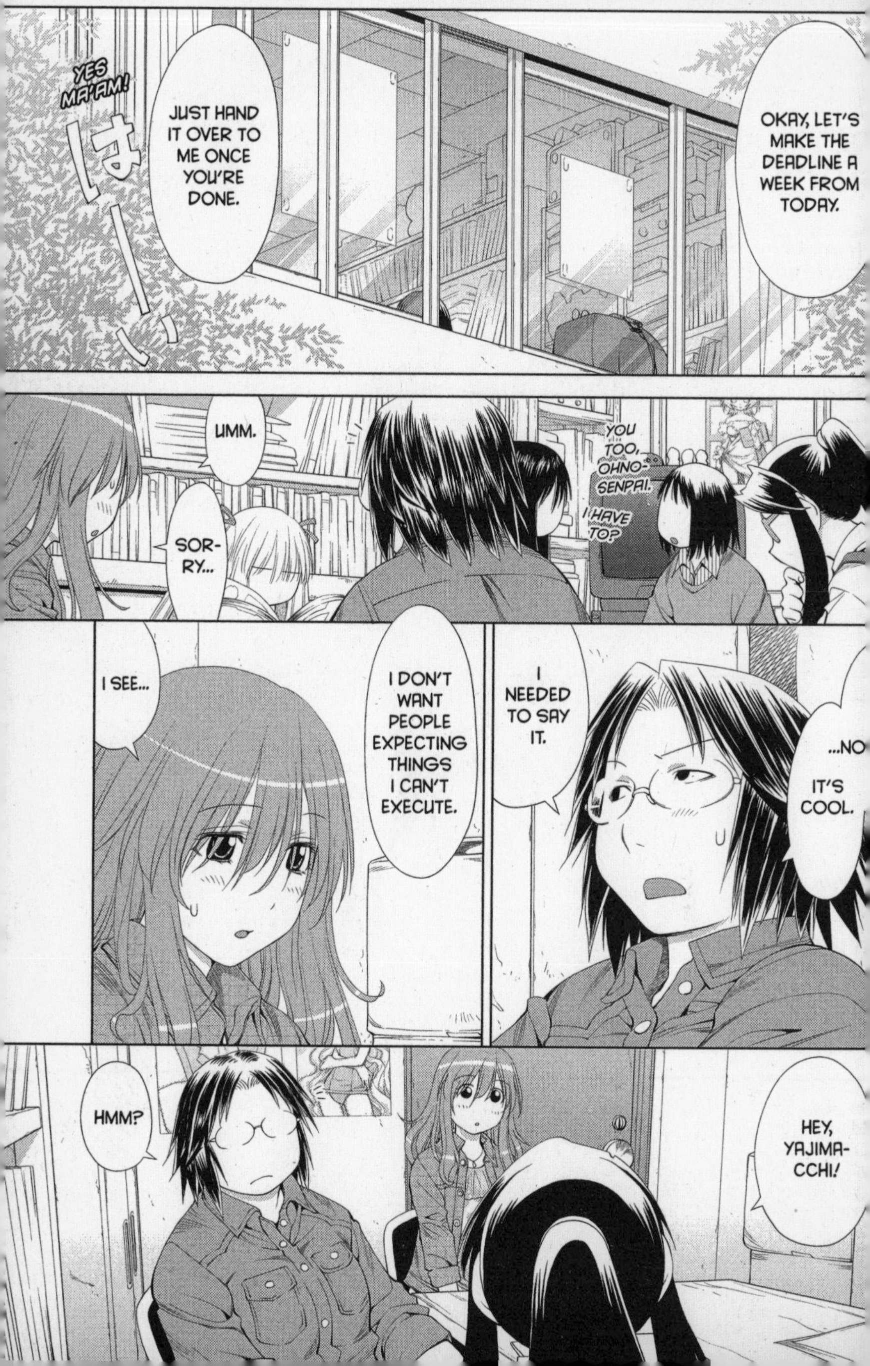
OKAY, LET'S MAKE THE DEADLINE A WEEK FROM TODAY.
JUST HAND IT OVER TO ME ONCE YOU'RE DONE.
はーい、
YES MA'AM!
YOU TOO, OHNO-SENPAI.
I HAVE TO?
UMM.
SOR-RY...
...NO IT'S COOL.
I NEEDED TO SAY IT.
I DON'T WANT PEOPLE EXPECTING THINGS I CAN'T EXECUTE.
I SEE...
HEY, YAJIMA-CCHI!
HMM?

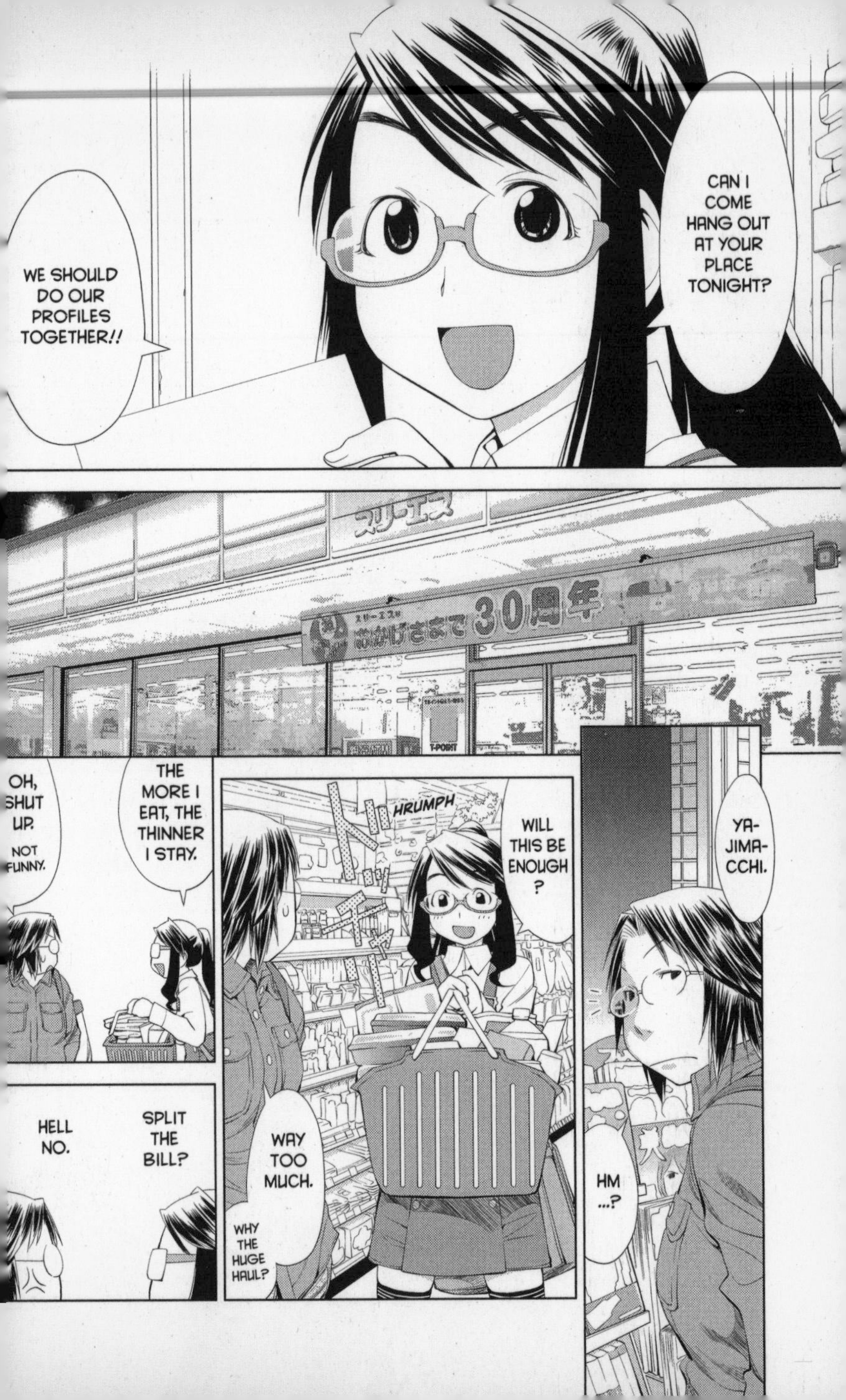
CAN I COME HANG OUT AT YOUR PLACE TONIGHT?
WE SHOULD DO OUR PROFILES TOGETHER!!
スリーエス
おかげさまで 30周年
T-POINT
YA-JIMA-CCHI.
HM ...?
WILL THIS BE ENOUGH?
HRUMPH
WAY TOO MUCH.
WHY THE HUGE HAUL?
THE MORE I EAT, THE THINNER I STAY.
OH, SHUT UP.
NOT FUNNY.
SPLIT THE BILL?
HELL NO.

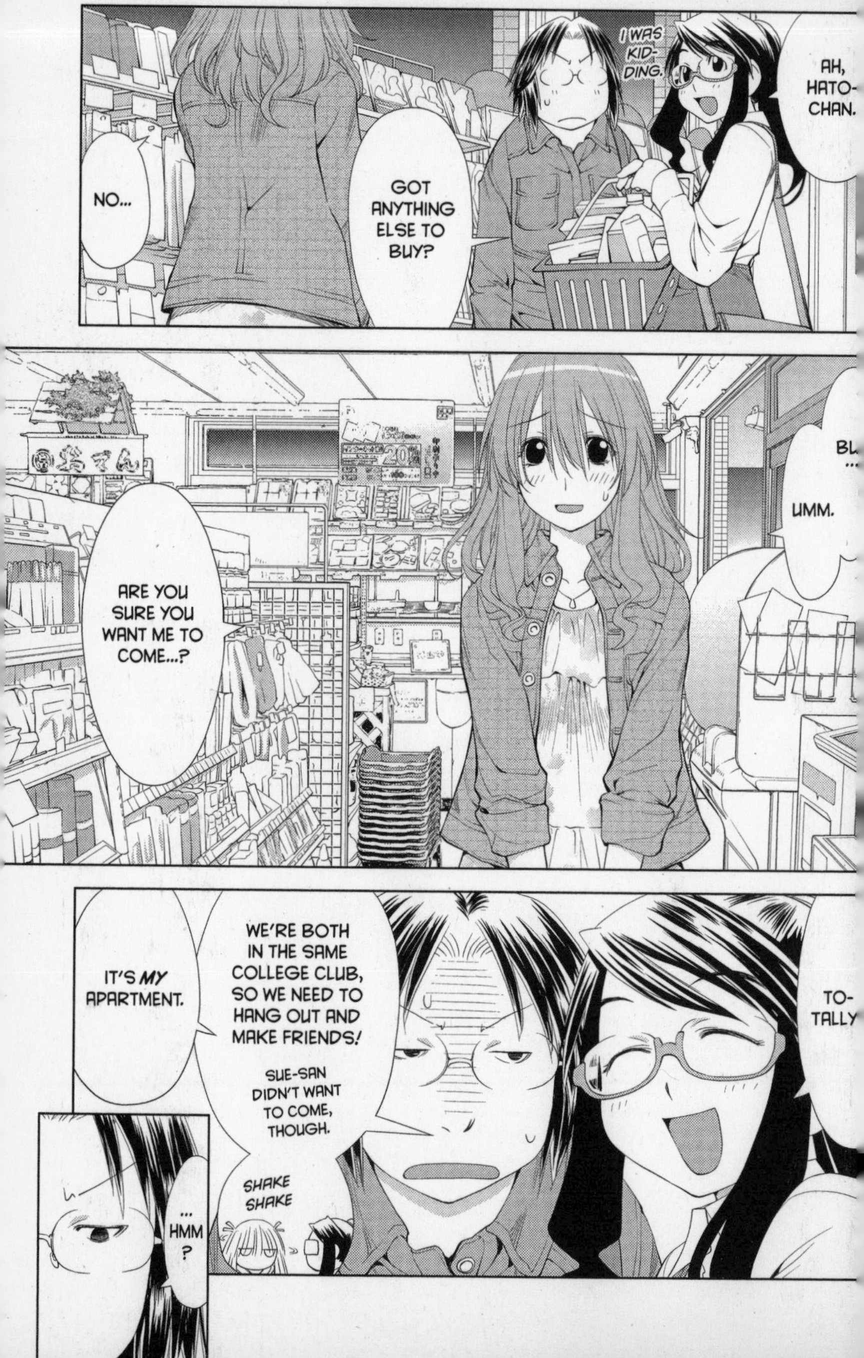
AH, HATO-CHAN.
I WAS KID-DING.
GOT ANYTHING ELSE TO BUY?
NO...
UMM.
ARE YOU SURE YOU WANT ME TO COME...?
TO-TALLY
WE'RE BOTH IN THE SAME COLLEGE CLUB, SO WE NEED TO HANG OUT AND MAKE FRIENDS!
IT'S *MY* APARTMENT.
SUE-SAN DIDN'T WANT TO COME, THOUGH.
SHAKE SHAKE
...HMM?

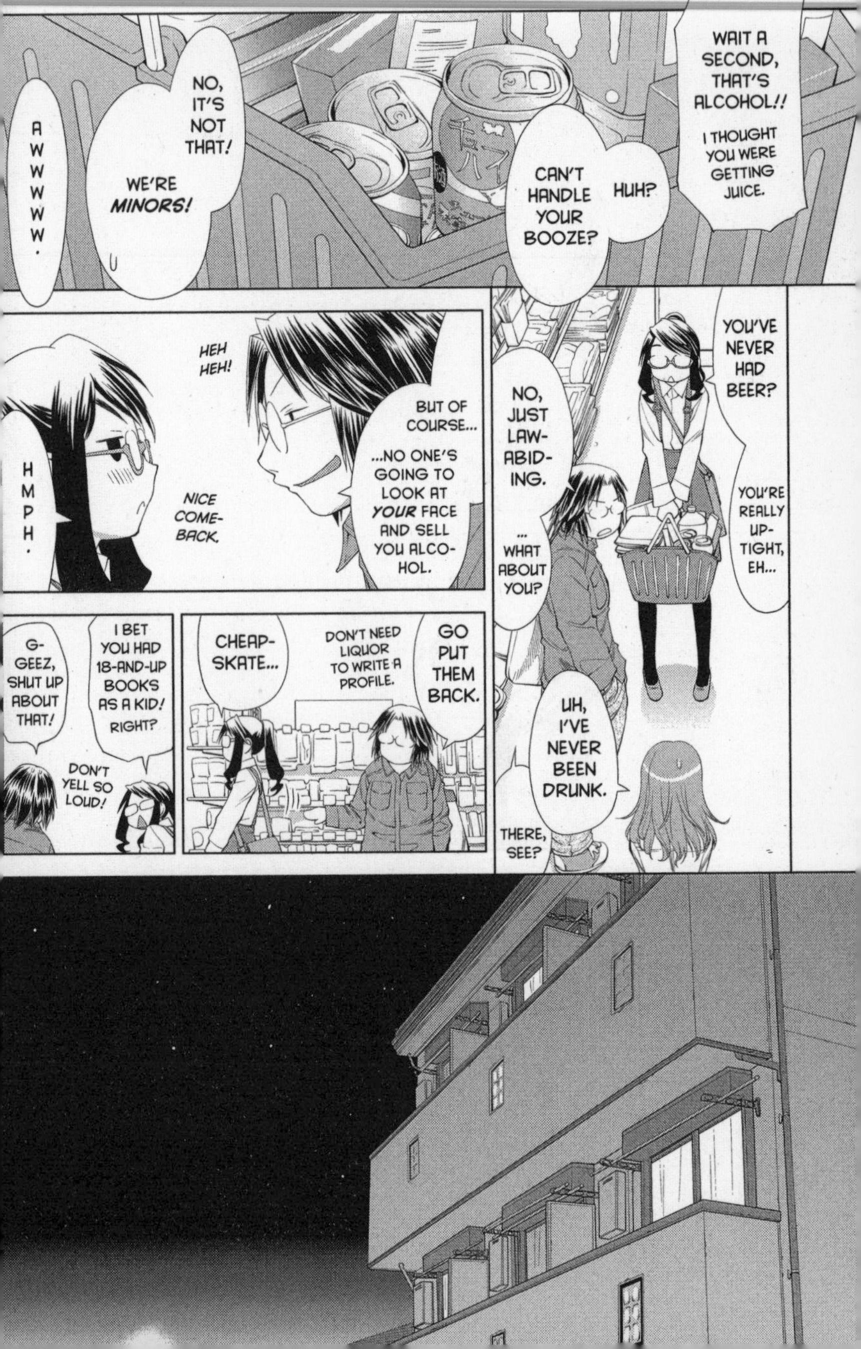
WAIT A SECOND, THAT'S ALCOHOL!!
I THOUGHT YOU WERE GETTING JUICE.
HUH?
CAN'T HANDLE YOUR BOOZE?
NO, IT'S NOT THAT!
WE'RE *MINORS!*
AWWWWWW.
YOU'VE NEVER HAD BEER?
YOU'RE REALLY UP-TIGHT, EH...
NO, JUST LAW-ABID-ING.
...WHAT ABOUT YOU?
UH, I'VE NEVER BEEN DRUNK.
THERE, SEE?
HEH HEH!
BUT OF COURSE...
...NO ONE'S GOING TO LOOK AT *YOUR* FACE AND SELL YOU ALCO-HOL.
NICE COME-BACK.
HMPH.
GO PUT THEM BACK.
DON'T NEED LIQUOR TO WRITE A PROFILE.
CHEAP-SKATE...
I BET YOU HAD 18-AND-UP BOOKS AS A KID! RIGHT?
G-GEEZ, SHUT UP ABOUT THAT!
DON'T YELL SO LOUD!

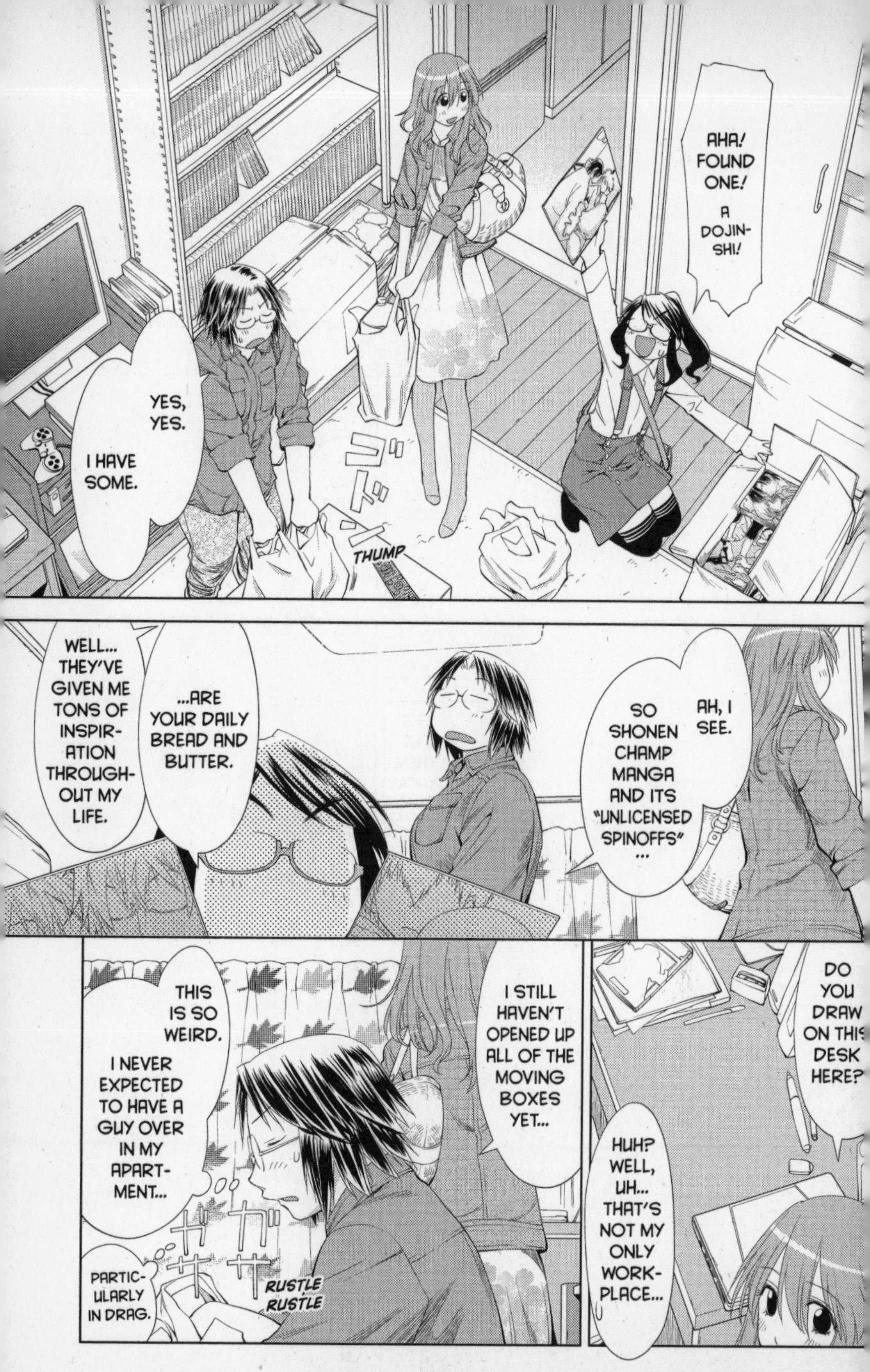
AHA! FOUND ONE!
A DOJIN-SHI!
THUMP
YES, YES.
I HAVE SOME.
AH, I SEE.
SO SHONEN CHAMP MANGA AND ITS "UNLICENSED SPINOFFS"...
...ARE YOUR DAILY BREAD AND BUTTER.
WELL... THEY'VE GIVEN ME TONS OF INSPIR-ATION THROUGH-OUT MY LIFE.
DO YOU DRAW ON THIS DESK HERE?
HUH? WELL, UH... THAT'S NOT MY ONLY WORK-PLACE...
I STILL HAVEN'T OPENED UP ALL OF THE MOVING BOXES YET...
THIS IS SO WEIRD.
I NEVER EXPECTED TO HAVE A GUY OVER IN MY APART-MENT...
PARTIC-ULARLY IN DRAG.
RUSTLE RUSTLE

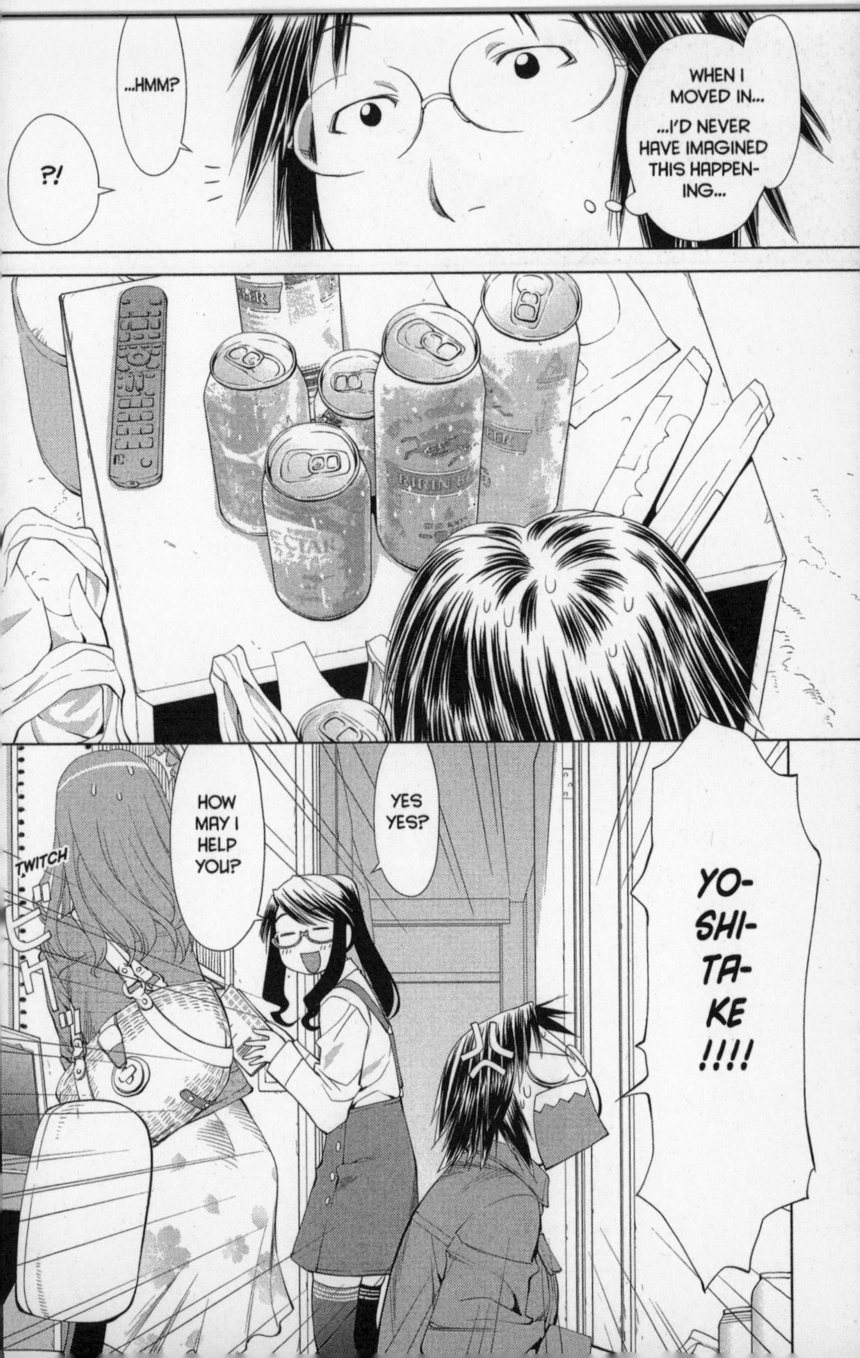

WHEN I MOVED IN... ...I'D NEVER HAVE IMAGINED THIS HAPPEN-ING...
...HMM?
?!
YO-SHI-TA-KE!!!!
YES YES?
HOW MAY I HELP YOU?
TWITCH

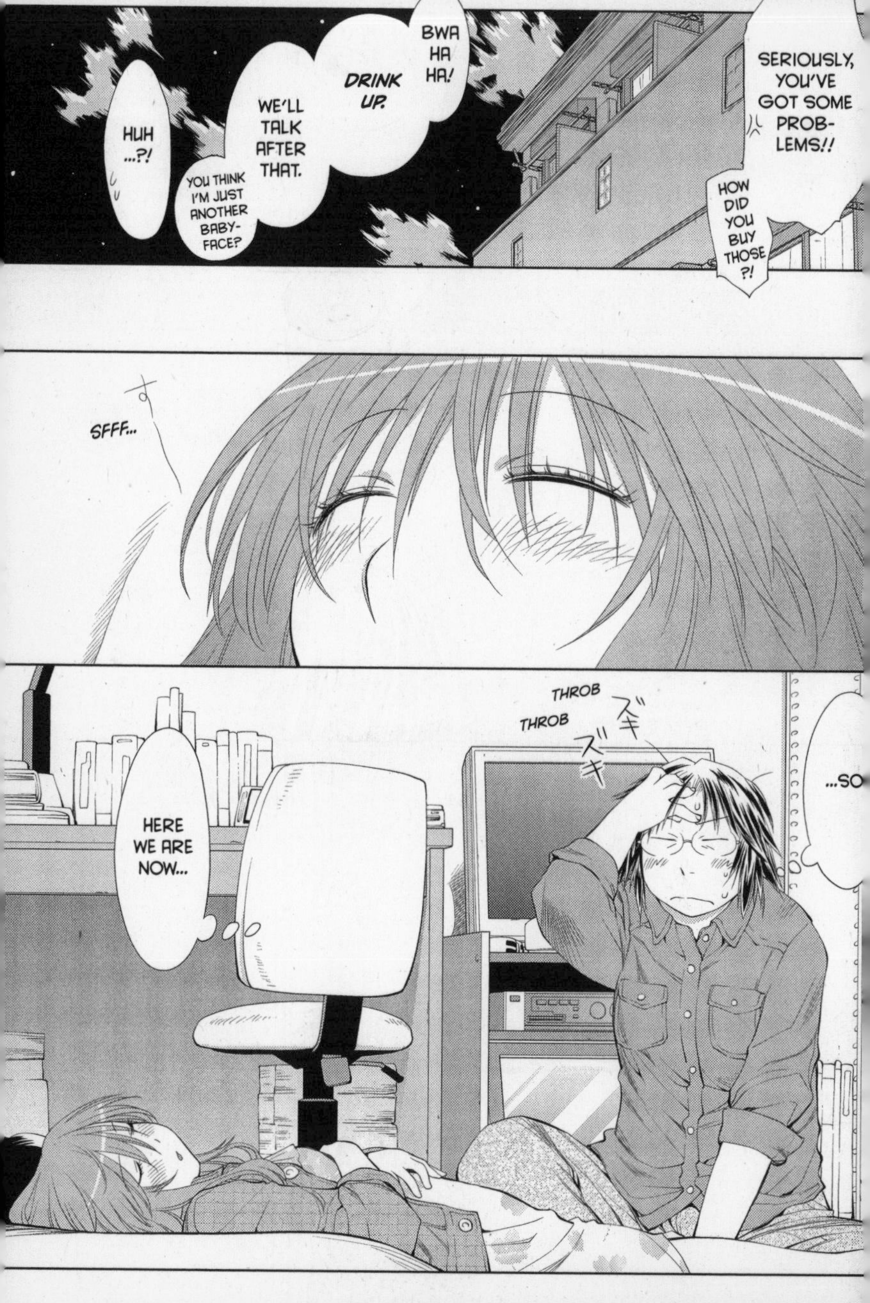
SERIOUSLY, YOU'VE GOT SOME PROB-LEMS!!
HOW DID YOU BUY THOSE ?!
BWA HA HA!
DRINK UP.
WE'LL TALK AFTER THAT.
YOU THINK I'M JUST ANOTHER BABY-FACE?
HUH ...?!
SFFF...
す
...SO
THROB
ズキ
THROB
ズキ
HERE WE ARE NOW...

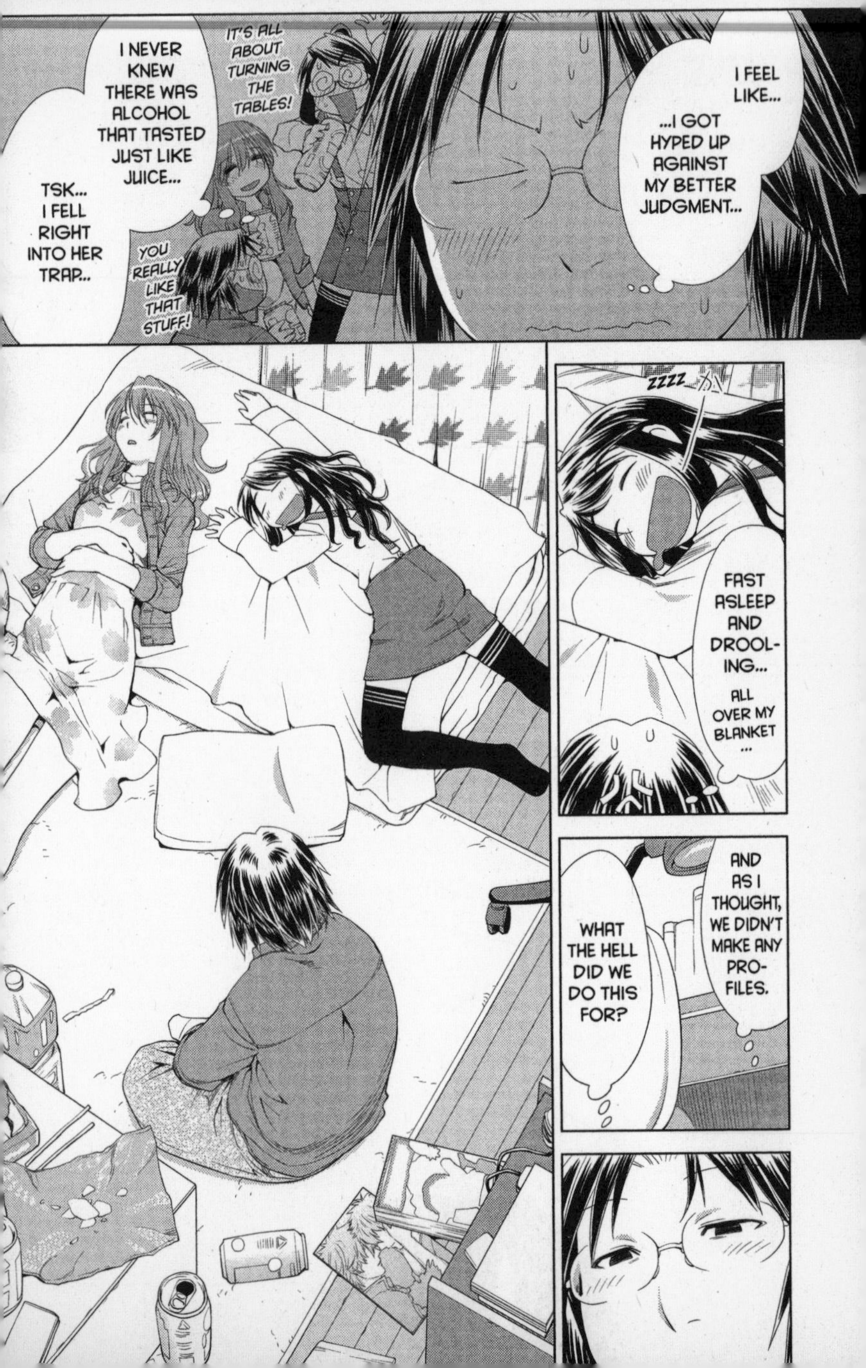
I FEEL LIKE...
...I GOT HYPED UP AGAINST MY BETTER JUDGMENT...
IT'S ALL ABOUT TURNING THE TABLES!
I NEVER KNEW THERE WAS ALCOHOL THAT TASTED JUST LIKE JUICE...
YOU REALLY LIKE THAT STUFF!
TSK... I FELL RIGHT INTO HER TRAP...
ZZZZ
FAST ASLEEP AND DROOLING...
ALL OVER MY BLANKET...
AND AS I THOUGHT, WE DIDN'T MAKE ANY PRO-FILES.
WHAT THE HELL DID WE DO THIS FOR?

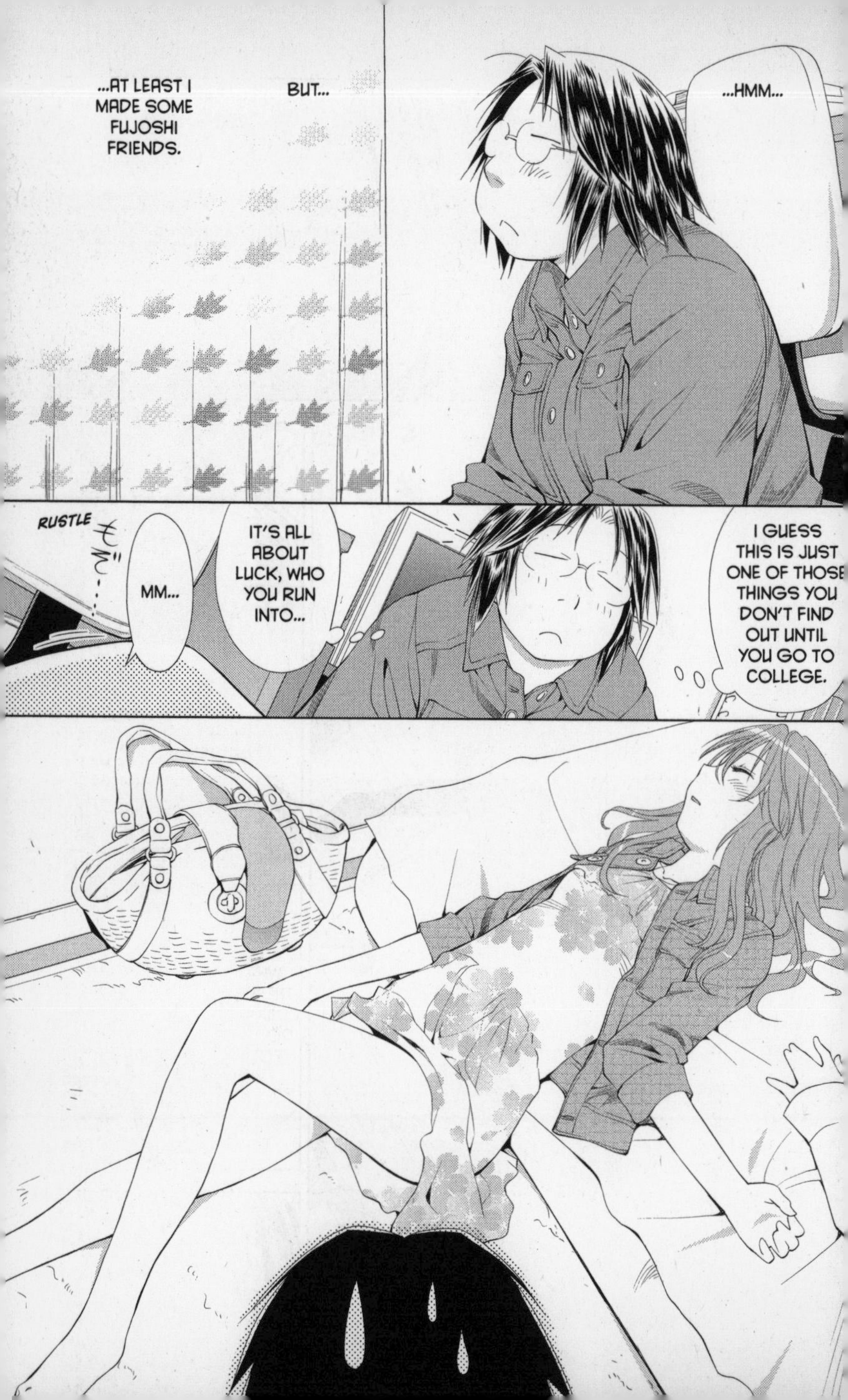
...HMM...
BUT...
...AT LEAST I MADE SOME FUJOSHI FRIENDS.
I GUESS THIS IS JUST ONE OF THOSE THINGS YOU DON'T FIND OUT UNTIL YOU GO TO COLLEGE.
IT'S ALL ABOUT LUCK, WHO YOU RUN INTO...
MM...
もぞ…
RUSTLE

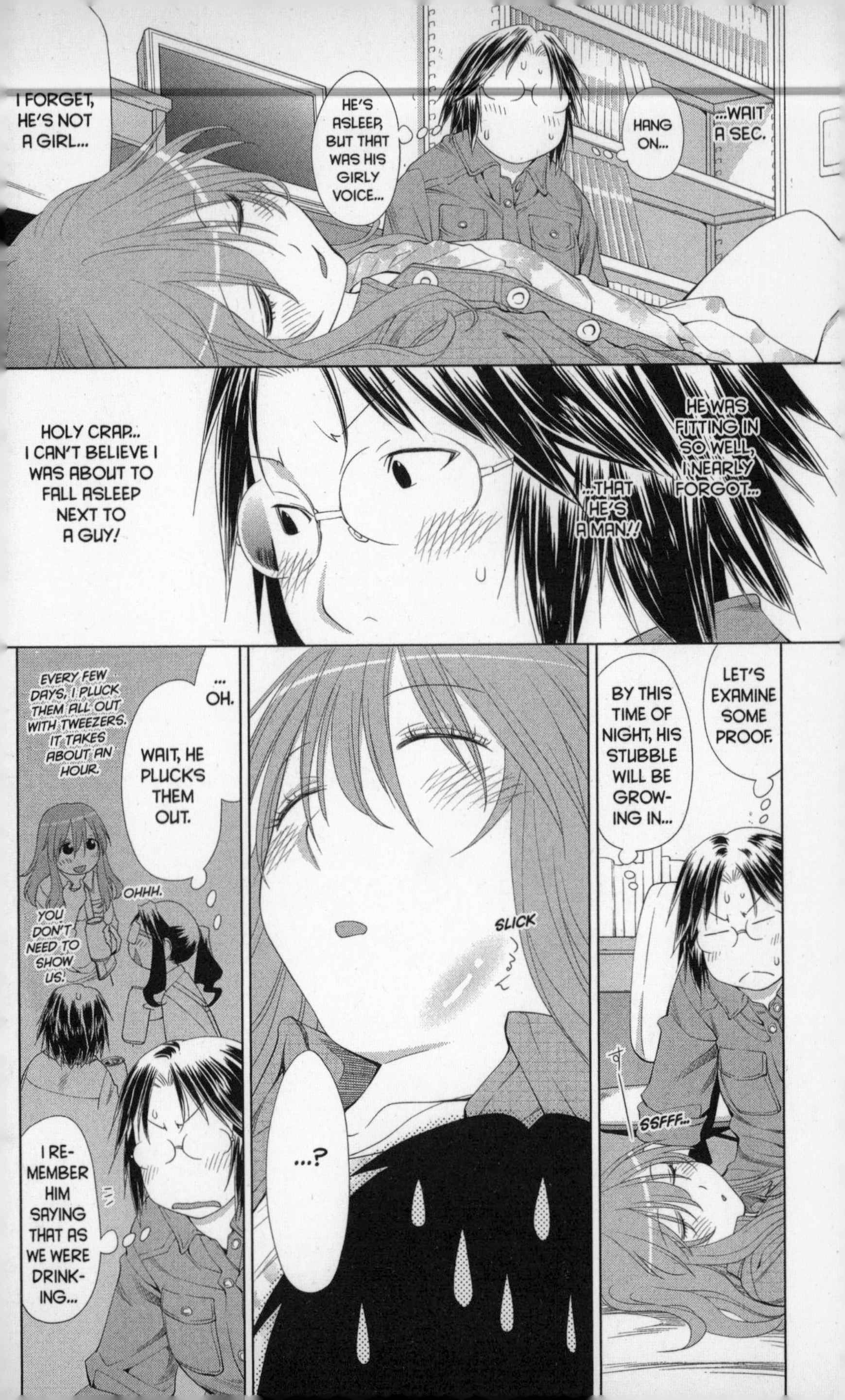
...WAIT A SEC.
HANG ON...
HE'S ASLEEP, BUT THAT WAS HIS GIRLY VOICE...
I FORGET, HE'S NOT A GIRL...
HE WAS FITTING IN SO WELL, I NEARLY FORGOT...
...THAT HE'S A MAN!!
HOLY CRAP... I CAN'T BELIEVE I WAS ABOUT TO FALL ASLEEP NEXT TO A GUY!
LET'S EXAMINE SOME PROOF.
BY THIS TIME OF NIGHT, HIS STUBBLE WILL BE GROW-ING IN...
SSFFF...
SLICK
...?
... OH.
WAIT, HE PLUCKS THEM OUT.
EVERY FEW DAYS, I PLUCK THEM ALL OUT WITH TWEEZERS. IT TAKES ABOUT AN HOUR.
OHHH.
YOU DON'T NEED TO SHOW US!
I RE-MEMBER HIM SAYING THAT AS WE WERE DRINK-ING...

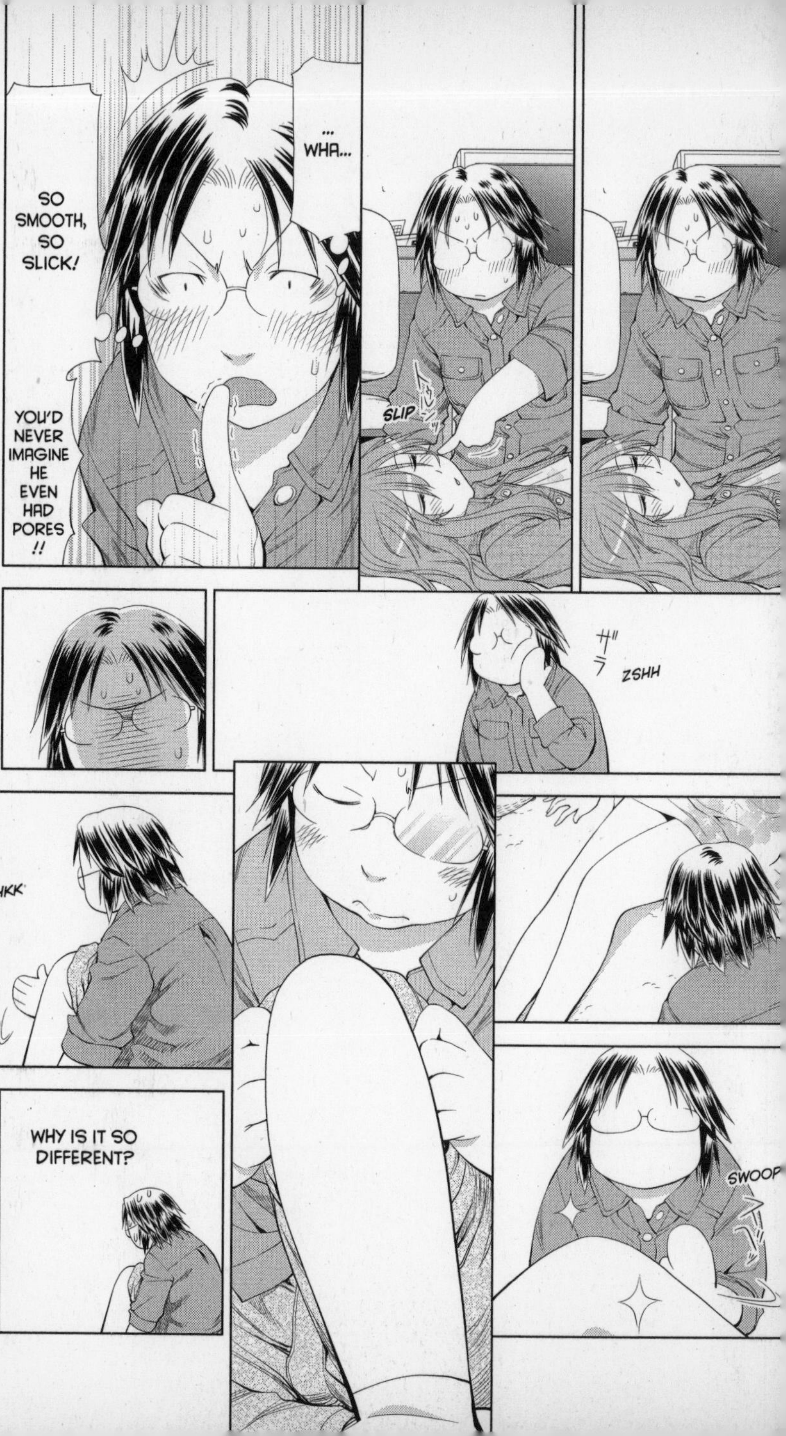
SLIP
... WHA...
SO SMOOTH, SO SLICK!
YOU'D NEVER IMAGINE HE EVEN HAD PORES!!
ザラ
ZSHH
SWOOP
GRSHKK
モジャラッ
WHY IS IT SO DIFFERENT?

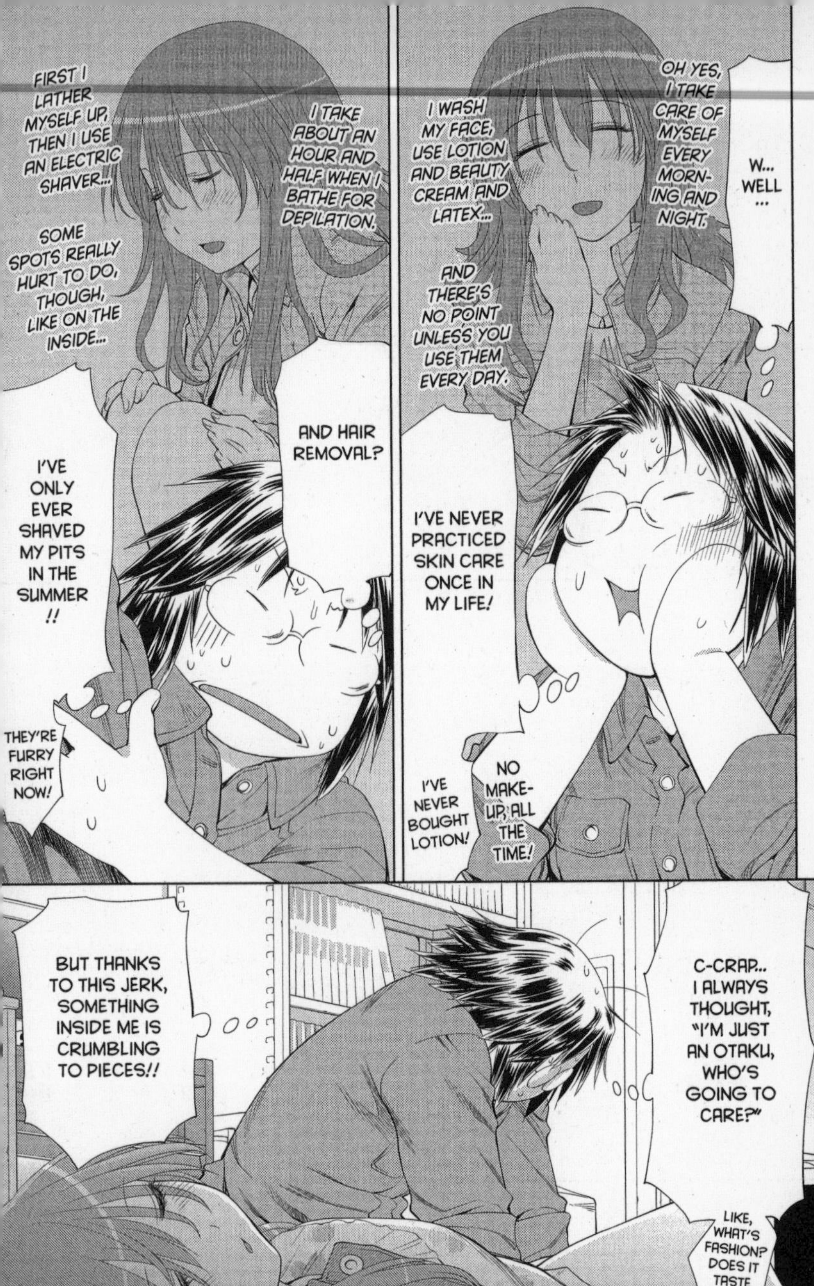
W... WELL ...
OH YES, I TAKE CARE OF MYSELF EVERY MORNING AND NIGHT.
I WASH MY FACE, USE LOTION AND BEAUTY CREAM AND LATEX...
AND THERE'S NO POINT UNLESS YOU USE THEM EVERY DAY.
I'VE NEVER PRACTICED SKIN CARE ONCE IN MY LIFE!
NO MAKE-UP, ALL THE TIME!
I'VE NEVER BOUGHT LOTION!
I TAKE ABOUT AN HOUR AND HALF WHEN I BATHE FOR DEPILATION.
FIRST I LATHER MYSELF UP, THEN I USE AN ELECTRIC SHAVER...
SOME SPOTS REALLY HURT TO DO, THOUGH, LIKE ON THE INSIDE...
AND HAIR REMOVAL?
I'VE ONLY EVER SHAVED MY PITS IN THE SUMMER !!
THEY'RE FURRY RIGHT NOW!
C-CRAP... I ALWAYS THOUGHT, "I'M JUST AN OTAKU, WHO'S GOING TO CARE?"
LIKE, WHAT'S FASHION? DOES IT TASTE GOOD?
BUT THANKS TO THIS JERK, SOMETHING INSIDE ME IS CRUMBLING TO PIECES!!

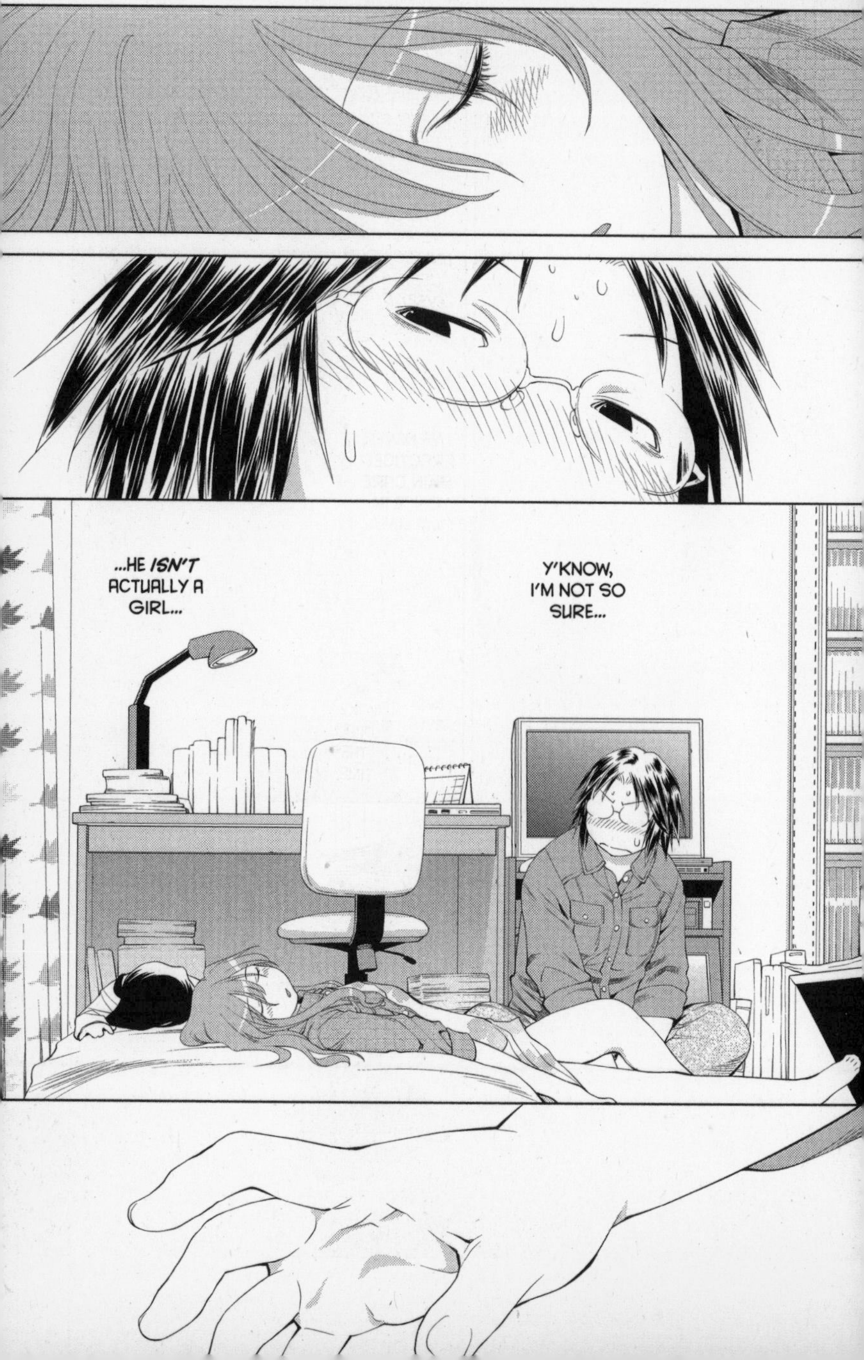
Y'KNOW, I'M NOT SO SURE...
...HE *ISN'T* ACTUALLY A GIRL...

...

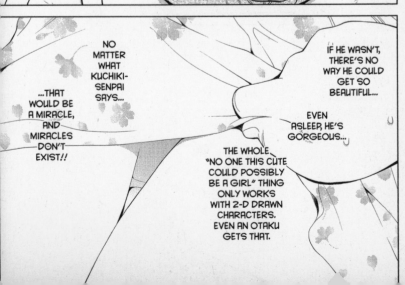

IF HE WASN'T, THERE'S NO WAY HE COULD GET SO BEAUTIFUL...

EVEN ASLEEP, HE'S GORGEOUS...

THE WHOLE "NO ONE THIS CUTE COULD POSSIBLY BE A GIRL" THING ONLY WORKS WITH 2-D DRAWN CHARACTERS. EVEN AN OTAKU GETS THAT.

NO MATTER WHAT KUCHIKI-SENPAI SAYS...

...THAT WOULD BE A MIRACLE, AND MIRACLES DON'T EXIST!!

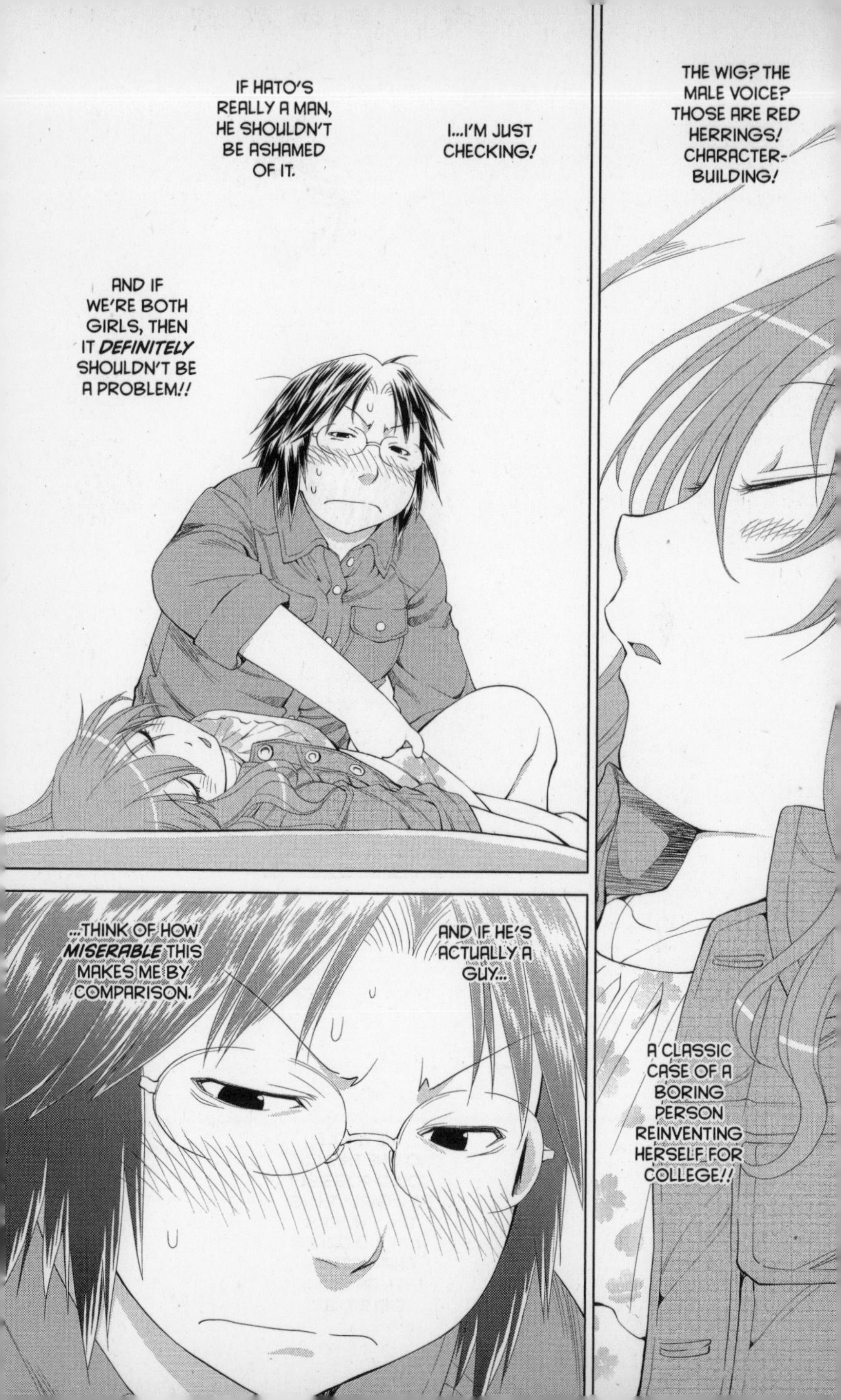
THE WIG? THE MALE VOICE? THOSE ARE RED HERRINGS! CHARACTER-BUILDING!
A CLASSIC CASE OF A BORING PERSON REINVENTING HERSELF FOR COLLEGE!!
I...I'M JUST CHECKING!
IF HATO'S REALLY A MAN, HE SHOULDN'T BE ASHAMED OF IT.
AND IF WE'RE BOTH GIRLS, THEN IT *DEFINITELY* SHOULDN'T BE A PROBLEM!!
AND IF HE'S ACTUALLY A GUY...
...THINK OF HOW *MISERABLE* THIS MAKES ME BY COMPARISON.

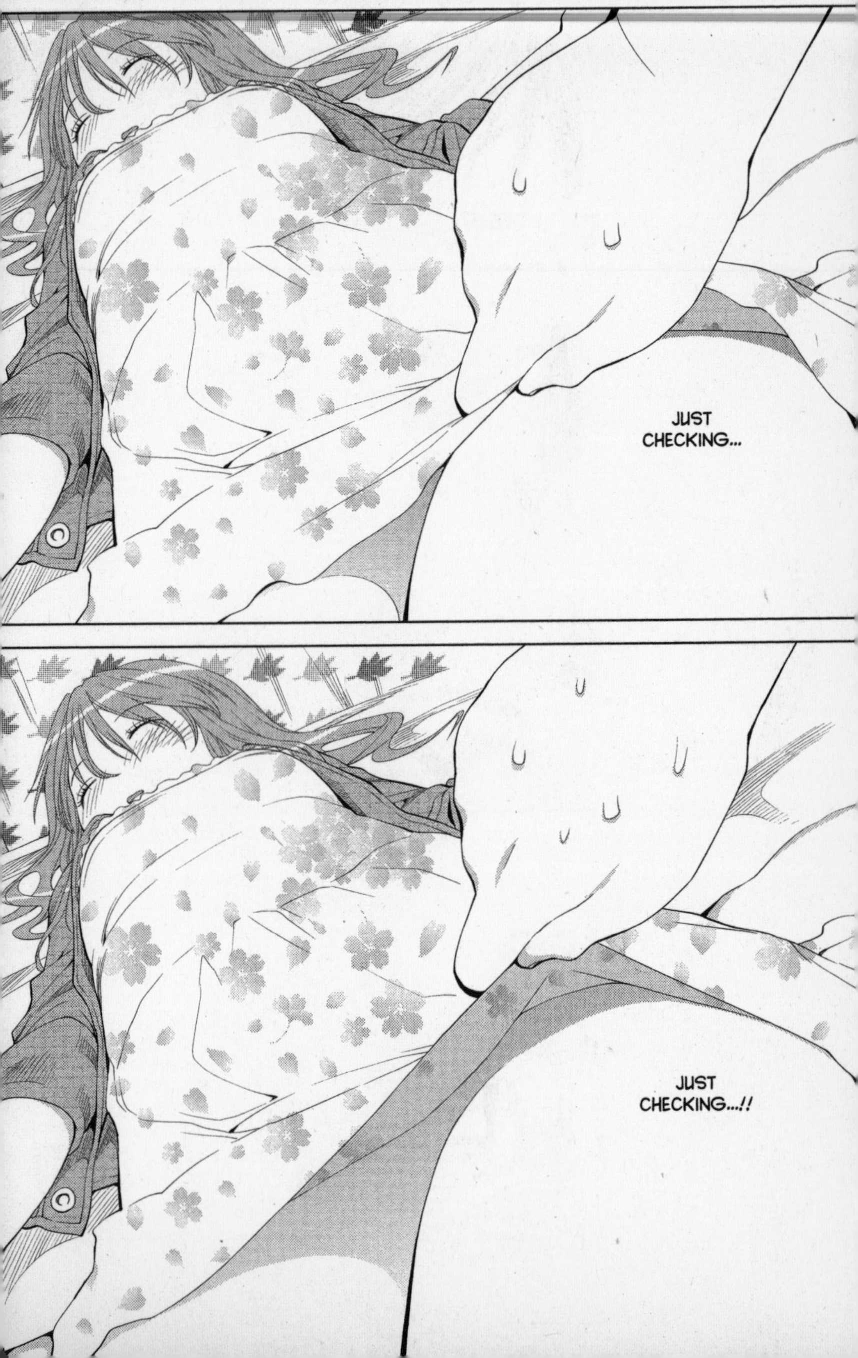
JUST CHECKING...
JUST CHECKING...!!

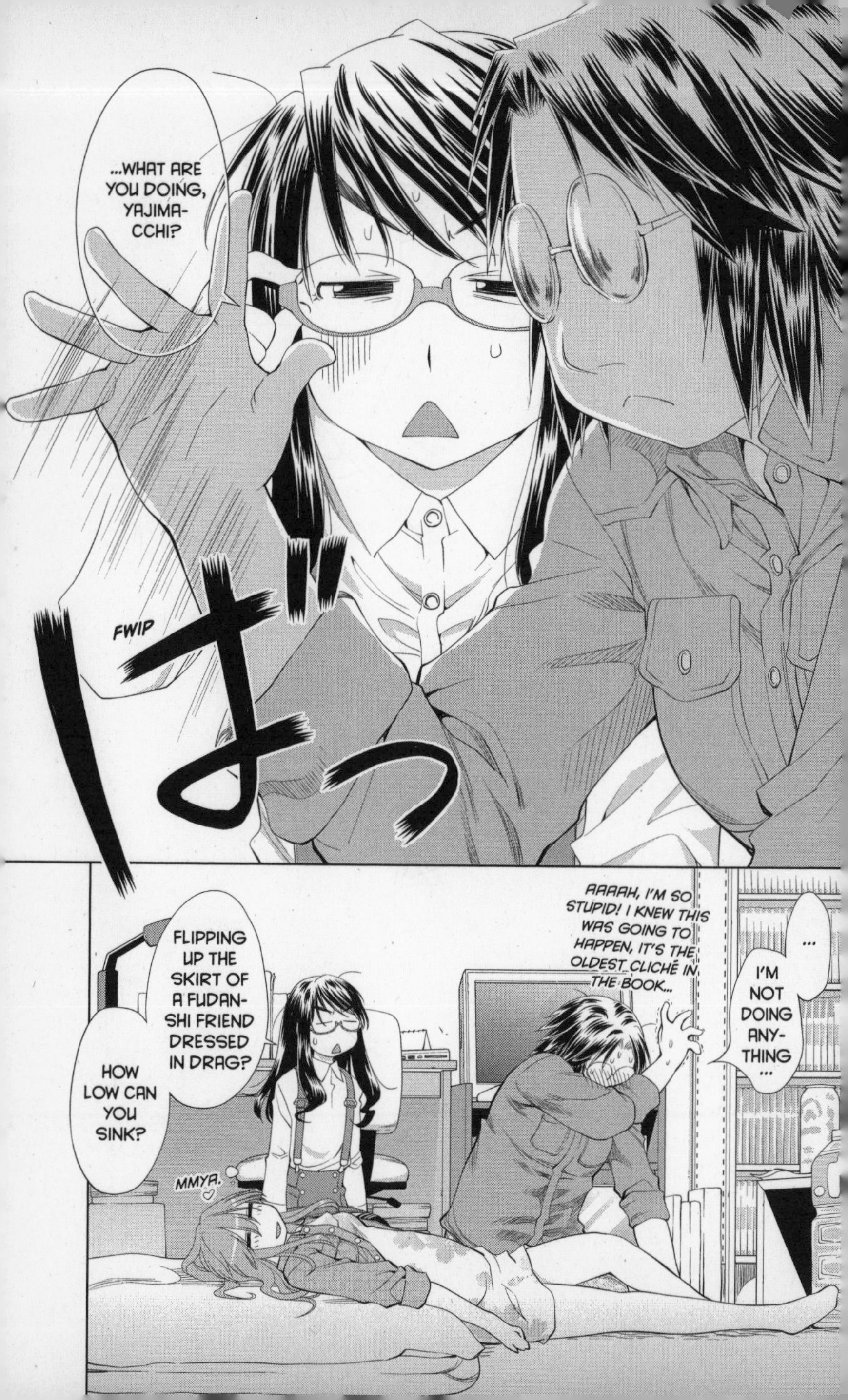
...WHAT ARE YOU DOING, YAJIMA-CCHI?
FWIP
ばっ
... I'M NOT DOING ANYTHING...
AAAAH, I'M SO STUPID! I KNEW THIS WAS GOING TO HAPPEN, IT'S THE OLDEST CLICHÉ IN THE BOOK...
FLIPPING UP THE SKIRT OF A FUDAN-SHI FRIEND DRESSED IN DRAG?
HOW LOW CAN YOU SINK?
MMYA.

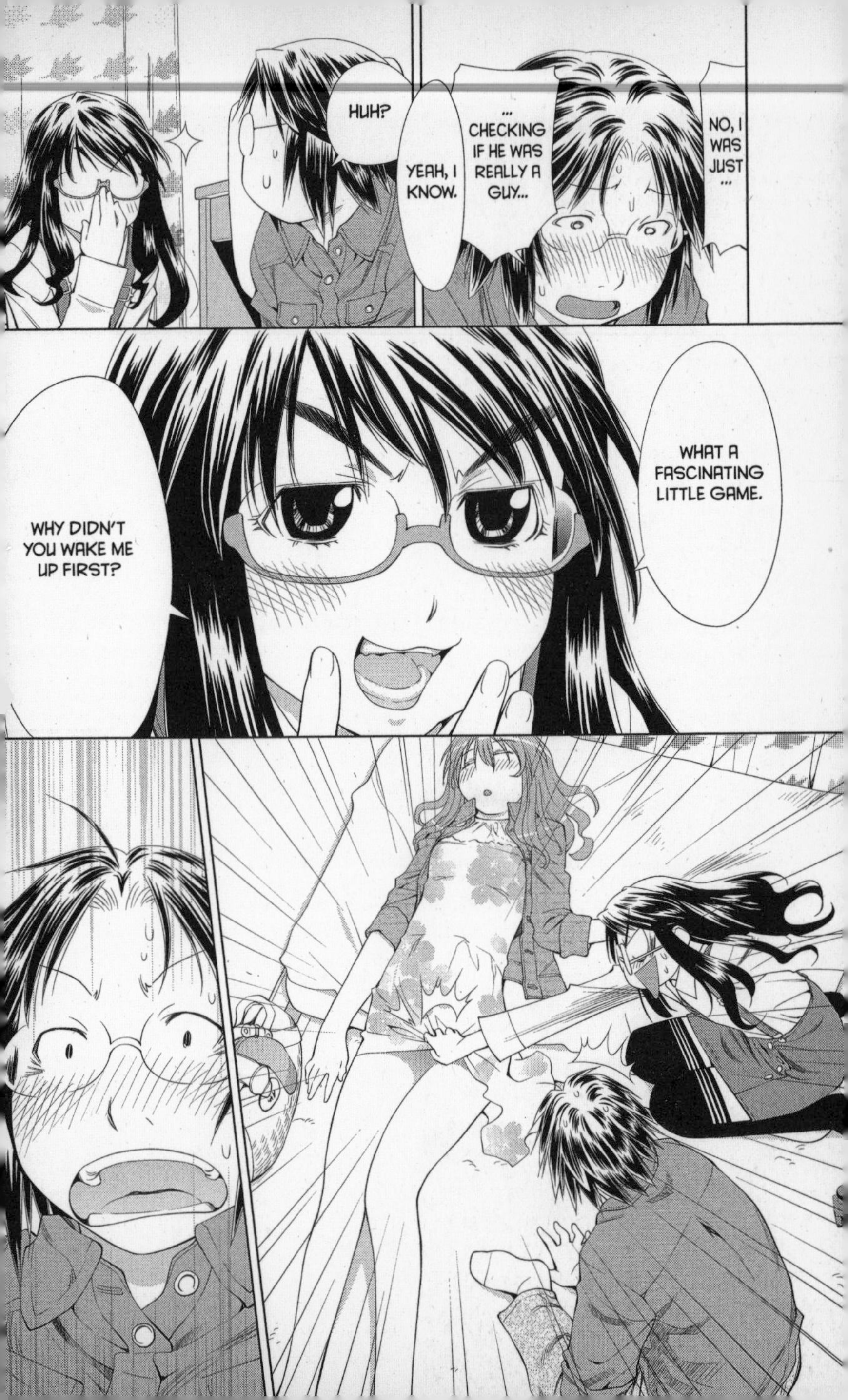
NO, I WAS JUST ...
... CHECKING IF HE WAS REALLY A GUY...
YEAH, I KNOW.
HUH?
WHAT A FASCINATING LITTLE GAME.
WHY DIDN'T YOU WAKE ME UP FIRST?

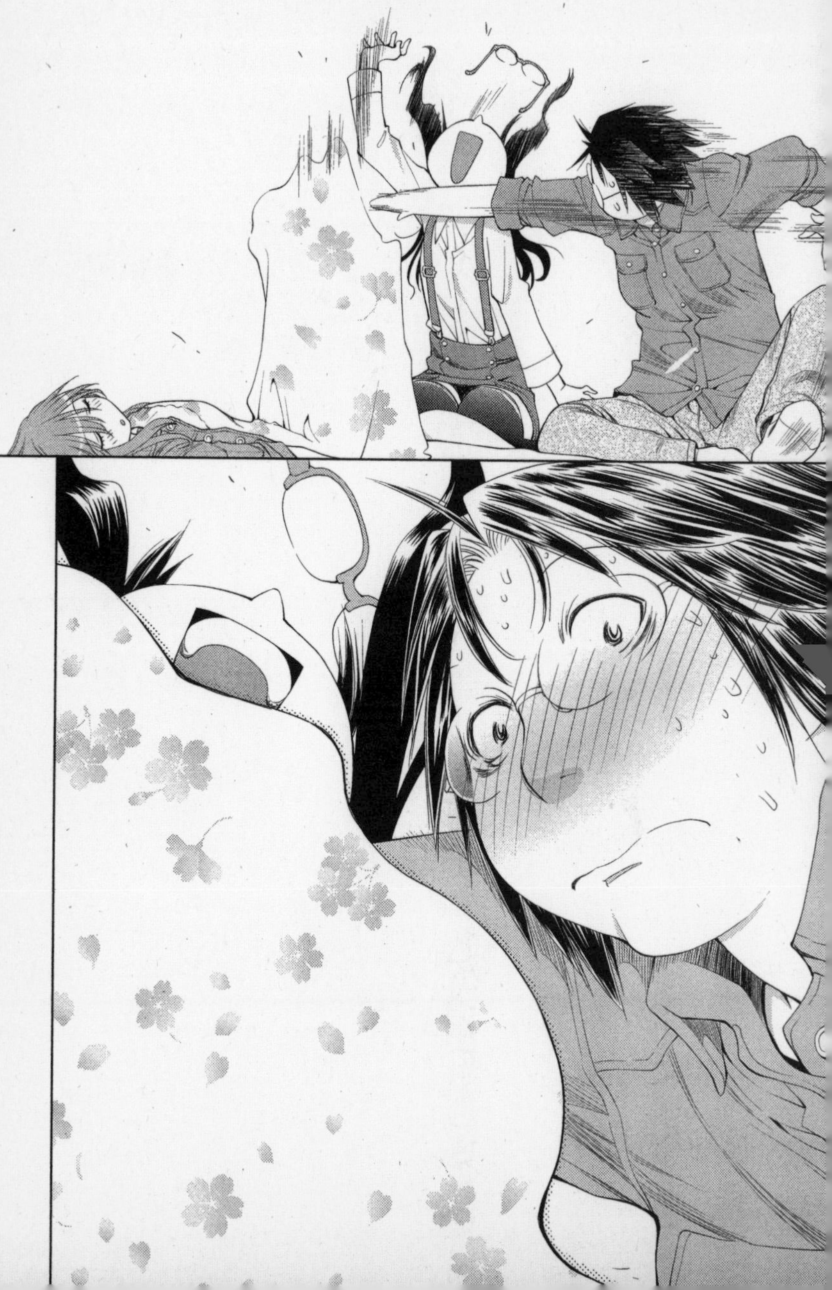

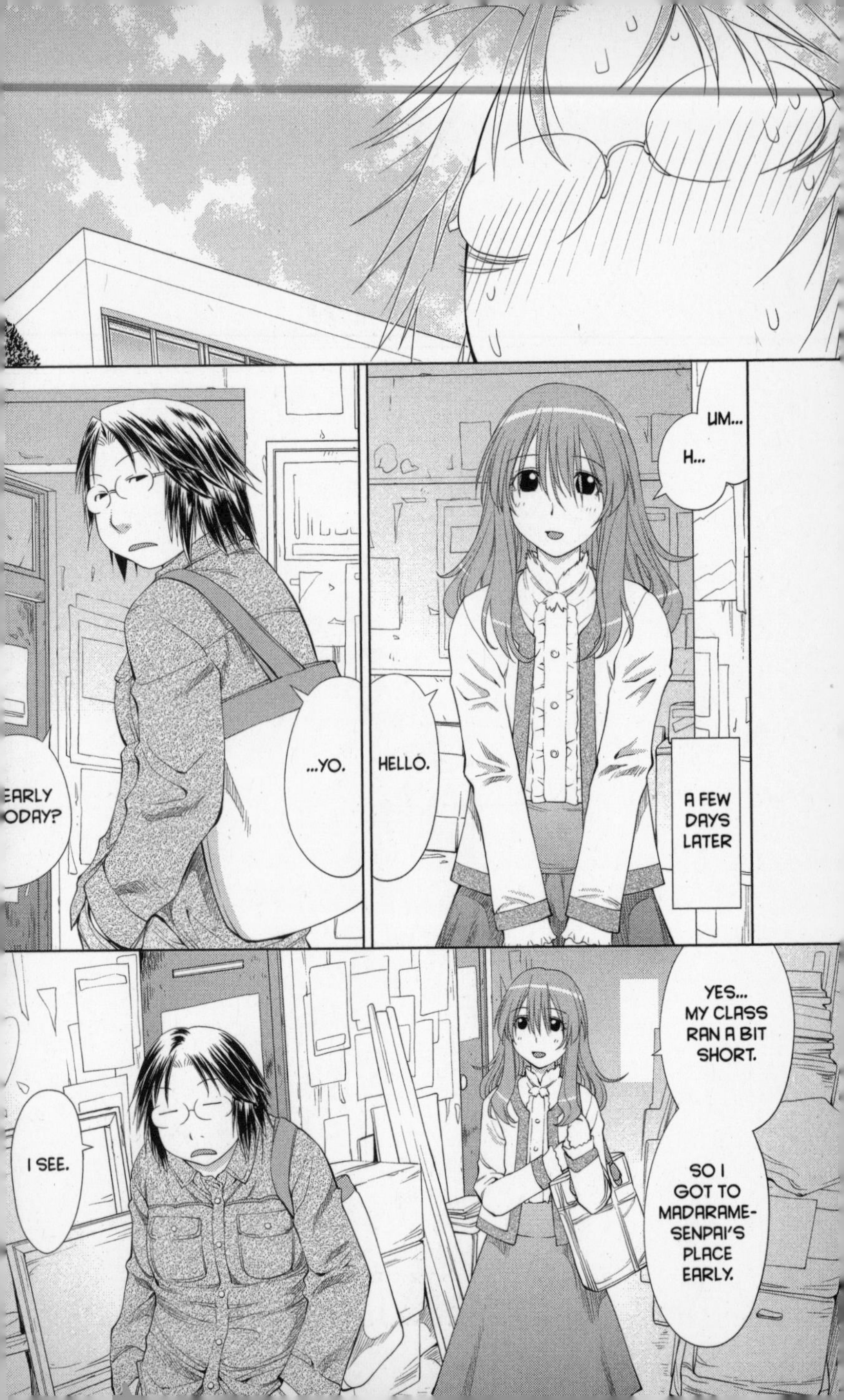
UM...
H...
A FEW DAYS LATER
HELLO.
...YO.
EARLY ODAY?
YES... MY CLASS RAN A BIT SHORT.
SO I GOT TO MADARAME-SENPAI'S PLACE EARLY.
I SEE.

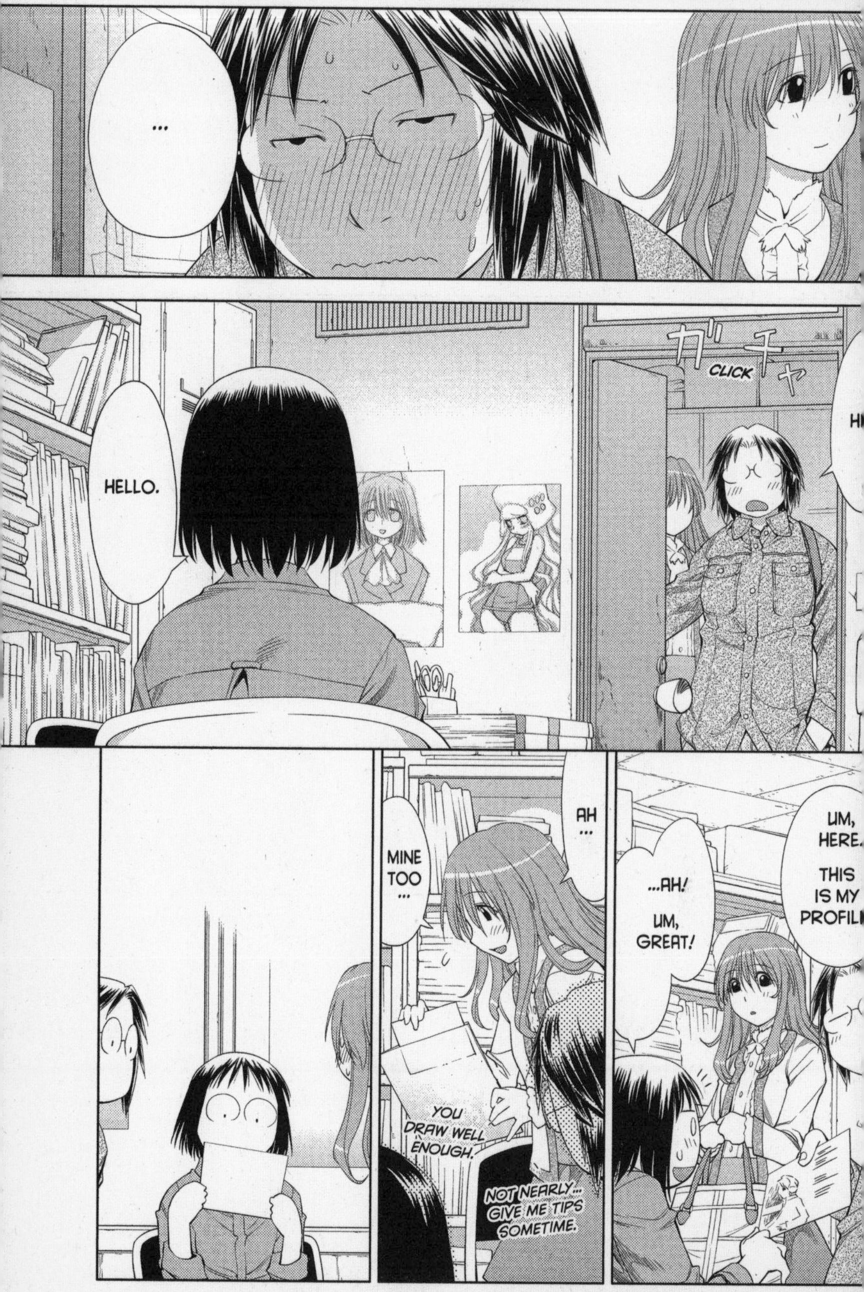
...
ガチャ
CLICK
HELLO.
UM, HERE.
THIS IS MY PROFIL
...AH!
UM, GREAT!
AH ...
MINE TOO ...
YOU DRAW WELL ENOUGH.
NOT NEARLY... GIVE ME TIPS SOMETIME.

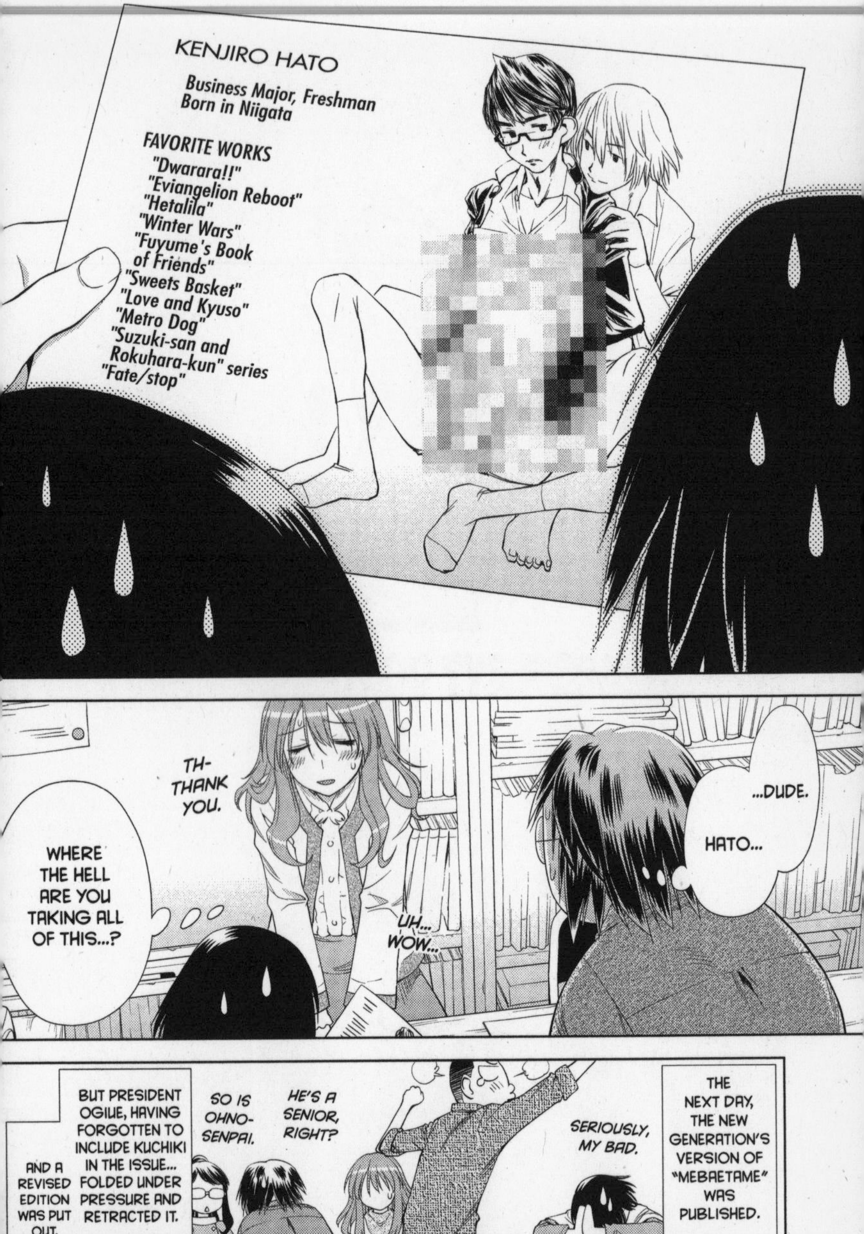
KENJIRO HATO
Business Major, Freshman
Born in Niigata
FAVORITE WORKS
"Dwarara!!"
"Eviangelion Reboot"
"Hetalila"
"Winter Wars"
"Fuyume's Book of Friends"
"Sweets Basket"
"Love and Kyuso"
"Metro Dog"
"Suzuki-san and Rokuhara-kun" series
"Fate/stop"
...DUDE.
HATO...
UH... WOW...
TH- THANK YOU.
WHERE THE HELL ARE YOU TAKING ALL OF THIS...?
THE NEXT DAY, THE NEW GENERATION'S VERSION OF "MEBAETAME" WAS PUBLISHED.
SERIOUSLY, MY BAD.
HE'S A SENIOR, RIGHT?
SO IS OHNO-SENPAI.
BUT PRESIDENT OGIUE, HAVING FORGOTTEN TO INCLUDE KUCHIKI IN THE ISSUE... FOLDED UNDER PRESSURE AND RETRACTED IT.
AND A REVISED EDITION WAS PUT OUT.

CHAPTER 58 -- END

CHIKA OGIUE

(NARUYUKI OGINO)

LIBERAL ARTS, JUNIOR
BORN IN YAMAGATA
MARCH 28TH, TYPE A

FAVORITE WORKS
"HAREGAN"
"KUJI-UN"
"ZENNICHI NO KYOJIN"

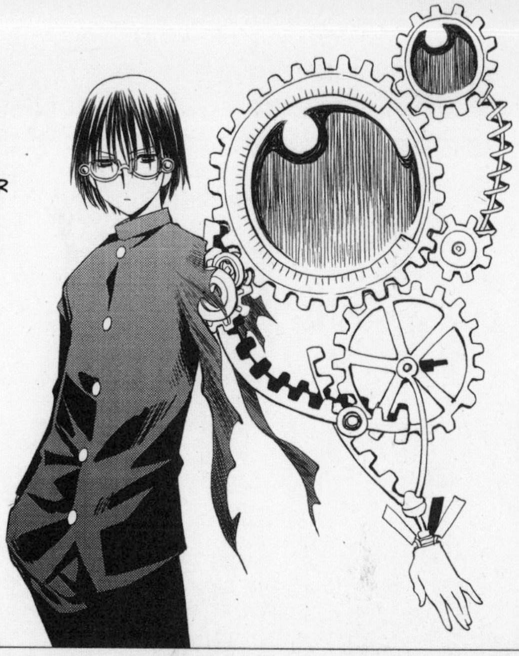

WANT TO COSPLAY? CONTACT KANAKO OHNO!!

- FULL AND VARIED LINEUP!
- ALL MADE-TO-ORDER AND PERFECTLY FITTING!
- COMES WITH FREE PHOTOGRAPHY!
- WE HELP YOU PLAN YOUR EVENT APPEARANCES!!

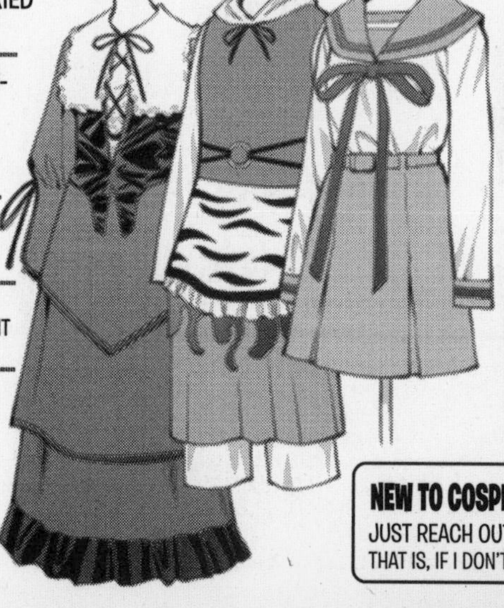

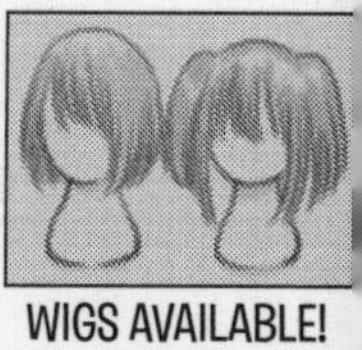

WIGS AVAILABLE!

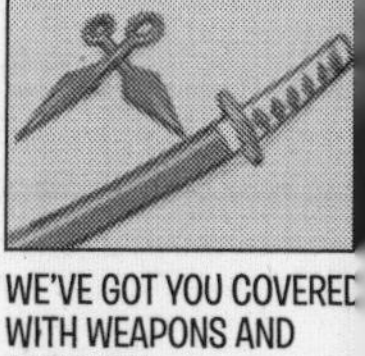

WE'VE GOT YOU COVERED WITH WEAPONS AND ARTICLES!

NEW TO COSPLAY? NO WORRIES!
JUST REACH OUT AND CONTACT ME!!
THAT IS, IF I DON'T CONTACT YOU FIRST ♡

STRIP STRIP

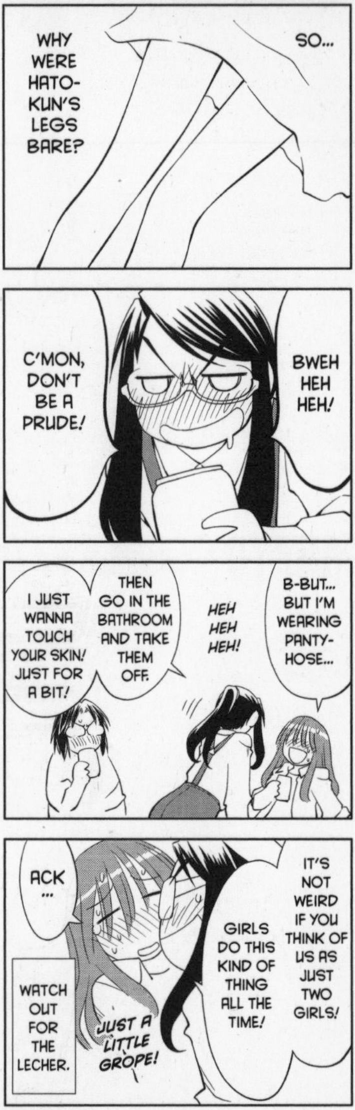
SO...
WHY WERE HATO-KUN'S LEGS BARE?
BWEH HEH HEH!
C'MON, DON'T BE A PRUDE!
B-BUT... BUT I'M WEARING PANTY-HOSE...
HEH HEH HEH!
THEN GO IN THE BATHROOM AND TAKE THEM OFF.
I JUST WANNA TOUCH YOUR SKIN! JUST FOR A BIT!
IT'S NOT WEIRD IF YOU THINK OF US AS JUST TWO GIRLS!
GIRLS DO THIS KIND OF THING ALL THE TIME!
ACK ...
JUST A LITTLE GROPE!
WATCH OUT FOR THE LECHER.

SLIDE SLIDE

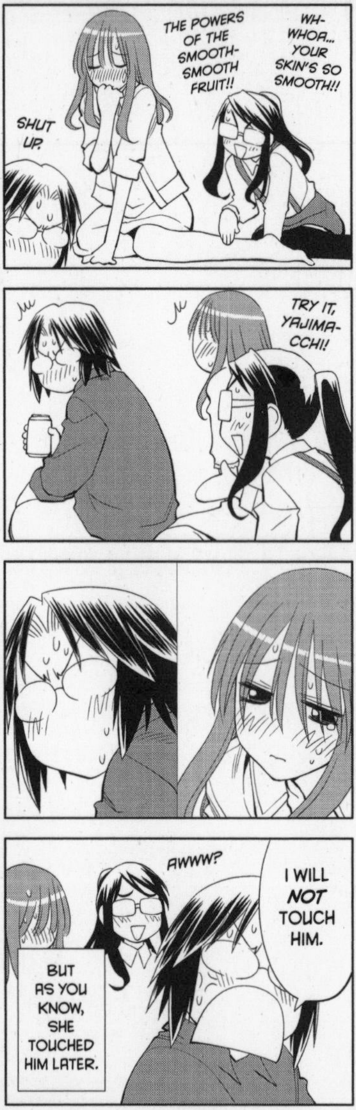
WH-WHOA... YOUR SKIN'S SO SMOOTH!!
THE POWERS OF THE SMOOTH-SMOOTH FRUIT!!
SHUT UP.
TRY IT, YAJIMA-CCHI!
I WILL NOT TOUCH HIM.
AWWW?
BUT AS YOU KNOW, SHE TOUCHED HIM LATER.

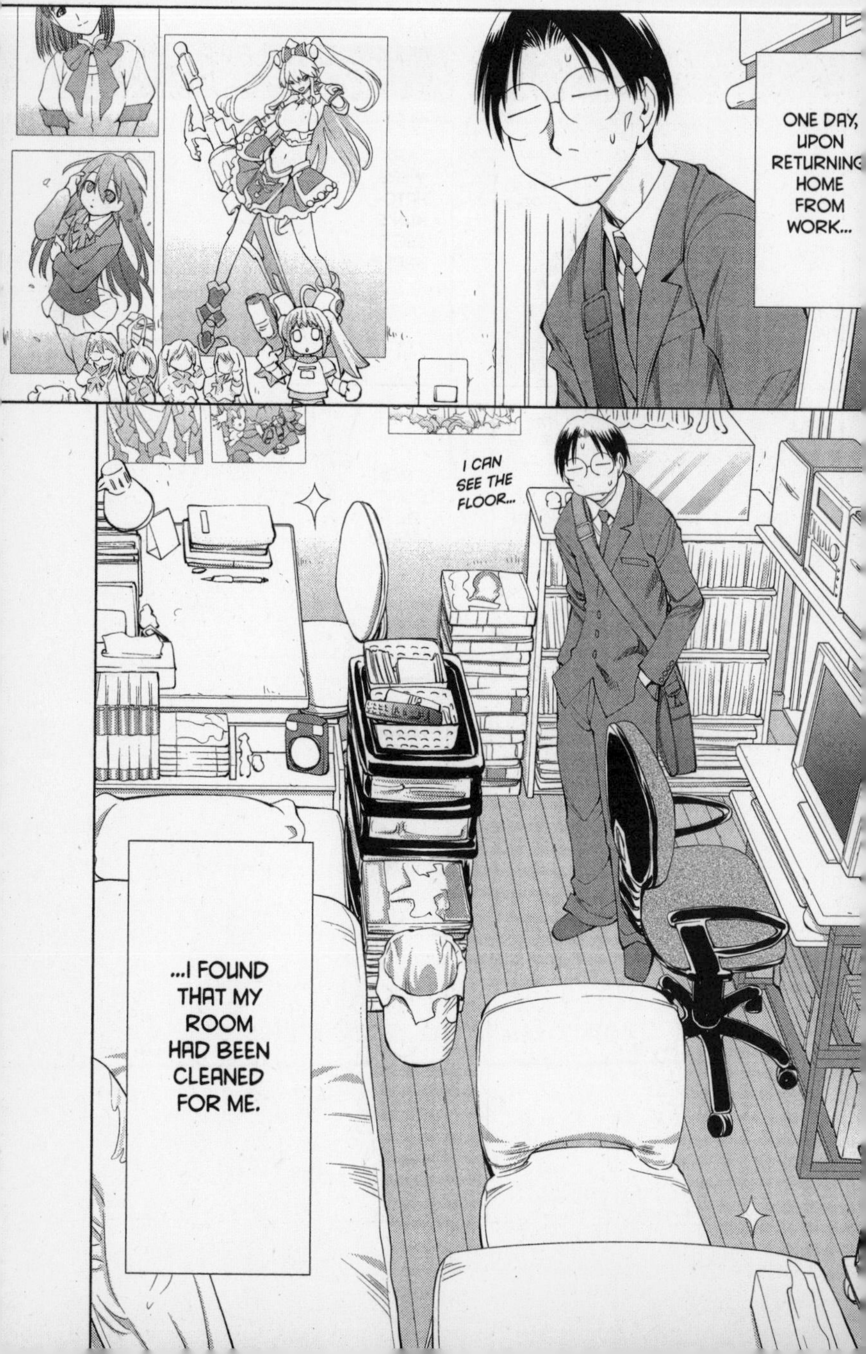
ONE DAY, UPON RETURNING HOME FROM WORK...
I CAN SEE THE FLOOR...
...I FOUND THAT MY ROOM HAD BEEN CLEANED FOR ME.

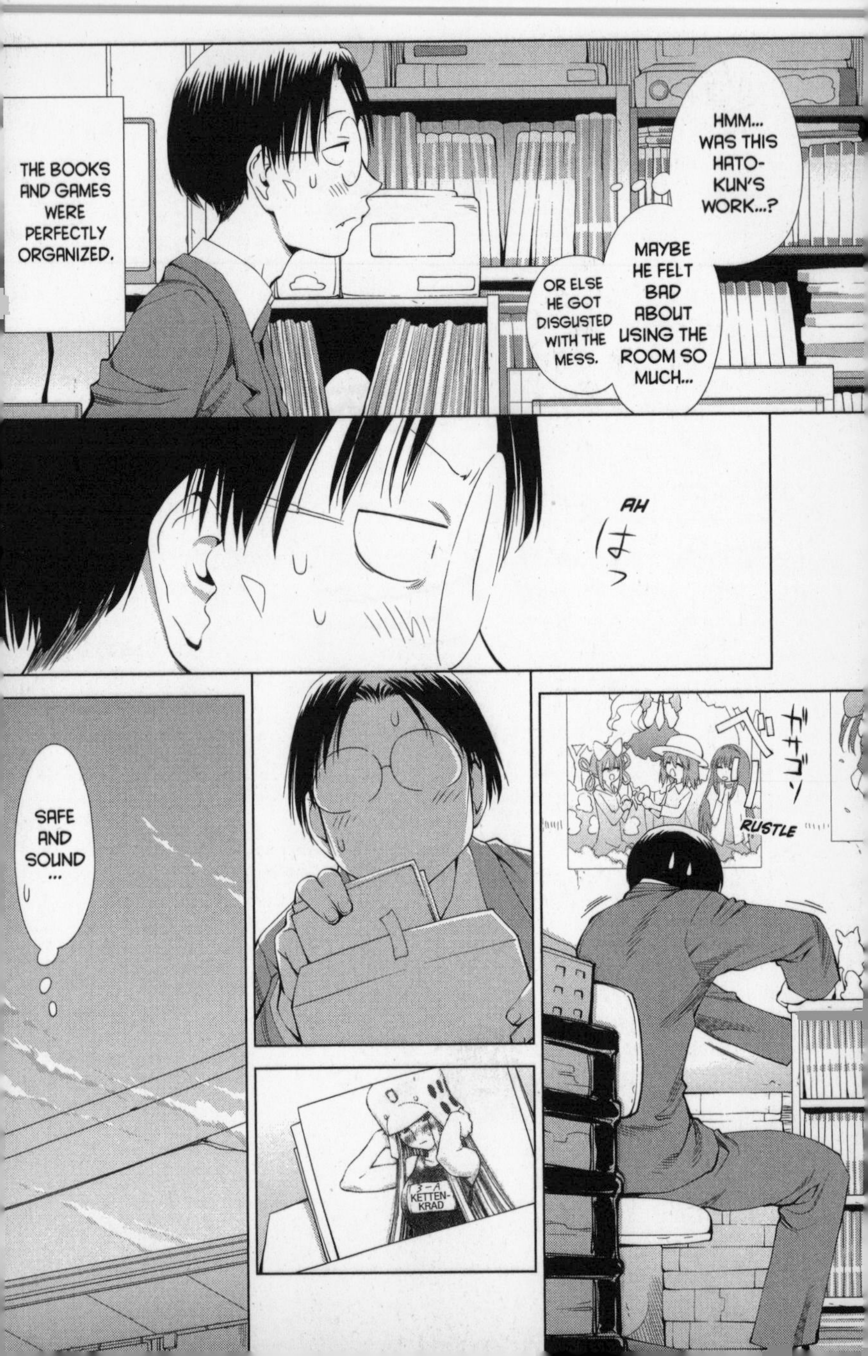
HMM... WAS THIS HATO-KUN'S WORK...?
MAYBE HE FELT BAD ABOUT USING THE ROOM SO MUCH...
OR ELSE HE GOT DISGUSTED WITH THE MESS.
THE BOOKS AND GAMES WERE PERFECTLY ORGANIZED.
AH
はっ
ガサゴソ
RUSTLE
3-A KETTEN-KRAD
SAFE AND SOUND ...

CHAPTER 59: MINESWEEPER

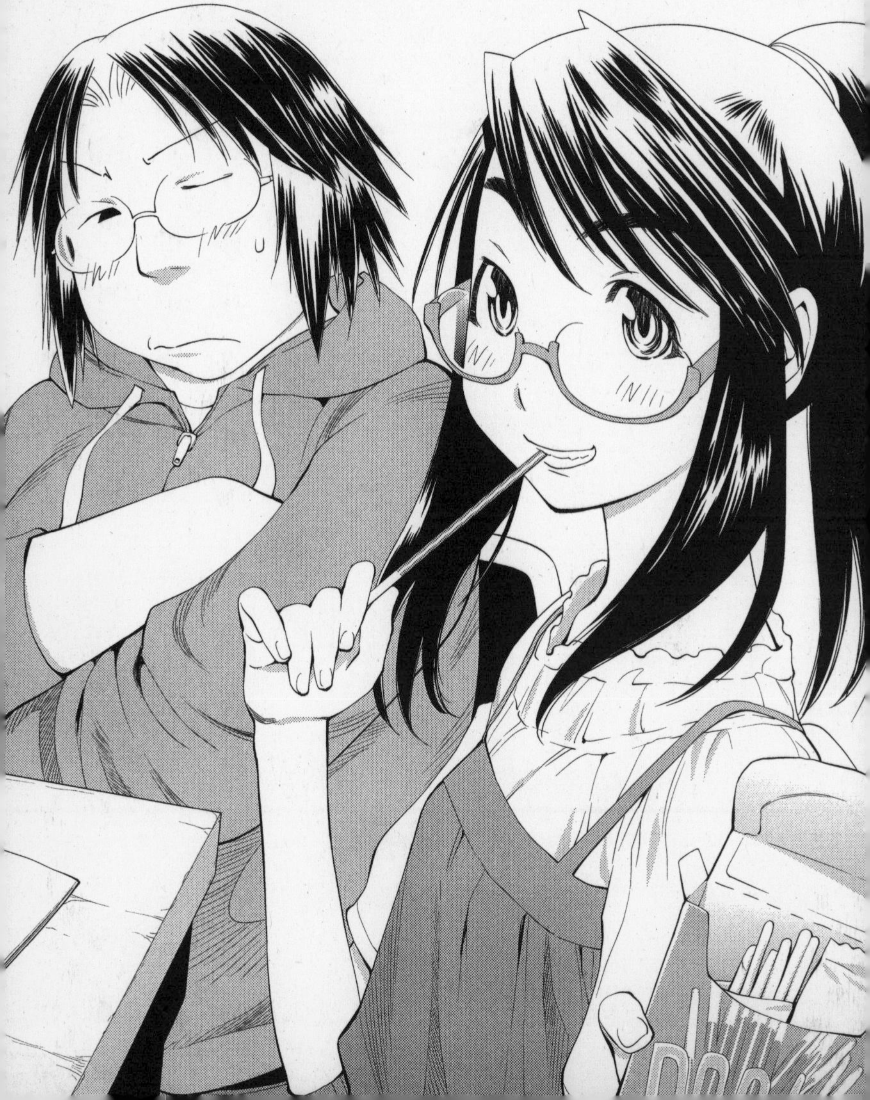

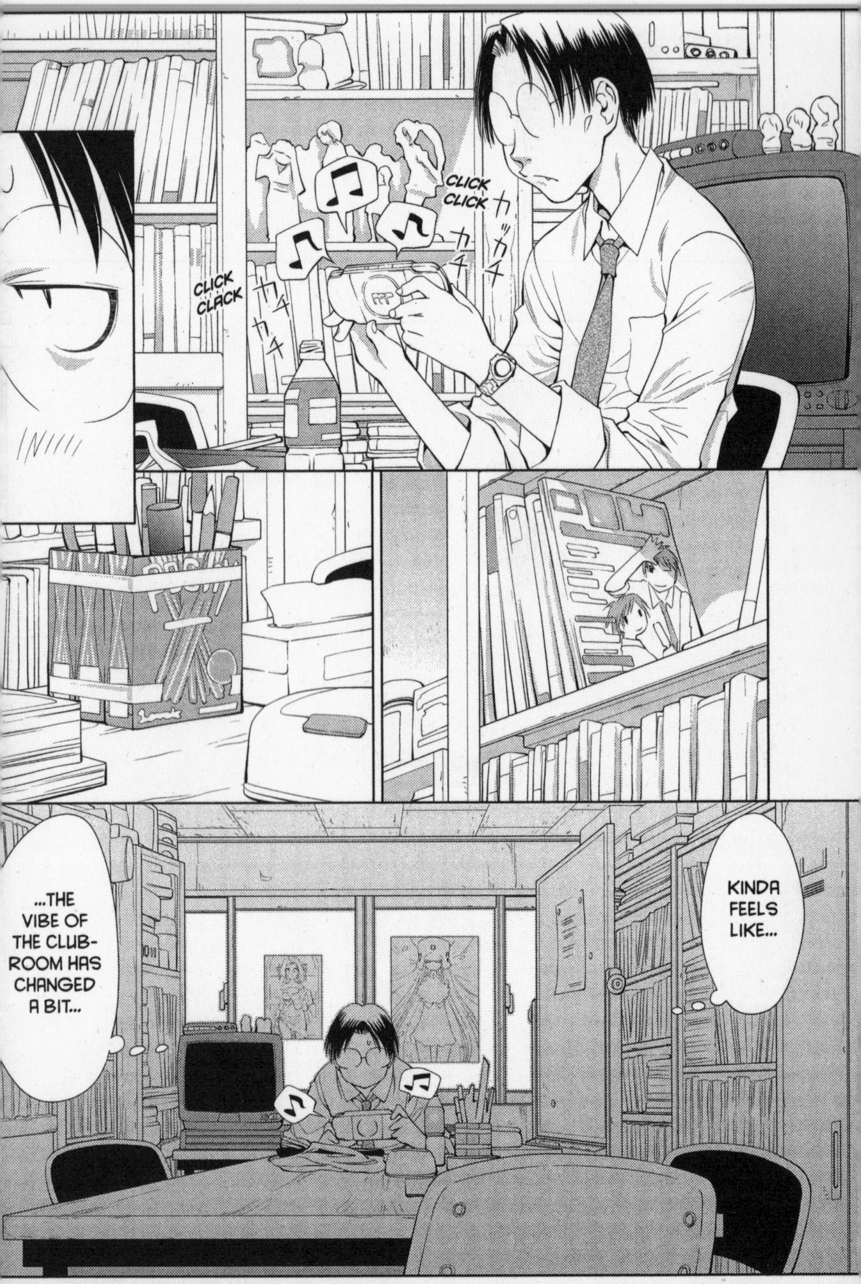

CLICK CLICK
カッカチ
カチ
CLICK CLACK
カチカチ
KINDA FEELS LIKE...
...THE VIBE OF THE CLUB-ROOM HAS CHANGED A BIT...

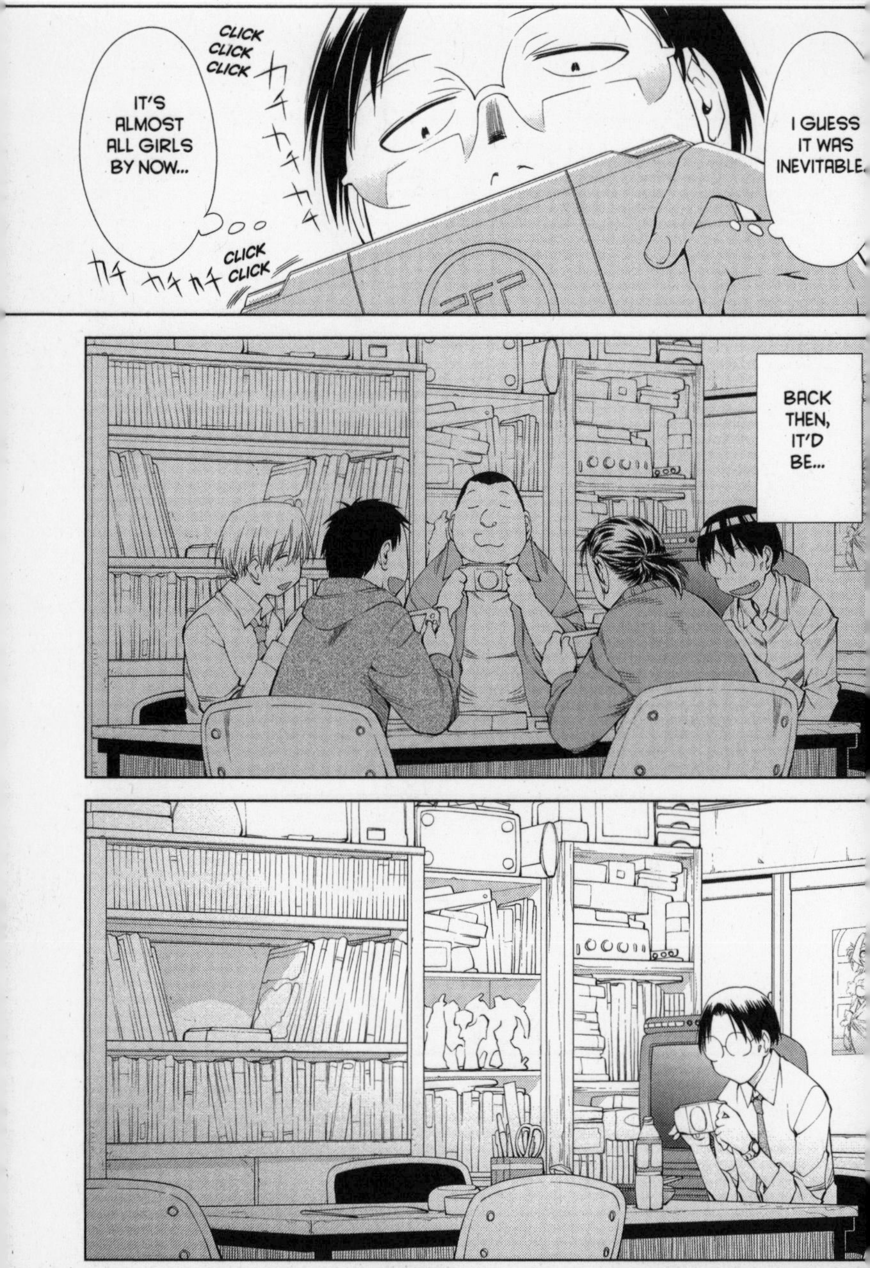
I GUESS IT WAS INEVITABLE.
CLICK CLICK CLICK
カチカチカチカチ
IT'S ALMOST ALL GIRLS BY NOW...
CLICK CLICK
カチ カチカチ
BACK THEN, IT'D BE...

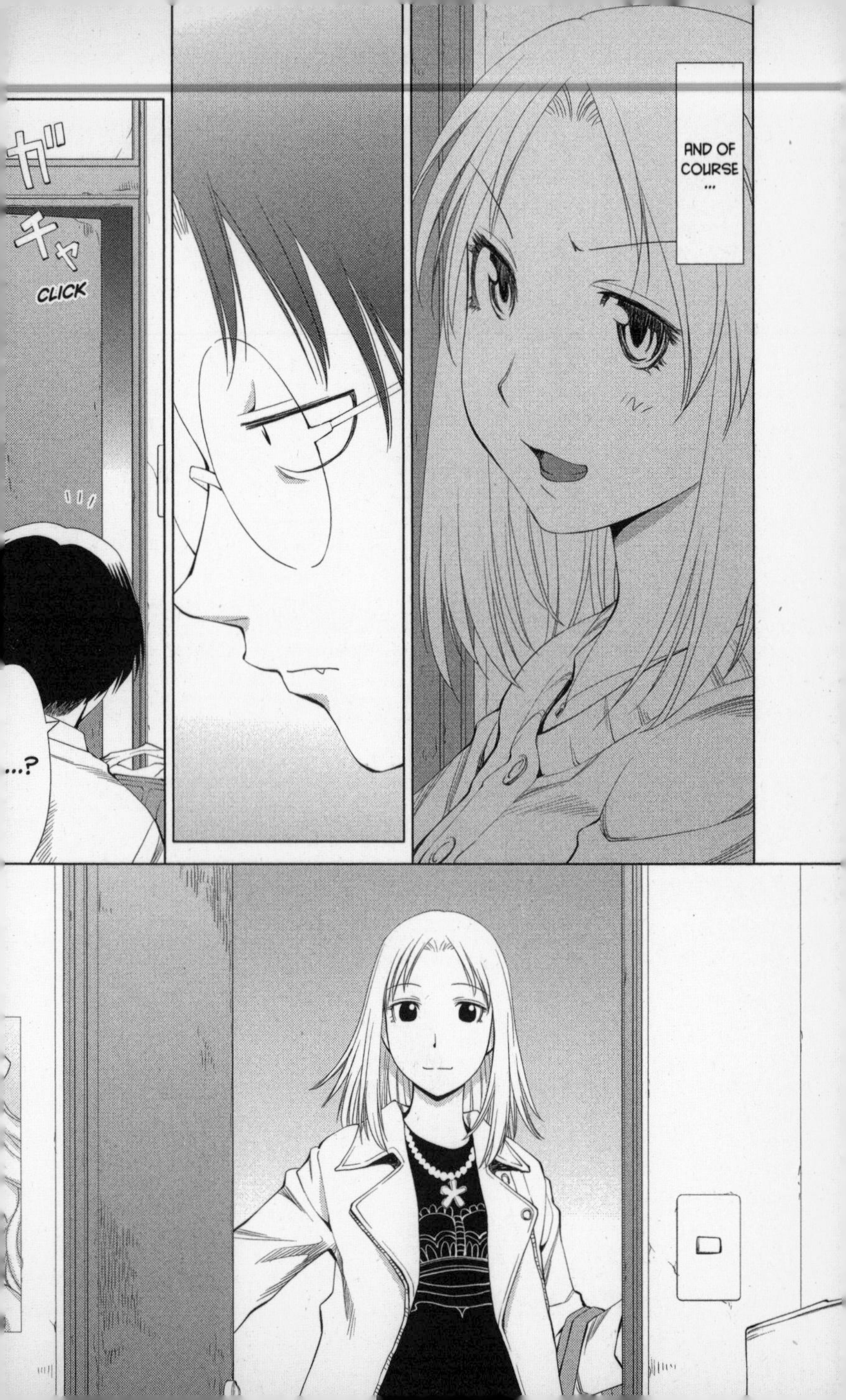
AND OF COURSE ...
ガチャ
CLICK
...?

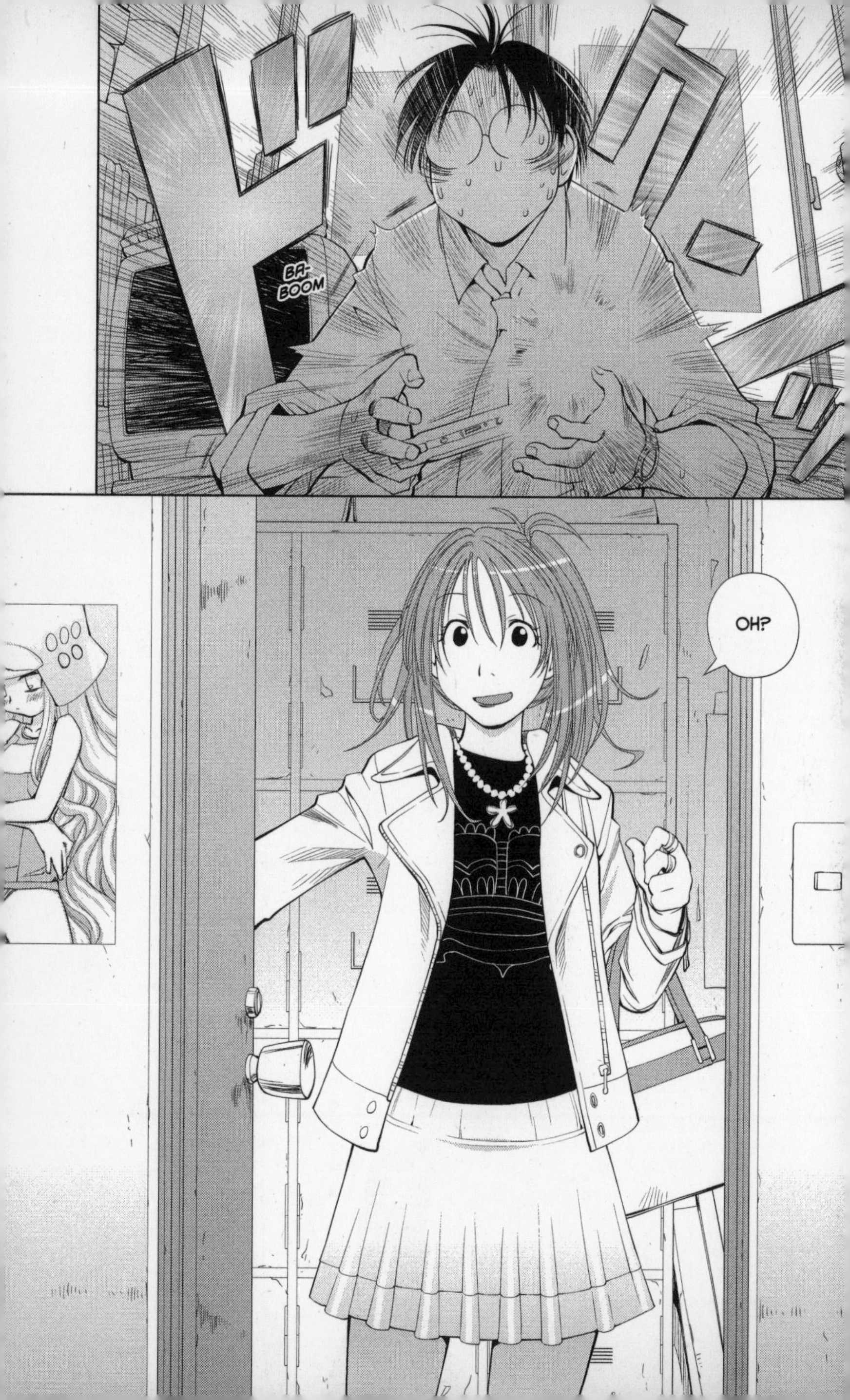
BA-
BOOM
OH?

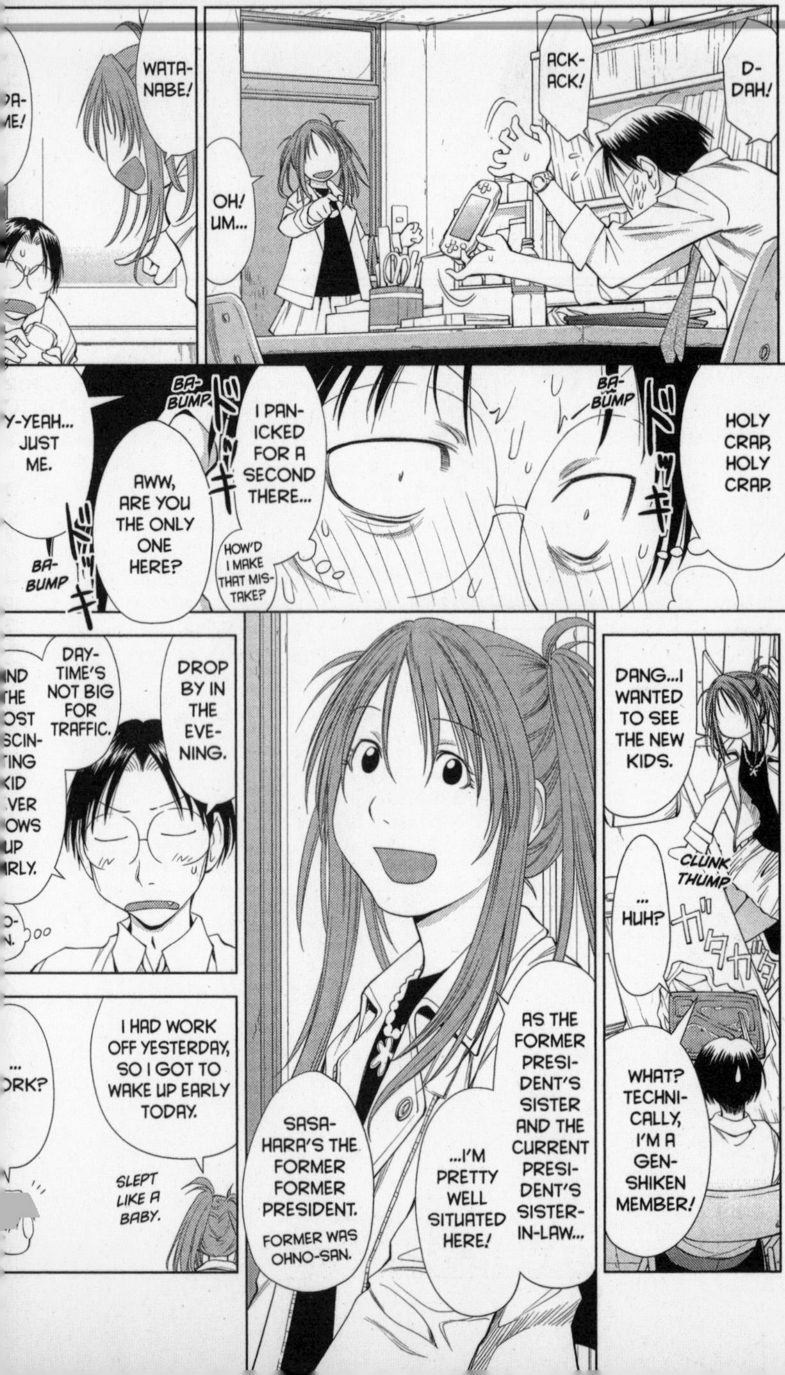

D-DAH!
ACK-ACK!
OH! UM...
WATA-NABE!
PA-ME!
HOLY CRAP, HOLY CRAP.
BA-BUMP
I PANICKED FOR A SECOND THERE...
HOW'D I MAKE THAT MISTAKE?
BA-BUMP
AWW, ARE YOU THE ONLY ONE HERE?
Y-YEAH... JUST ME.
BA-BUMP
DANG...I WANTED TO SEE THE NEW KIDS.
CLUNK THUMP
... HUH?
WHAT? TECHNICALLY, I'M A GENSHIKEN MEMBER!
AS THE FORMER PRESIDENT'S SISTER AND THE CURRENT PRESIDENT'S SISTER-IN-LAW...
...I'M PRETTY WELL SITUATED HERE!
SASAHARA'S THE FORMER FORMER PRESIDENT.
FORMER WAS OHNO-SAN.
DROP BY IN THE EVENING.
DAYTIME'S NOT BIG FOR TRAFFIC.
ND THE OST SCIN-TING KID VER OWS UP RLY.
I HAD WORK OFF YESTERDAY, SO I GOT TO WAKE UP EARLY TODAY.
SLEPT LIKE A BABY.
... ORK?

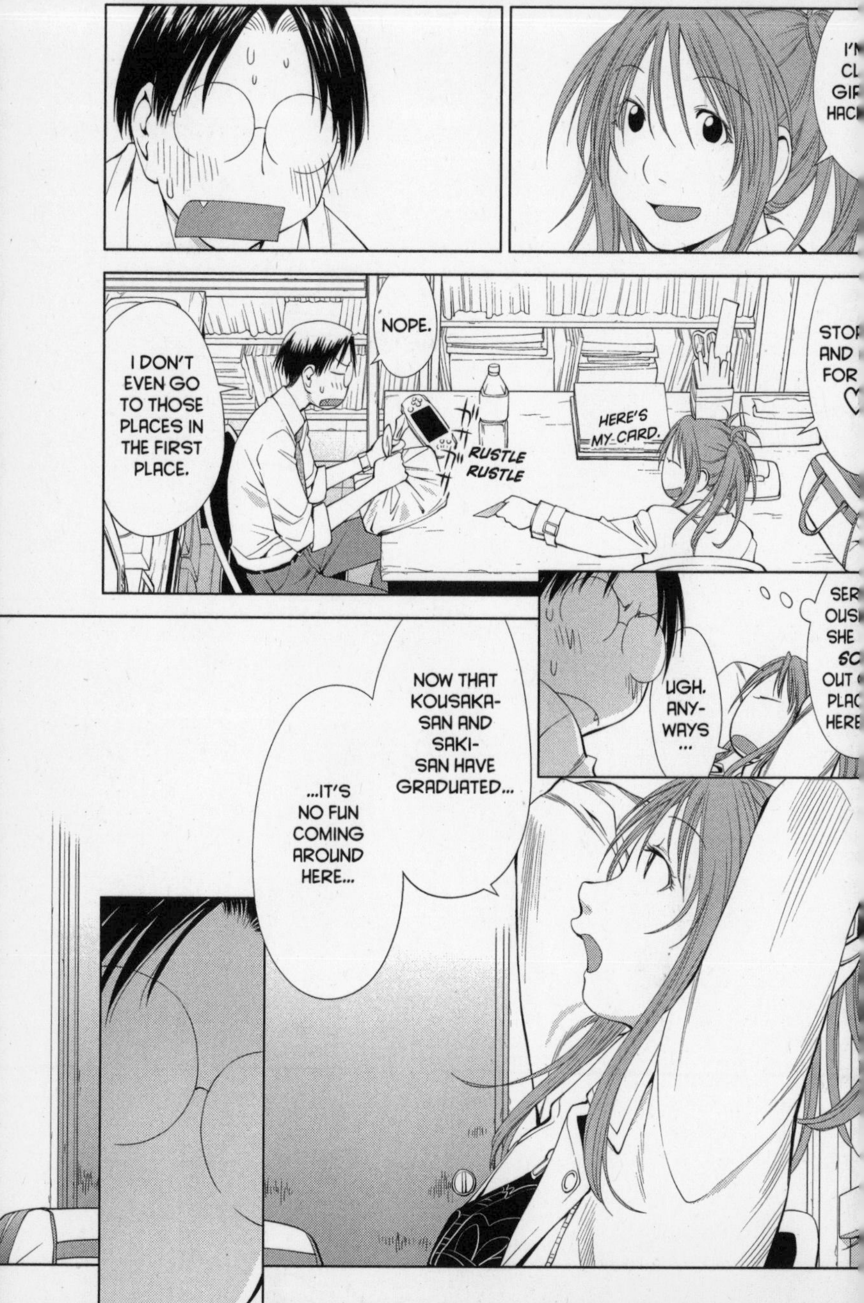
I'M CL GIR HACK
STOP AND FOR ♡
HERE'S MY CARD.
RUSTLE RUSTLE
NOPE.
I DON'T EVEN GO TO THOSE PLACES IN THE FIRST PLACE.
SER OUSL SHE SC OUT PLAC HERE
UGH. ANYWAYS...
NOW THAT KOUSAKA-SAN AND SAKI-SAN HAVE GRADUATED...
...IT'S NO FUN COMING AROUND HERE...

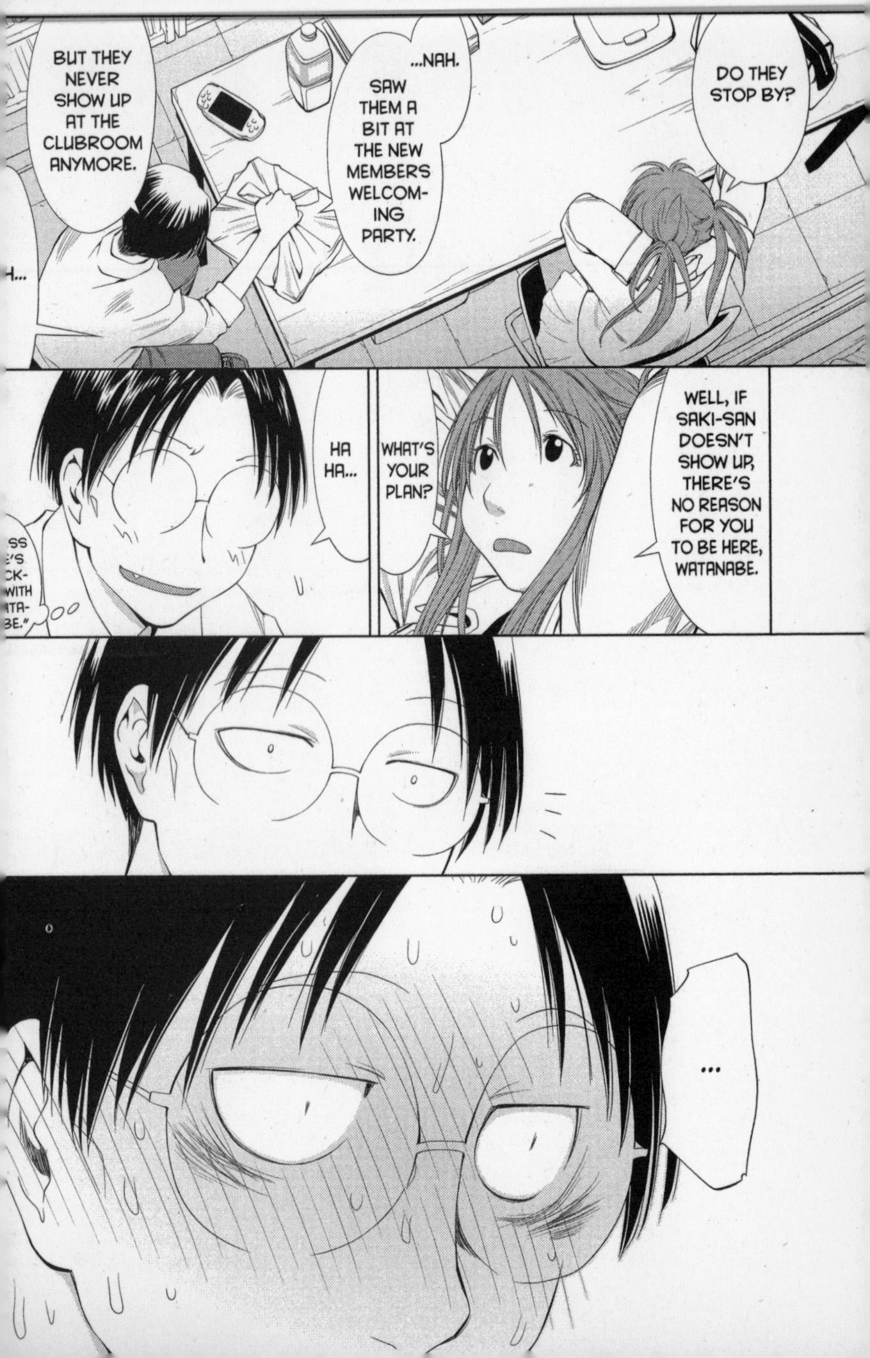
DO THEY STOP BY?
...NAH. SAW THEM A BIT AT THE NEW MEMBERS WELCOMING PARTY.
BUT THEY NEVER SHOW UP AT THE CLUBROOM ANYMORE.
WELL, IF SAKI-SAN DOESN'T SHOW UP, THERE'S NO REASON FOR YOU TO BE HERE, WATANABE.
WHAT'S YOUR PLAN?
HA HA...
...

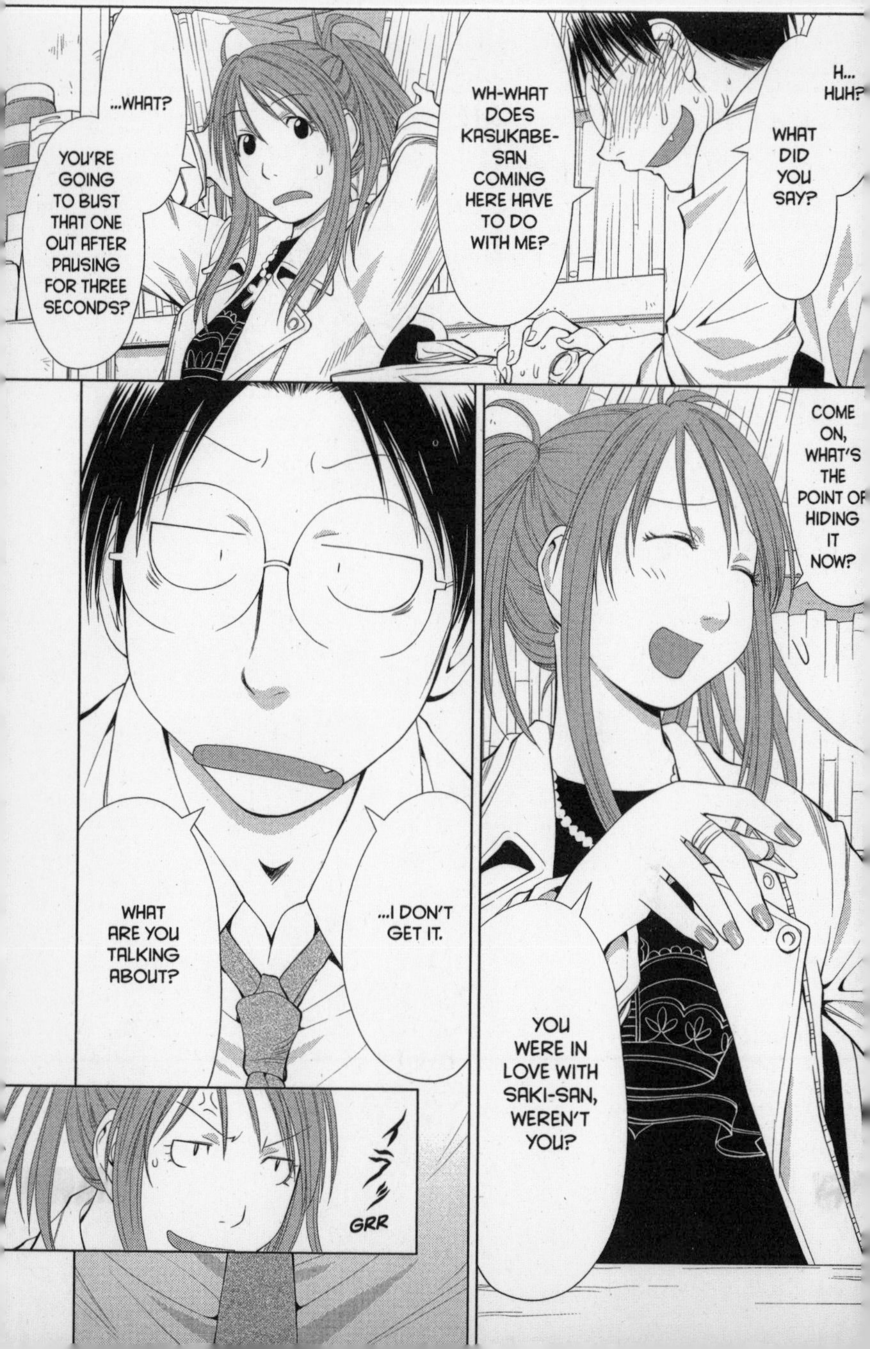
H... HUH?
WHAT DID YOU SAY?
WH-WHAT DOES KASUKABE-SAN COMING HERE HAVE TO DO WITH ME?
...WHAT?
YOU'RE GOING TO BUST THAT ONE OUT AFTER PAUSING FOR THREE SECONDS?
COME ON, WHAT'S THE POINT OF HIDING IT NOW?
YOU WERE IN LOVE WITH SAKI-SAN, WEREN'T YOU?
...I DON'T GET IT.
WHAT ARE YOU TALKING ABOUT?
GRR

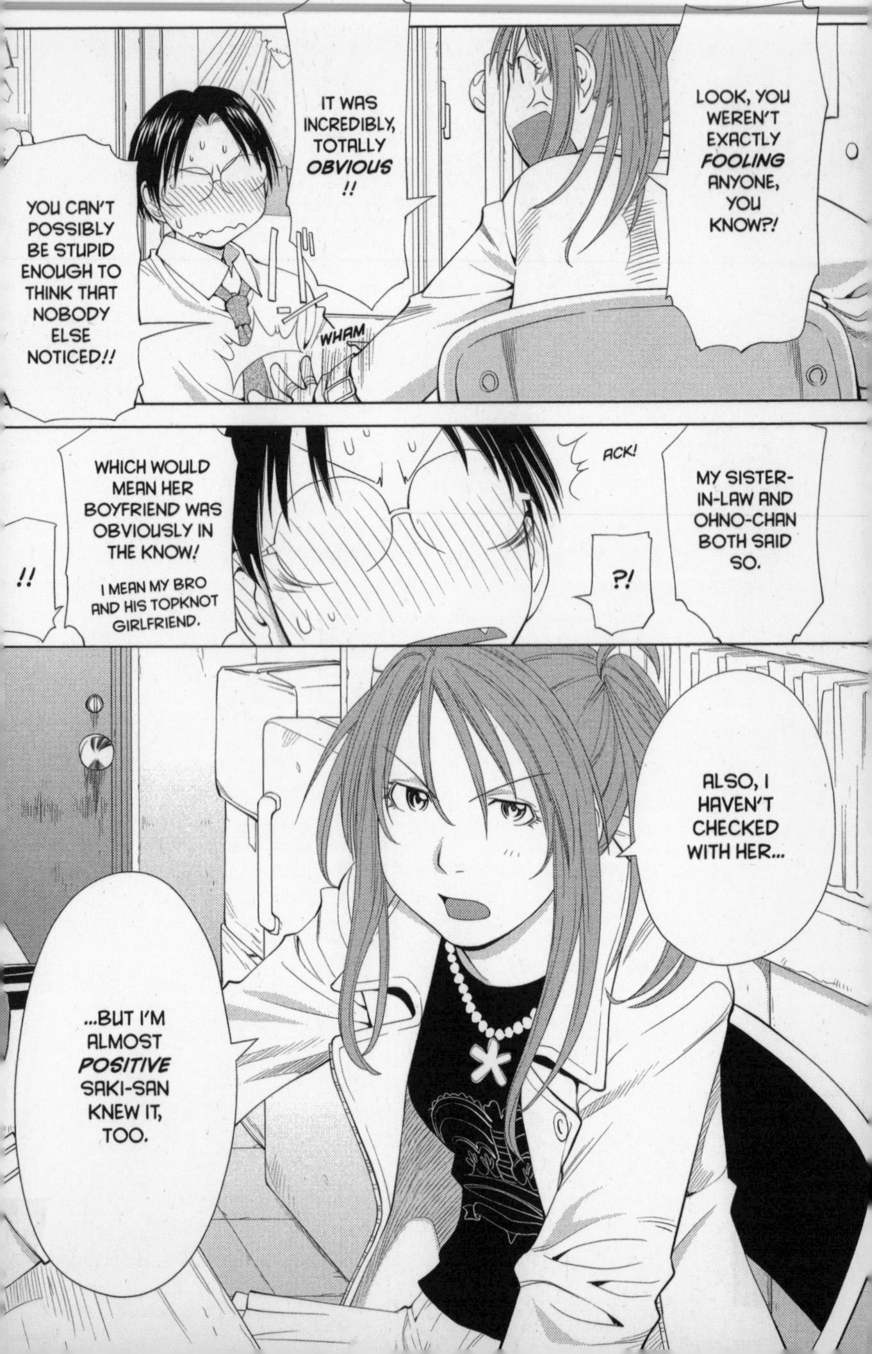
LOOK, YOU WEREN'T EXACTLY *FOOLING* ANYONE, YOU KNOW?!
IT WAS INCREDIBLY, TOTALLY *OBVIOUS* !!
WHAM
YOU CAN'T POSSIBLY BE STUPID ENOUGH TO THINK THAT NOBODY ELSE NOTICED!!
MY SISTER-IN-LAW AND OHNO-CHAN BOTH SAID SO.
ACK!
?!
WHICH WOULD MEAN HER BOYFRIEND WAS OBVIOUSLY IN THE KNOW!
I MEAN MY BRO AND HIS TOPKNOT GIRLFRIEND.
!!
ALSO, I HAVEN'T CHECKED WITH HER...
...BUT I'M ALMOST *POSITIVE* SAKI-SAN KNEW IT, TOO.

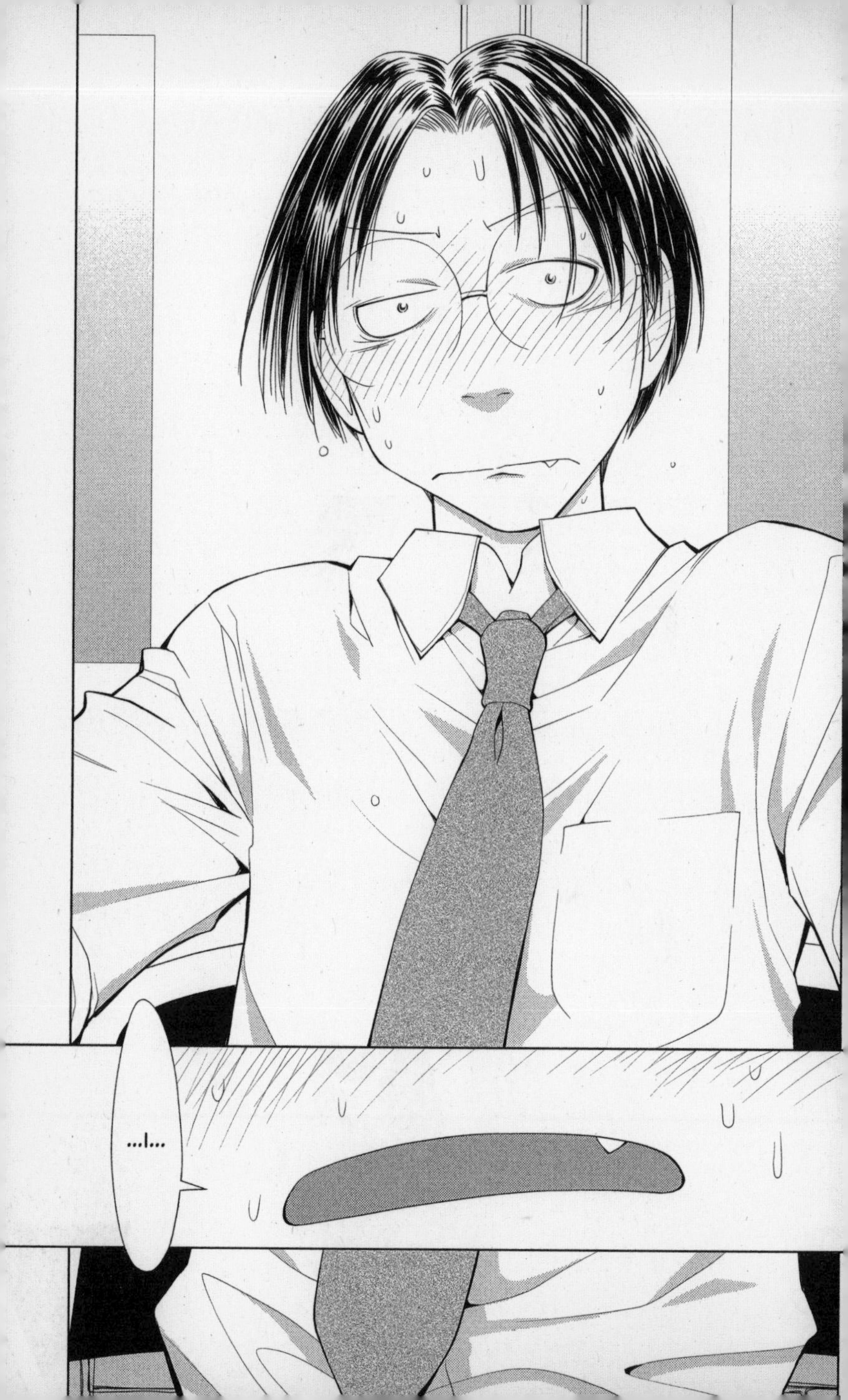
...I...

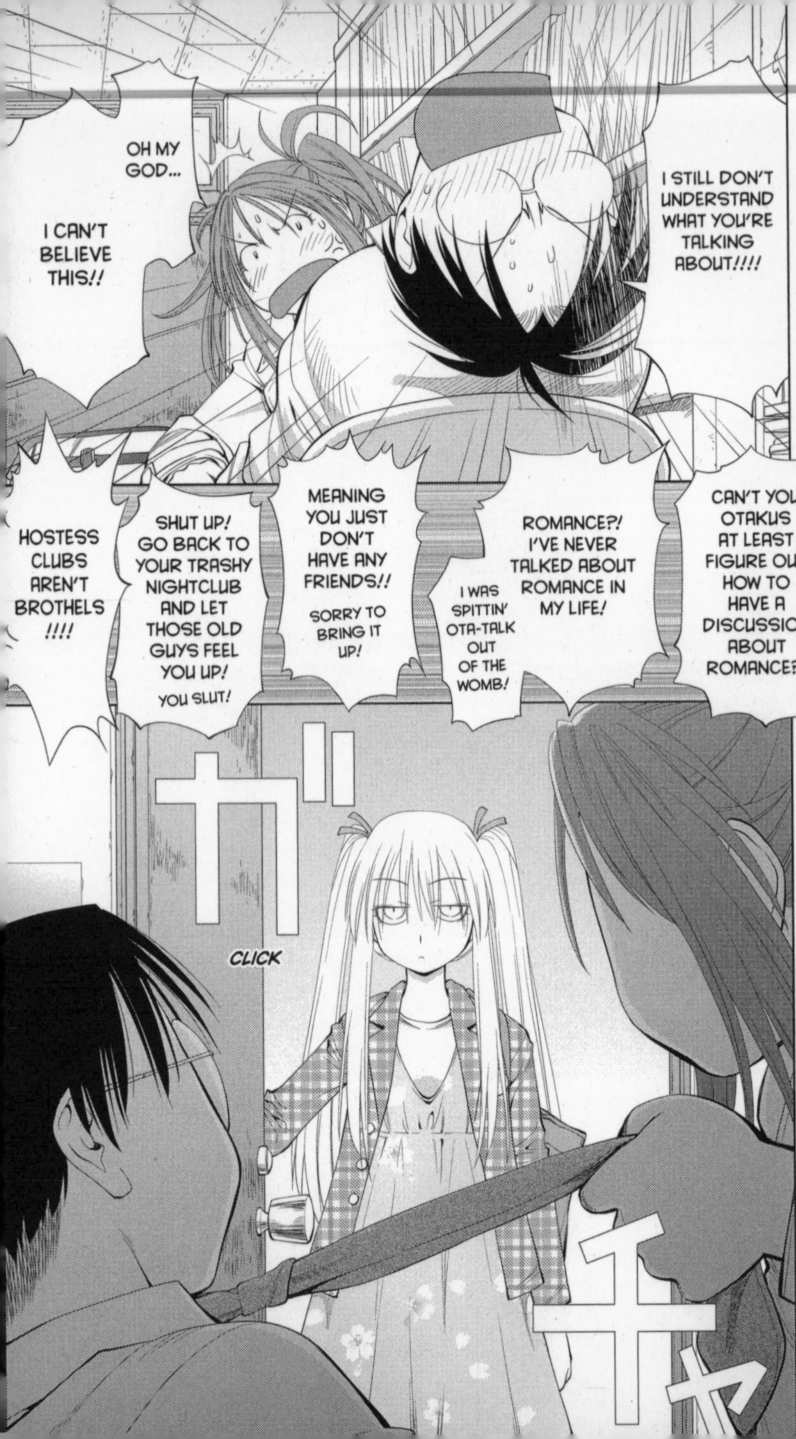

I STILL DON'T UNDERSTAND WHAT YOU'RE TALKING ABOUT!!!!
OH MY GOD...
I CAN'T BELIEVE THIS!!
CAN'T YOU OTAKUS AT LEAST FIGURE OUT HOW TO HAVE A DISCUSSION ABOUT ROMANCE?!
ROMANCE?! I'VE NEVER TALKED ABOUT ROMANCE IN MY LIFE!
I WAS SPITTIN' OTA-TALK OUT OF THE WOMB!
MEANING YOU JUST DON'T HAVE ANY FRIENDS!!
SORRY TO BRING IT UP!
SHUT UP! GO BACK TO YOUR TRASHY NIGHTCLUB AND LET THOSE OLD GUYS FEEL YOU UP!
YOU SLUT!
HOSTESS CLUBS AREN'T BROTHELS!!!!
ガチャ
CLICK

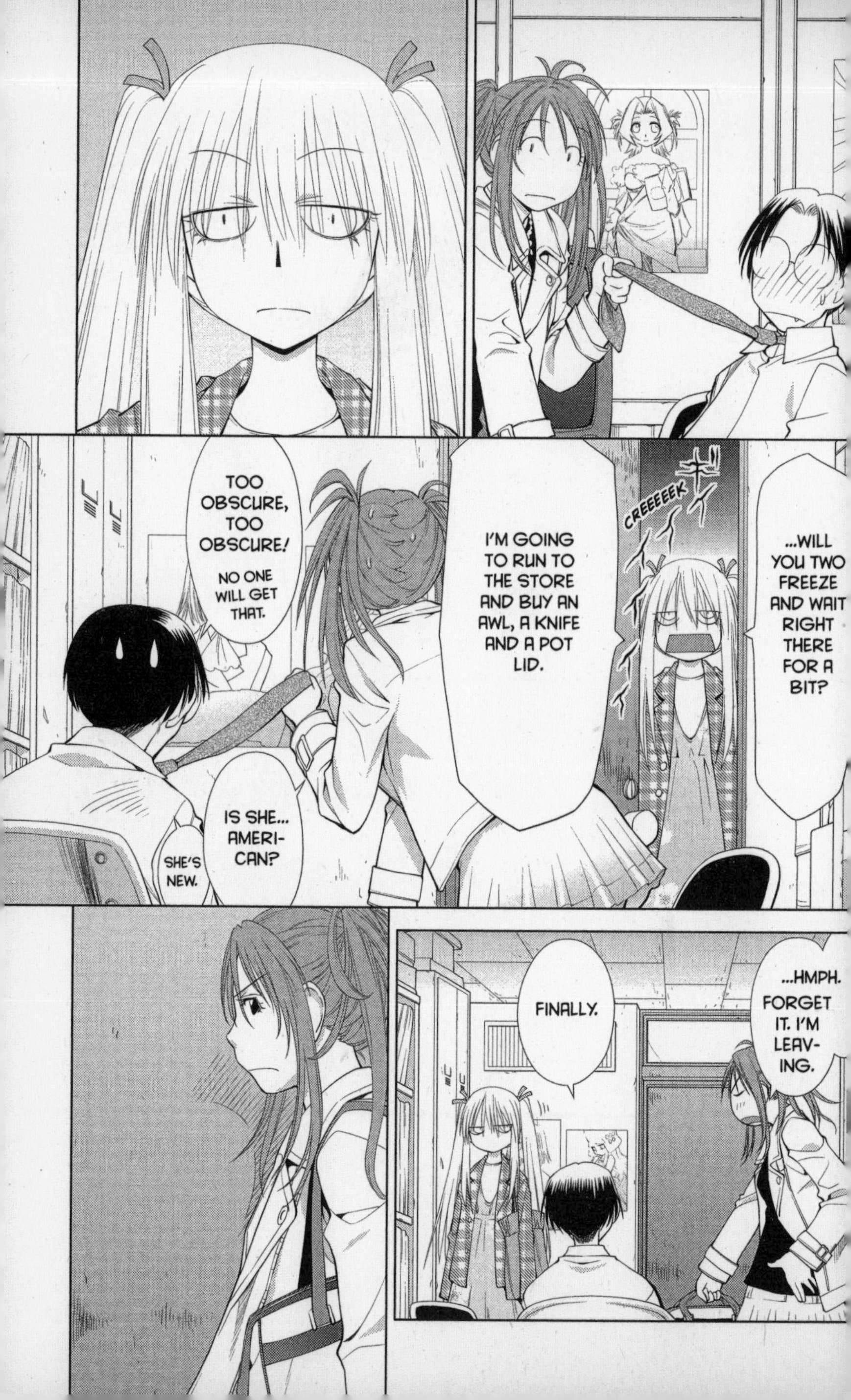
...WILL YOU TWO FREEZE AND WAIT RIGHT THERE FOR A BIT?
CREEEEEK
I'M GOING TO RUN TO THE STORE AND BUY AN AWL, A KNIFE AND A POT LID.
TOO OBSCURE, TOO OBSCURE!
NO ONE WILL GET THAT.
IS SHE... AMERI-CAN?
SHE'S NEW.
...HMPH. FORGET IT. I'M LEAV-ING.
FINALLY.

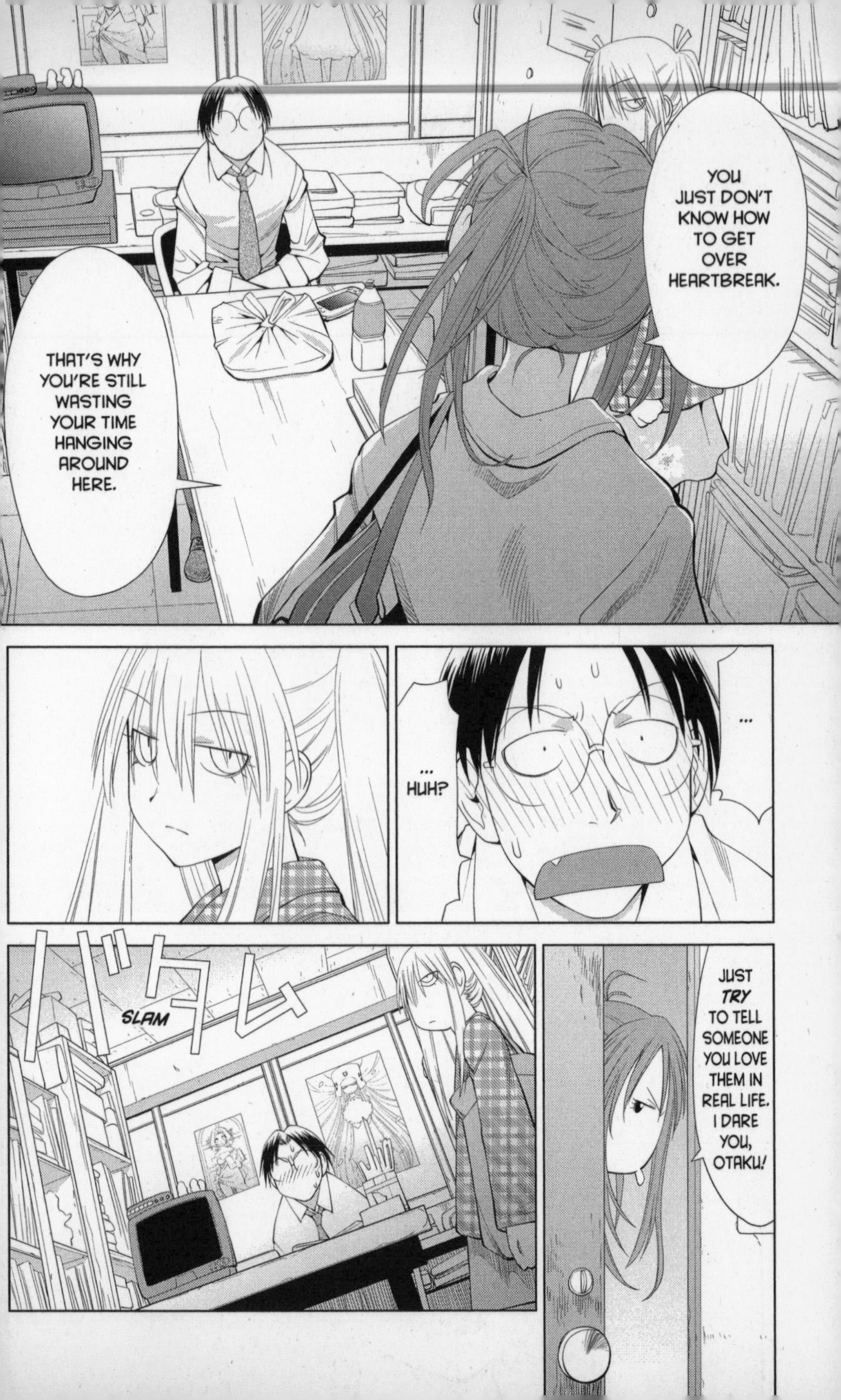
YOU JUST DON'T KNOW HOW TO GET OVER HEARTBREAK.
THAT'S WHY YOU'RE STILL WASTING YOUR TIME HANGING AROUND HERE.
...
... HUH?
JUST *TRY* TO TELL SOMEONE YOU LOVE THEM IN REAL LIFE. I DARE YOU, OTAKU!
バタム
SLAM

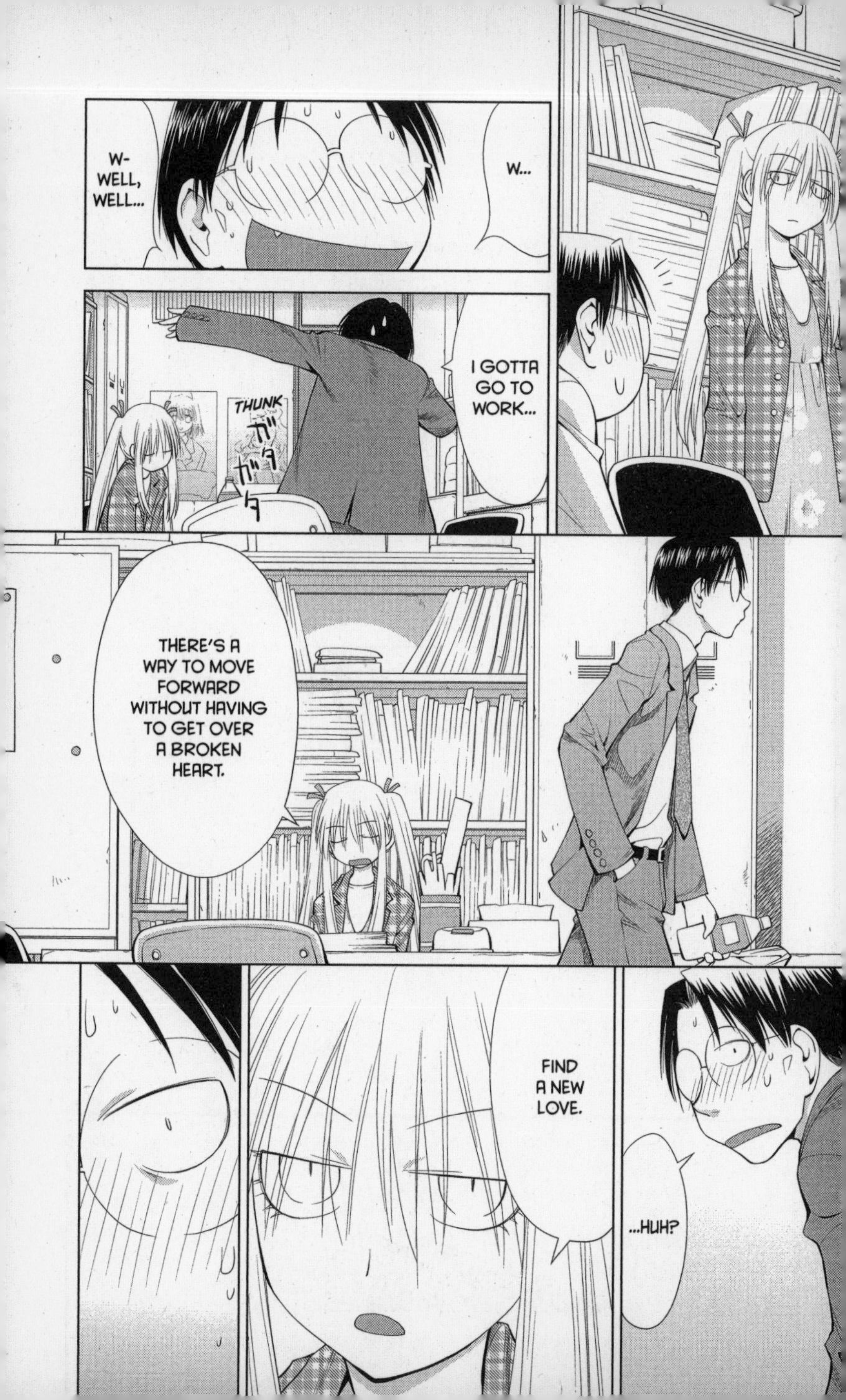
W...
W-WELL, WELL...
I GOTTA GO TO WORK...
THUNK
ガタガタ
THERE'S A WAY TO MOVE FORWARD WITHOUT HAVING TO GET OVER A BROKEN HEART.
...HUH?
FIND A NEW LOVE.

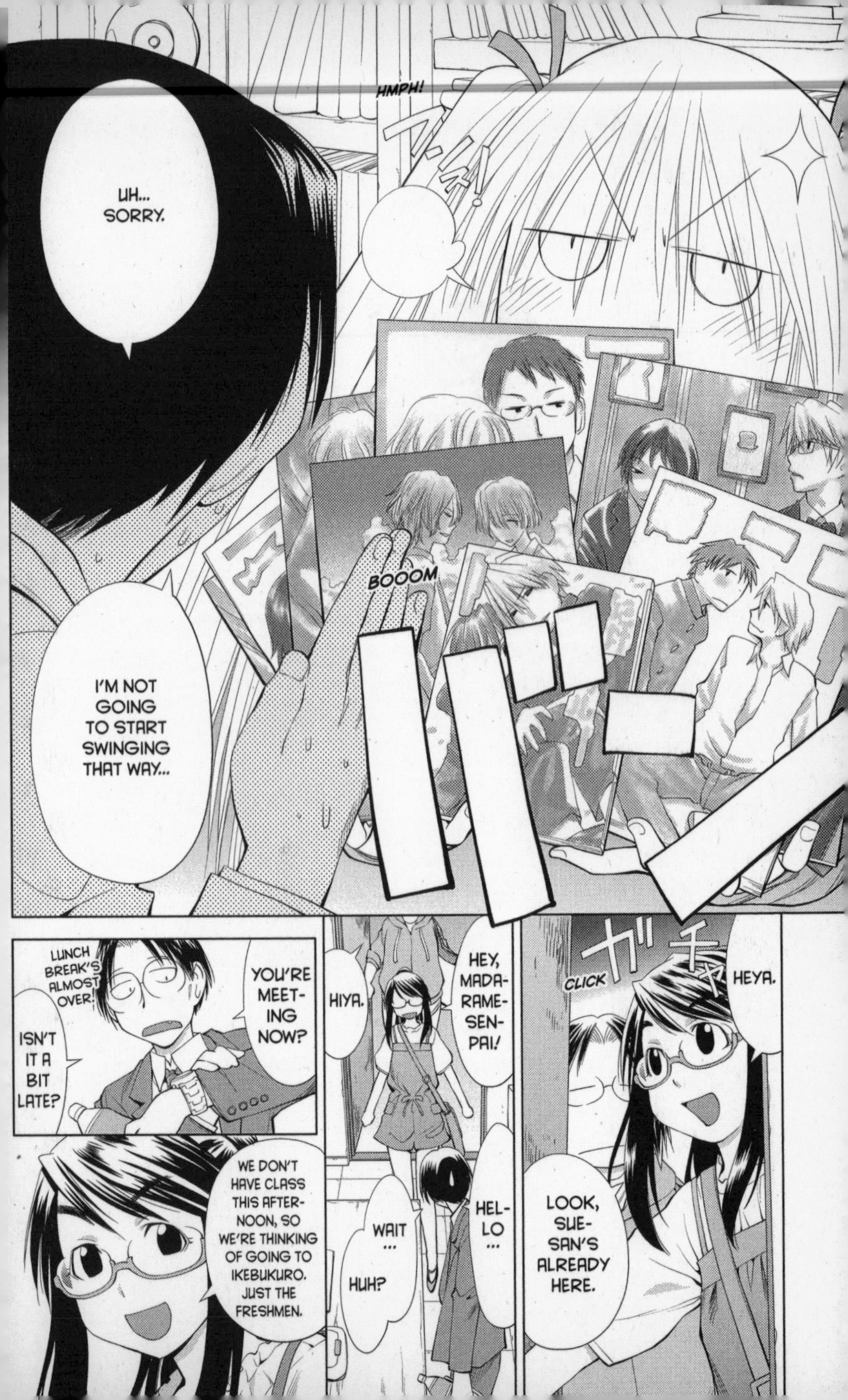

HMPH!
UH... SORRY.
BOOOM
I'M NOT GOING TO START SWINGING THAT WAY...
CLICK
HEYA.
LOOK, SUE-SAN'S ALREADY HERE.
HEY, MADARAME-SENPAI!
HIYA.
HELLO...
WAIT... HUH?
YOU'RE MEETING NOW?
LUNCH BREAK'S ALMOST OVER!
ISN'T IT A BIT LATE?
WE DON'T HAVE CLASS THIS AFTERNOON, SO WE'RE THINKING OF GOING TO IKEBUKURO. JUST THE FRESHMEN.

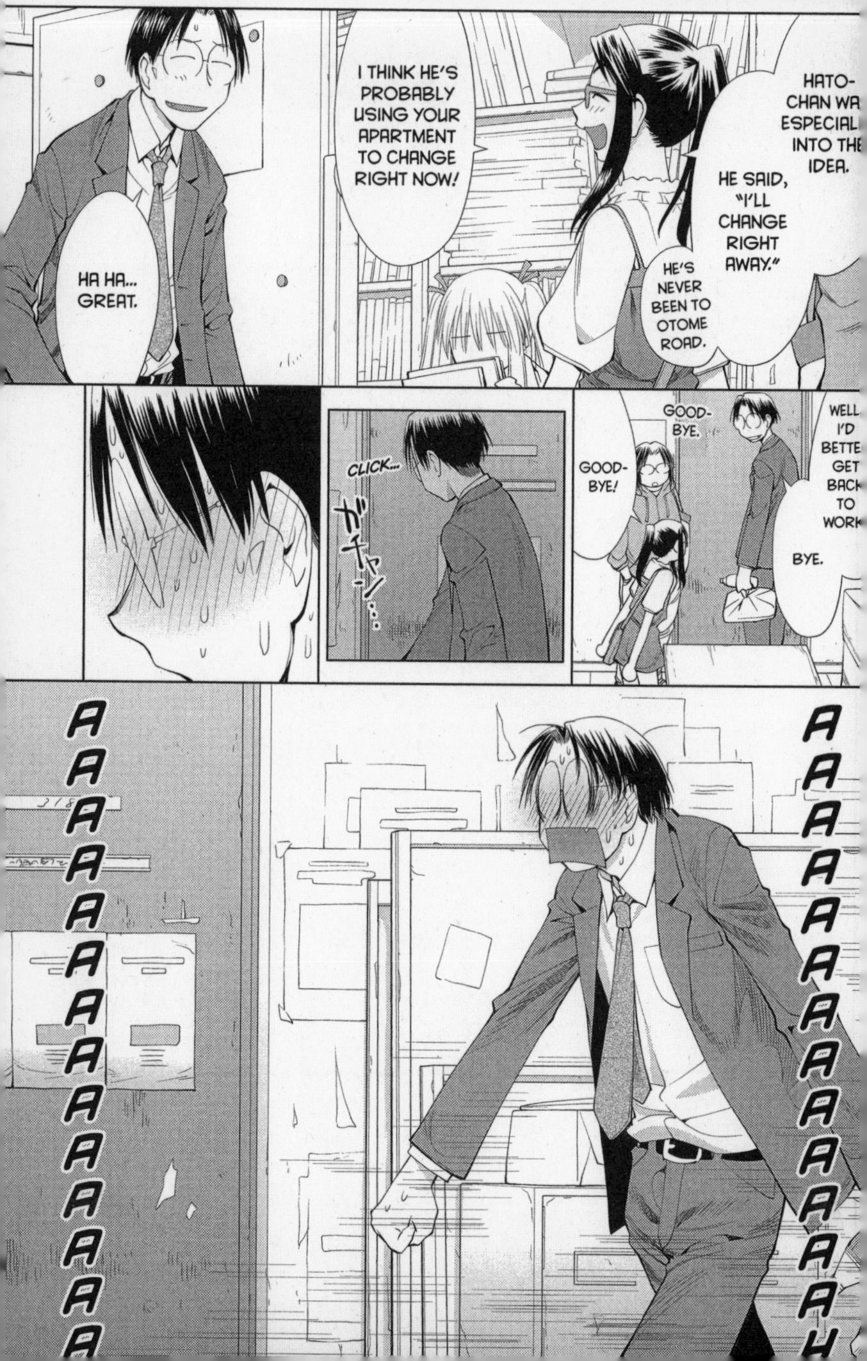
HATO-CHAN WA ESPECIAL INTO THE IDEA.
HE SAID, "I'LL CHANGE RIGHT AWAY."
HE'S NEVER BEEN TO OTOME ROAD.
I THINK HE'S PROBABLY USING YOUR APARTMENT TO CHANGE RIGHT NOW!
HA HA... GREAT.
WELL I'D BETTE GET BACK TO WORK
BYE.
GOOD-BYE.
GOOD-BYE!
CLICK...
ガチャン…
AAAAAAAAAAAAAAAH
AAAAAAAAAAAAAAAAA

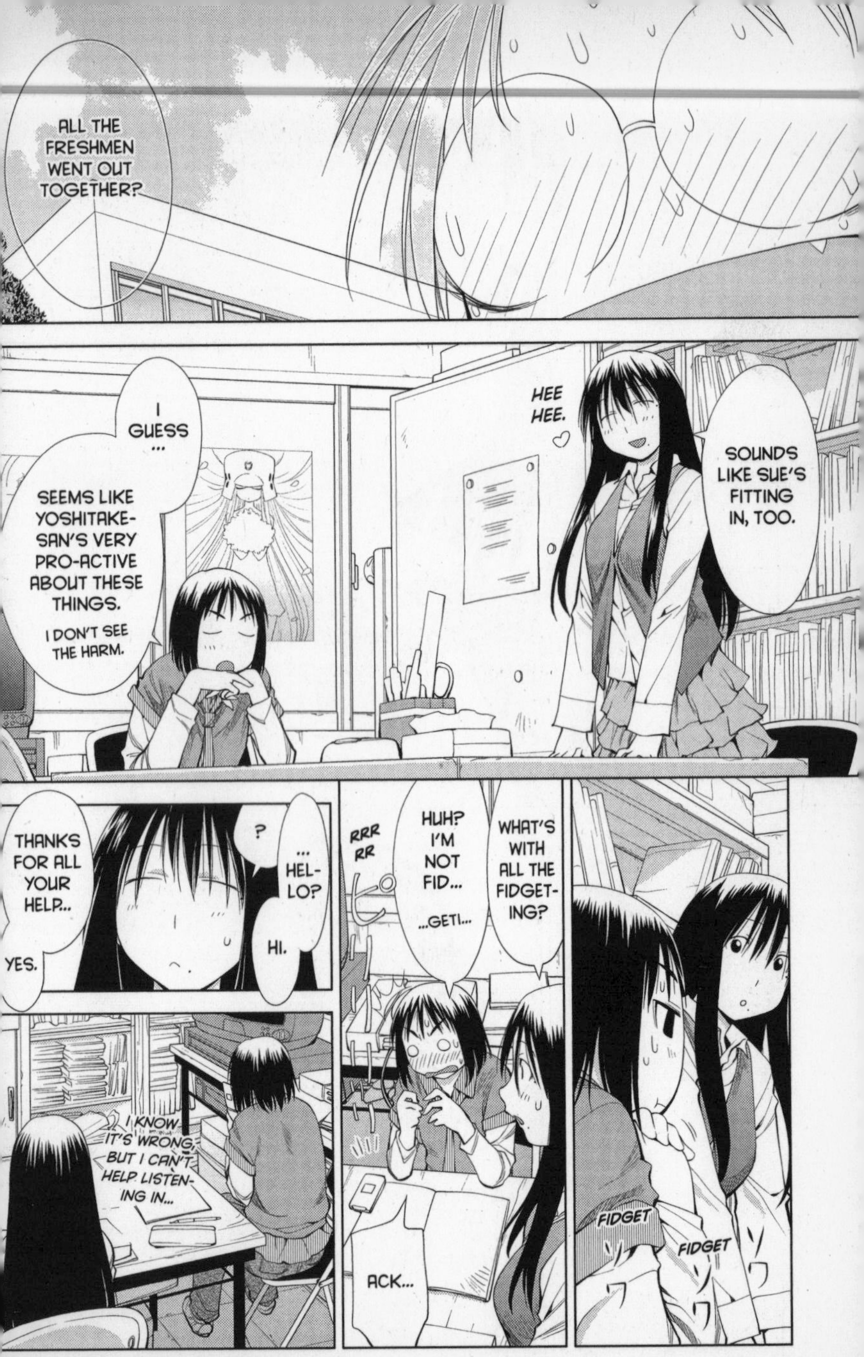
ALL THE FRESHMEN WENT OUT TOGETHER?
SOUNDS LIKE SUE'S FITTING IN, TOO.
HEE HEE.
I GUESS...
SEEMS LIKE YOSHITAKE-SAN'S VERY PRO-ACTIVE ABOUT THESE THINGS.
I DON'T SEE THE HARM.
WHAT'S WITH ALL THE FIDGET-ING?
FIDGET
FIDGET
HUH? I'M NOT FID...
...GETI...
RRR RR
ACK...
... HEL-LO?
?
HI.
THANKS FOR ALL YOUR HELP...
YES.
I KNOW IT'S WRONG, BUT I CAN'T HELP LISTEN-ING IN...

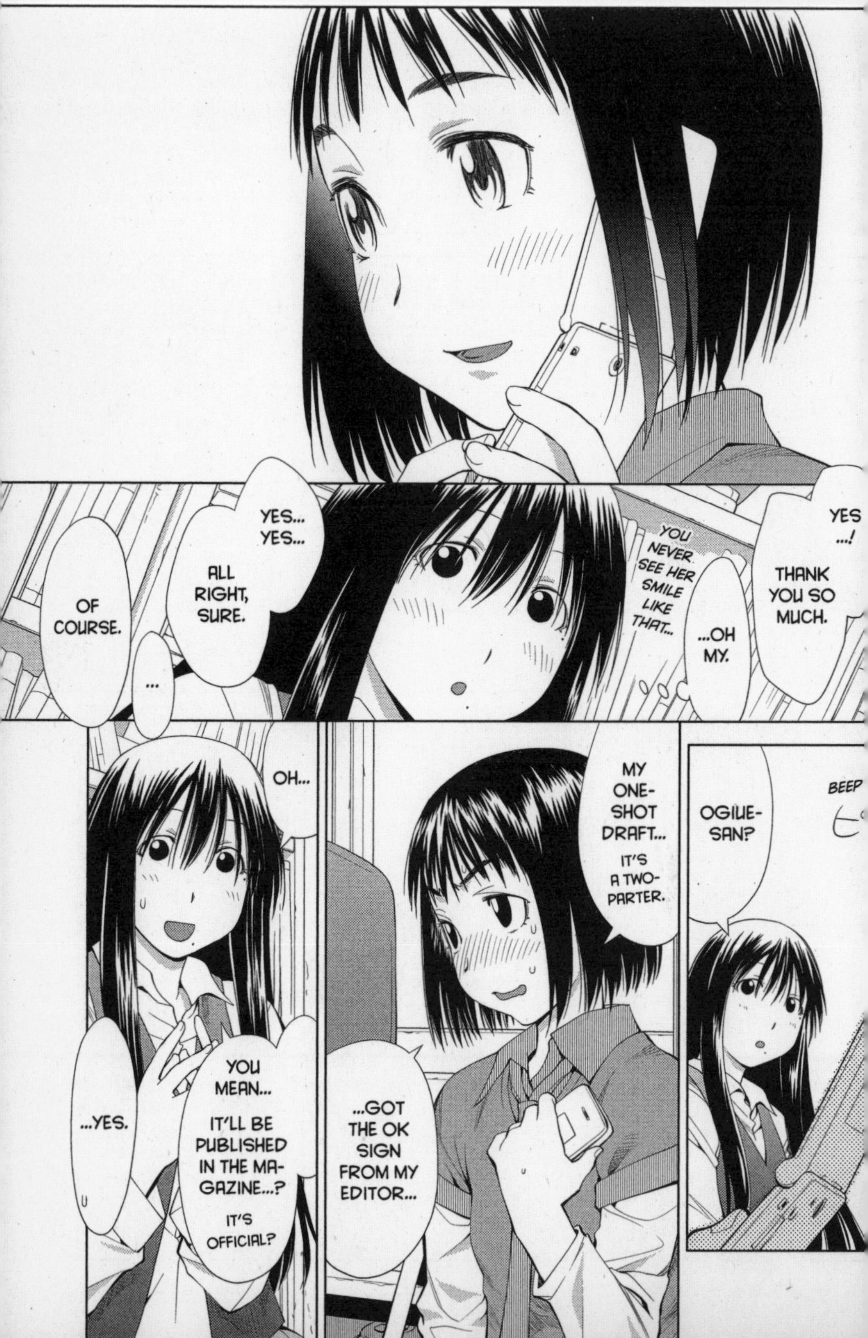
YES ...! THANK YOU SO MUCH.
...OH MY.
YOU NEVER SEE HER SMILE LIKE THAT...
YES... YES...
ALL RIGHT, SURE.
...
OF COURSE.
BEEP
OGIUE-SAN?
MY ONE-SHOT DRAFT... IT'S A TWO-PARTER.
...GOT THE OK SIGN FROM MY EDITOR...
OH...
YOU MEAN... IT'LL BE PUBLISHED IN THE MA-GAZINE...? IT'S OFFICIAL?
...YES.

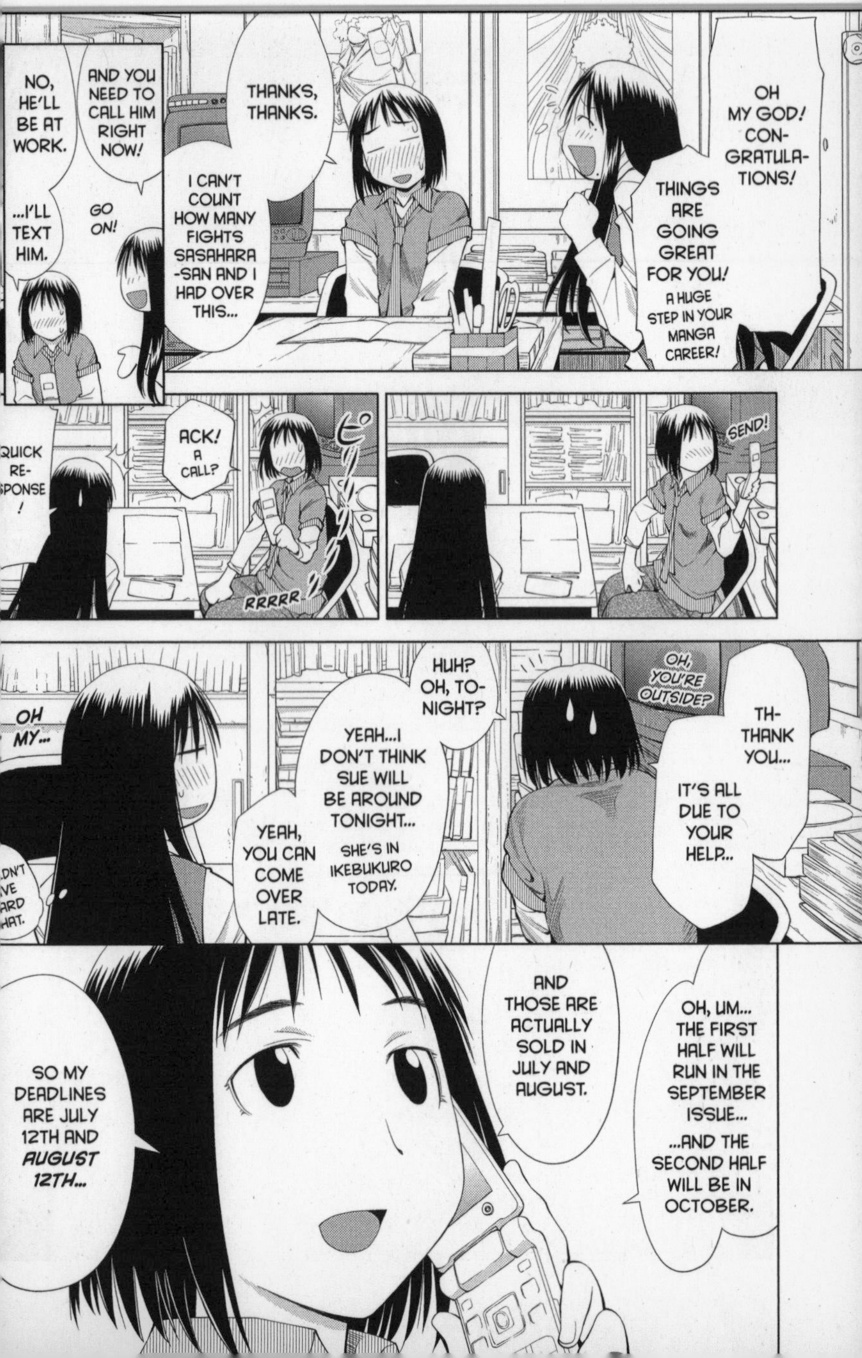
OH MY GOD! CON-GRATULA-TIONS!
THINGS ARE GOING GREAT FOR YOU!
A HUGE STEP IN YOUR MANGA CAREER!
THANKS, THANKS.
I CAN'T COUNT HOW MANY FIGHTS SASAHARA-SAN AND I HAD OVER THIS...
AND YOU NEED TO CALL HIM RIGHT NOW!
NO, HE'LL BE AT WORK.
GO ON!
...I'LL TEXT HIM.
SEND!
ACK! A CALL?
QUICK RE-SPONSE!
RRRRR
OH, YOU'RE OUTSIDE?
TH-THANK YOU...
IT'S ALL DUE TO YOUR HELP...
HUH? OH, TO-NIGHT?
YEAH...I DON'T THINK SUE WILL BE AROUND TONIGHT...
SHE'S IN IKEBUKURO TODAY.
YEAH, YOU CAN COME OVER LATE.
OH MY...
OH, UM... THE FIRST HALF WILL RUN IN THE SEPTEMBER ISSUE...
...AND THE SECOND HALF WILL BE IN OCTOBER.
AND THOSE ARE ACTUALLY SOLD IN JULY AND AUGUST.
SO MY DEADLINES ARE JULY 12TH AND AUGUST 12TH...

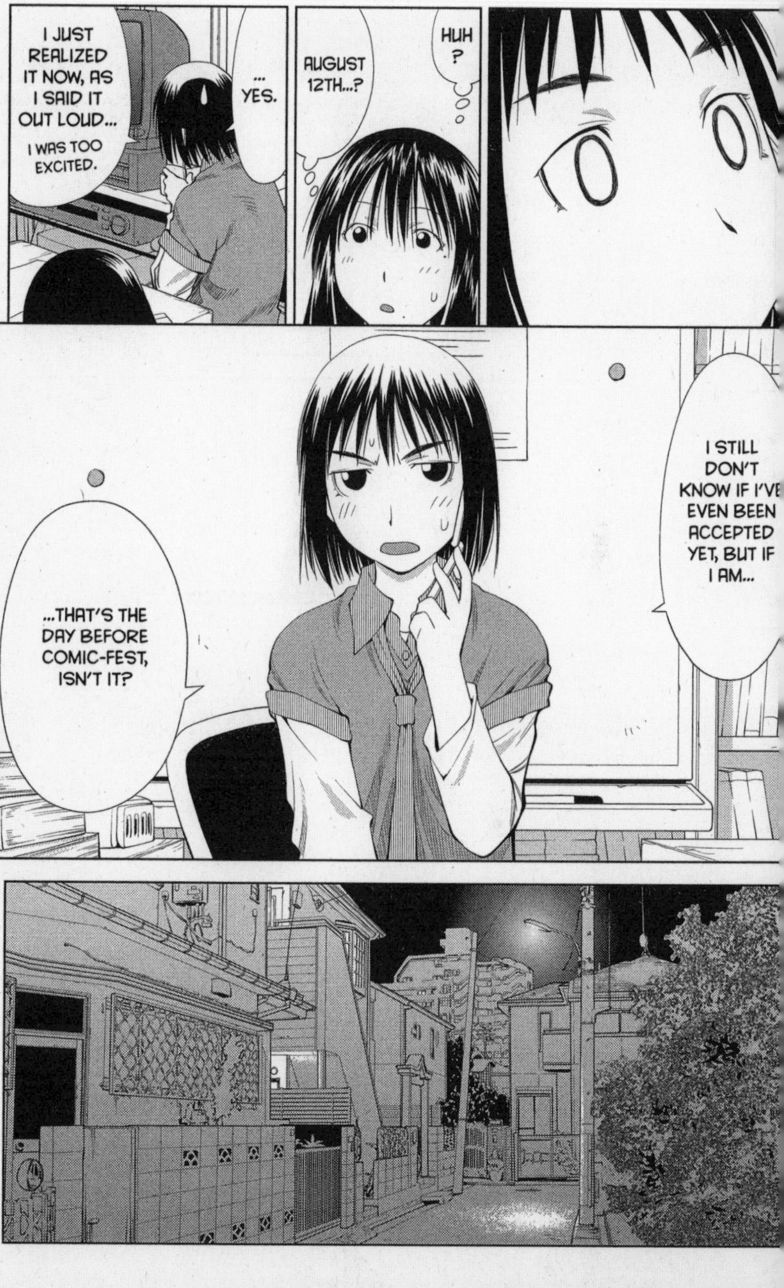
HUH?
AUGUST 12TH...?
... YES.
I JUST REALIZED IT NOW, AS I SAID IT OUT LOUD...
I WAS TOO EXCITED.
I STILL DON'T KNOW IF I'VE EVEN BEEN ACCEPTED YET, BUT IF I AM...
...THAT'S THE DAY BEFORE COMIC-FEST, ISN'T IT?

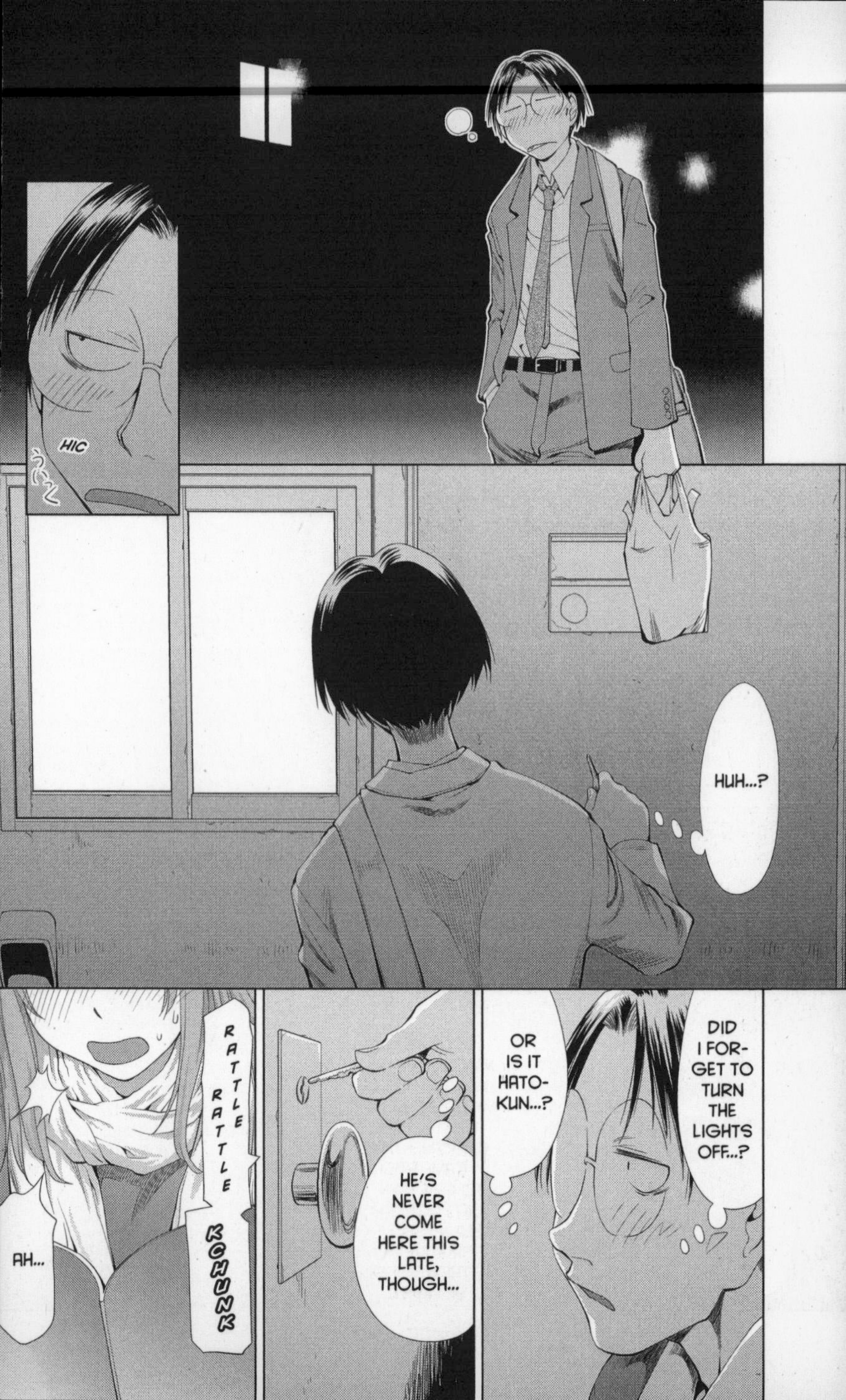
HIC
HUH...?
DID I FOR-GET TO TURN THE LIGHTS OFF...?
OR IS IT HATO-KUN...?
HE'S NEVER COME HERE THIS LATE, THOUGH...
RATTLE RATTLE
KCHUNK
AH...

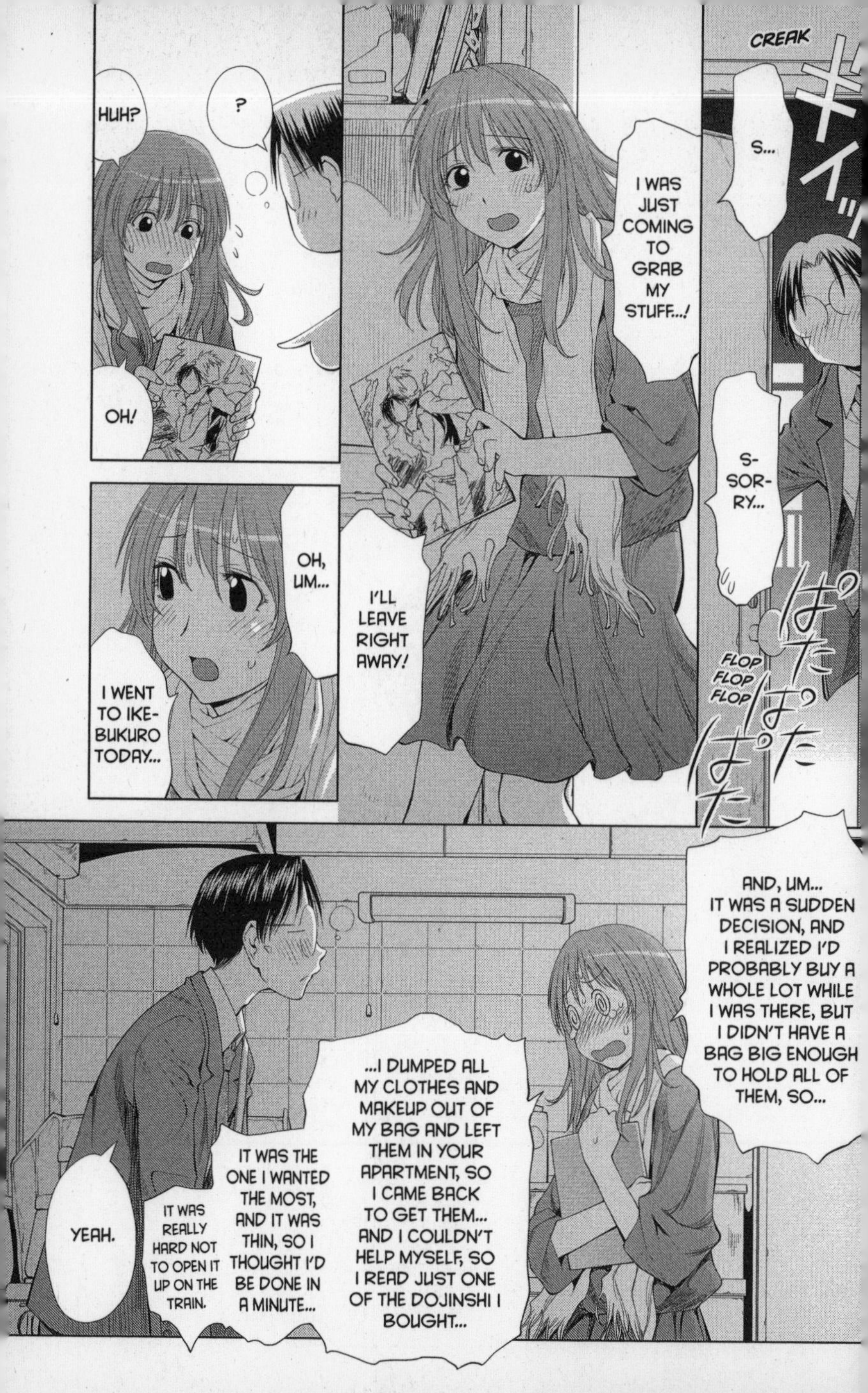
CREAK
ギイッ
S...
S-SORRY...
FLOP FLOP FLOP
ぱたぱたぱた
I WAS JUST COMING TO GRAB MY STUFF...!
I'LL LEAVE RIGHT AWAY!
?
HUH?
OH!
OH, UM...
I WENT TO IKE-BUKURO TODAY...
AND, UM... IT WAS A SUDDEN DECISION, AND I REALIZED I'D PROBABLY BUY A WHOLE LOT WHILE I WAS THERE, BUT I DIDN'T HAVE A BAG BIG ENOUGH TO HOLD ALL OF THEM, SO...
...I DUMPED ALL MY CLOTHES AND MAKEUP OUT OF MY BAG AND LEFT THEM IN YOUR APARTMENT, SO I CAME BACK TO GET THEM... AND I COULDN'T HELP MYSELF, SO I READ JUST ONE OF THE DOJINSHI I BOUGHT...
IT WAS THE ONE I WANTED THE MOST, AND IT WAS THIN, SO I THOUGHT I'D BE DONE IN A MINUTE...
IT WAS REALLY HARD NOT TO OPEN IT UP ON THE TRAIN.
YEAH.

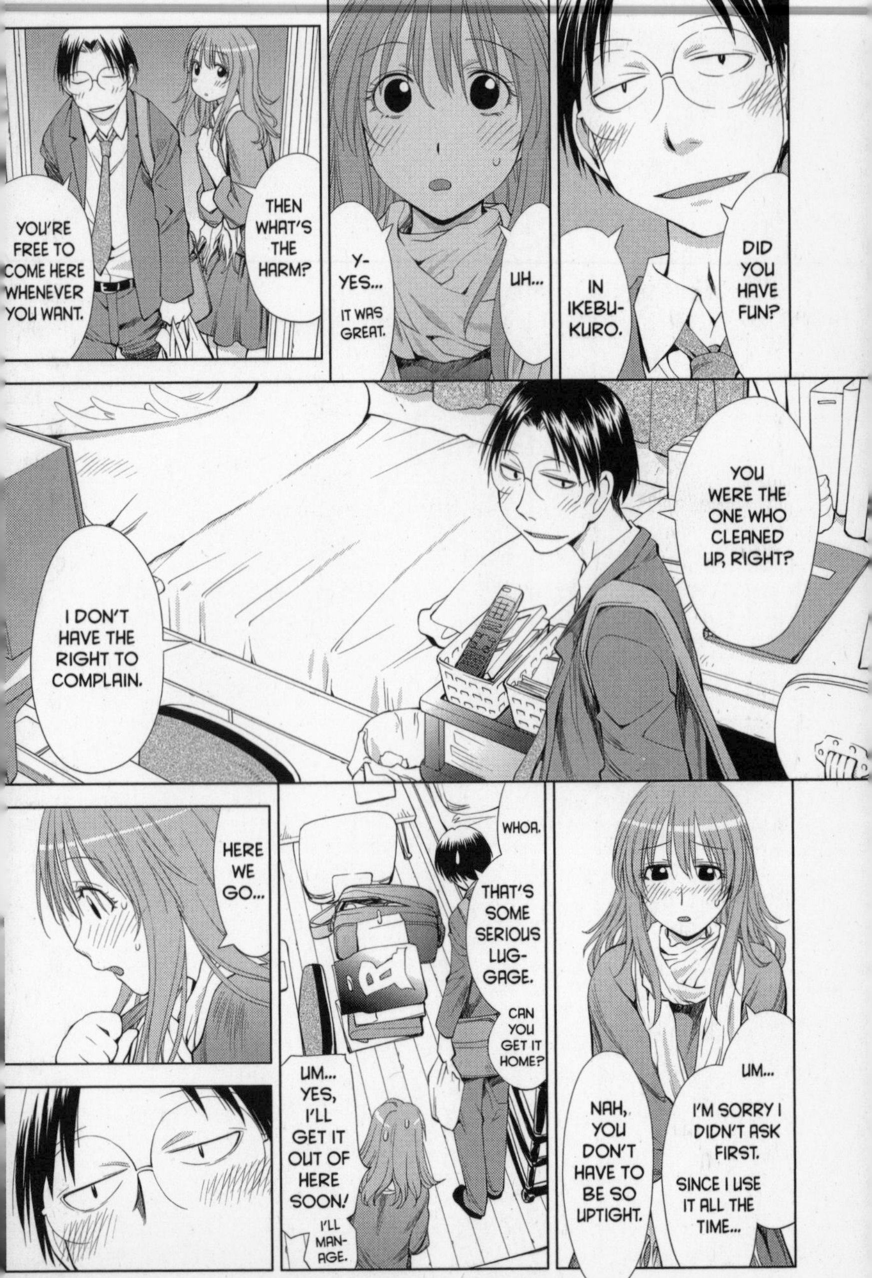
DID YOU HAVE FUN?
IN IKEBUKURO.
UH...
Y-YES...
IT WAS GREAT.
THEN WHAT'S THE HARM?
YOU'RE FREE TO COME HERE WHENEVER YOU WANT.
YOU WERE THE ONE WHO CLEANED UP, RIGHT?
I DON'T HAVE THE RIGHT TO COMPLAIN.
UM...
I'M SORRY I DIDN'T ASK FIRST.
SINCE I USE IT ALL THE TIME...
NAH, YOU DON'T HAVE TO BE SO UPTIGHT.
WHOA.
THAT'S SOME SERIOUS LUG-GAGE.
CAN YOU GET IT HOME?
UM... YES, I'LL GET IT OUT OF HERE SOON!
I'LL MAN-AGE.
HERE WE GO...

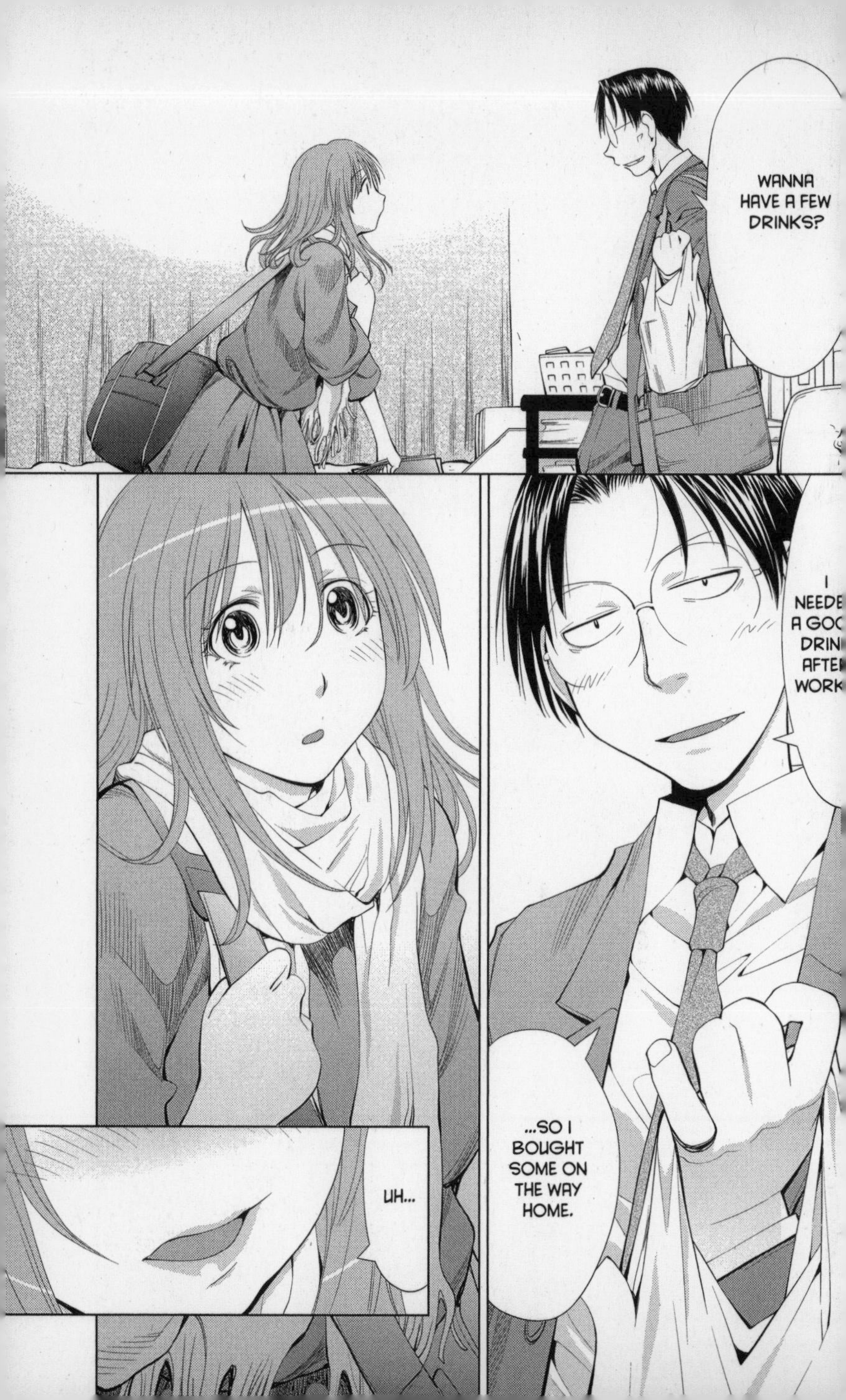
WANNA HAVE A FEW DRINKS?
I NEEDE A GOO DRIN AFTE WORK
...SO I BOUGHT SOME ON THE WAY HOME.
UH...

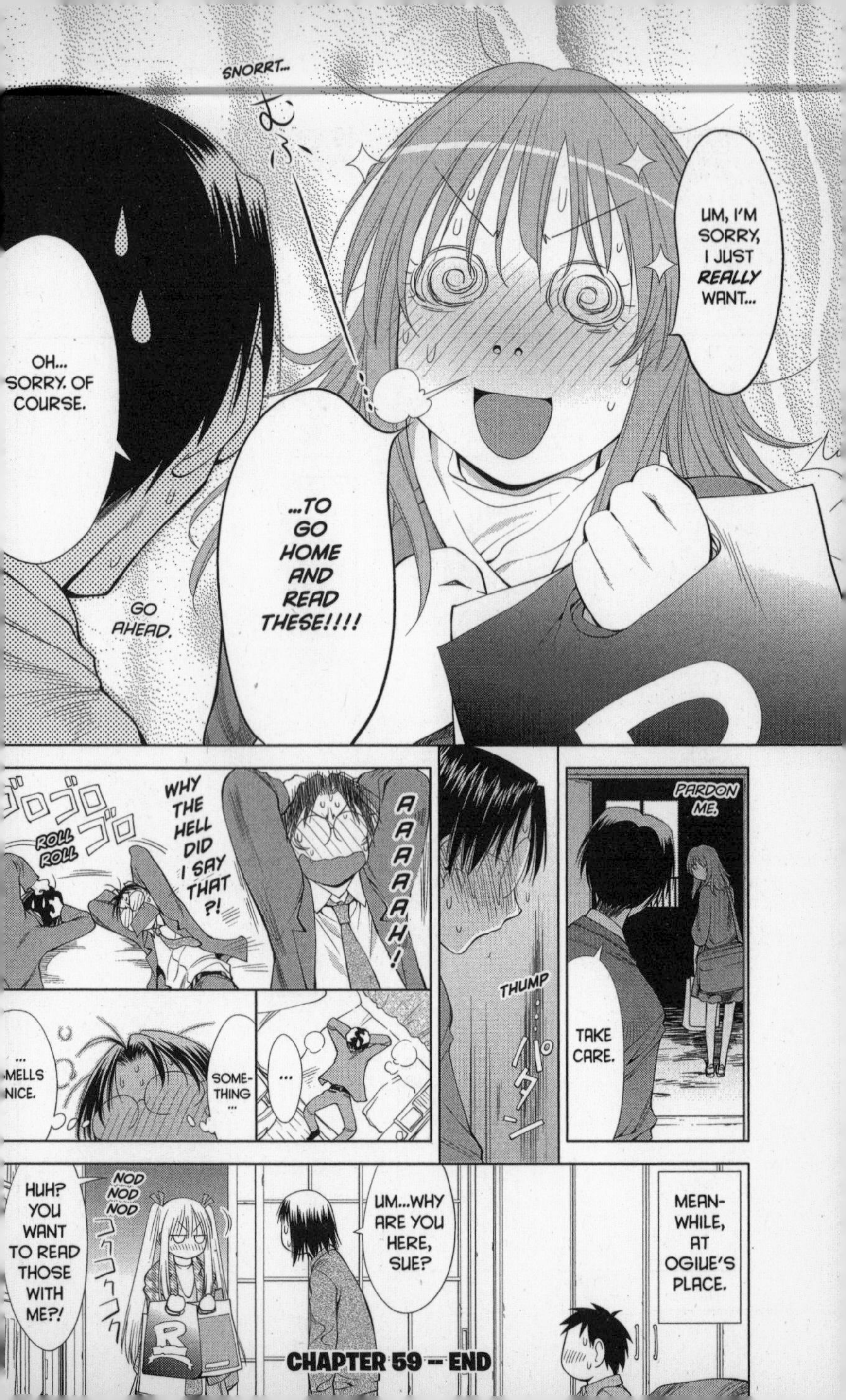
SNORRT...
UM, I'M SORRY, I JUST *REALLY* WANT...
...TO GO HOME AND READ THESE!!!!
OH... SORRY. OF COURSE.
GO AHEAD.
PARDON ME.
TAKE CARE.
THUMP
WHY THE HELL DID I SAY THAT?!
AAAAAAH!
ROLL ROLL
SOME-THING...
...
... MELLS NICE.
MEAN-WHILE, AT OGIUE'S PLACE.
UM...WHY ARE YOU HERE, SUE?
NOD NOD NOD
HUH? YOU WANT TO READ THOSE WITH ME?!
CHAPTER 59 -- END

SASA'S LITTLE SISTER CAN'T BE THIS CUTE

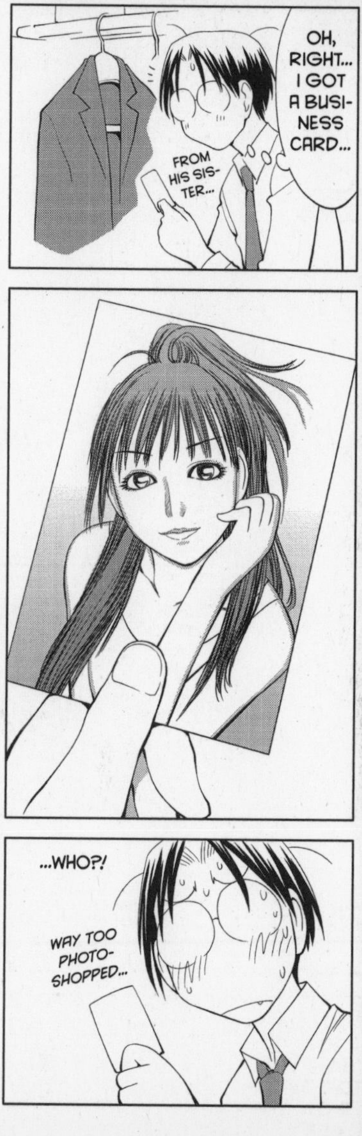
OH, RIGHT... I GOT A BUSINESS CARD...
FROM HIS SISTER...
...WHO?!
WAY TOO PHOTOSHOPPED...

I CAN'T ASK...

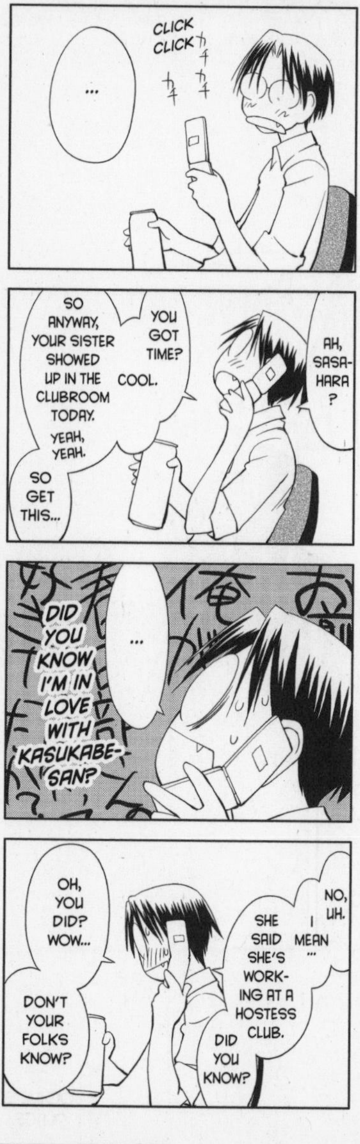
CLICK CLICK カチ カチ カチ
...
AH, SASAHARA?
YOU GOT TIME?
COOL.
SO ANYWAY, YOUR SISTER SHOWED UP IN THE CLUBROOM TODAY.
YEAH, YEAH.
SO GET THIS...
...
DID YOU KNOW I'M IN LOVE WITH KASUKABE-SAN?
NO, UH. I MEAN...
SHE SAID SHE'S WORKING AT A HOSTESS CLUB.
DID YOU KNOW?
OH, YOU DID? WOW...
DON'T YOUR FOLKS KNOW?

CHAOS

ぐび
GLUG
ぐびぐび
ぐびぐび
GLUG
GLUG
GLUG
ぐる
SPIN
ぐる
SPIN
ぐるん
SPIN
ぐるん
SPIN
ぐるん
SPIN
AAAAAAAAH!
DAMMIT!

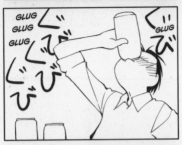

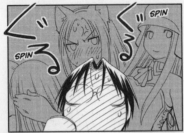

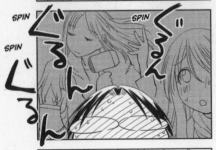

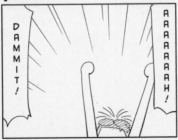

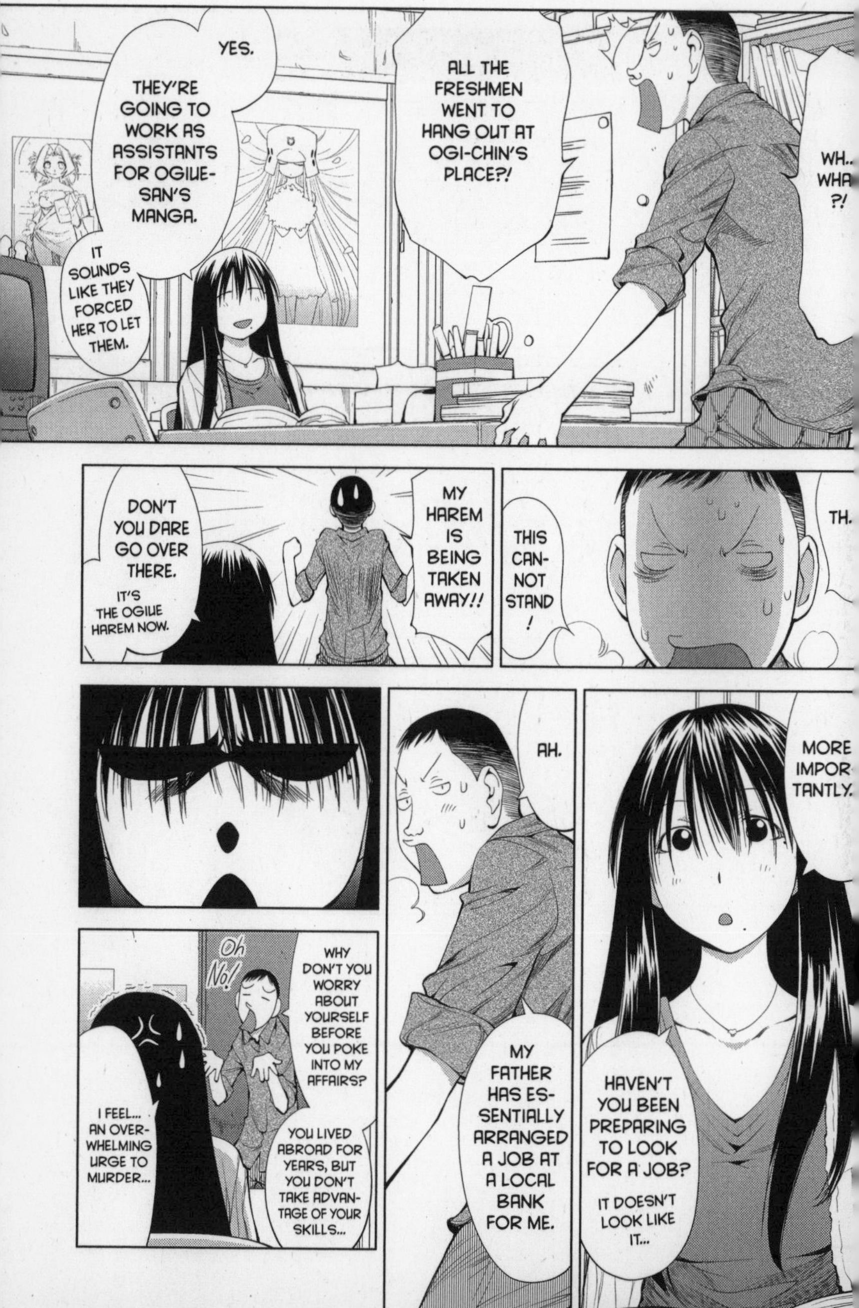
WH.. WHA ?!
ALL THE FRESHMEN WENT TO HANG OUT AT OGI-CHIN'S PLACE?!
YES.
THEY'RE GOING TO WORK AS ASSISTANTS FOR OGIUE-SAN'S MANGA.
IT SOUNDS LIKE THEY FORCED HER TO LET THEM.
TH.
THIS CAN-NOT STAND!
MY HAREM IS BEING TAKEN AWAY!!
DON'T YOU DARE GO OVER THERE.
IT'S THE OGIUE HAREM NOW.
MORE IMPOR TANTLY.
HAVEN'T YOU BEEN PREPARING TO LOOK FOR A JOB?
IT DOESN'T LOOK LIKE IT...
AH.
MY FATHER HAS ES-SENTIALLY ARRANGED A JOB AT A LOCAL BANK FOR ME.
Oh No!
WHY DON'T YOU WORRY ABOUT YOURSELF BEFORE YOU POKE INTO MY AFFAIRS?
YOU LIVED ABROAD FOR YEARS, BUT YOU DON'T TAKE ADVAN-TAGE OF YOUR SKILLS...
I FEEL... AN OVER-WHELMING URGE TO MURDER...

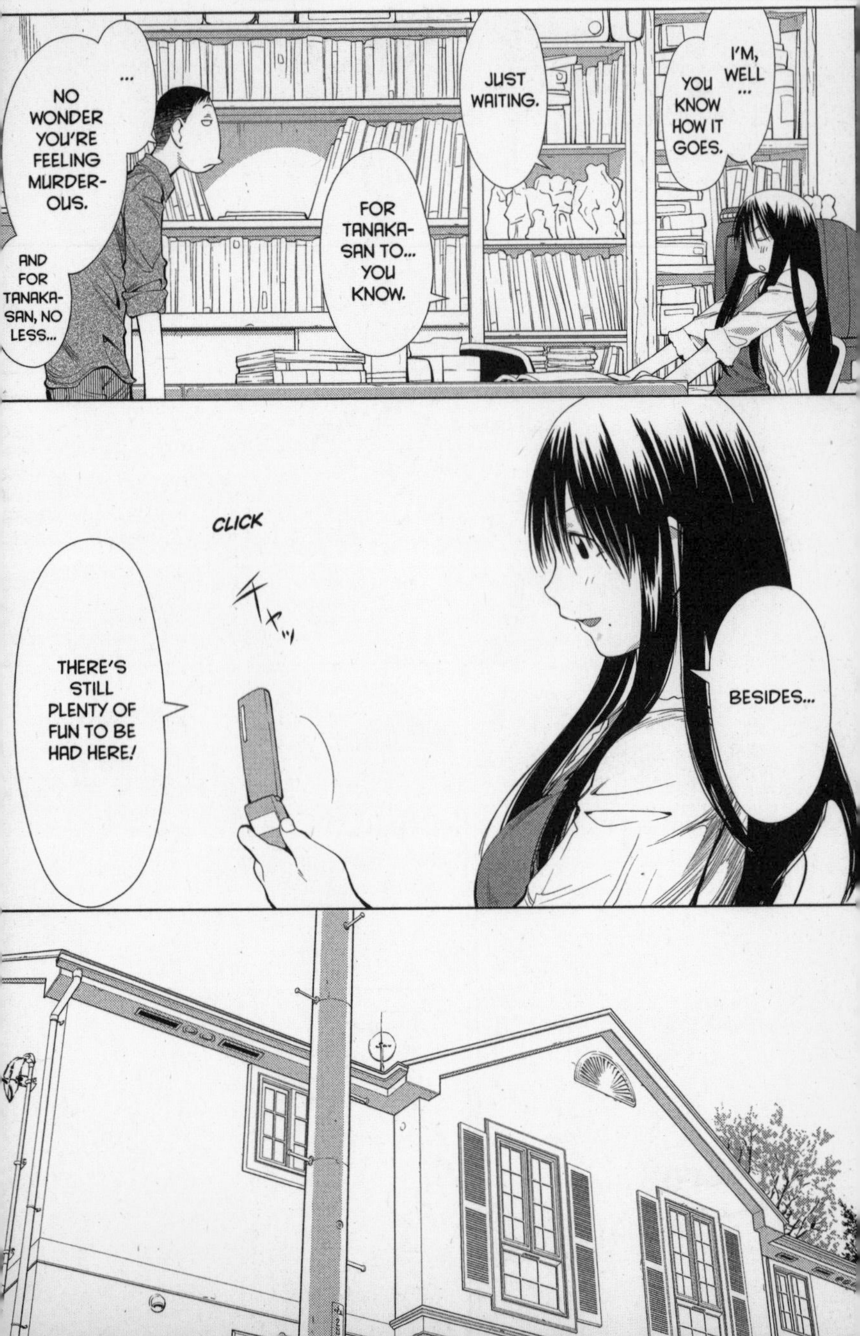
I'M, WELL ... YOU KNOW HOW IT GOES.
JUST WAITING.
FOR TANAKA-SAN TO... YOU KNOW.
... NO WONDER YOU'RE FEELING MURDER-OUS.
AND FOR TANAKA-SAN, NO LESS...
BESIDES...
CLICK
THERE'S STILL PLENTY OF FUN TO BE HAD HERE!

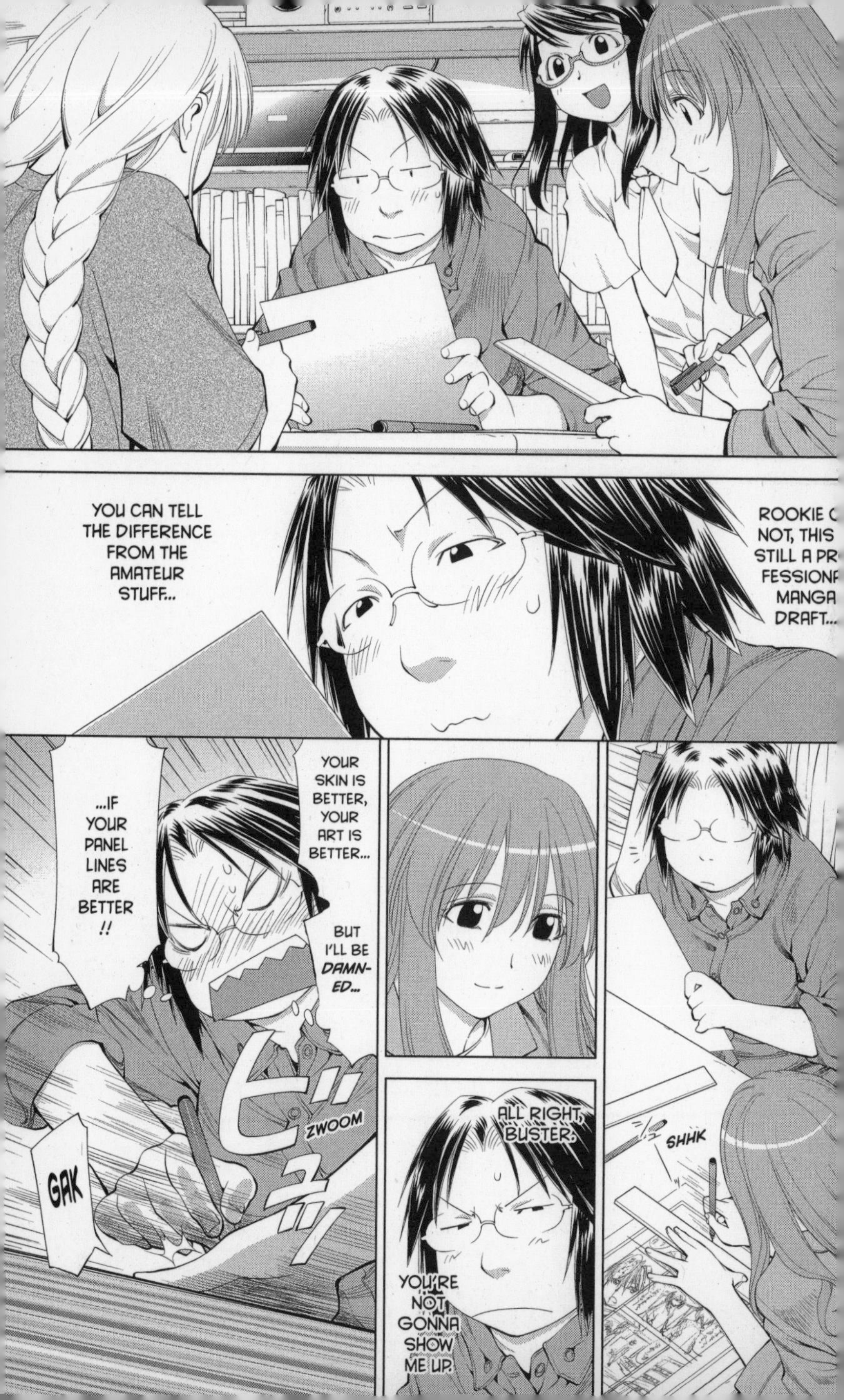
ROOKIE O
NOT, THIS
STILL A PR
FESSIONA
MANGA
DRAFT...
YOU CAN TELL THE DIFFERENCE FROM THE AMATEUR STUFF...
SHHK
YOUR SKIN IS BETTER, YOUR ART IS BETTER...
BUT I'LL BE DAMNED...
ALL RIGHT, BUSTER.
YOU'RE NOT GONNA SHOW ME UP.
...IF YOUR PANEL LINES ARE BETTER!!
ZWOOM
GAK

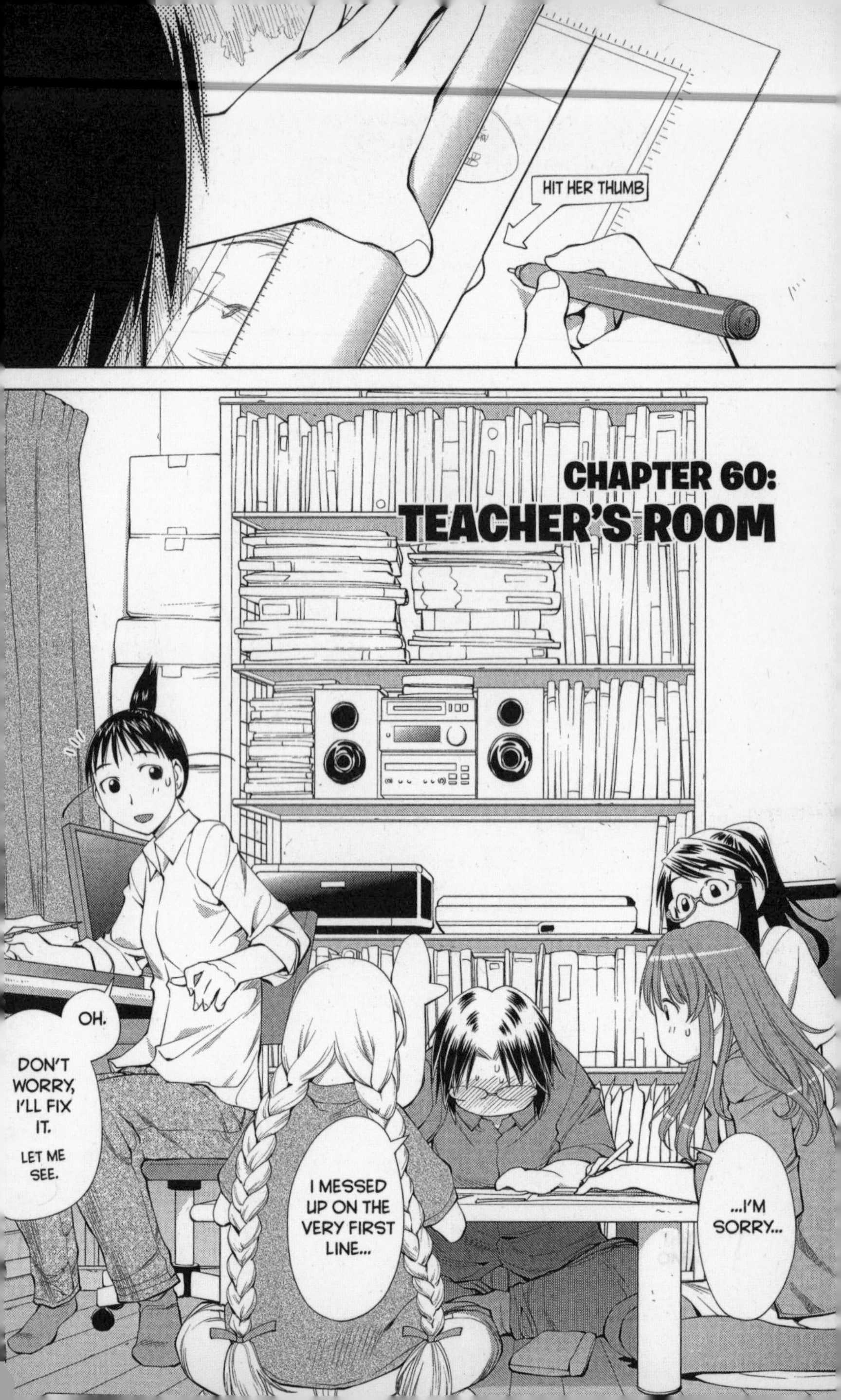
HIT HER THUMB
CHAPTER 60: TEACHER'S ROOM
...I'M SORRY...
I MESSED UP ON THE VERY FIRST LINE...
OH.
DON'T WORRY, I'LL FIX IT.
LET ME SEE.

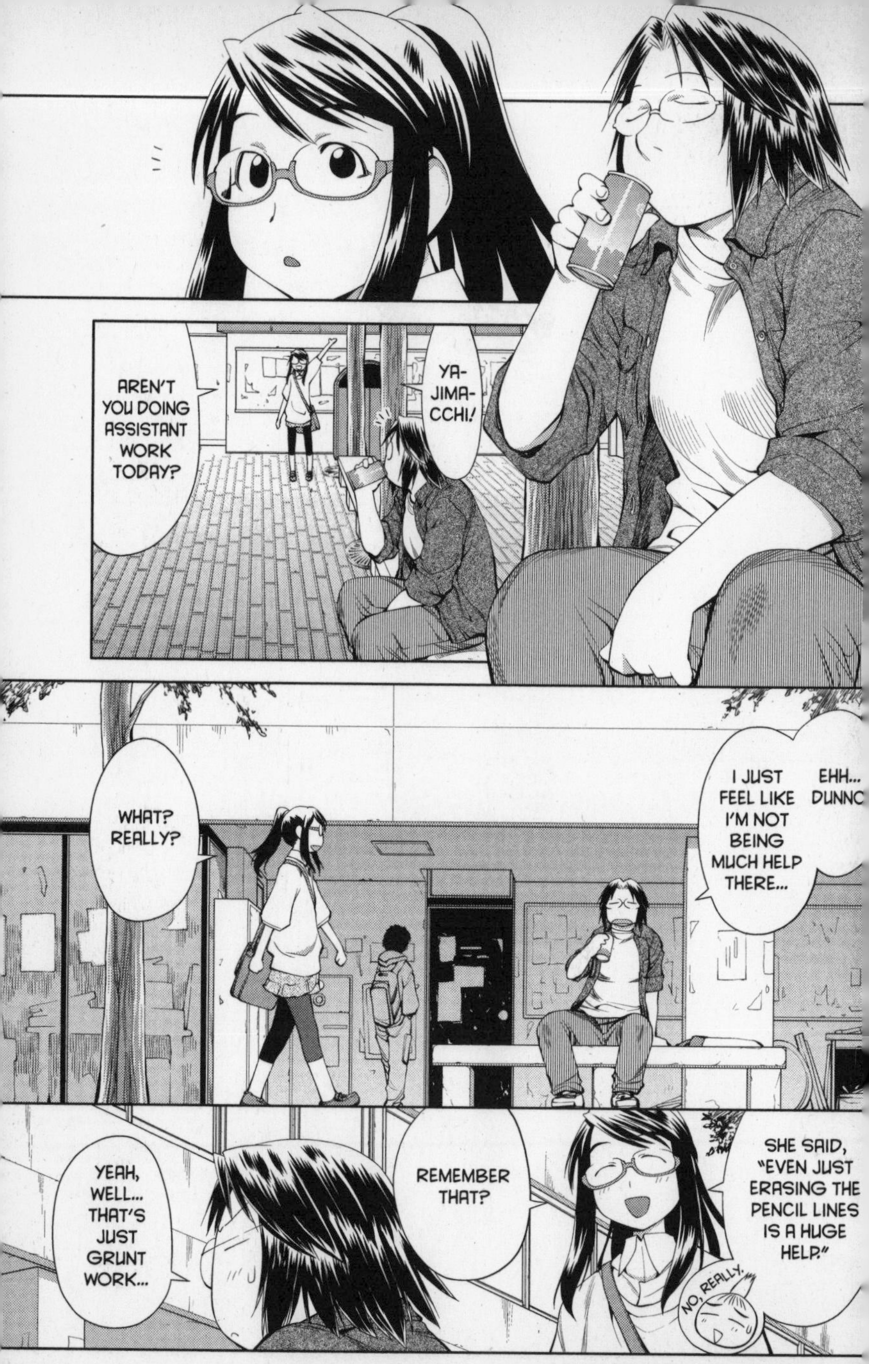
YA-JIMACCHI!
AREN'T YOU DOING ASSISTANT WORK TODAY?
EHH... DUNNO
I JUST FEEL LIKE I'M NOT BEING MUCH HELP THERE...
WHAT? REALLY?
SHE SAID, "EVEN JUST ERASING THE PENCIL LINES IS A HUGE HELP."
NO, REALLY.
REMEMBER THAT?
YEAH, WELL... THAT'S JUST GRUNT WORK...

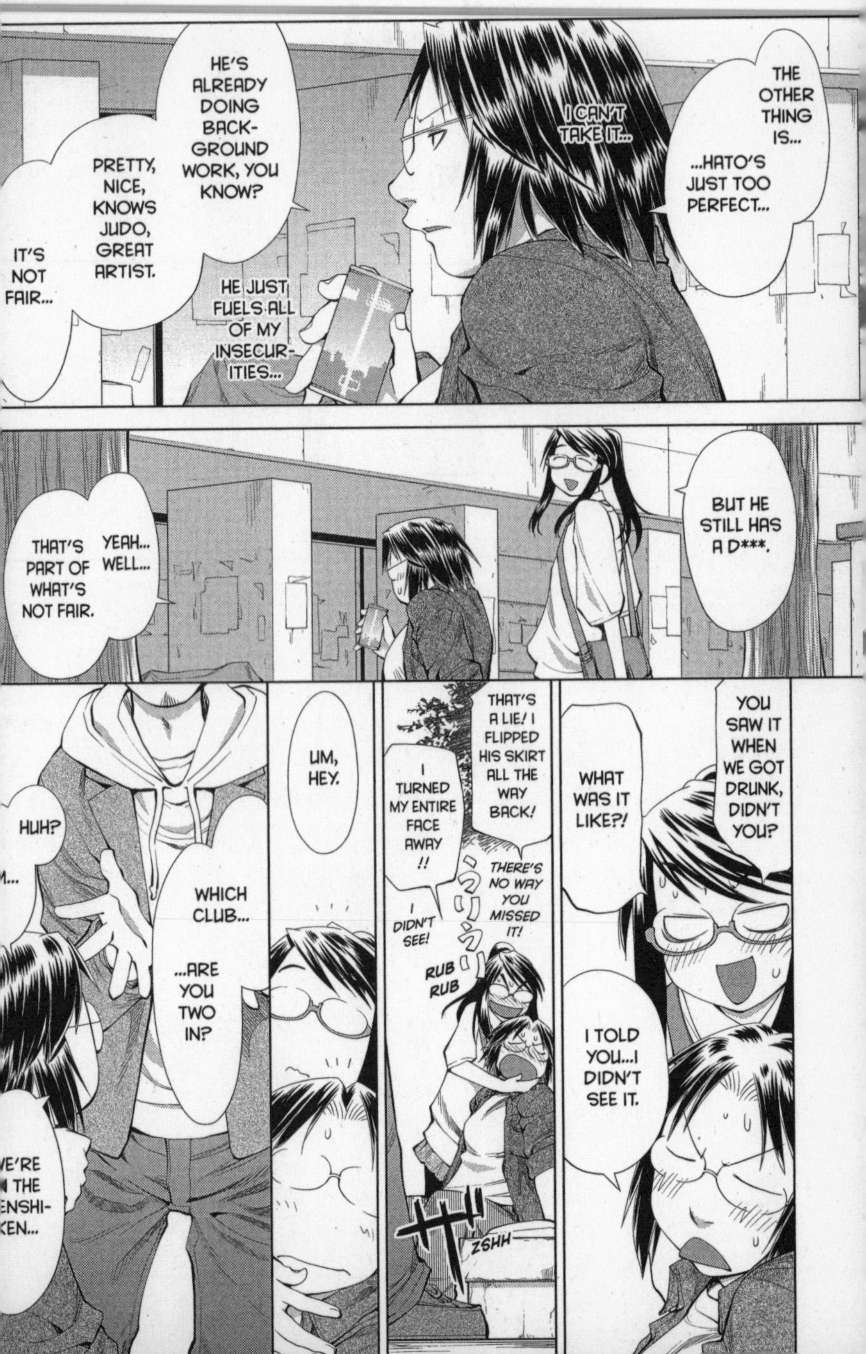
THE OTHER THING IS...
...HATO'S JUST TOO PERFECT...
I CAN'T TAKE IT...
HE'S ALREADY DOING BACK-GROUND WORK, YOU KNOW?
HE JUST FUELS ALL OF MY INSECUR-ITIES...
PRETTY, NICE, KNOWS JUDO, GREAT ARTIST.
IT'S NOT FAIR...
BUT HE STILL HAS A D***.
YEAH... WELL...
THAT'S PART OF WHAT'S NOT FAIR.
YOU SAW IT WHEN WE GOT DRUNK, DIDN'T YOU?
WHAT WAS IT LIKE?!
I TOLD YOU...I DIDN'T SEE IT.
THAT'S A LIE! I FLIPPED HIS SKIRT ALL THE WAY BACK!
I TURNED MY ENTIRE FACE AWAY!!
THERE'S NO WAY YOU MISSED IT!
I DIDN'T SEE!
RUB RUB
ZSHH
UM, HEY.
WHICH CLUB...
...ARE YOU TWO IN?
HUH?
E'RE N THE ENSHI-KEN...

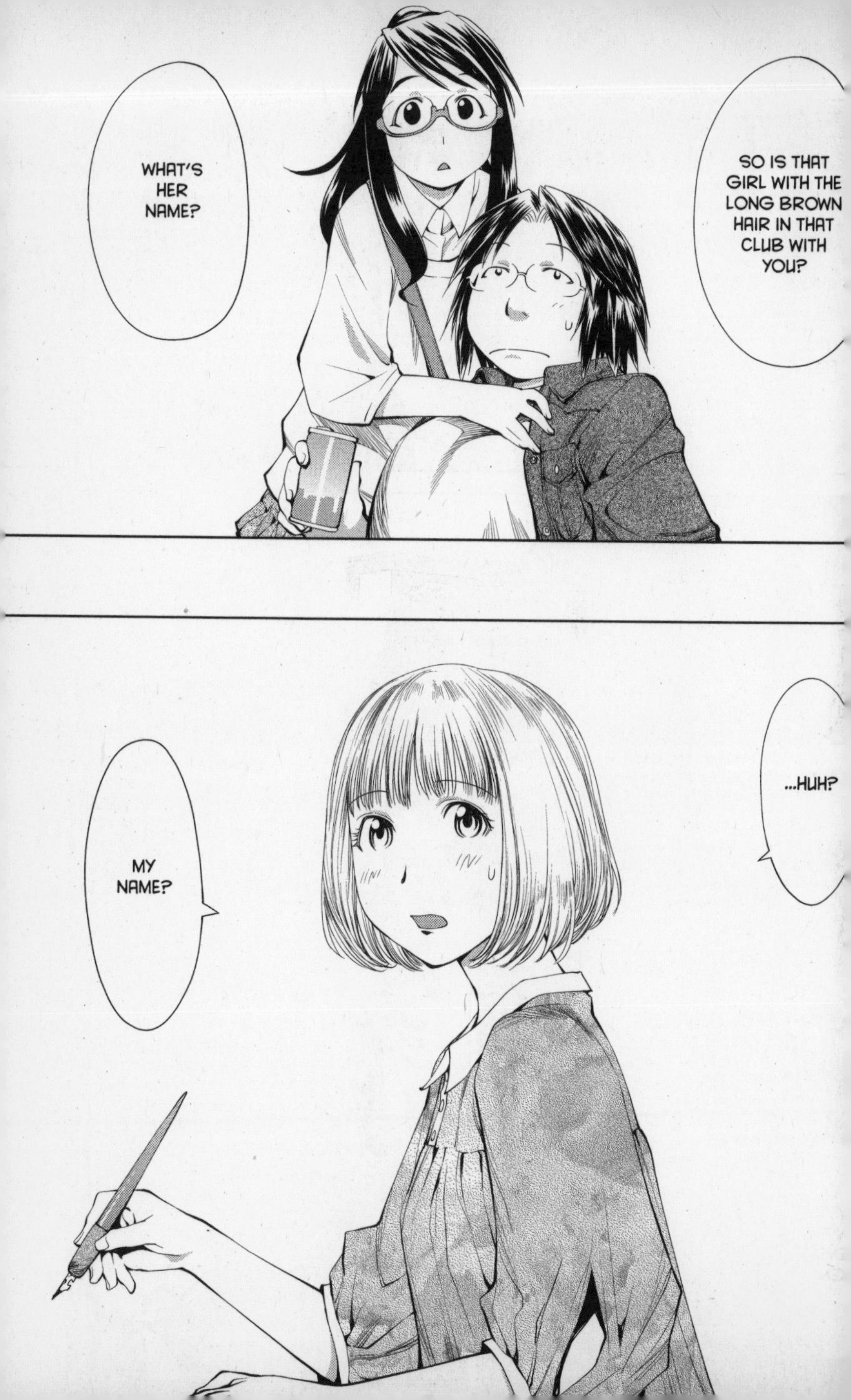
SO IS THAT GIRL WITH THE LONG BROWN HAIR IN THAT CLUB WITH YOU?
WHAT'S HER NAME?
...HUH?
MY NAME?

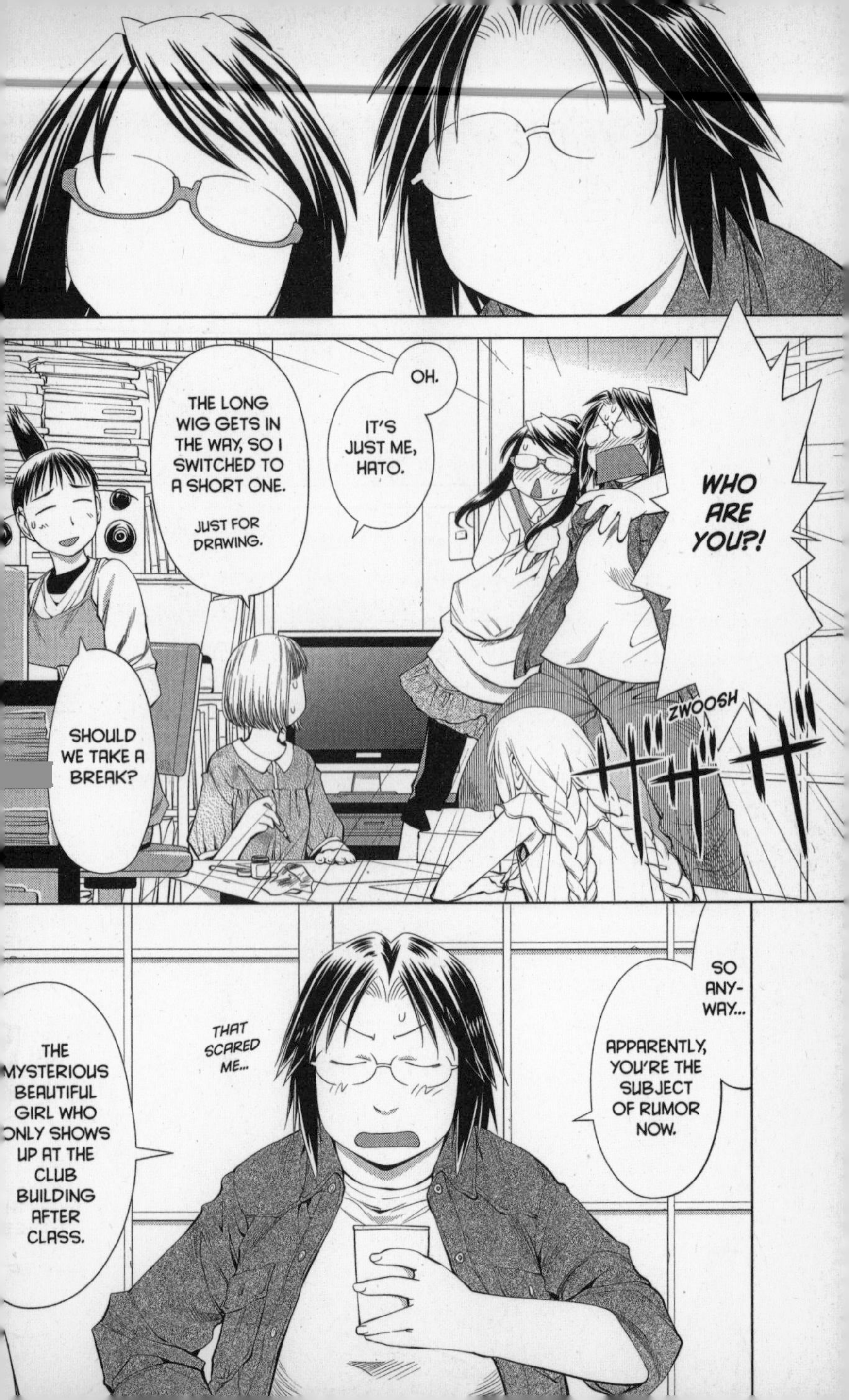
WHO ARE YOU?!
ZWOOSH
OH.
IT'S JUST ME, HATO.
THE LONG WIG GETS IN THE WAY, SO I SWITCHED TO A SHORT ONE.
JUST FOR DRAWING.
SHOULD WE TAKE A BREAK?
SO ANY-WAY...
APPARENTLY, YOU'RE THE SUBJECT OF RUMOR NOW.
THAT SCARED ME...
THE MYSTERIOUS BEAUTIFUL GIRL WHO ONLY SHOWS UP AT THE CLUB BUILDING AFTER CLASS.

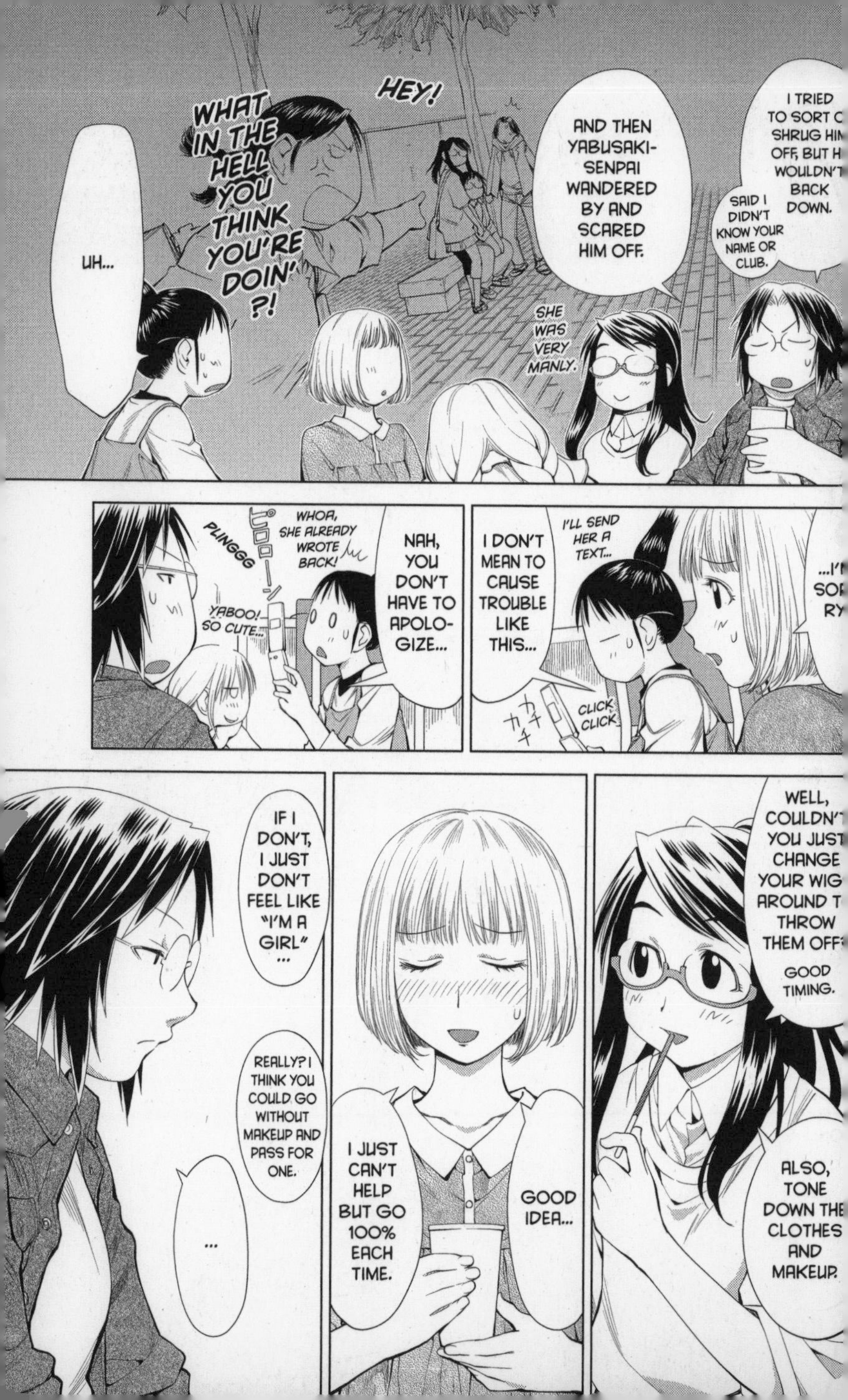
I TRIED TO SORT O SHRUG HIM OFF, BUT H WOULDN'T BACK DOWN.
SAID I DIDN'T KNOW YOUR NAME OR CLUB.
AND THEN YABUSAKI-SENPAI WANDERED BY AND SCARED HIM OFF.
SHE WAS VERY MANLY.
HEY!
WHAT IN THE HELL YOU THINK YOU'RE DOIN'?!
UH...
...I' SOR RY
I'LL SEND HER A TEXT...
I DON'T MEAN TO CAUSE TROUBLE LIKE THIS...
カチカチ
CLICK CLICK
NAH, YOU DON'T HAVE TO APOLOGIZE...
WHOA, SHE ALREADY WROTE BACK!
ピロローン
PLINGGG
YABOO! SO CUTE...
WELL, COULDN'T YOU JUST CHANGE YOUR WIG AROUND T THROW THEM OFF?
GOOD TIMING.
ALSO, TONE DOWN THE CLOTHES AND MAKEUP.
GOOD IDEA...
I JUST CAN'T HELP BUT GO 100% EACH TIME.
IF I DON'T, I JUST DON'T FEEL LIKE "I'M A GIRL" ...
REALLY? I THINK YOU COULD GO WITHOUT MAKEUP AND PASS FOR ONE.
...

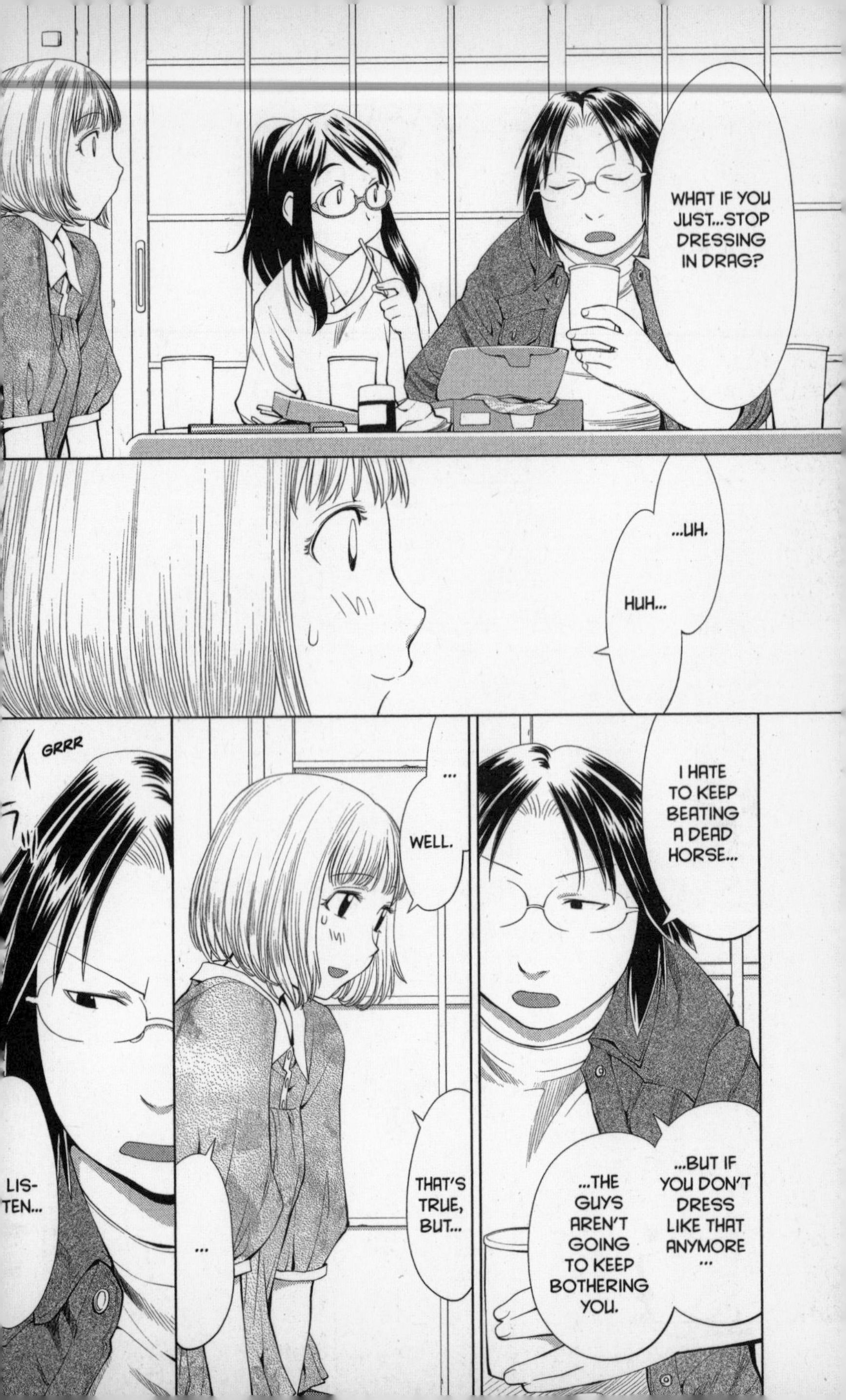

WHAT IF YOU JUST...STOP DRESSING IN DRAG?
...UH.
HUH...
I HATE TO KEEP BEATING A DEAD HORSE...
...BUT IF YOU DON'T DRESS LIKE THAT ANYMORE...
...THE GUYS AREN'T GOING TO KEEP BOTHERING YOU.
... WELL.
THAT'S TRUE, BUT...
...
GRRR
LIS-TEN...

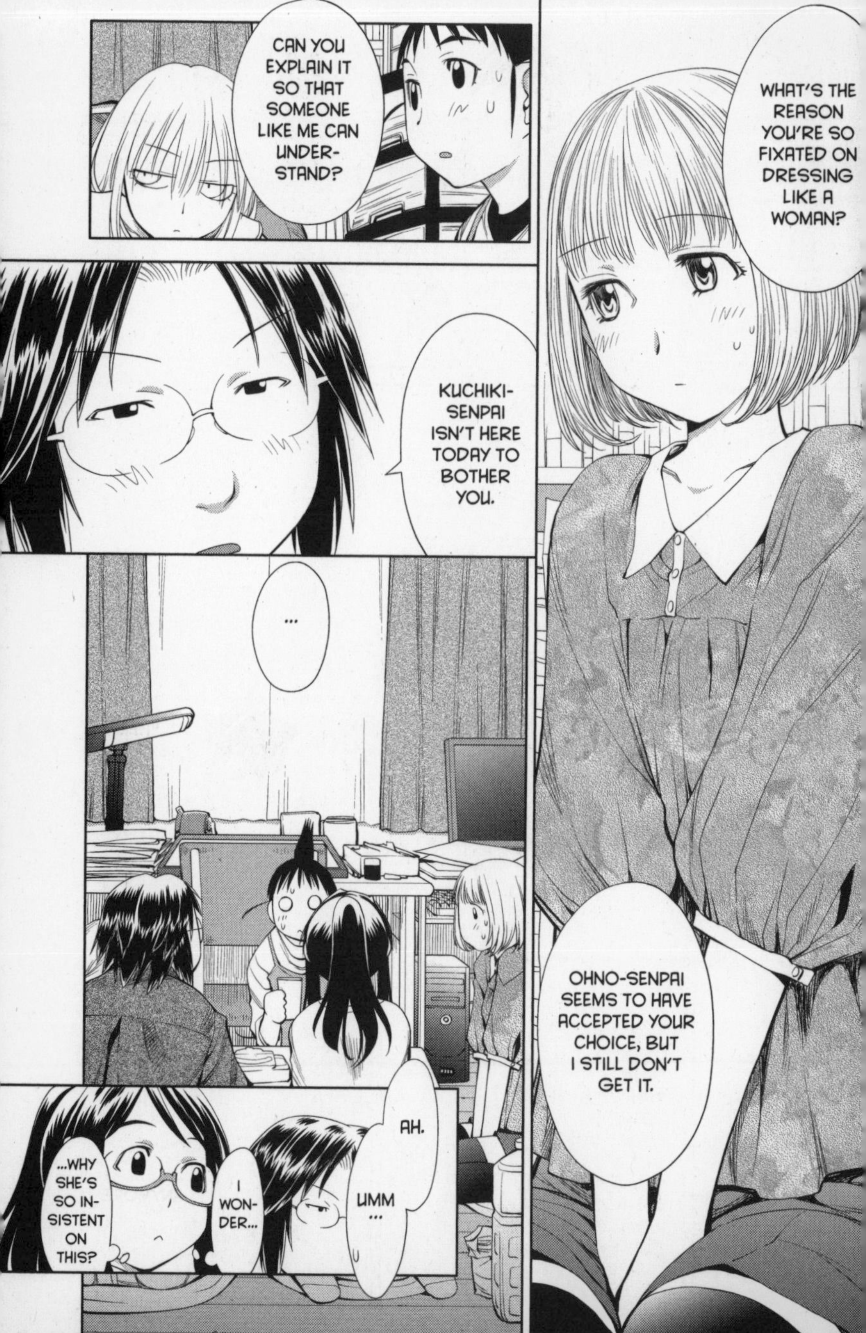
WHAT'S THE REASON YOU'RE SO FIXATED ON DRESSING LIKE A WOMAN?
OHNO-SENPAI SEEMS TO HAVE ACCEPTED YOUR CHOICE, BUT I STILL DON'T GET IT.
CAN YOU EXPLAIN IT SO THAT SOMEONE LIKE ME CAN UNDER-STAND?
KUCHIKI-SENPAI ISN'T HERE TODAY TO BOTHER YOU.
...
AH.
UMM ...
I WONDER...
...WHY SHE'S SO IN-SISTENT ON THIS?

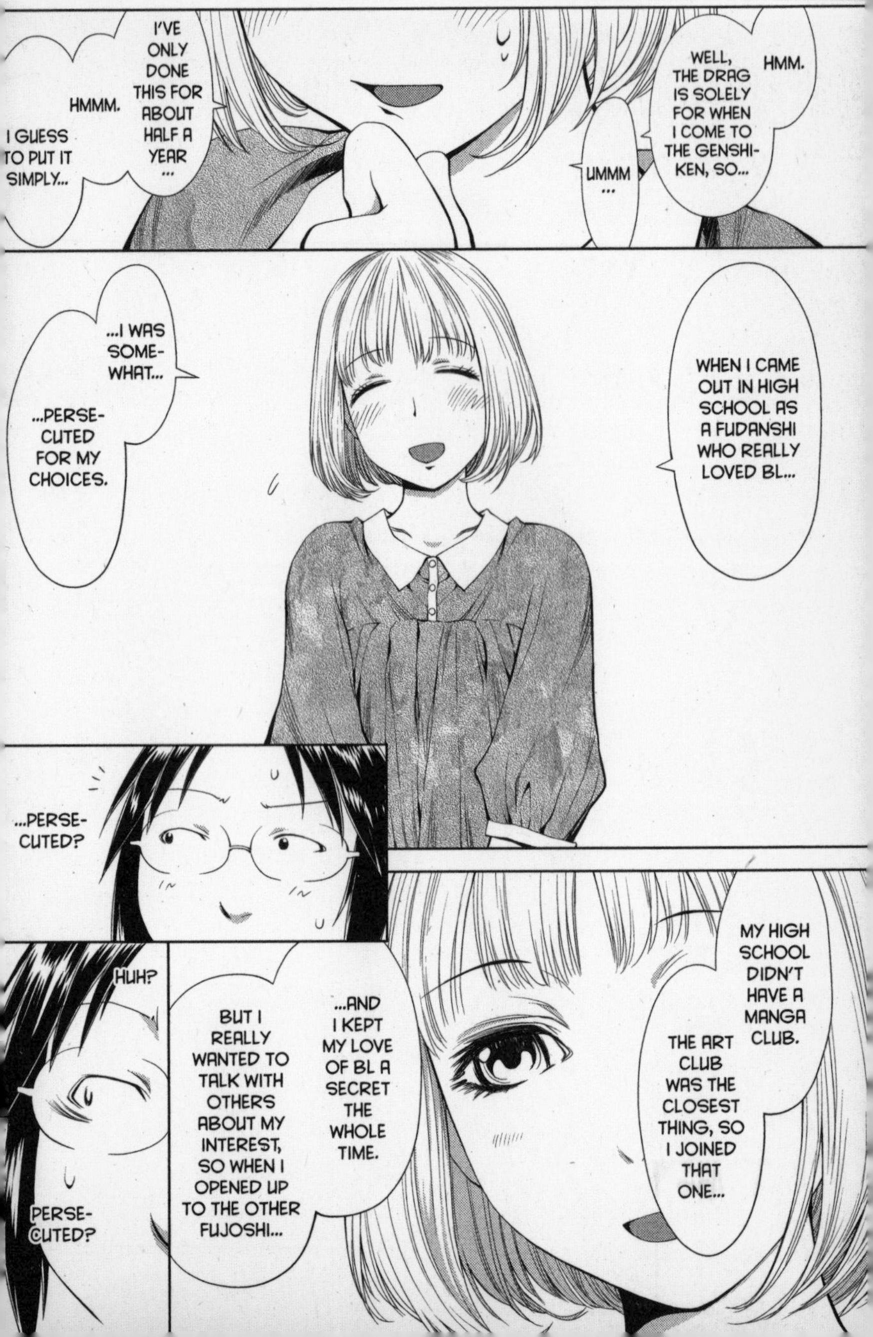

HMM.
WELL, THE DRAG IS SOLELY FOR WHEN I COME TO THE GENSHIKEN, SO...
UMMM ...
I'VE ONLY DONE THIS FOR ABOUT HALF A YEAR ...
HMMM.
I GUESS TO PUT IT SIMPLY...
WHEN I CAME OUT IN HIGH SCHOOL AS A FUDANSHI WHO REALLY LOVED BL...
...I WAS SOME-WHAT...
...PERSE-CUTED FOR MY CHOICES.
...PERSE-CUTED?
MY HIGH SCHOOL DIDN'T HAVE A MANGA CLUB.
THE ART CLUB WAS THE CLOSEST THING, SO I JOINED THAT ONE...
...AND I KEPT MY LOVE OF BL A SECRET THE WHOLE TIME.
BUT I REALLY WANTED TO TALK WITH OTHERS ABOUT MY INTEREST, SO WHEN I OPENED UP TO THE OTHER FUJOSHI...
HUH?
PERSE-CUTED?

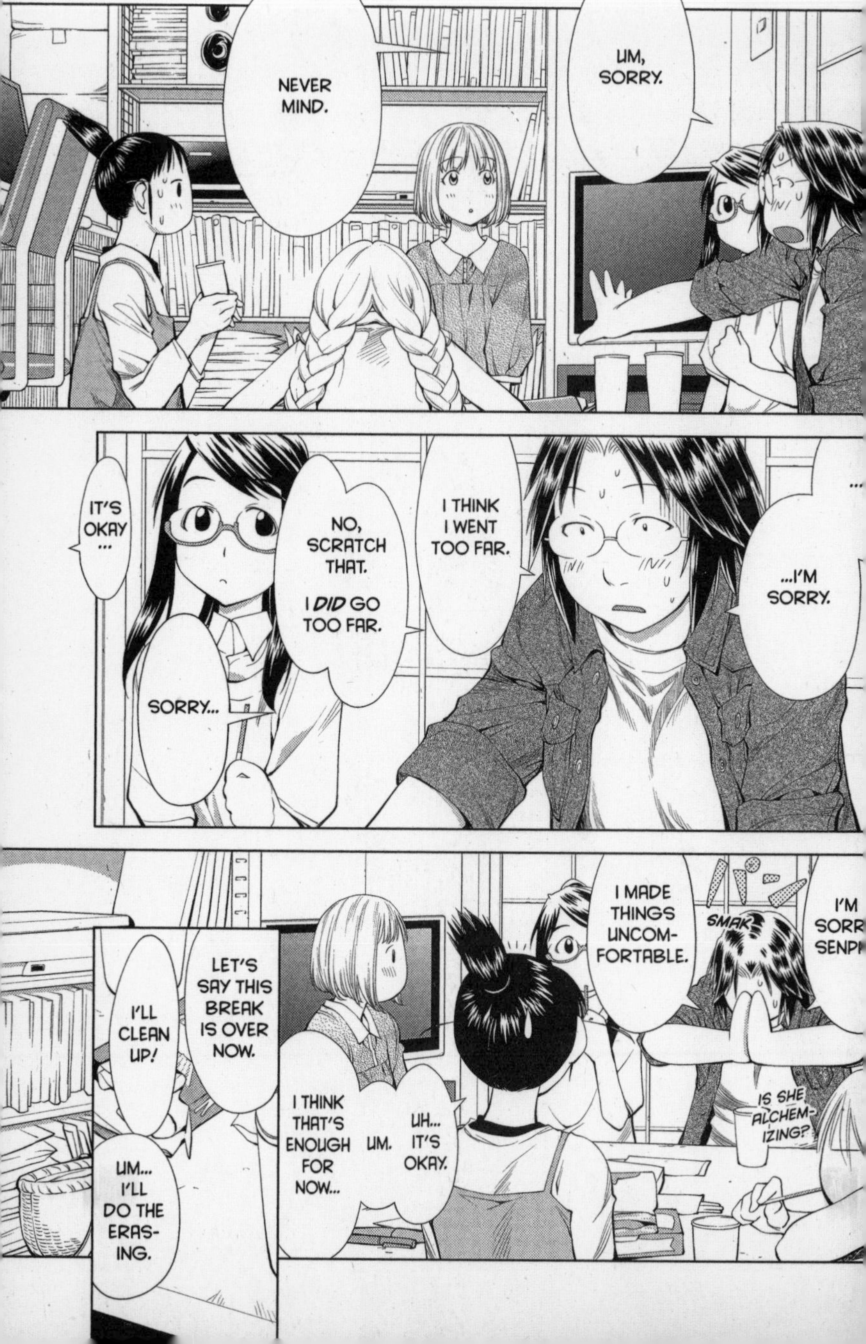
UM, SORRY.
NEVER MIND.
...
...I'M SORRY.
I THINK I WENT TOO FAR.
NO, SCRATCH THAT. I *DID* GO TOO FAR.
IT'S OKAY ...
SORRY...
I'M SORR SENP
SMAK
I MADE THINGS UNCOM-FORTABLE.
IS SHE ALCHEM-IZING?
UH... IT'S OKAY.
UM.
I THINK THAT'S ENOUGH FOR NOW...
LET'S SAY THIS BREAK IS OVER NOW.
I'LL CLEAN UP!
UM... I'LL DO THE ERAS-ING.

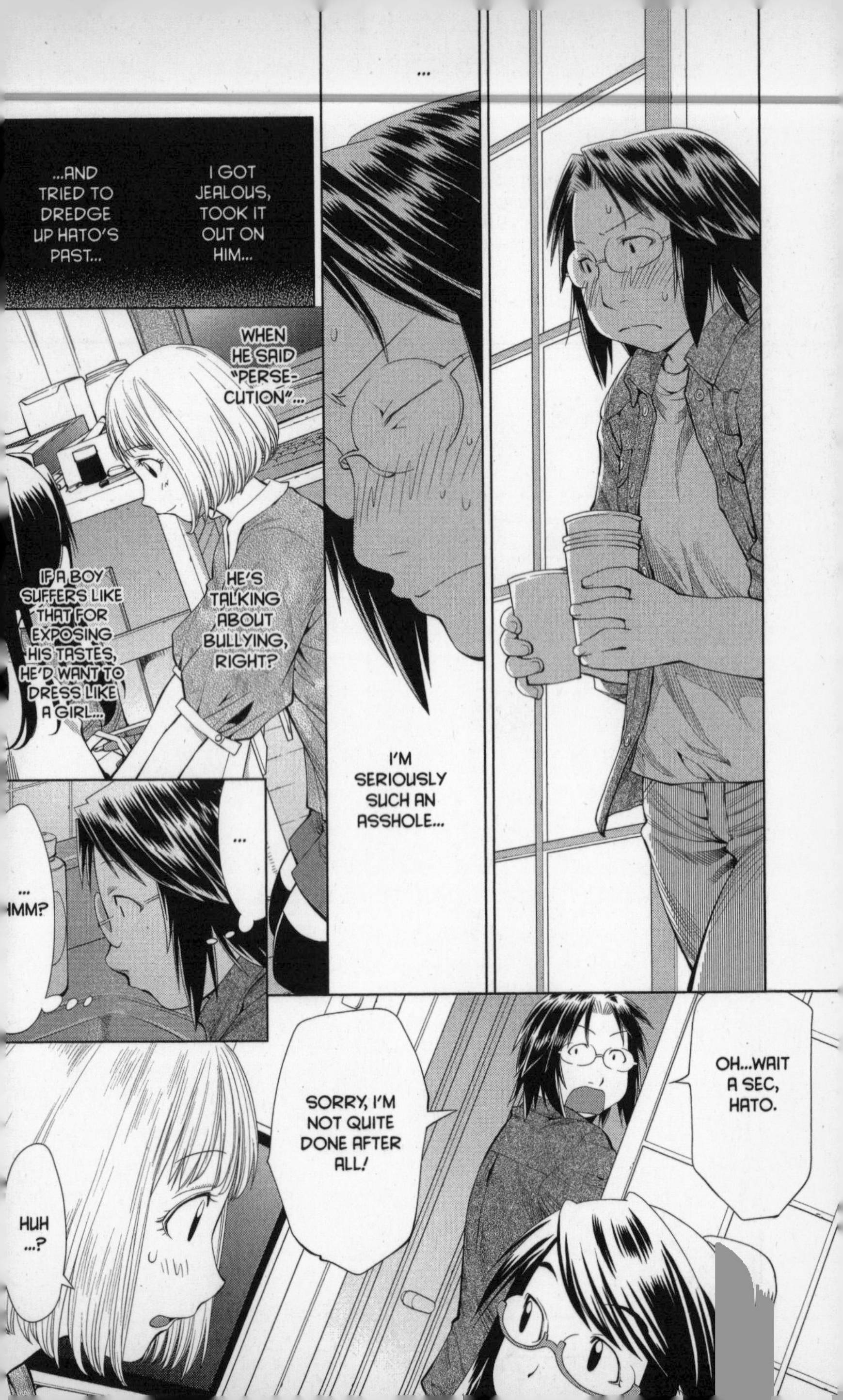
...
I'M SERIOUSLY SUCH AN ASSHOLE...
I GOT JEALOUS, TOOK IT OUT ON HIM...
...AND TRIED TO DREDGE UP HATO'S PAST...
WHEN HE SAID "PERSE-CUTION"...
HE'S TALKING ABOUT BULLYING, RIGHT?
IF A BOY SUFFERS LIKE THAT FOR EXPOSING HIS TASTES, HE'D WANT TO DRESS LIKE A GIRL...
...
... HMM?
OH...WAIT A SEC, HATO.
SORRY, I'M NOT QUITE DONE AFTER ALL!
HUH ...?

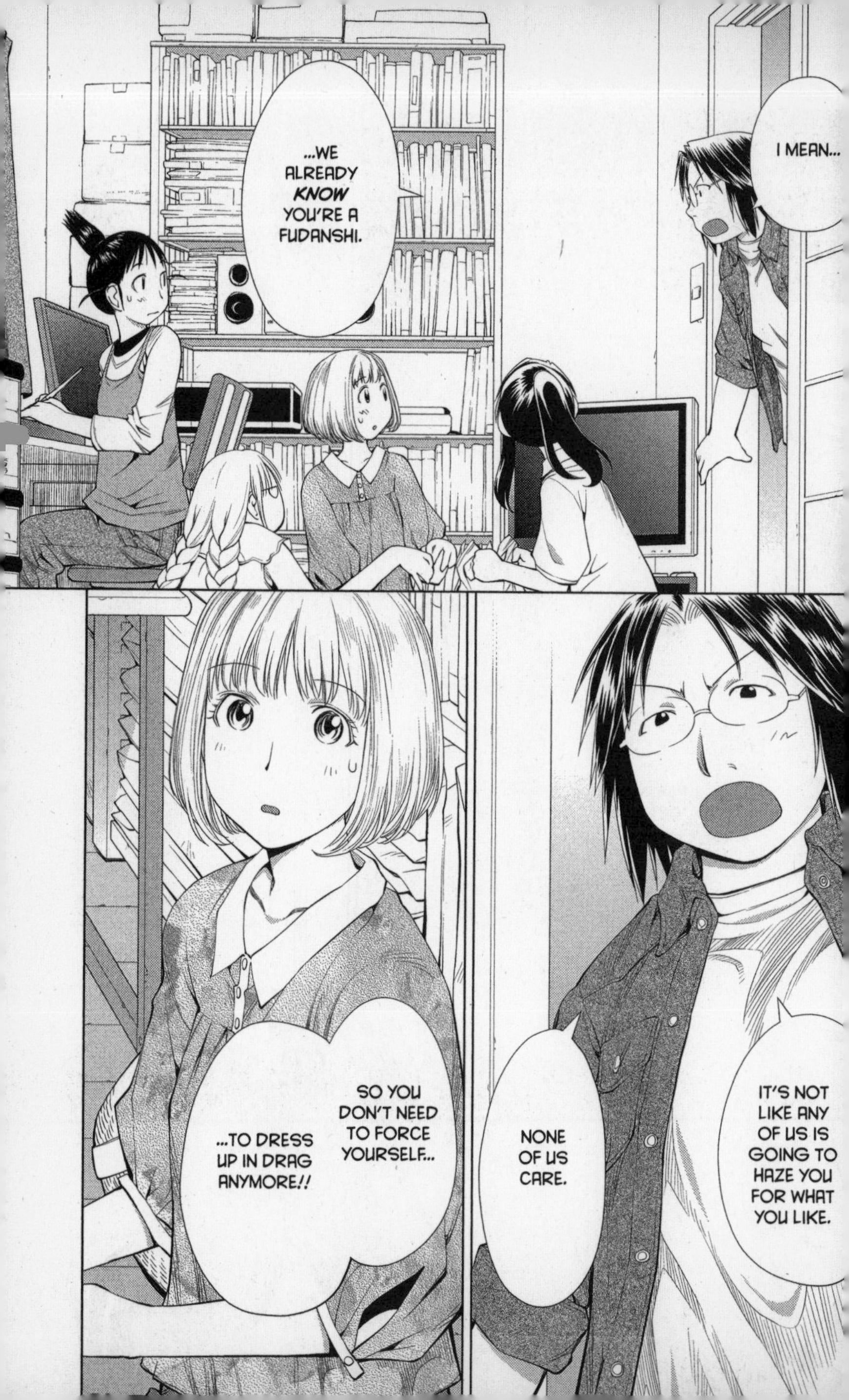
I MEAN...
...WE ALREADY *KNOW* YOU'RE A FUDANSHI.
IT'S NOT LIKE ANY OF US IS GOING TO HAZE YOU FOR WHAT YOU LIKE.
NONE OF US CARE.
SO YOU DON'T NEED TO FORCE YOURSELF...
...TO DRESS UP IN DRAG ANYMORE!!

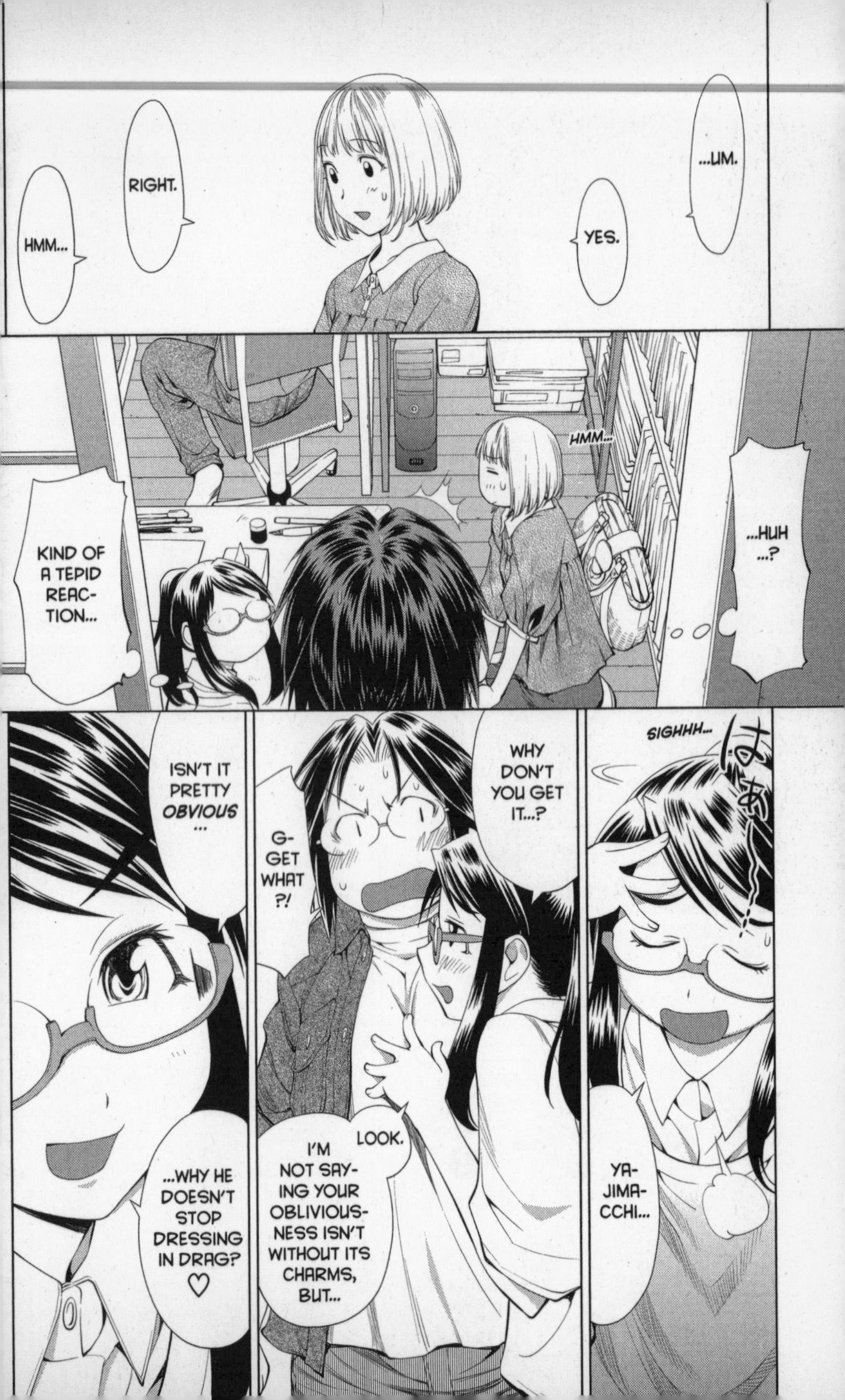

...UM.
YES.
RIGHT.
HMM...
...HUH ...?
HMM...
KIND OF A TEPID REACTION...
SIGHHH...
はあ
YA-JIMA-CCHI...
WHY DON'T YOU GET IT...?
G-GET WHAT?!
LOOK.
I'M NOT SAYING YOUR OBLIVIOUSNESS ISN'T WITHOUT ITS CHARMS, BUT...
ISN'T IT PRETTY *OBVIOUS*...
...WHY HE DOESN'T STOP DRESSING IN DRAG? ♡

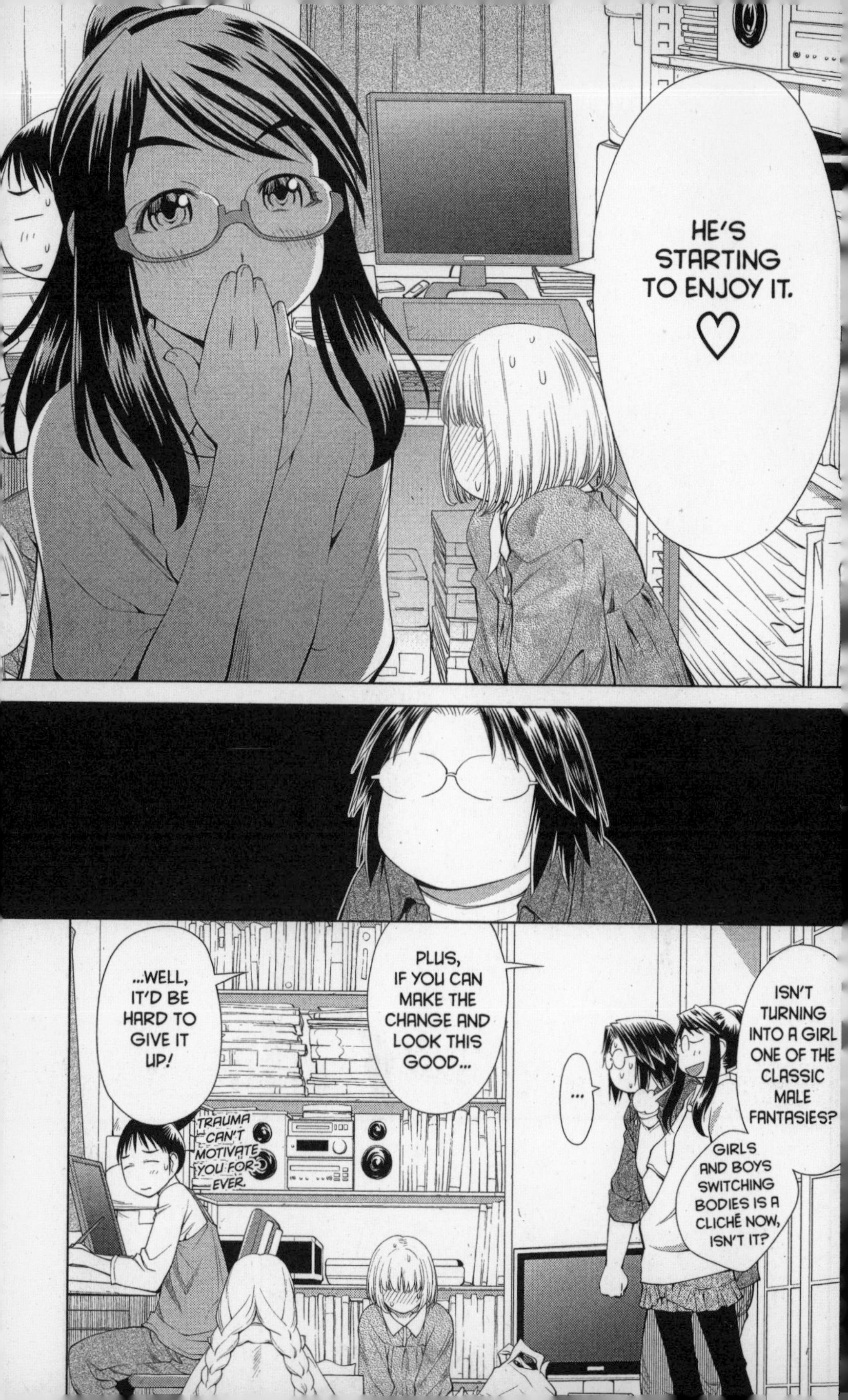
HE'S STARTING TO ENJOY IT. ♥
ISN'T TURNING INTO A GIRL ONE OF THE CLASSIC MALE FANTASIES?
GIRLS AND BOYS SWITCHING BODIES IS A CLICHÉ NOW, ISN'T IT?
...
PLUS, IF YOU CAN MAKE THE CHANGE AND LOOK THIS GOOD...
...WELL, IT'D BE HARD TO GIVE IT UP!
TRAUMA CAN'T MOTIVATE YOU FOREVER.

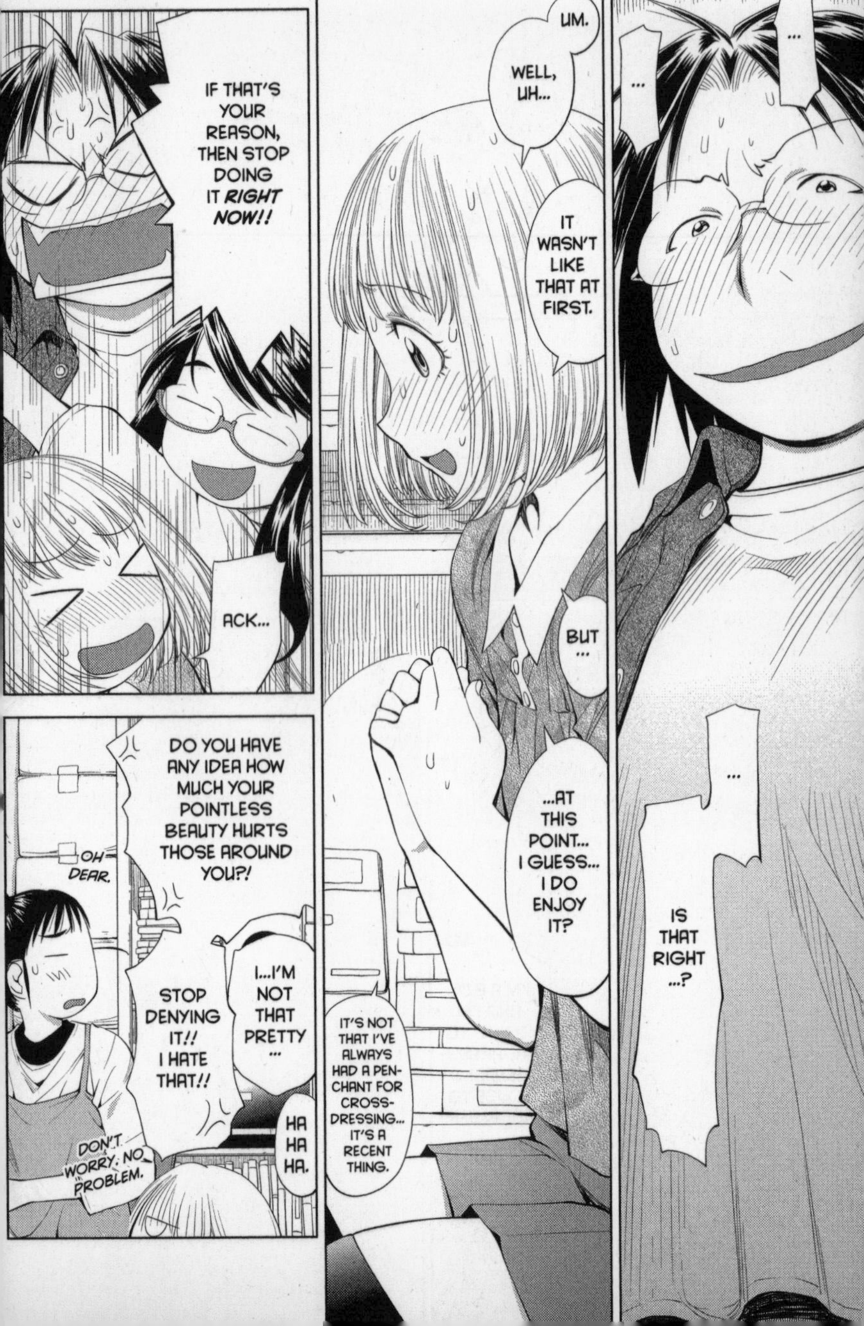
...
...
...
IS THAT RIGHT...?
UM.
WELL, UH...
IT WASN'T LIKE THAT AT FIRST.
BUT...
...AT THIS POINT... I GUESS... I DO ENJOY IT?
IT'S NOT THAT I'VE ALWAYS HAD A PEN-CHANT FOR CROSS-DRESSING... IT'S A RECENT THING.
IF THAT'S YOUR REASON, THEN STOP DOING IT RIGHT NOW!!
ACK...
DO YOU HAVE ANY IDEA HOW MUCH YOUR POINTLESS BEAUTY HURTS THOSE AROUND YOU?!
OH DEAR.
I...I'M NOT THAT PRETTY...
STOP DENYING IT!! I HATE THAT!!
HA HA HA.
DON'T WORRY. NO PROBLEM.

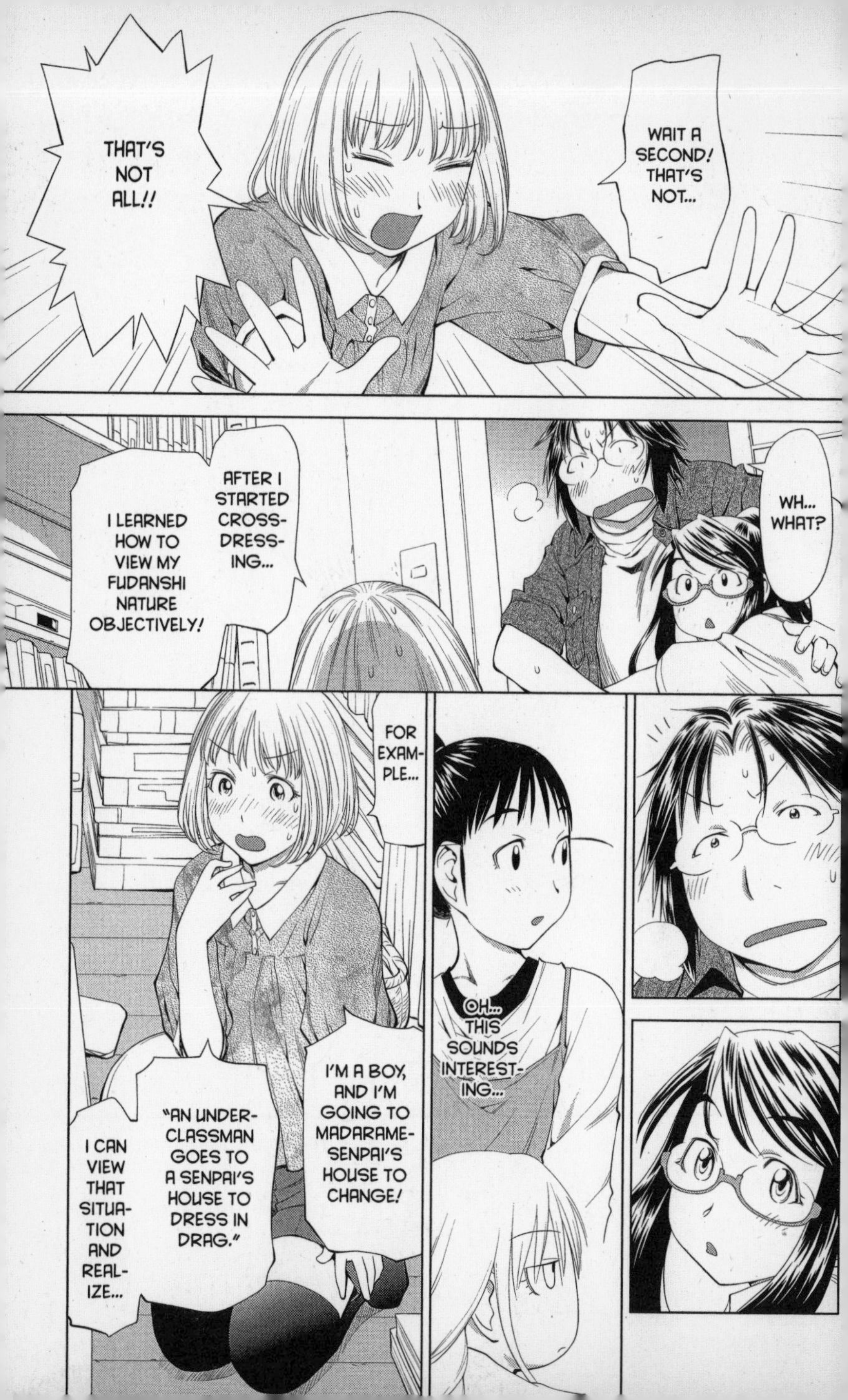
WAIT A SECOND! THAT'S NOT...
THAT'S NOT ALL!!
WH... WHAT?
AFTER I STARTED CROSS-DRESSING...
I LEARNED HOW TO VIEW MY FUDANSHI NATURE OBJECTIVELY!
OH... THIS SOUNDS INTERESTING...
FOR EXAMPLE...
I'M A BOY, AND I'M GOING TO MADARAME-SENPAI'S HOUSE TO CHANGE!
"AN UNDERCLASSMAN GOES TO A SENPAI'S HOUSE TO DRESS IN DRAG."
I CAN VIEW THAT SITUATION AND REALIZE...

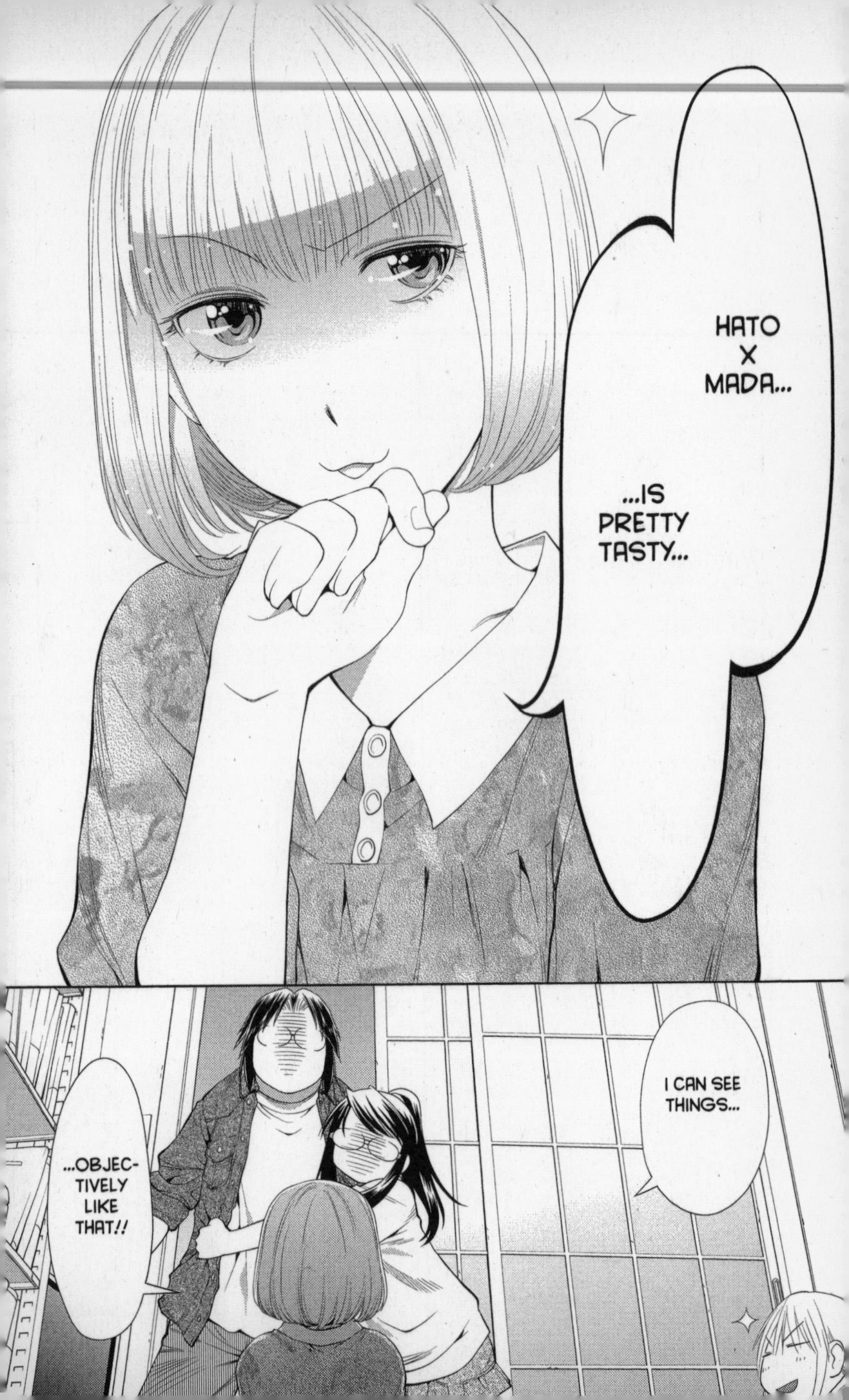
HATO X MADA...
...IS PRETTY TASTY...
I CAN SEE THINGS...
...OBJECTIVELY LIKE THAT!!

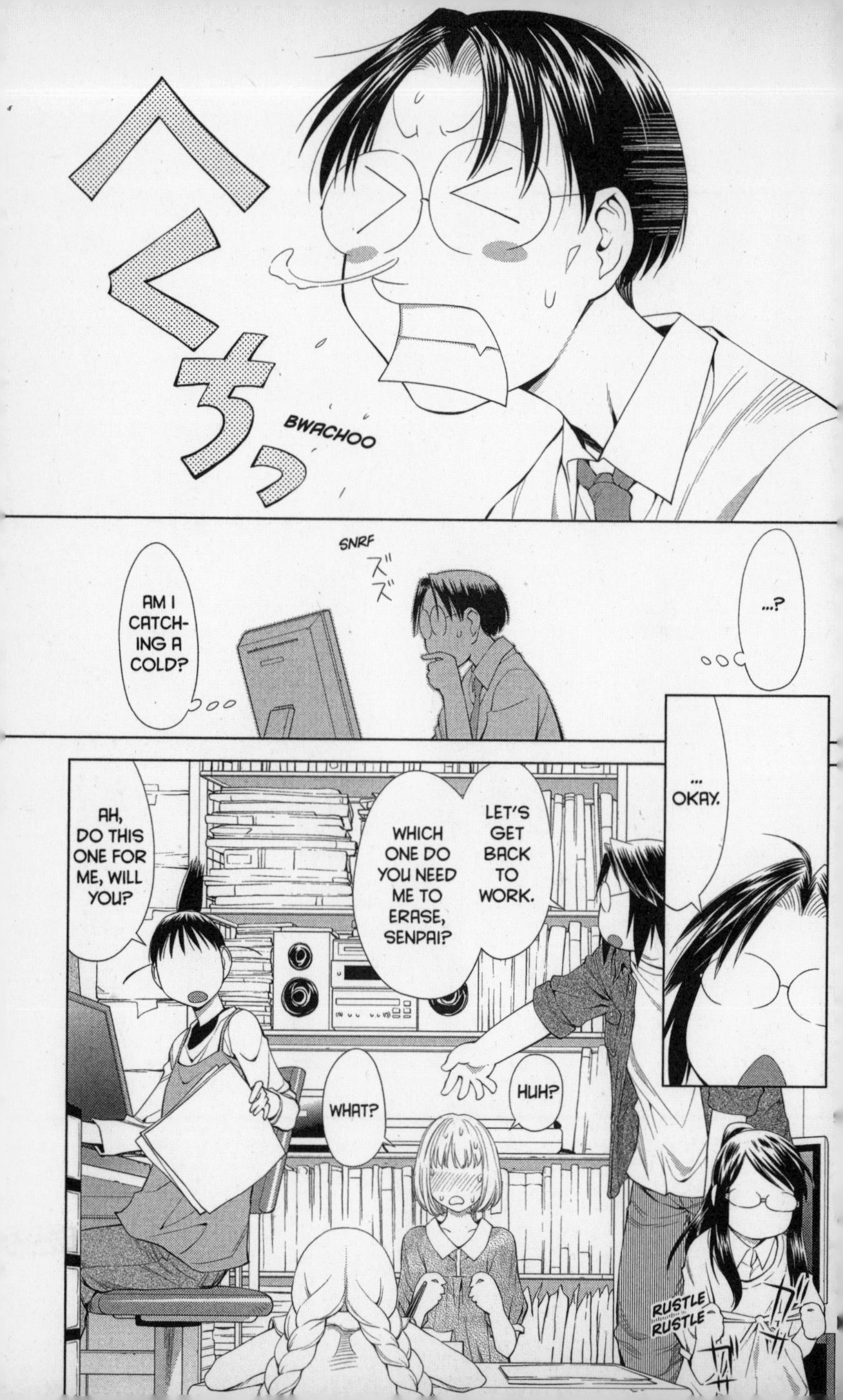
へくちっ
BWACHOO
SNRF
ズズ
AM I CATCHING A COLD?
...?
... OKAY.
LET'S GET BACK TO WORK.
WHICH ONE DO YOU NEED ME TO ERASE, SENPAI?
AH, DO THIS ONE FOR ME, WILL YOU?
HUH?
WHAT?
RUSTLE RUSTLE

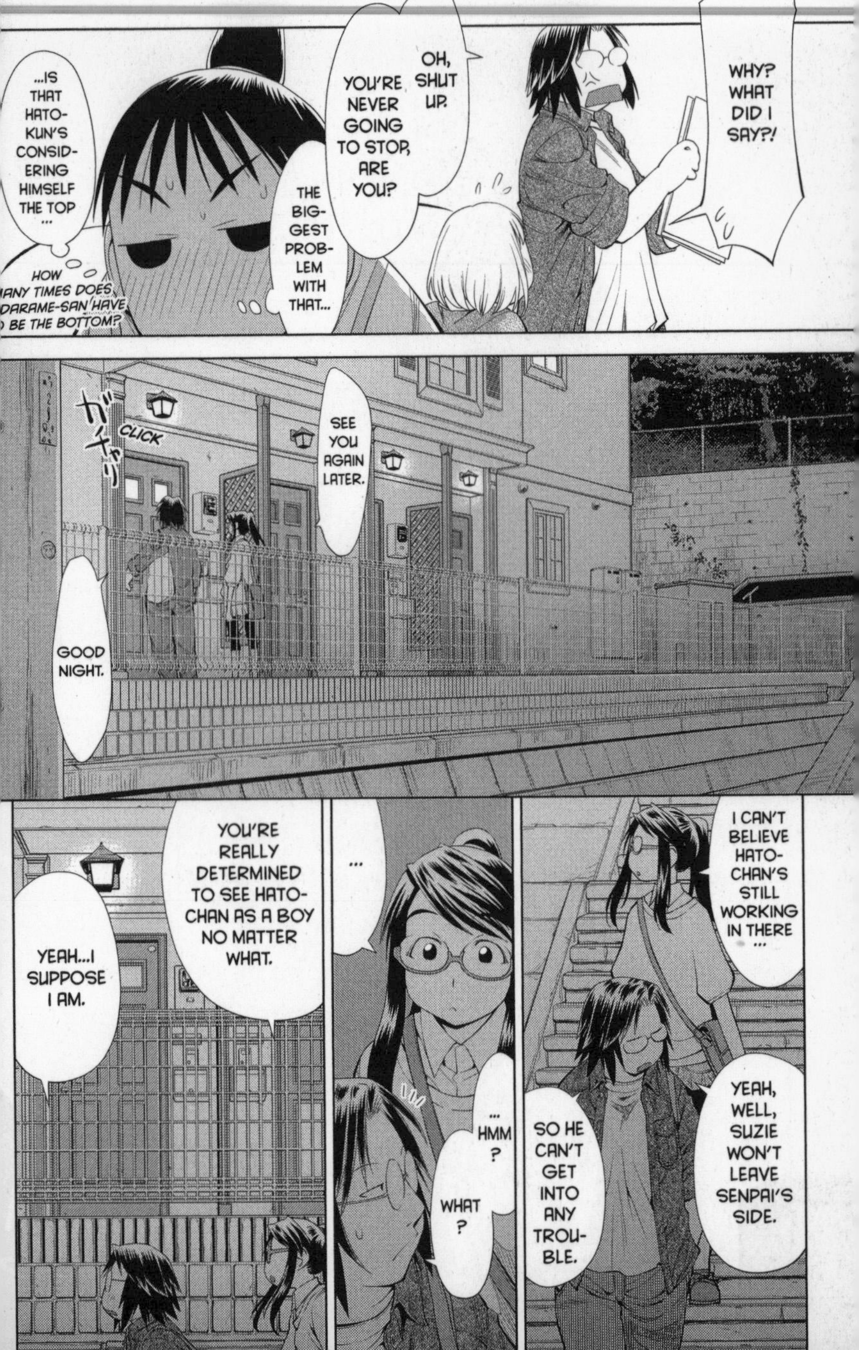
WHY? WHAT DID I SAY?!
OH, SHUT UP.
YOU'RE NEVER GOING TO STOP, ARE YOU?
THE BIG-GEST PROB-LEM WITH THAT...
...IS THAT HATO-KUN'S CONSID-ERING HIMSELF THE TOP...
HOW ANY TIMES DOES DARAME-SAN HAVE BE THE BOTTOM?
ガチャリ
CLICK
SEE YOU AGAIN LATER.
GOOD NIGHT.
I CAN'T BELIEVE HATO-CHAN'S STILL WORKING IN THERE...
YEAH, WELL, SUZIE WON'T LEAVE SENPAI'S SIDE.
SO HE CAN'T GET INTO ANY TROU-BLE.
...
...HMM?
WHAT?
YOU'RE REALLY DETERMINED TO SEE HATO-CHAN AS A BOY NO MATTER WHAT.
YEAH...I SUPPOSE I AM.

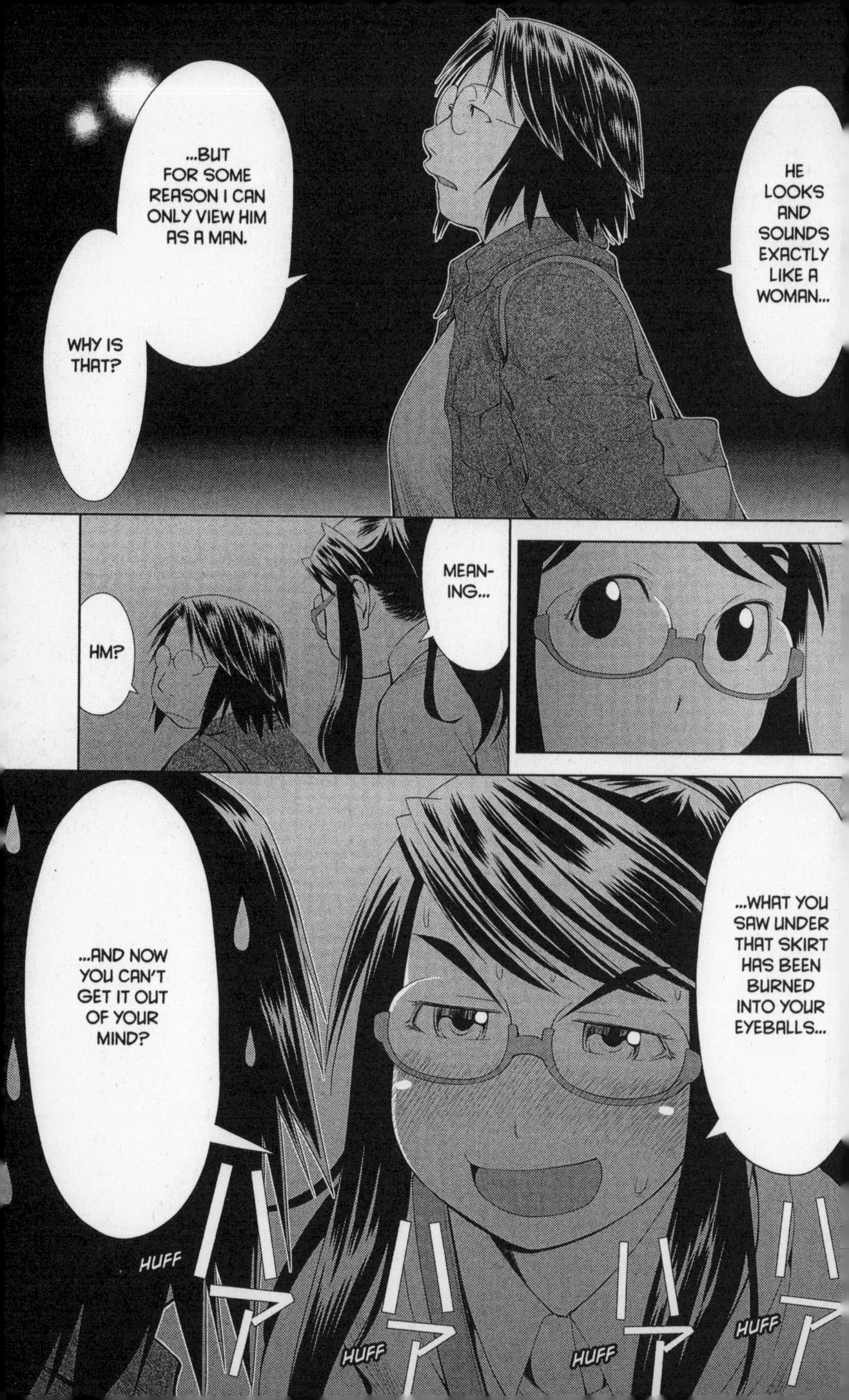
HE LOOKS AND SOUNDS EXACTLY LIKE A WOMAN...
...BUT FOR SOME REASON I CAN ONLY VIEW HIM AS A MAN.
WHY IS THAT?
MEAN-ING...
HM?
...WHAT YOU SAW UNDER THAT SKIRT HAS BEEN BURNED INTO YOUR EYEBALLS...
...AND NOW YOU CAN'T GET IT OUT OF YOUR MIND?
HUFF
HUFF
HUFF
HUFF
HUFF

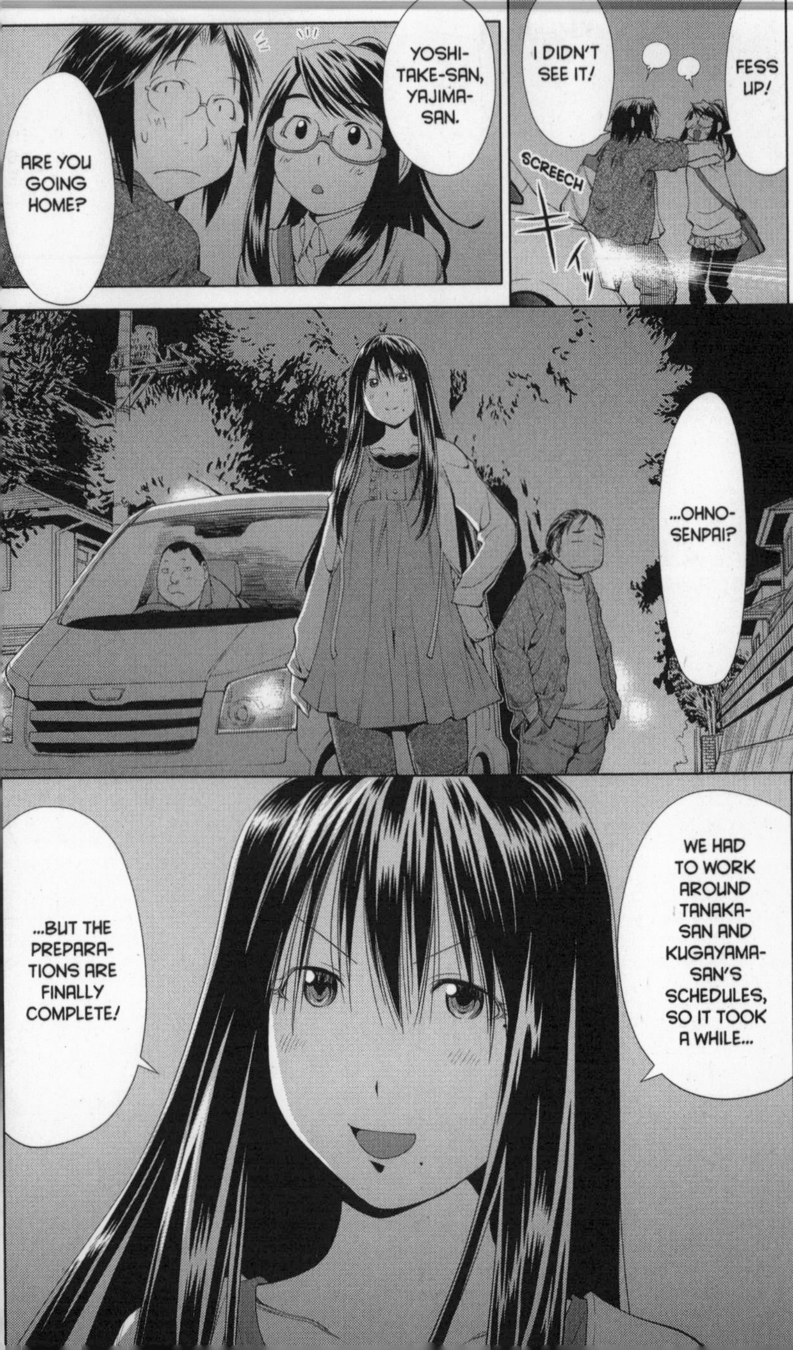
FESS UP!
I DIDN'T SEE IT!
SCREECH
YOSHI-TAKE-SAN, YAJIMA-SAN.
ARE YOU GOING HOME?
...OHNO-SENPAI?
WE HAD TO WORK AROUND TANAKA-SAN AND KUGAYAMA-SAN'S SCHEDULES, SO IT TOOK A WHILE...
...BUT THE PREPARA-TIONS ARE FINALLY COMPLETE!

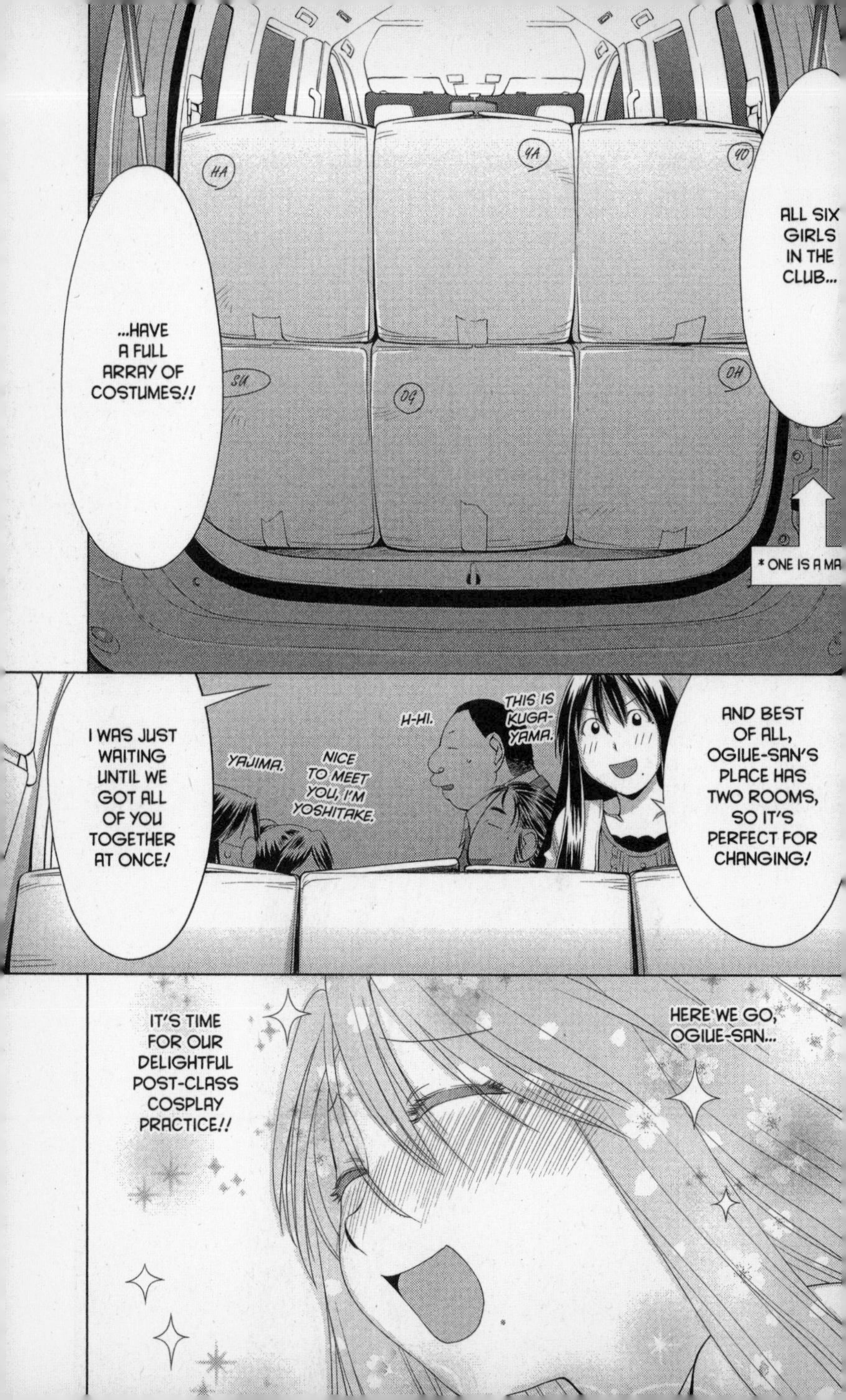
ALL SIX GIRLS IN THE CLUB...
YO
YA
HA
OH
OG
SU
* ONE IS A MA
...HAVE A FULL ARRAY OF COSTUMES!!
AND BEST OF ALL, OGIUE-SAN'S PLACE HAS TWO ROOMS, SO IT'S PERFECT FOR CHANGING!
THIS IS KUGA-YAMA.
H-HI.
NICE TO MEET YOU, I'M YOSHITAKE.
YAJIMA.
I WAS JUST WAITING UNTIL WE GOT ALL OF YOU TOGETHER AT ONCE!
HERE WE GO, OGIUE-SAN...
IT'S TIME FOR OUR DELIGHTFUL POST-CLASS COSPLAY PRACTICE!!

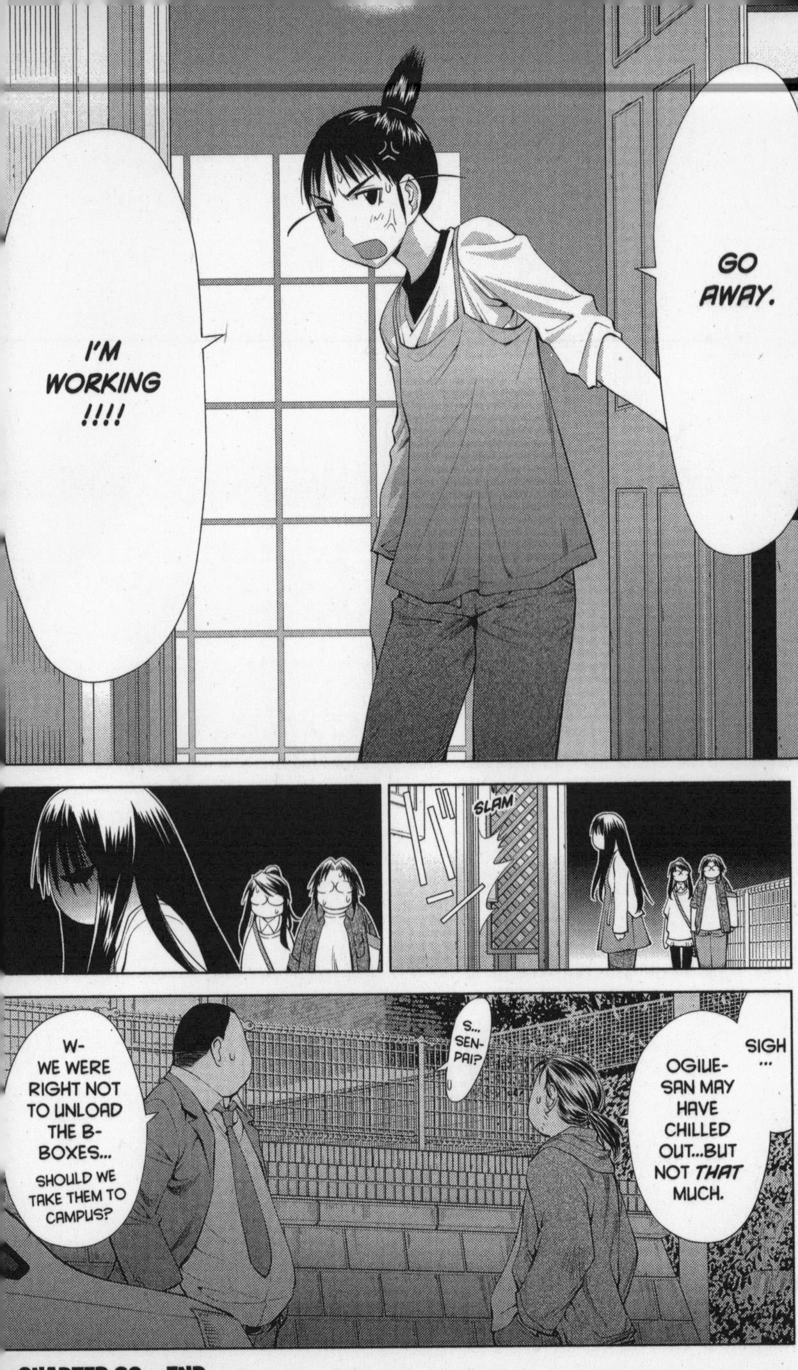
GO AWAY.
I'M WORKING !!!!
SLAM
SIGH ...
OGIUE-SAN MAY HAVE CHILLED OUT...BUT NOT *THAT* MUCH.
S... SEN-PAI?
W- WE WERE RIGHT NOT TO UNLOAD THE B-BOXES...
SHOULD WE TAKE THEM TO CAMPUS?

CHAPTER 60 -- END

MIREI YAJIMA

LIBERAL ARTS, FRESHMAN
BORN IN TOCHIGI
NOVEMBER 7TH, TYPE A

FAVORITE WORKS

"PAKUMAN"
"KINTAMA"
"TEN PIECE"
"MENMA"
"BUGBEAR: RISE OF THE MONSTER CLAN"

A neverending Ogiue!
Suzama Hopkins

EVEN FURTHER IN THE PAST

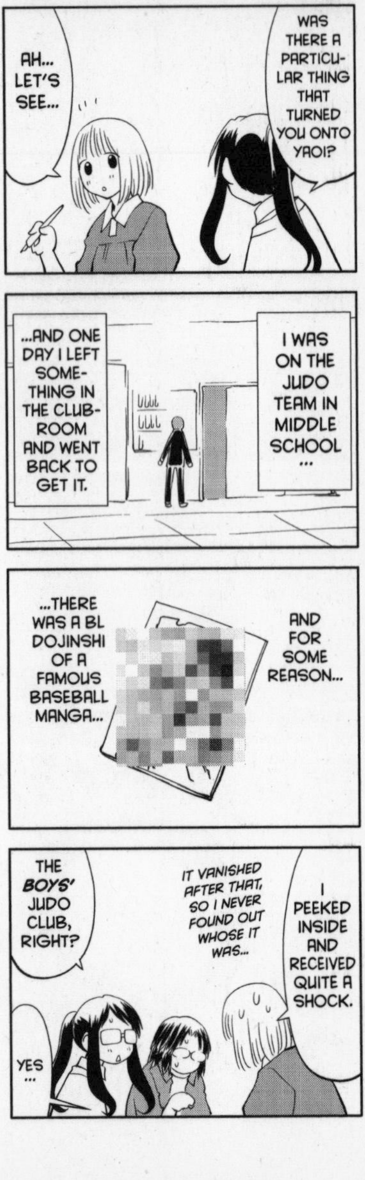
WAS THERE A PARTICULAR THING THAT TURNED YOU ONTO YAOI?
AH... LET'S SEE...
I WAS ON THE JUDO TEAM IN MIDDLE SCHOOL...
...AND ONE DAY I LEFT SOMETHING IN THE CLUBROOM AND WENT BACK TO GET IT.
AND FOR SOME REASON...
...THERE WAS A BL DOJINSHI OF A FAMOUS BASEBALL MANGA...
I PEEKED INSIDE AND RECEIVED QUITE A SHOCK.
IT VANISHED AFTER THAT, SO I NEVER FOUND OUT WHOSE IT WAS...
THE *BOYS'* JUDO CLUB, RIGHT?
YES...

DANGER: DO NOT TOUCH

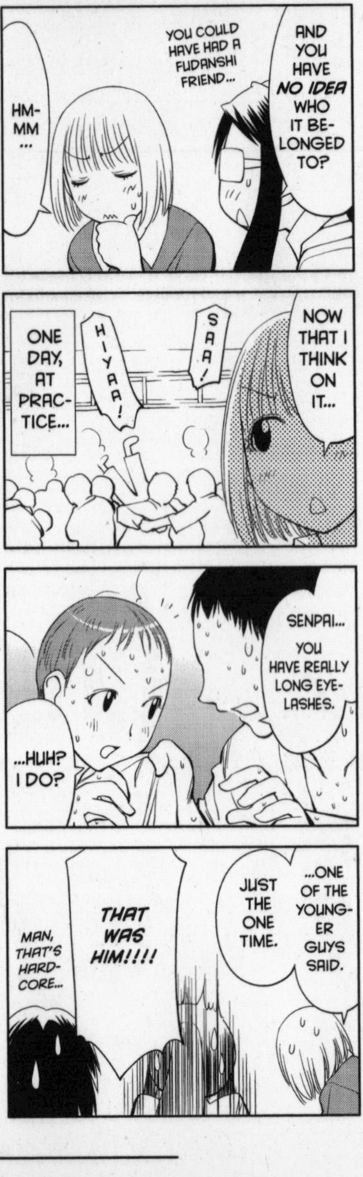
AND YOU HAVE *NO IDEA* WHO IT BELONGED TO?
YOU COULD HAVE HAD A FUDANSHI FRIEND...
HM-MM...
NOW THAT I THINK ON IT...
SAA!
HIYAA!
ONE DAY, AT PRACTICE...
SENPAI... YOU HAVE REALLY LONG EYELASHES.
...HUH? I DO?
...ONE OF THE YOUNGER GUYS SAID.
JUST THE ONE TIME.
THAT WAS HIM!!!!
MAN, THAT'S HARDCORE...

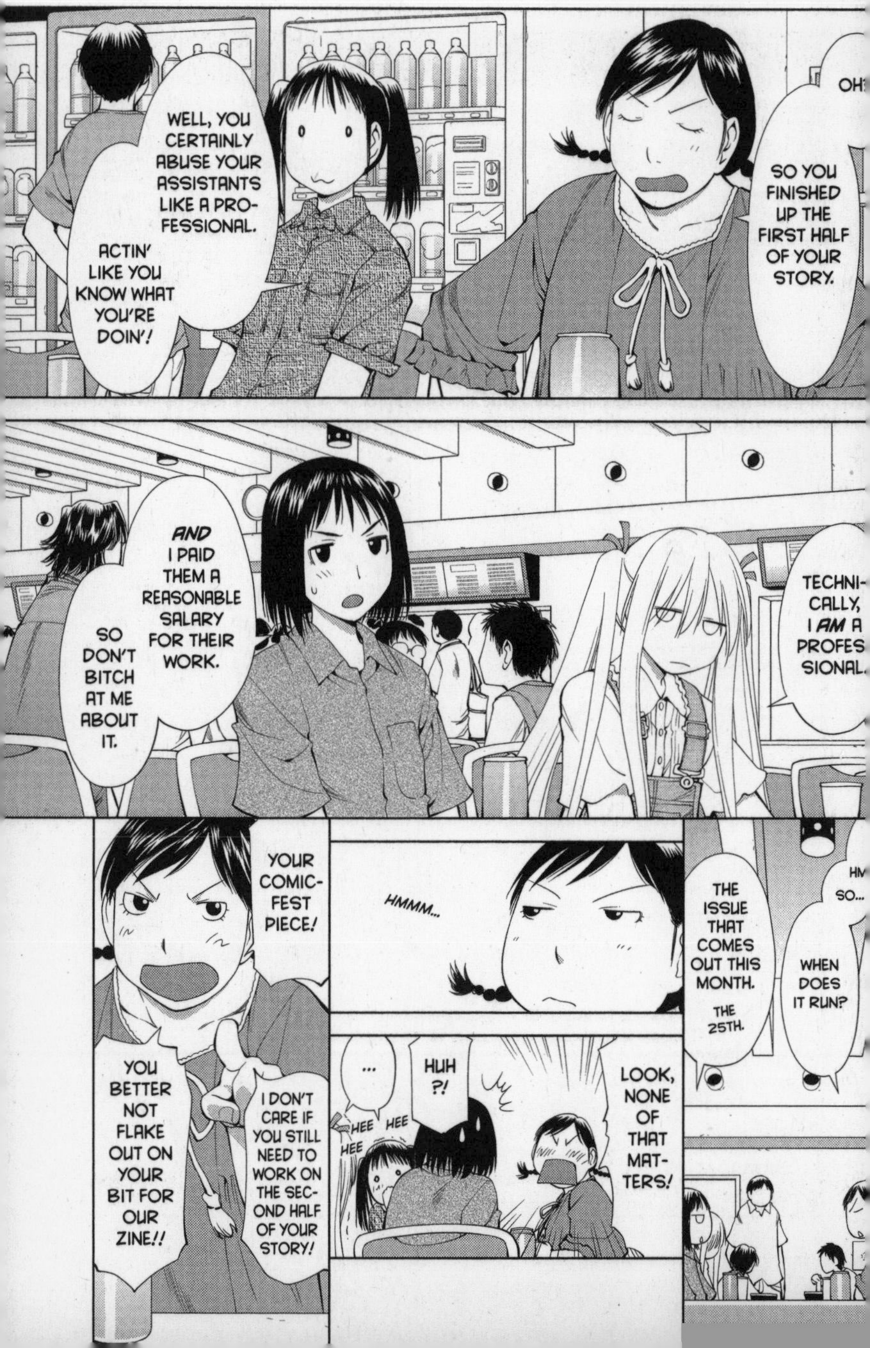
OH!
SO YOU FINISHED UP THE FIRST HALF OF YOUR STORY.
WELL, YOU CERTAINLY ABUSE YOUR ASSISTANTS LIKE A PROFESSIONAL.
ACTIN' LIKE YOU KNOW WHAT YOU'RE DOIN'!
TECHNICALLY, I *AM* A PROFESSIONAL.
AND I PAID THEM A REASONABLE SALARY FOR THEIR WORK.
SO DON'T BITCH AT ME ABOUT IT.
HM SO...
WHEN DOES IT RUN?
THE ISSUE THAT COMES OUT THIS MONTH.
THE 25TH.
HMMM...
LOOK, NONE OF THAT MATTERS!
HUH ?!
...
HEE HEE HEE
YOUR COMIC-FEST PIECE!
I DON'T CARE IF YOU STILL NEED TO WORK ON THE SECOND HALF OF YOUR STORY!
YOU BETTER NOT FLAKE OUT ON YOUR BIT FOR OUR ZINE!!

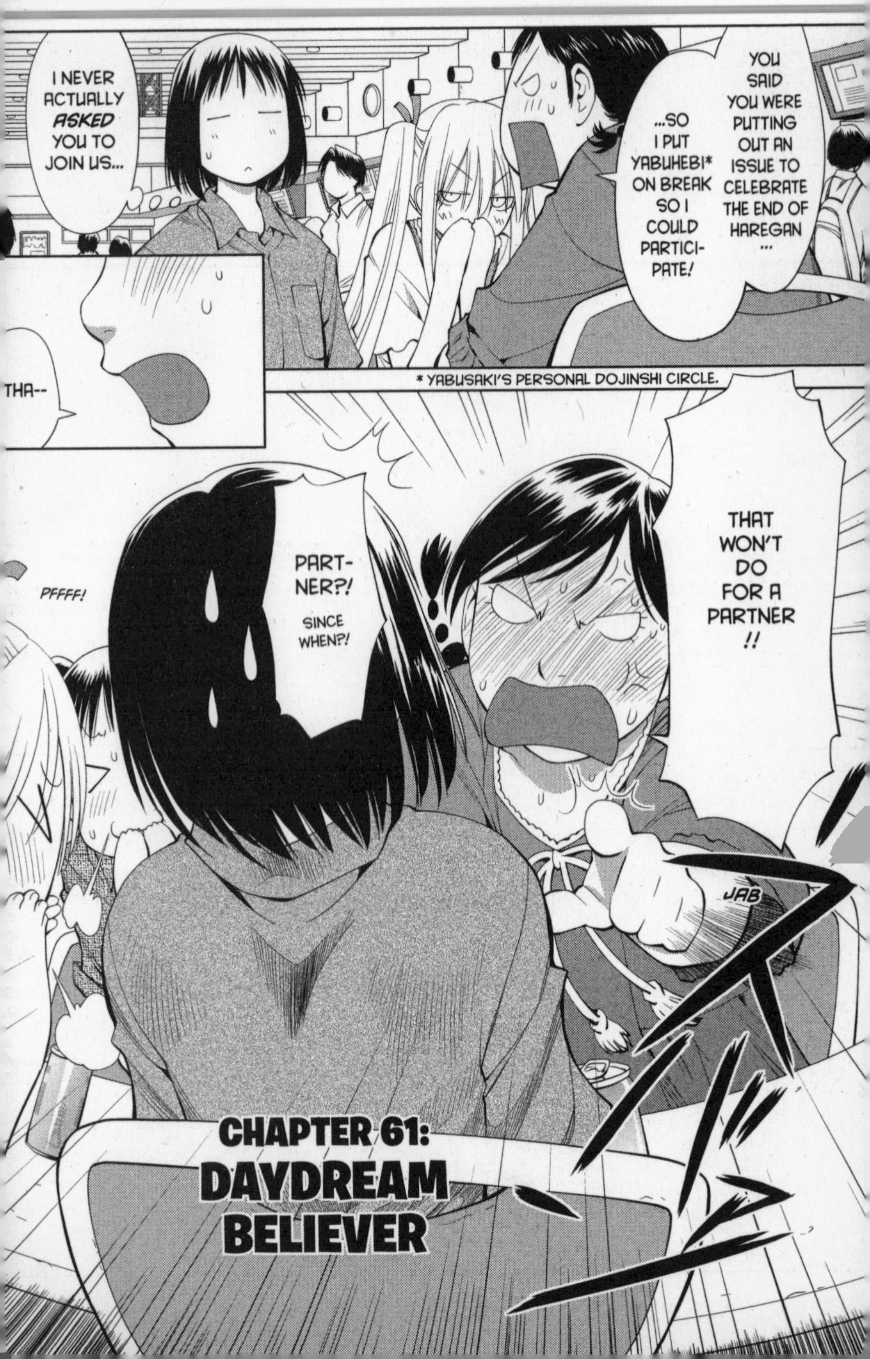
YOU SAID YOU WERE PUTTING OUT AN ISSUE TO CELEBRATE THE END OF HAREGAN ...
...SO I PUT YABUHEBI* ON BREAK SO I COULD PARTICI-PATE!
I NEVER ACTUALLY *ASKED* YOU TO JOIN US...
* YABUSAKI'S PERSONAL DOJINSHI CIRCLE.
THA--
THAT WON'T DO FOR A PARTNER !!
JAB
PART-NER?!
SINCE WHEN?!
PFFFF!
CHAPTER 61: DAYDREAM BELIEVER

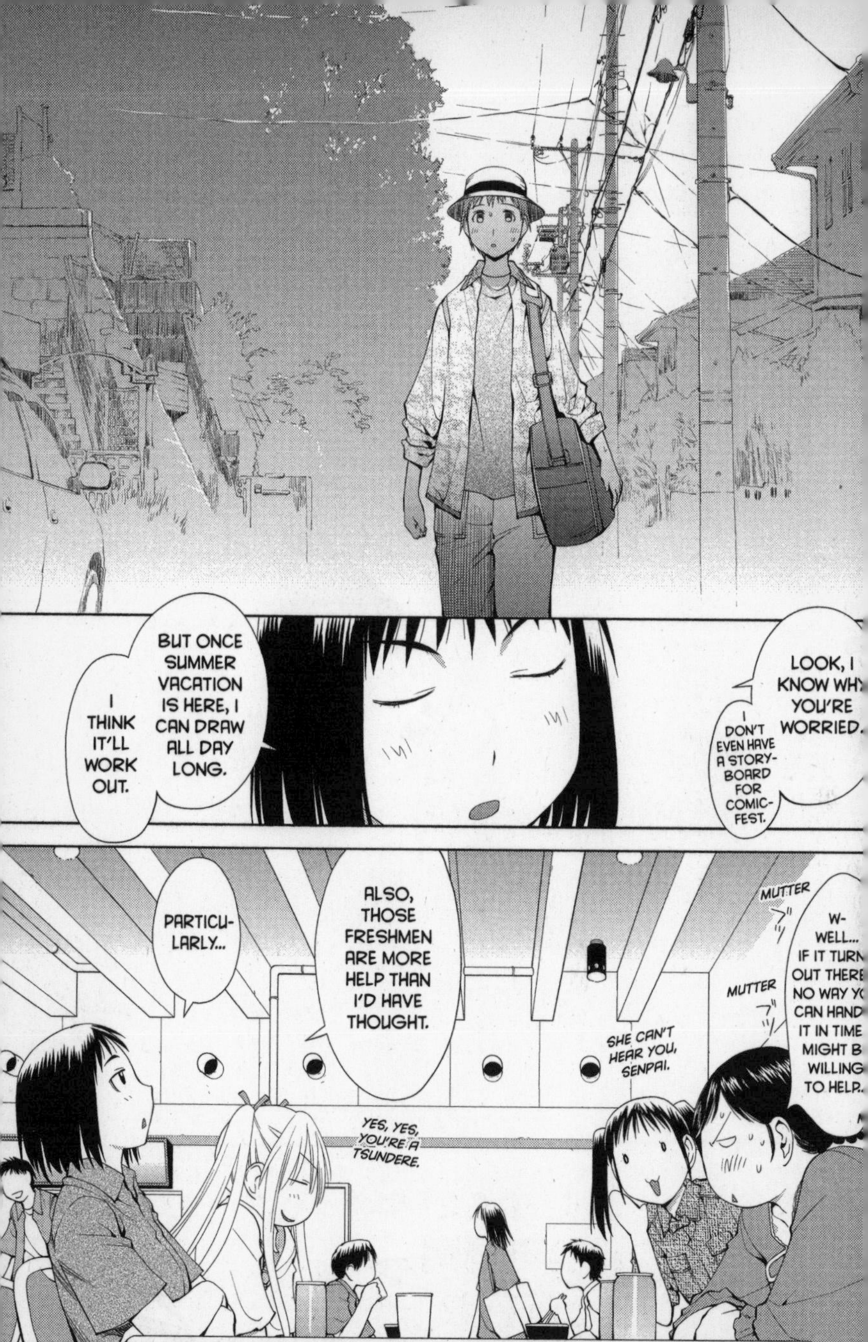
LOOK, I KNOW WHY YOU'RE WORRIED.
I DON'T EVEN HAVE A STORY-BOARD FOR COMIC-FEST.
BUT ONCE SUMMER VACATION IS HERE, I CAN DRAW ALL DAY LONG.
I THINK IT'LL WORK OUT.
W-WELL... IF IT TURN OUT THERE NO WAY Y CAN HAND IT IN TIME MIGHT B WILLING TO HELP...
MUTTER
MUTTER
SHE CAN'T HEAR YOU, SENPAI.
ALSO, THOSE FRESHMEN ARE MORE HELP THAN I'D HAVE THOUGHT.
PARTICU-LARLY...
YES, YES, YOU'RE A TSUNDERE.

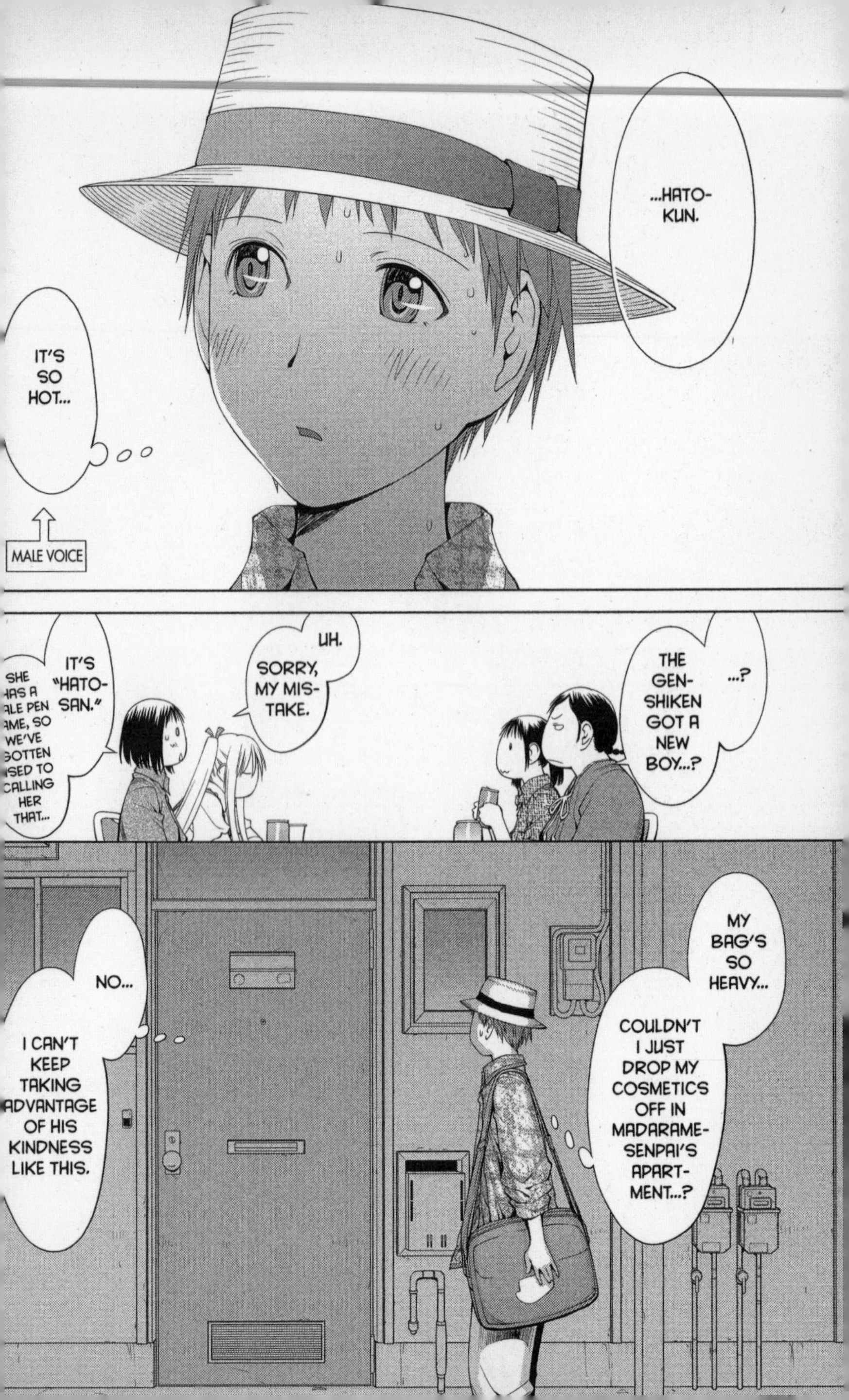
...HATO-KUN.
IT'S SO HOT...
MALE VOICE
...?
THE GEN-SHIKEN GOT A NEW BOY...?
UH. SORRY, MY MIS-TAKE.
IT'S "HATO-SAN."
SHE HAS A ALE PEN AME, SO WE'VE GOTTEN SED TO CALLING HER THAT...
MY BAG'S SO HEAVY...
COULDN'T I JUST DROP MY COSMETICS OFF IN MADARAME-SENPAI'S APART-MENT...?
NO...
I CAN'T KEEP TAKING DVANTAGE OF HIS KINDNESS LIKE THIS.

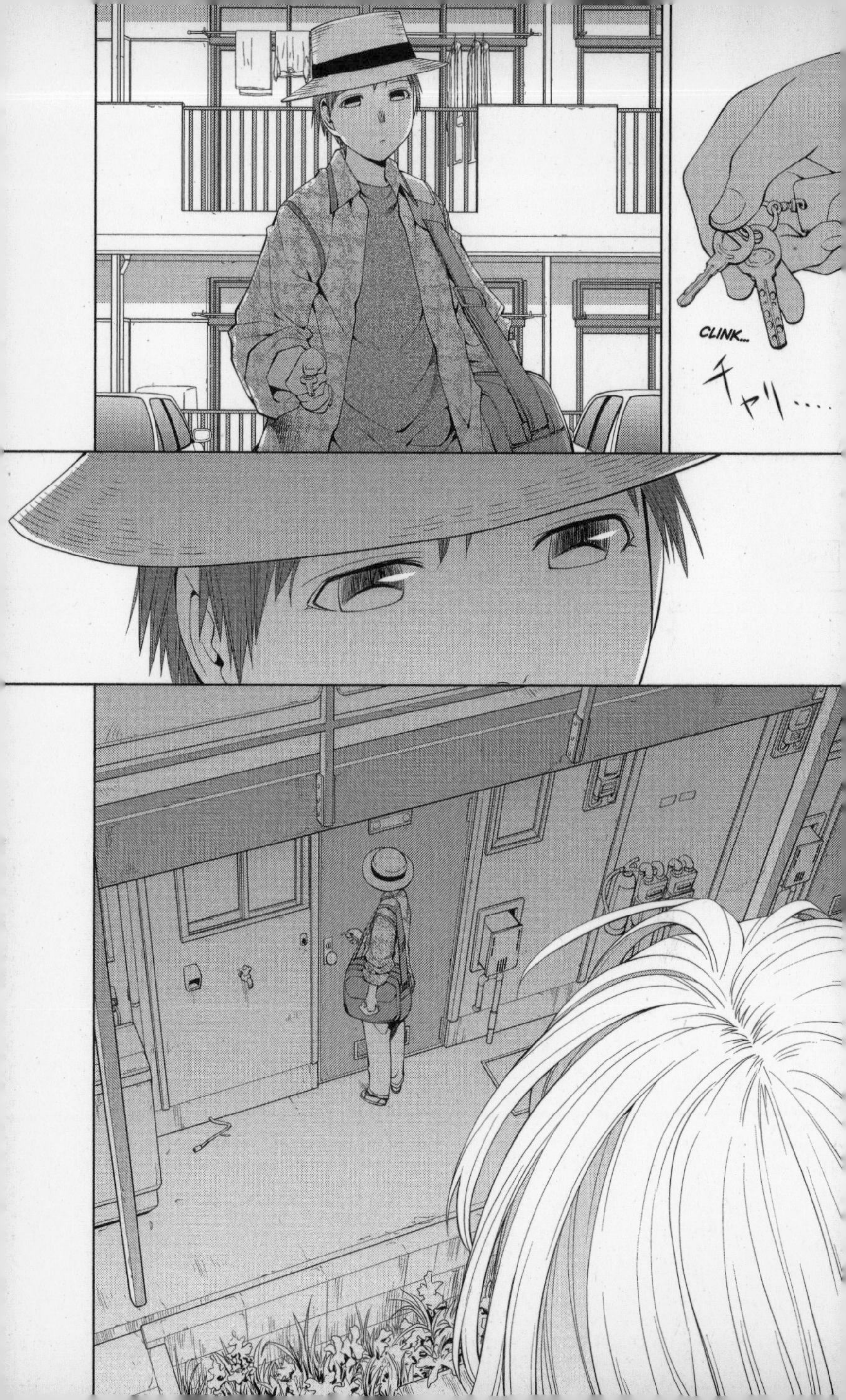
CLINK...
チャリ....

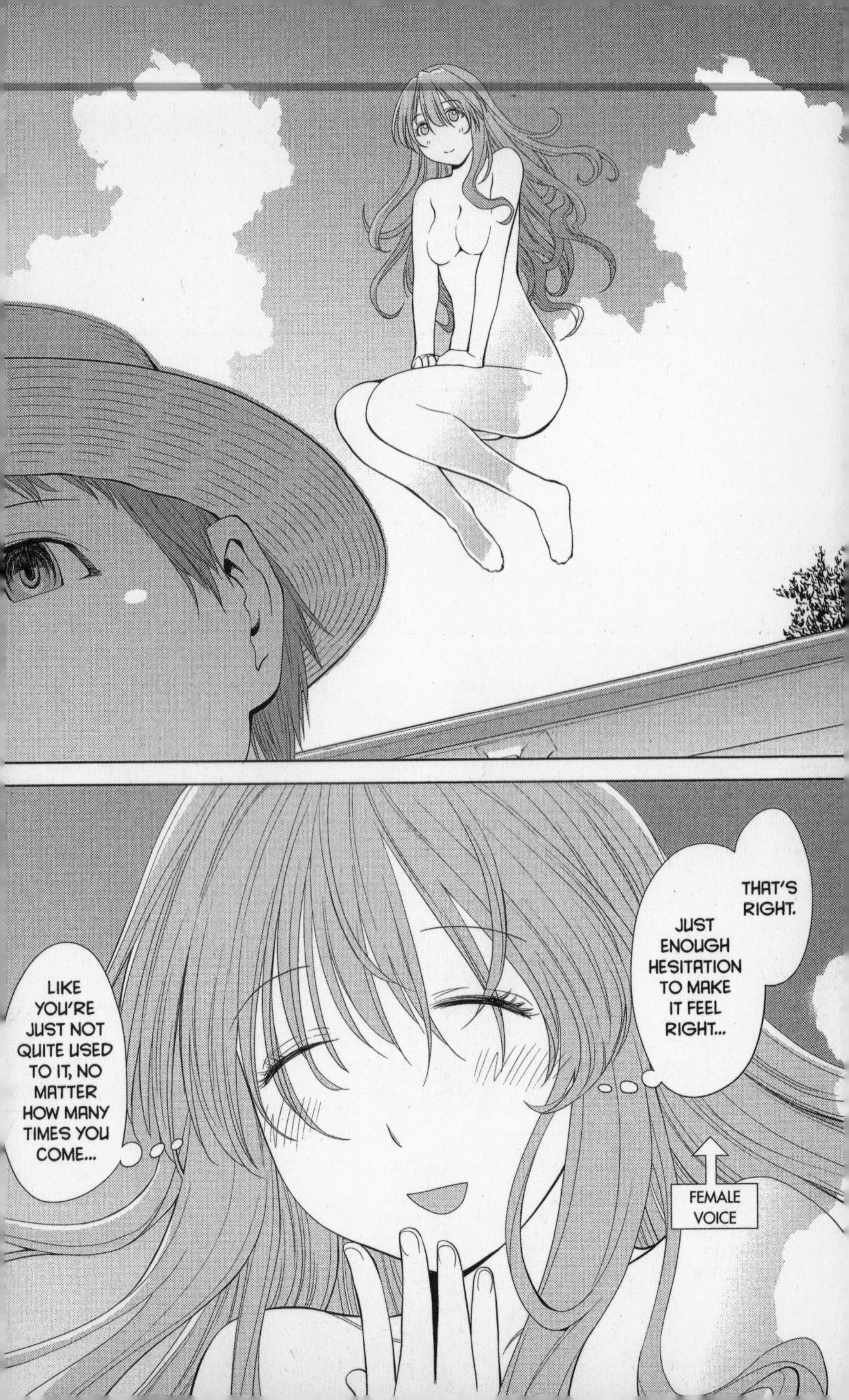
THAT'S RIGHT. JUST ENOUGH HESITATION TO MAKE IT FEEL RIGHT...
LIKE YOU'RE JUST NOT QUITE USED TO IT, NO MATTER HOW MANY TIMES YOU COME...
FEMALE VOICE

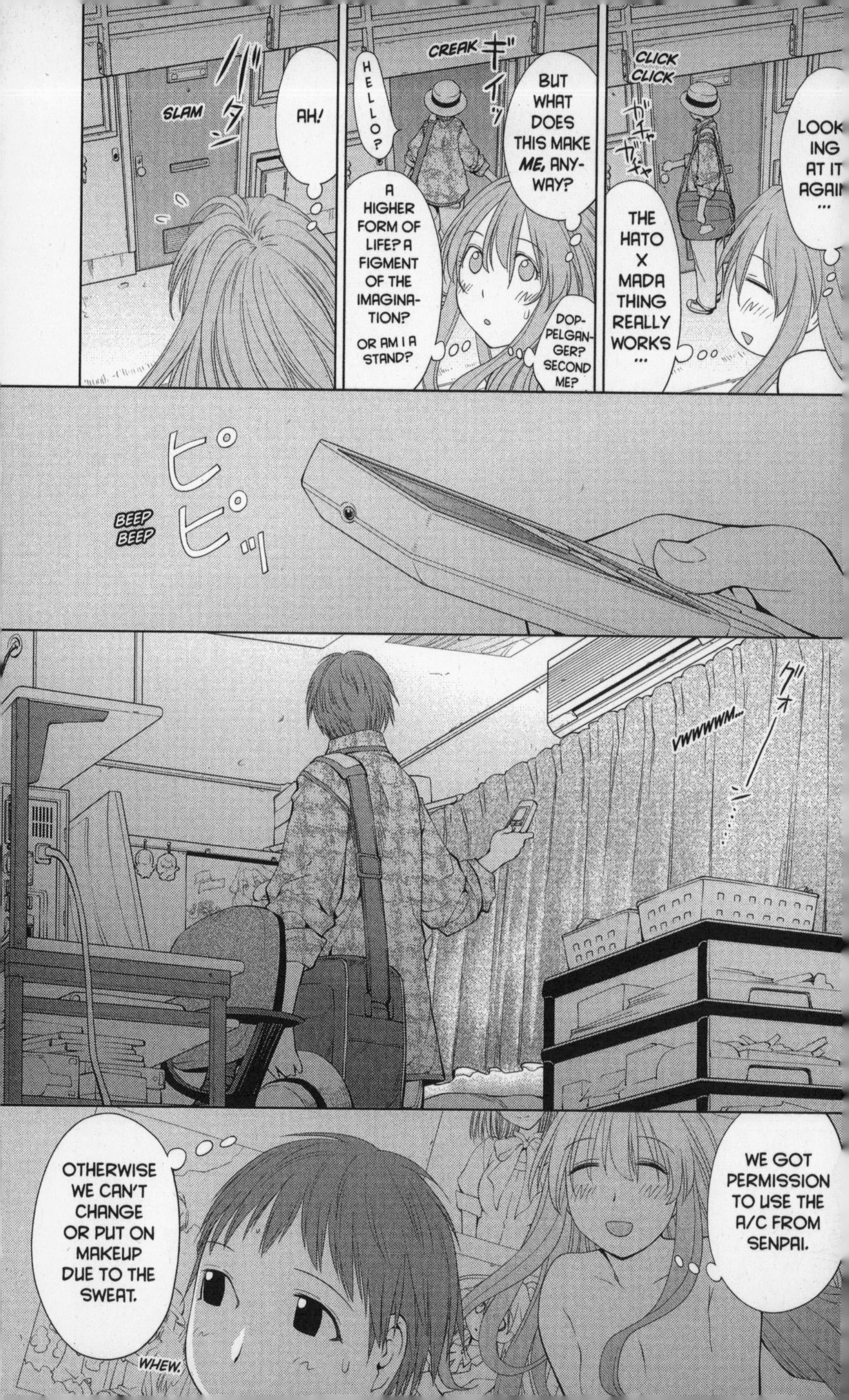

CLICK CLICK
ガチャガチャ
LOOKING AT IT AGAIN...
THE HATO X MADA THING REALLY WORKS...
CREAK
ギイッ
BUT WHAT DOES THIS MAKE *ME*, ANYWAY?
HELLO?
DOP-PELGANGER? SECOND ME?
A HIGHER FORM OF LIFE? A FIGMENT OF THE IMAGINATION?
OR AM I A STAND?
バタン
SLAM
AH!
ピピッ
BEEP BEEP
グオー
VWWWWM...
WE GOT PERMISSION TO USE THE A/C FROM SENPAI.
OTHERWISE WE CAN'T CHANGE OR PUT ON MAKEUP DUE TO THE SWEAT.
WHEW.

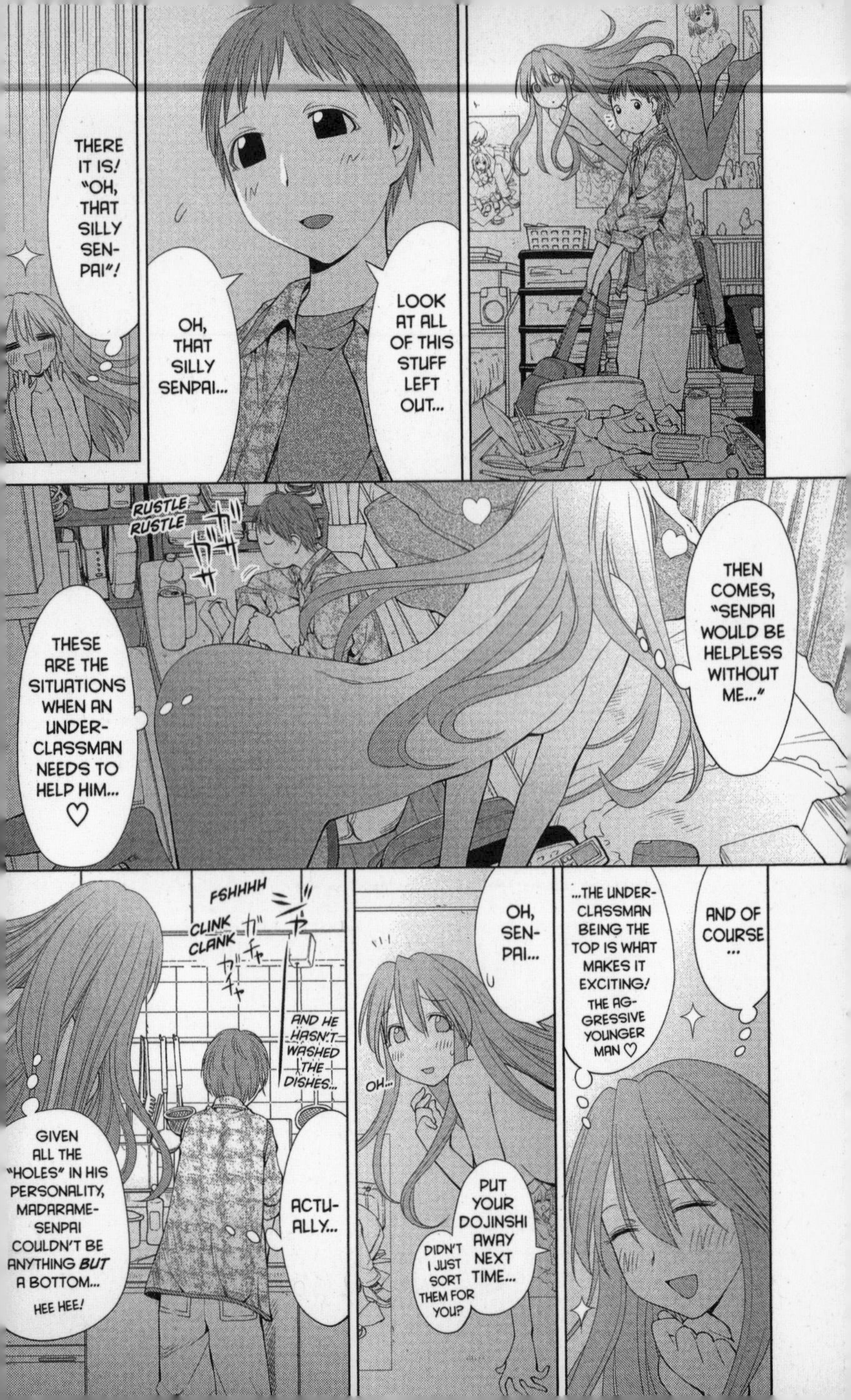
LOOK AT ALL OF THIS STUFF LEFT OUT...
OH, THAT SILLY SENPAI...
THERE IT IS! "OH, THAT SILLY SENPAI"!
RUSTLE RUSTLE
THEN COMES, "SENPAI WOULD BE HELPLESS WITHOUT ME..."
THESE ARE THE SITUATIONS WHEN AN UNDERCLASSMAN NEEDS TO HELP HIM... ♡
AND OF COURSE...
...THE UNDERCLASSMAN BEING THE TOP IS WHAT MAKES IT EXCITING! THE AGGRESSIVE YOUNGER MAN ♡
OH, SENPAI...
OH...
PUT YOUR DOJINSHI AWAY NEXT TIME...
DIDN'T I JUST SORT THEM FOR YOU?
FSHHHH
CLINK CLANK
AND HE HASN'T WASHED THE DISHES...
ACTUALLY...
GIVEN ALL THE "HOLES" IN HIS PERSONALITY, MADARAME-SENPAI COULDN'T BE ANYTHING *BUT* A BOTTOM... HEE HEE!

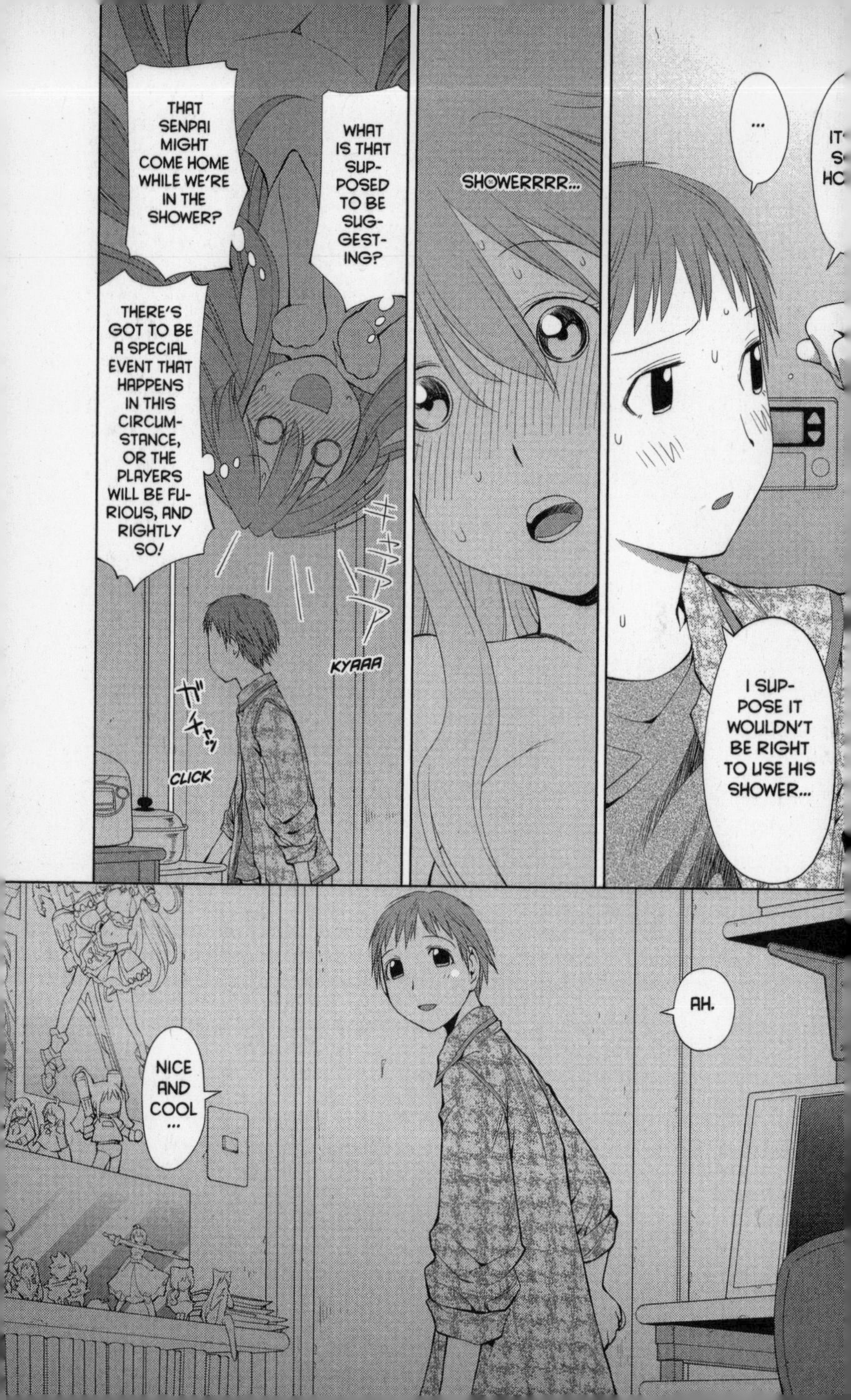
...
I SUPPOSE IT WOULDN'T BE RIGHT TO USE HIS SHOWER...
SHOWERRRR...
WHAT IS THAT SUPPOSED TO BE SUGGESTING?
THAT SENPAI MIGHT COME HOME WHILE WE'RE IN THE SHOWER?
THERE'S GOT TO BE A SPECIAL EVENT THAT HAPPENS IN THIS CIRCUMSTANCE, OR THE PLAYERS WILL BE FURIOUS, AND RIGHTLY SO!
KYAAA
CLICK
AH.
NICE AND COOL...

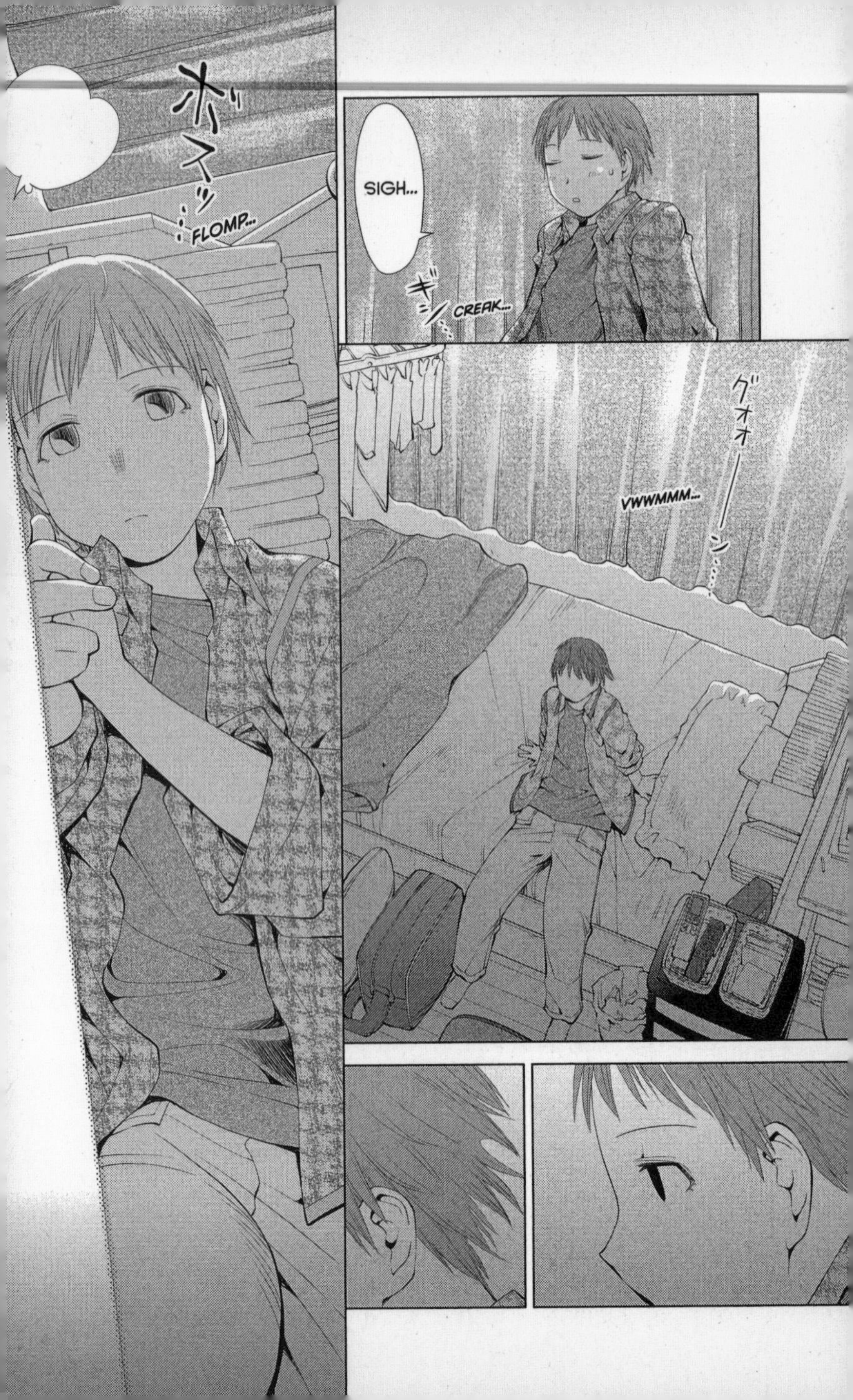
SIGH...
ギシ…
CREAK...
グオオーーン…
VWWMMM...
ボスッ…
FLOMP...

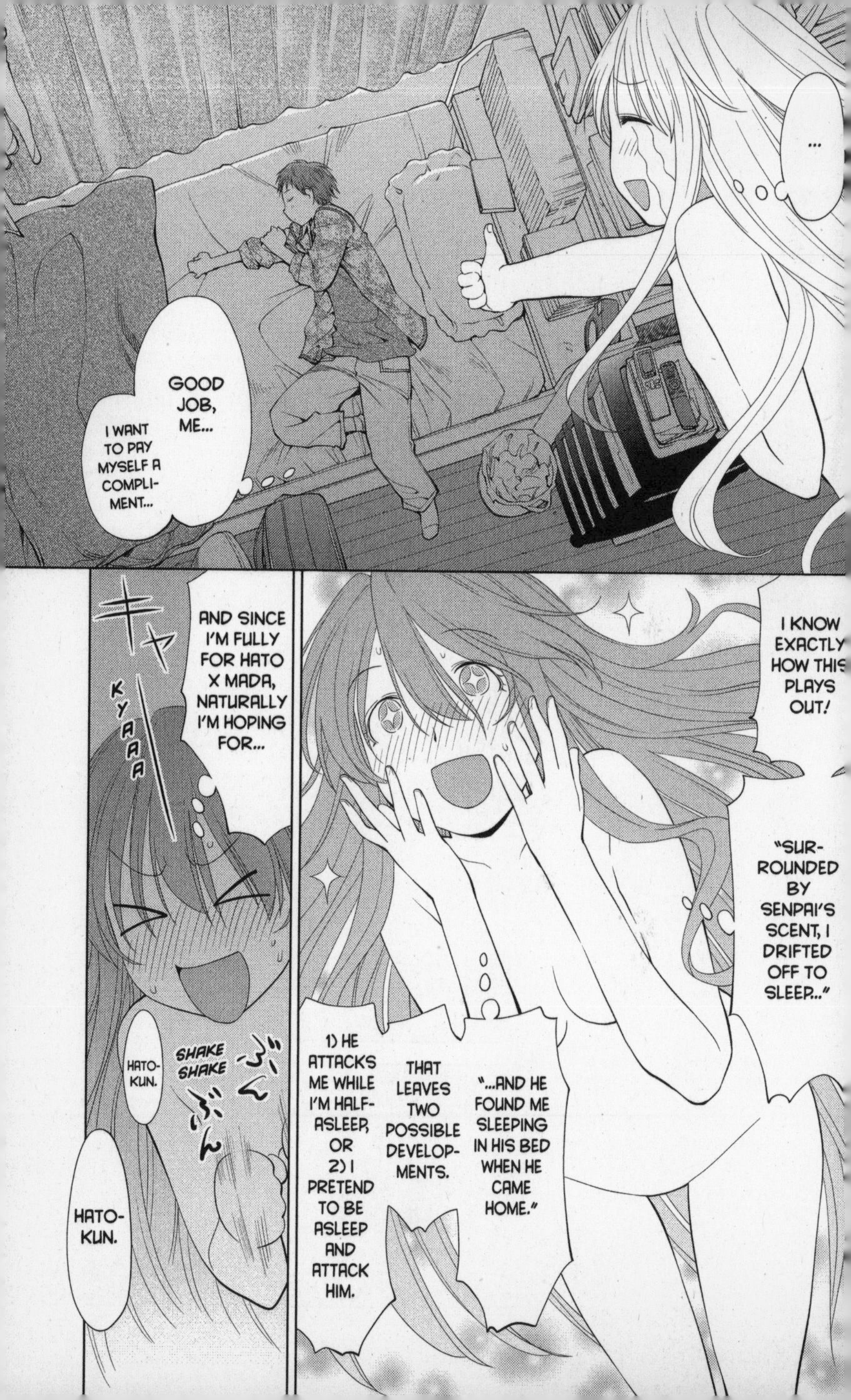
...
GOOD JOB, ME...
I WANT TO PAY MYSELF A COMPLIMENT...
I KNOW EXACTLY HOW THIS PLAYS OUT!
"SURROUNDED BY SENPAI'S SCENT, I DRIFTED OFF TO SLEEP..."
"...AND HE FOUND ME SLEEPING IN HIS BED WHEN HE CAME HOME."
THAT LEAVES TWO POSSIBLE DEVELOPMENTS.
1) HE ATTACKS ME WHILE I'M HALF-ASLEEP, OR 2) I PRETEND TO BE ASLEEP AND ATTACK HIM.
AND SINCE I'M FULLY FOR HATO X MADA, NATURALLY I'M HOPING FOR...
KYAAA
HATO-KUN.
SHAKE SHAKE
HATO-KUN.

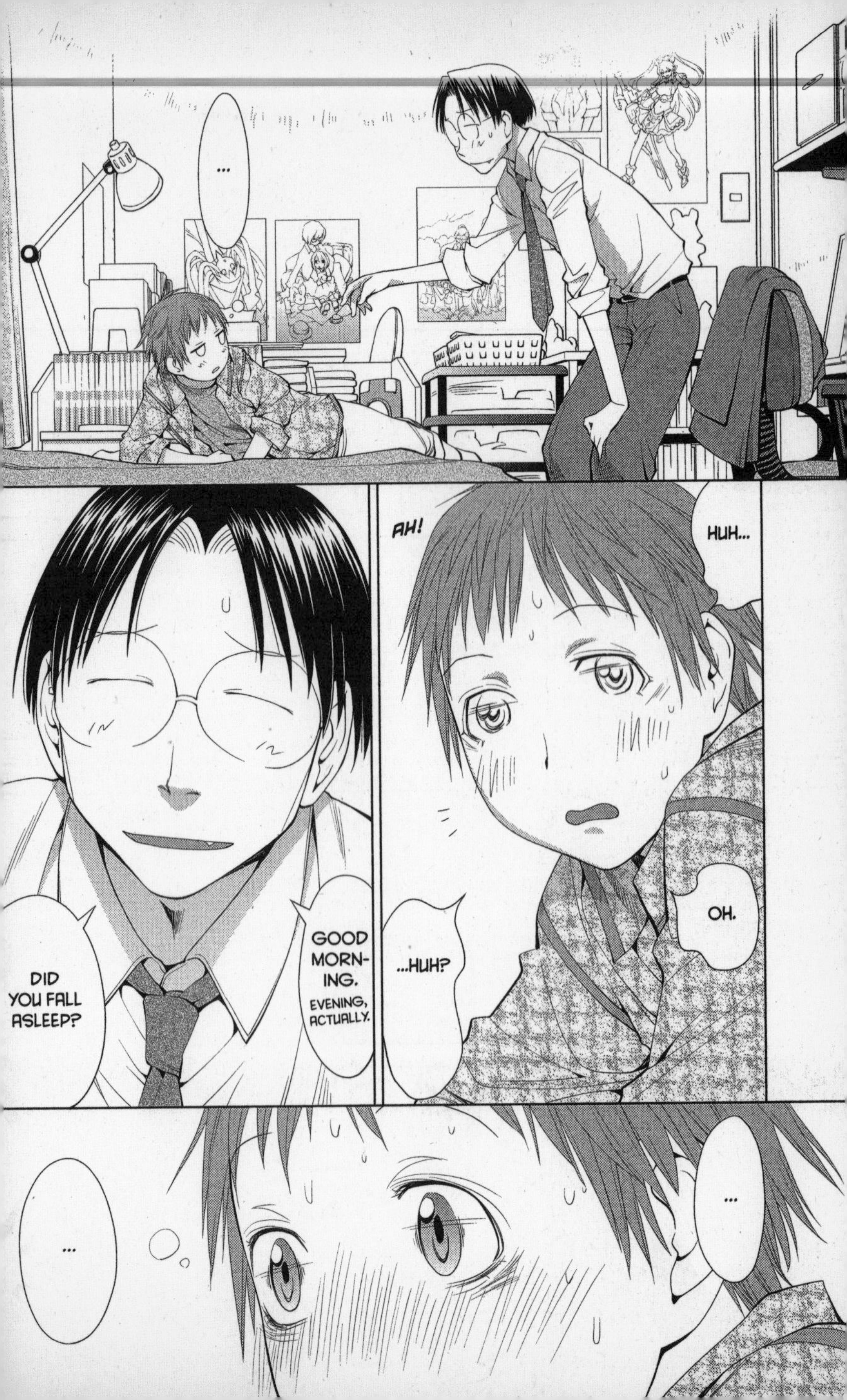
...
HUH...
AH!
OH.
...HUH?
GOOD MORN-ING.
EVENING, ACTUALLY.
DID YOU FALL ASLEEP?
...
...

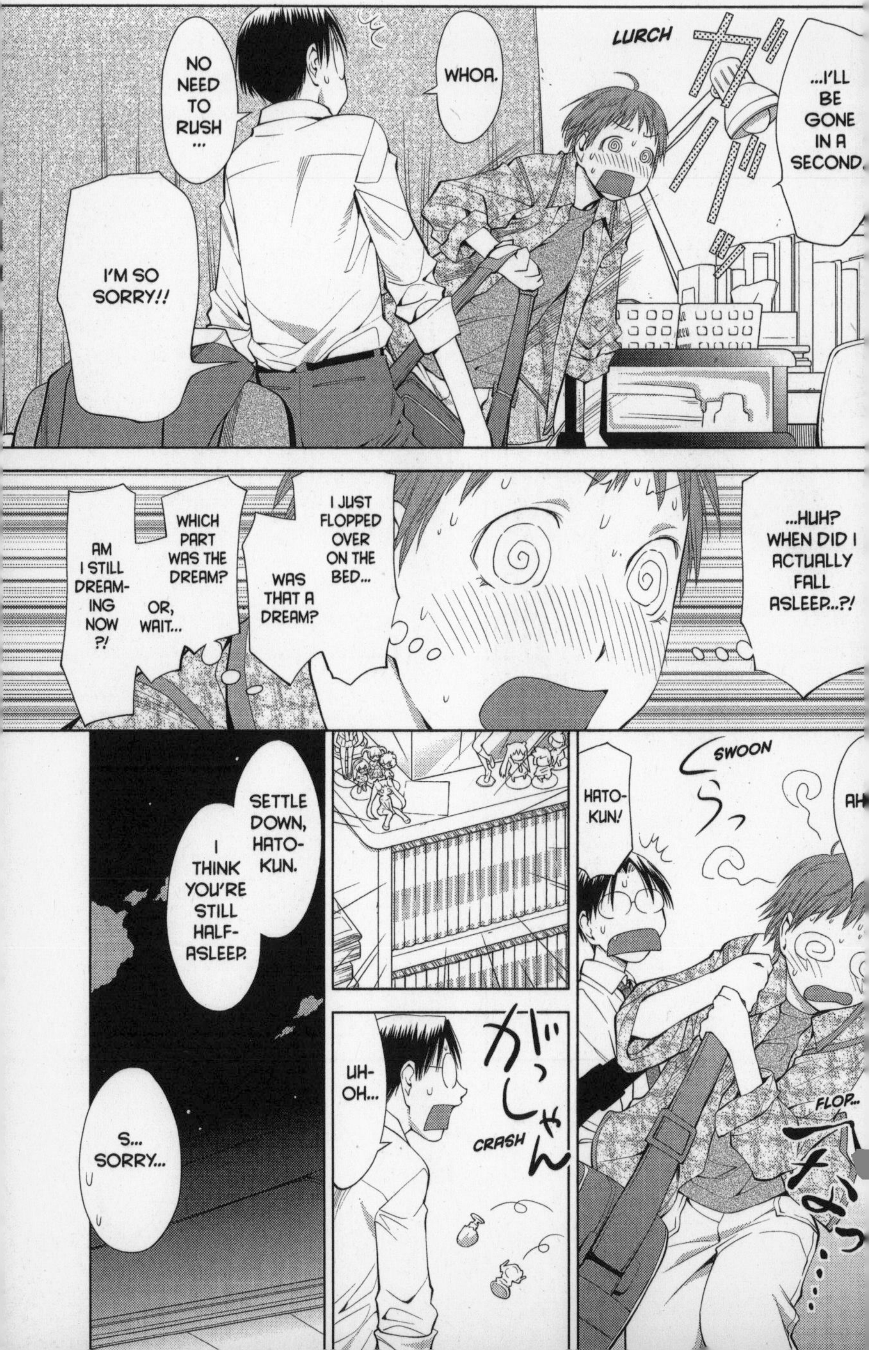
...I'LL BE GONE IN A SECOND.
LURCH
WHOA.
NO NEED TO RUSH...
I'M SO SORRY!!
...HUH? WHEN DID I ACTUALLY FALL ASLEEP...?!
I JUST FLOPPED OVER ON THE BED...
WAS THAT A DREAM?
WHICH PART WAS THE DREAM?
OR, WAIT...
AM I STILL DREAMING NOW?!
AH
SWOON
HATO-KUN!
FLOP...
CRASH
UH-OH...
SETTLE DOWN, HATO-KUN.
I THINK YOU'RE STILL HALF-ASLEEP.
S... SORRY...

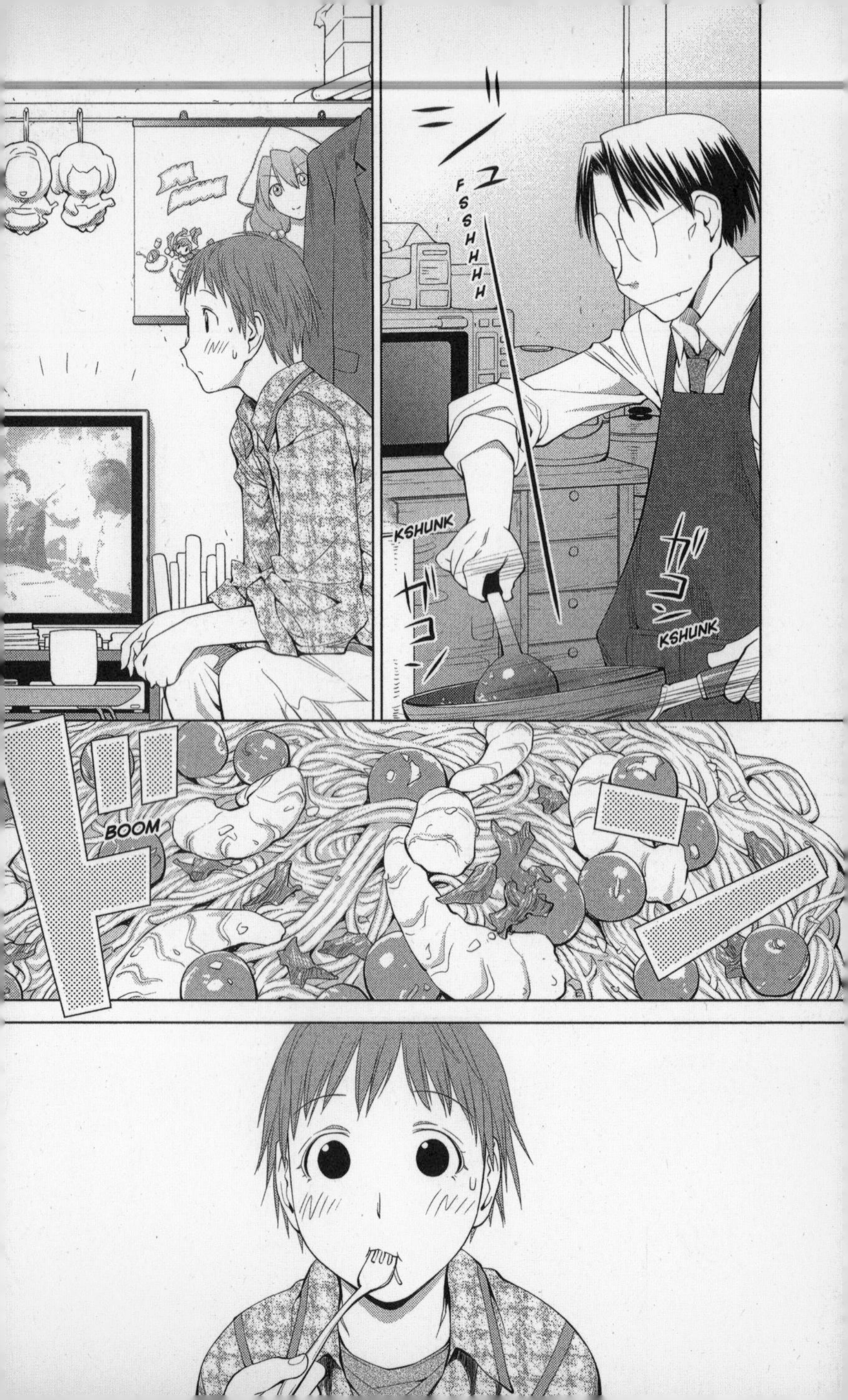
FSSHHHH
KSHUNK
KSHUNK
BOOM

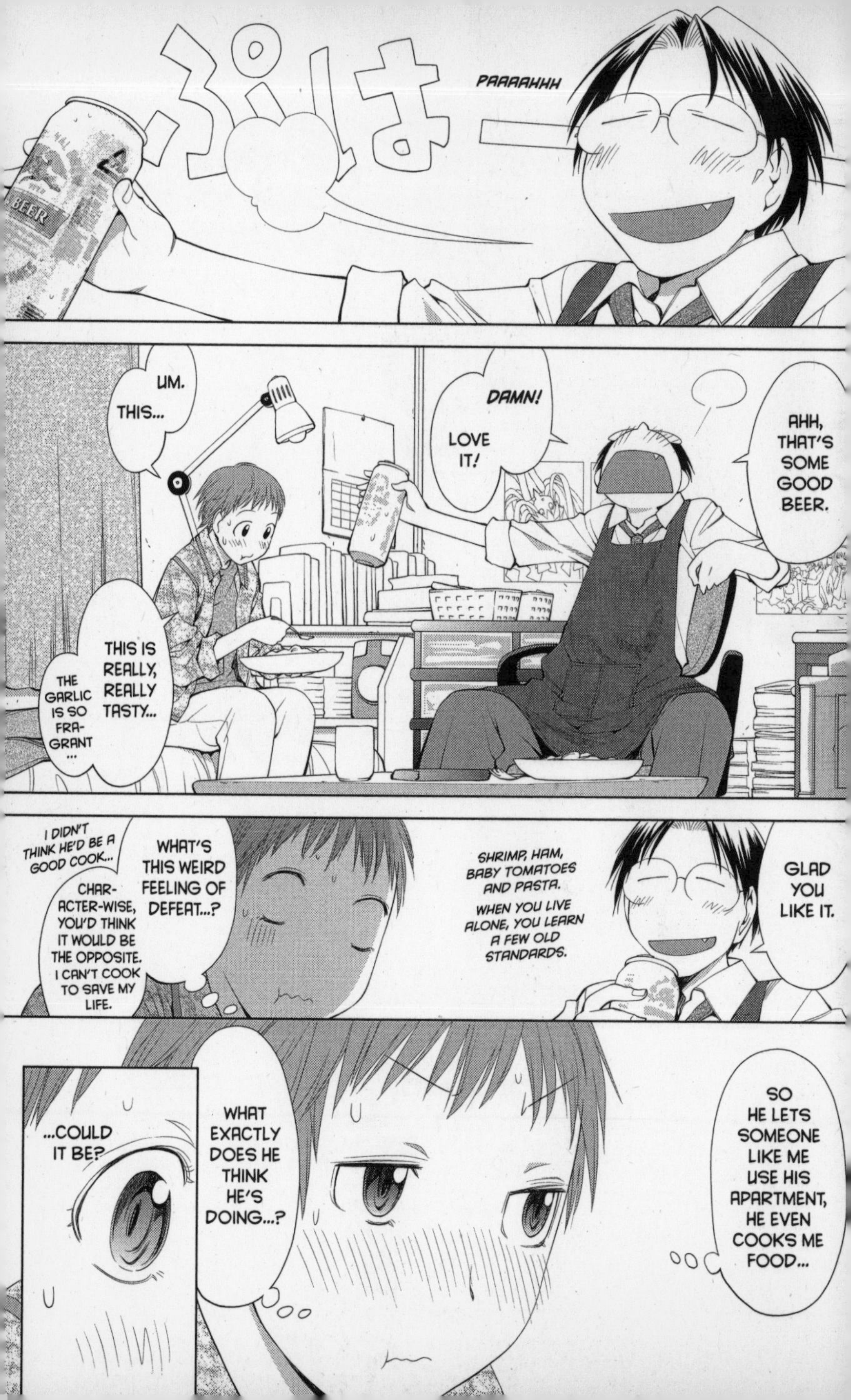
ぷはー
PAAAAHHH
AHH, THAT'S SOME GOOD BEER.
DAMN!
LOVE IT!
UM. THIS...
THIS IS REALLY, REALLY TASTY...
THE GARLIC IS SO FRA-GRANT ...
GLAD YOU LIKE IT.
SHRIMP, HAM, BABY TOMATOES AND PASTA.
WHEN YOU LIVE ALONE, YOU LEARN A FEW OLD STANDARDS.
WHAT'S THIS WEIRD FEELING OF DEFEAT...?
I DIDN'T THINK HE'D BE A GOOD COOK...
CHAR-ACTER-WISE, YOU'D THINK IT WOULD BE THE OPPOSITE. I CAN'T COOK TO SAVE MY LIFE.
SO HE LETS SOMEONE LIKE ME USE HIS APARTMENT, HE EVEN COOKS ME FOOD...
WHAT EXACTLY DOES HE THINK HE'S DOING...?
...COULD IT BE?

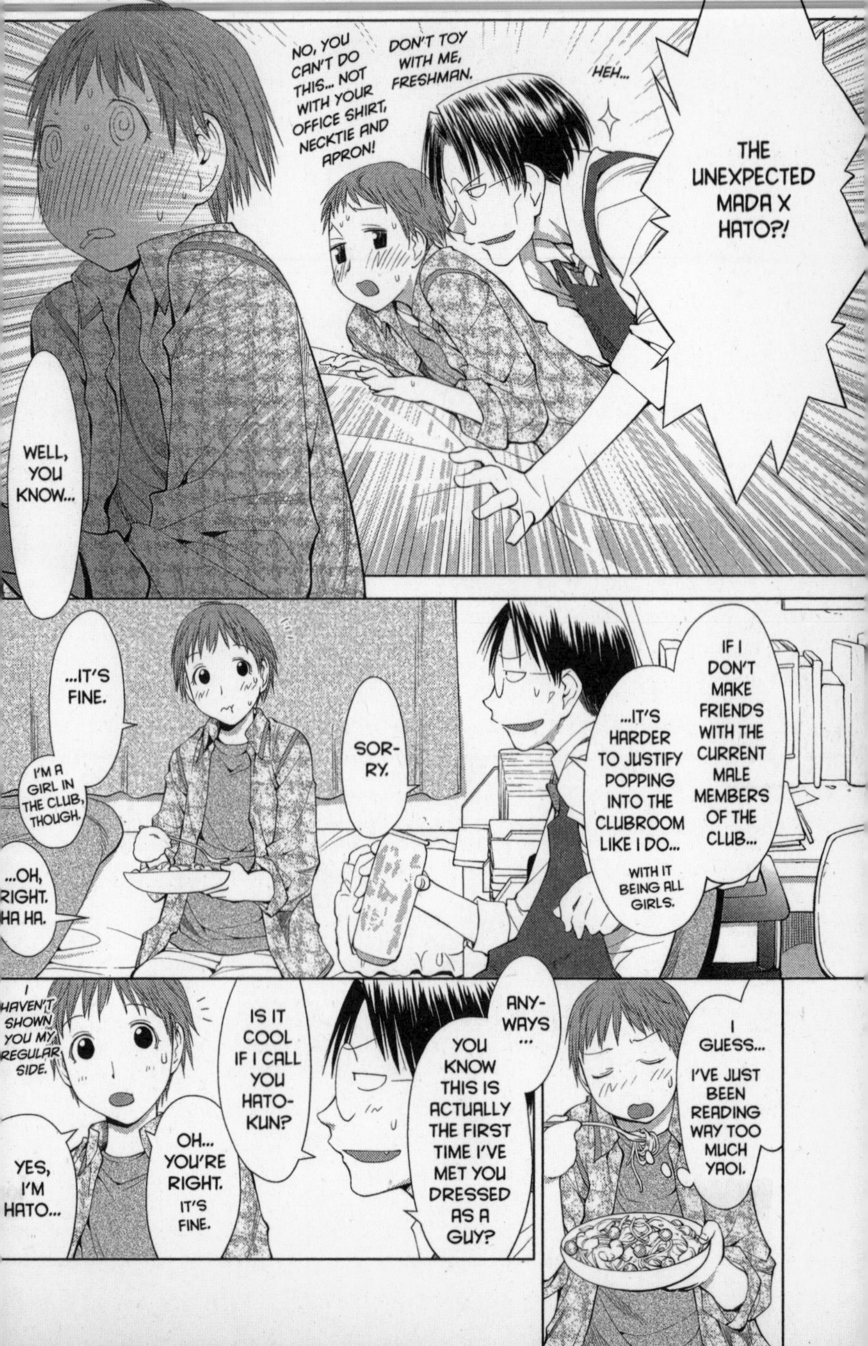
THE UNEXPECTED MADA X HATO?!
HEH...
DON'T TOY WITH ME, FRESHMAN.
NO, YOU CAN'T DO THIS... NOT WITH YOUR OFFICE SHIRT, NECKTIE AND APRON!
WELL, YOU KNOW...
IF I DON'T MAKE FRIENDS WITH THE CURRENT MALE MEMBERS OF THE CLUB...
...IT'S HARDER TO JUSTIFY POPPING INTO THE CLUBROOM LIKE I DO...
WITH IT BEING ALL GIRLS.
SORRY.
...IT'S FINE.
I'M A GIRL IN THE CLUB, THOUGH.
...OH, RIGHT. HA HA.
I GUESS...
I'VE JUST BEEN READING WAY TOO MUCH YAOI.
ANYWAYS...
YOU KNOW THIS IS ACTUALLY THE FIRST TIME I'VE MET YOU DRESSED AS A GUY?
IS IT COOL IF I CALL YOU HATO-KUN?
I HAVEN'T SHOWN YOU MY REGULAR SIDE.
OH... YOU'RE RIGHT. IT'S FINE.
YES, I'M HATO...

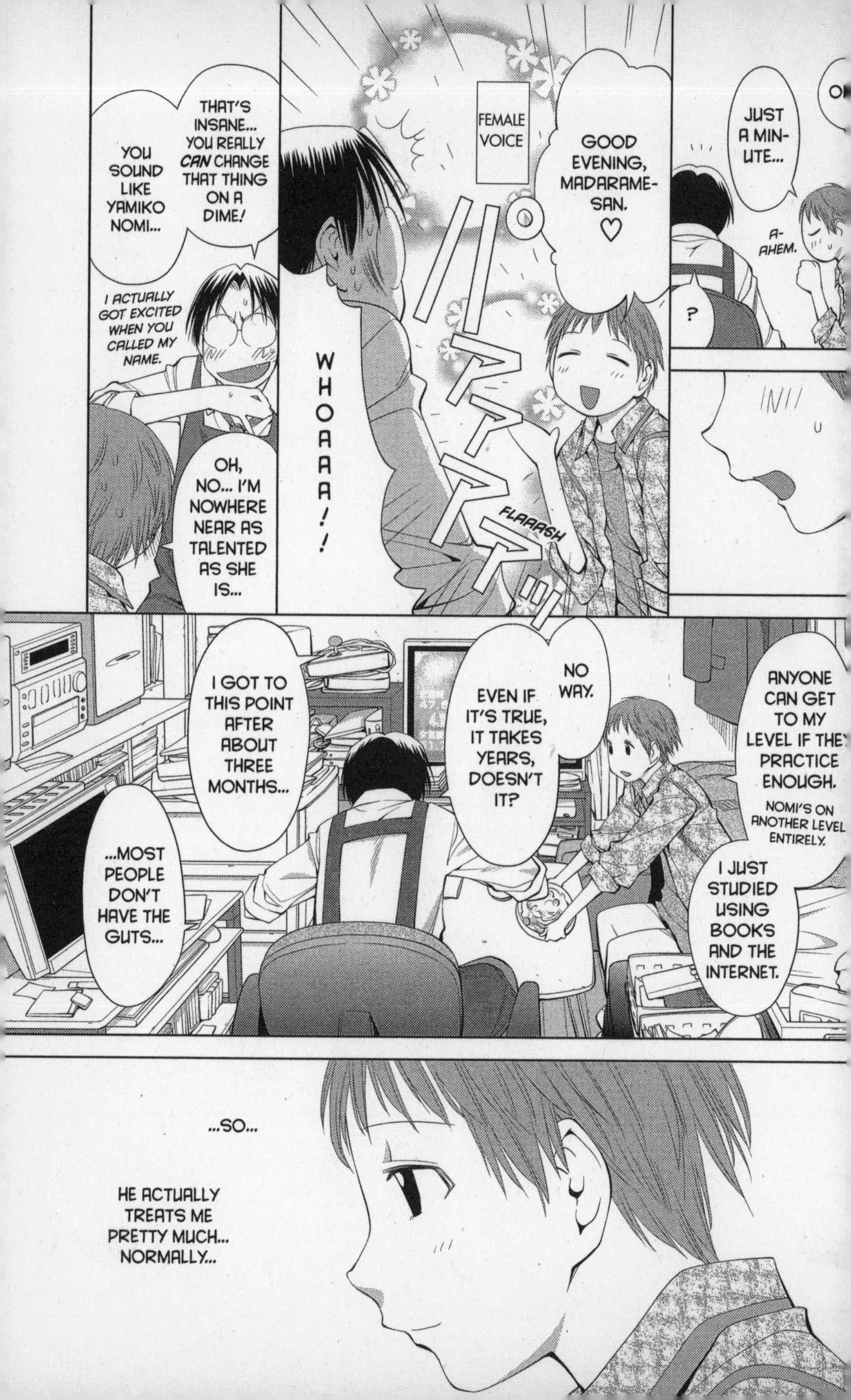
JUST A MIN-UTE...
A-AHEM.
?
FEMALE VOICE
GOOD EVENING, MADARAME-SAN. ♡
WHOAAAA!!
FLAAASH
THAT'S INSANE... YOU REALLY CAN CHANGE THAT THING ON A DIME!
YOU SOUND LIKE YAMIKO NOMI...
I ACTUALLY GOT EXCITED WHEN YOU CALLED MY NAME.
OH, NO... I'M NOWHERE NEAR AS TALENTED AS SHE IS...
ANYONE CAN GET TO MY LEVEL IF THE PRACTICE ENOUGH.
NOMI'S ON ANOTHER LEVEL ENTIRELY.
I JUST STUDIED USING BOOKS AND THE INTERNET.
NO WAY.
EVEN IF IT'S TRUE, IT TAKES YEARS, DOESN'T IT?
I GOT TO THIS POINT AFTER ABOUT THREE MONTHS...
...MOST PEOPLE DON'T HAVE THE GUTS...
...SO...
HE ACTUALLY TREATS ME PRETTY MUCH... NORMALLY...

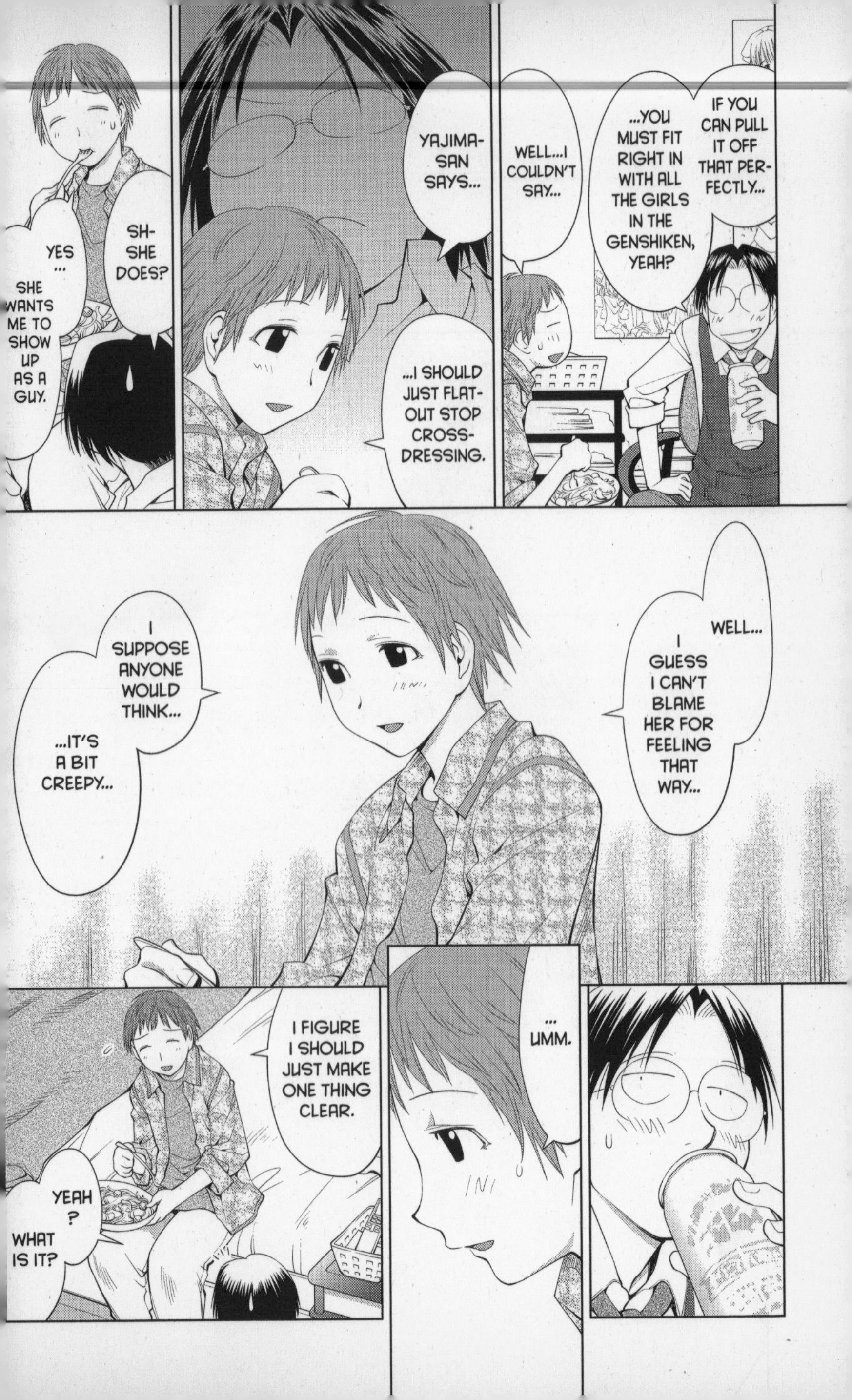
IF YOU CAN PULL IT OFF THAT PERFECTLY...
...YOU MUST FIT RIGHT IN WITH ALL THE GIRLS IN THE GENSHIKEN, YEAH?
WELL...I COULDN'T SAY...
YAJIMA-SAN SAYS...
...I SHOULD JUST FLAT-OUT STOP CROSS-DRESSING.
SH-SHE DOES?
YES... SHE WANTS ME TO SHOW UP AS A GUY.
WELL...
I GUESS I CAN'T BLAME HER FOR FEELING THAT WAY...
I SUPPOSE ANYONE WOULD THINK...
...IT'S A BIT CREEPY...
... UMM.
I FIGURE I SHOULD JUST MAKE ONE THING CLEAR.
YEAH? WHAT IS IT?

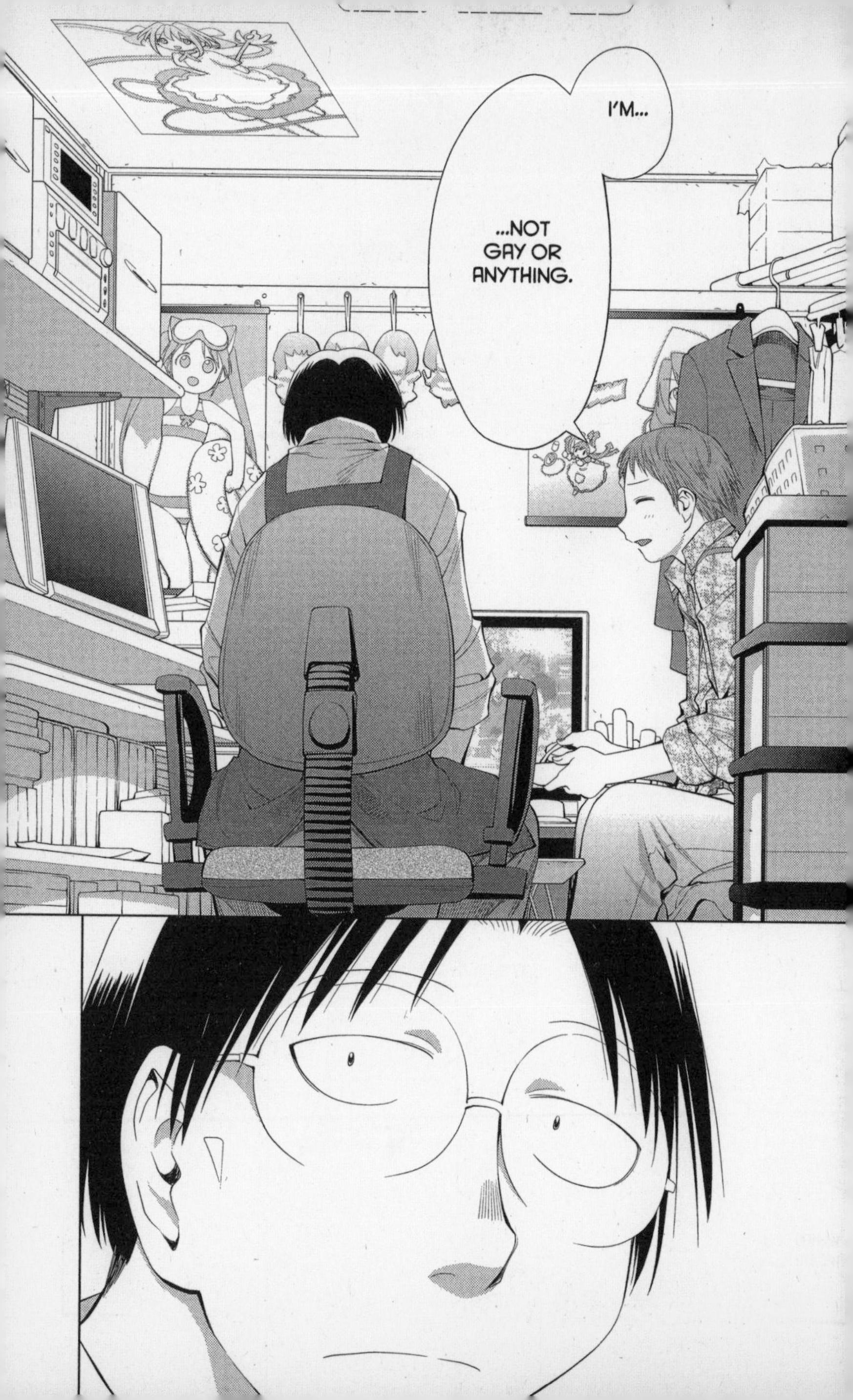
I'M...
...NOT GAY OR ANYTHING.

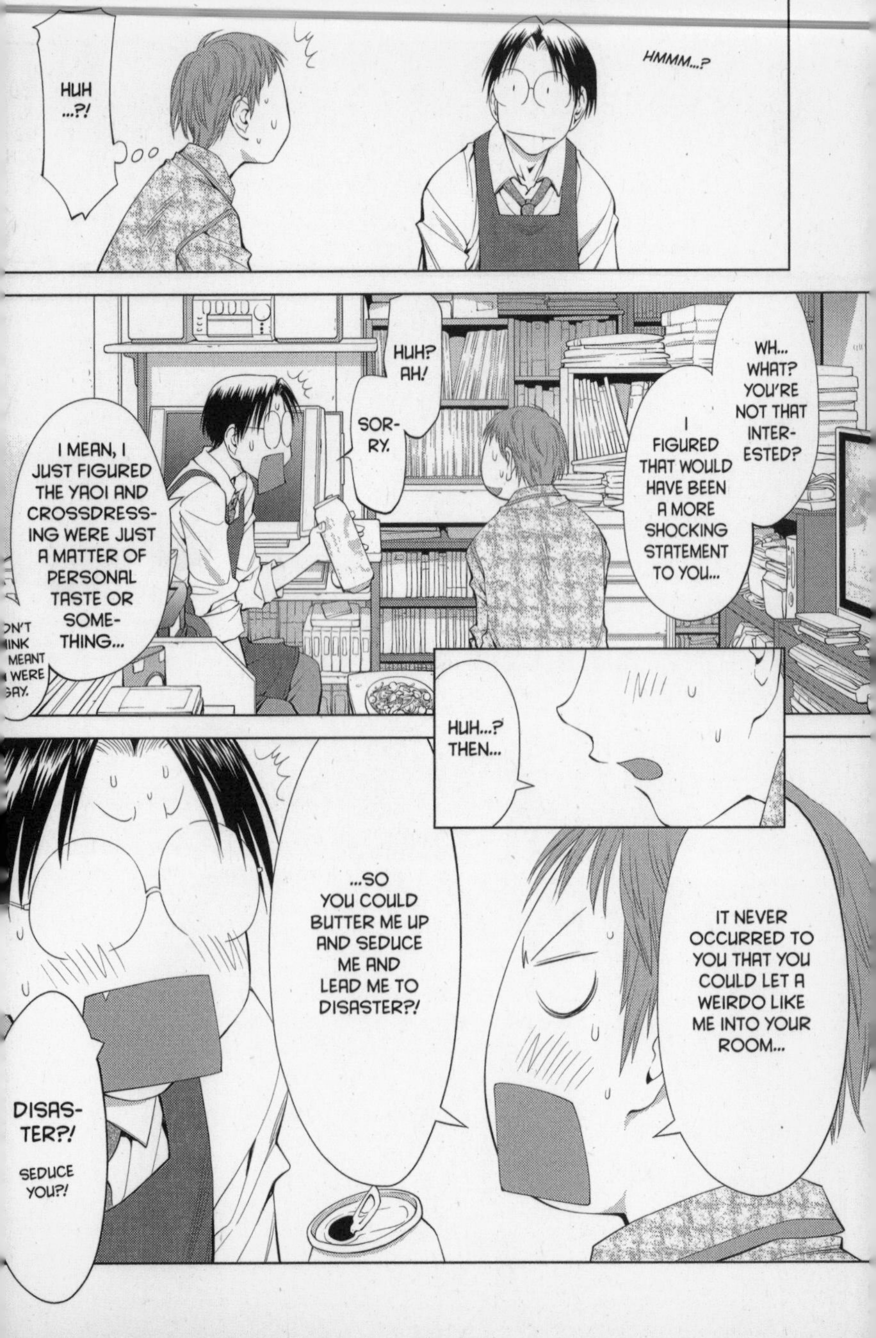
HMMM...?
HUH ...?!
WH... WHAT? YOU'RE NOT THAT INTERESTED?
I FIGURED THAT WOULD HAVE BEEN A MORE SHOCKING STATEMENT TO YOU...
HUH? AH! SORRY.
I MEAN, I JUST FIGURED THE YAOI AND CROSSDRESSING WERE JUST A MATTER OF PERSONAL TASTE OR SOMETHING...
HUH...? THEN...
IT NEVER OCCURRED TO YOU THAT YOU COULD LET A WEIRDO LIKE ME INTO YOUR ROOM...
...SO YOU COULD BUTTER ME UP AND SEDUCE ME AND LEAD ME TO DISASTER?!
DISASTER?!
SEDUCE YOU?!

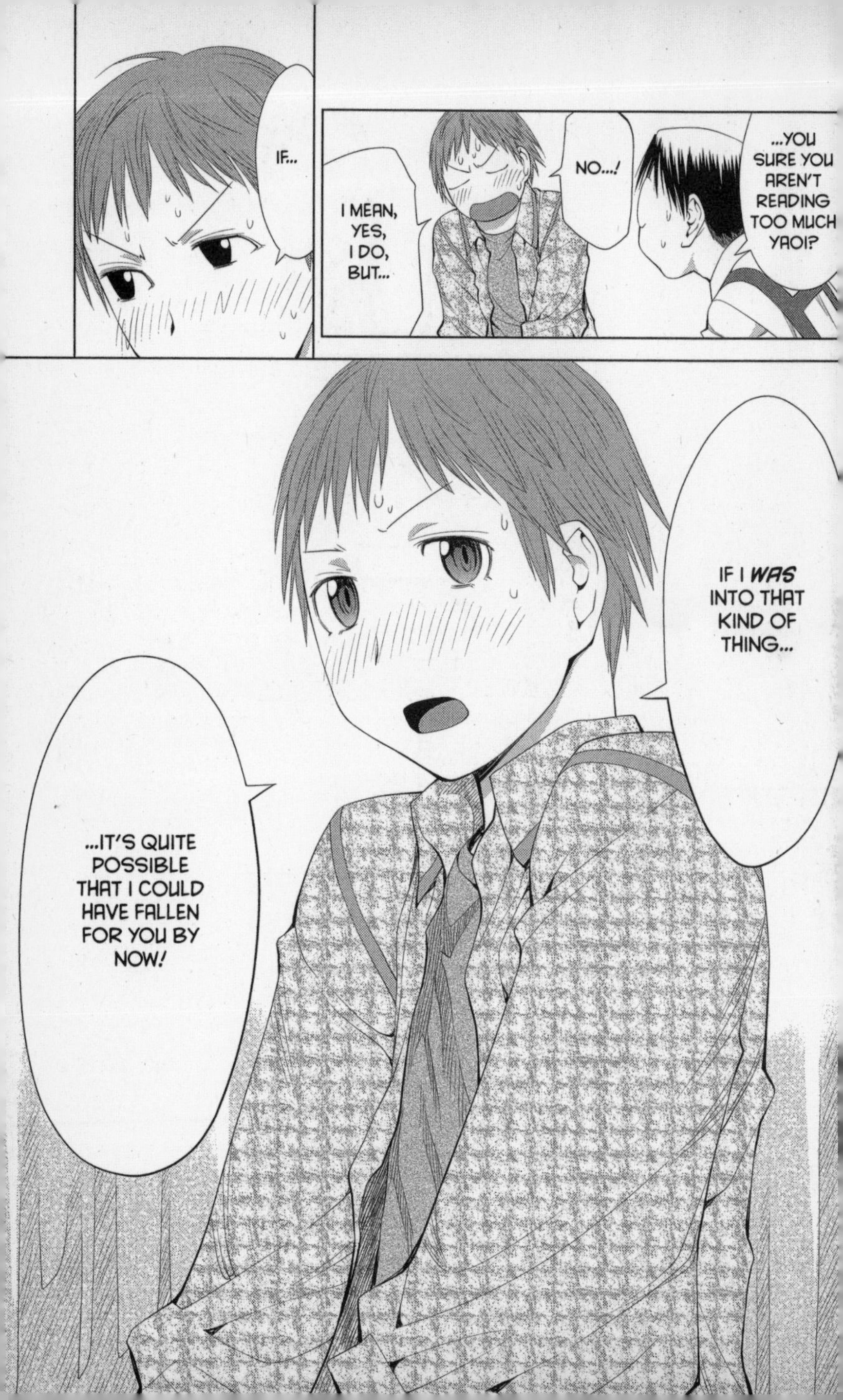
...YOU SURE YOU AREN'T READING TOO MUCH YAOI?
NO...!
I MEAN, YES, I DO, BUT...
IF...
IF I ***WAS*** INTO THAT KIND OF THING...
...IT'S QUITE POSSIBLE THAT I COULD HAVE FALLEN FOR YOU BY NOW!

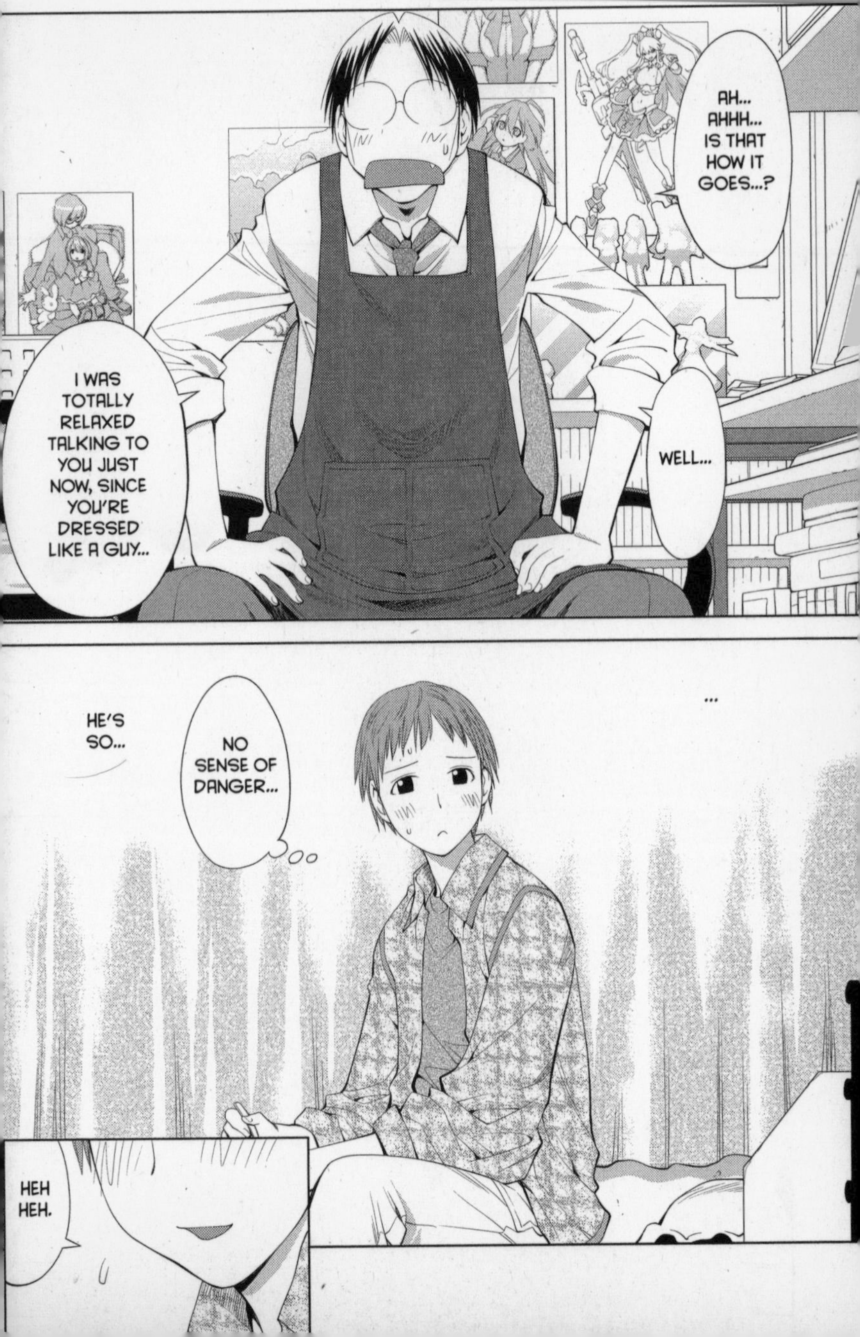
AH... AHHH... IS THAT HOW IT GOES...?
WELL...
I WAS TOTALLY RELAXED TALKING TO YOU JUST NOW, SINCE YOU'RE DRESSED LIKE A GUY...
...
NO SENSE OF DANGER...
HE'S SO...
HEH HEH.

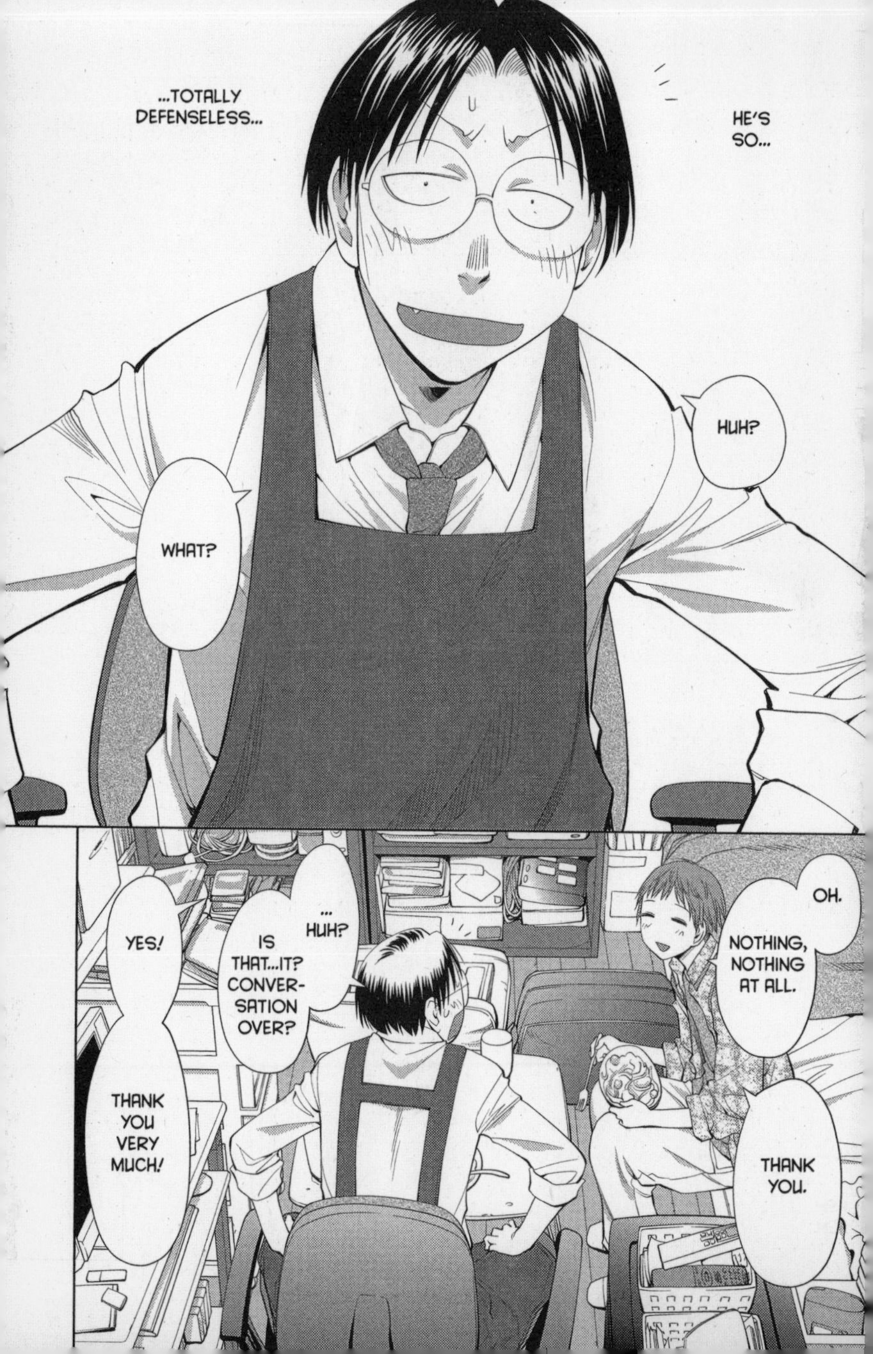
HE'S SO...
...TOTALLY DEFENSELESS...
HUH?
WHAT?
OH.
NOTHING, NOTHING AT ALL.
... HUH?
IS THAT...IT? CONVER-SATION OVER?
YES!
THANK YOU.
THANK YOU VERY MUCH!

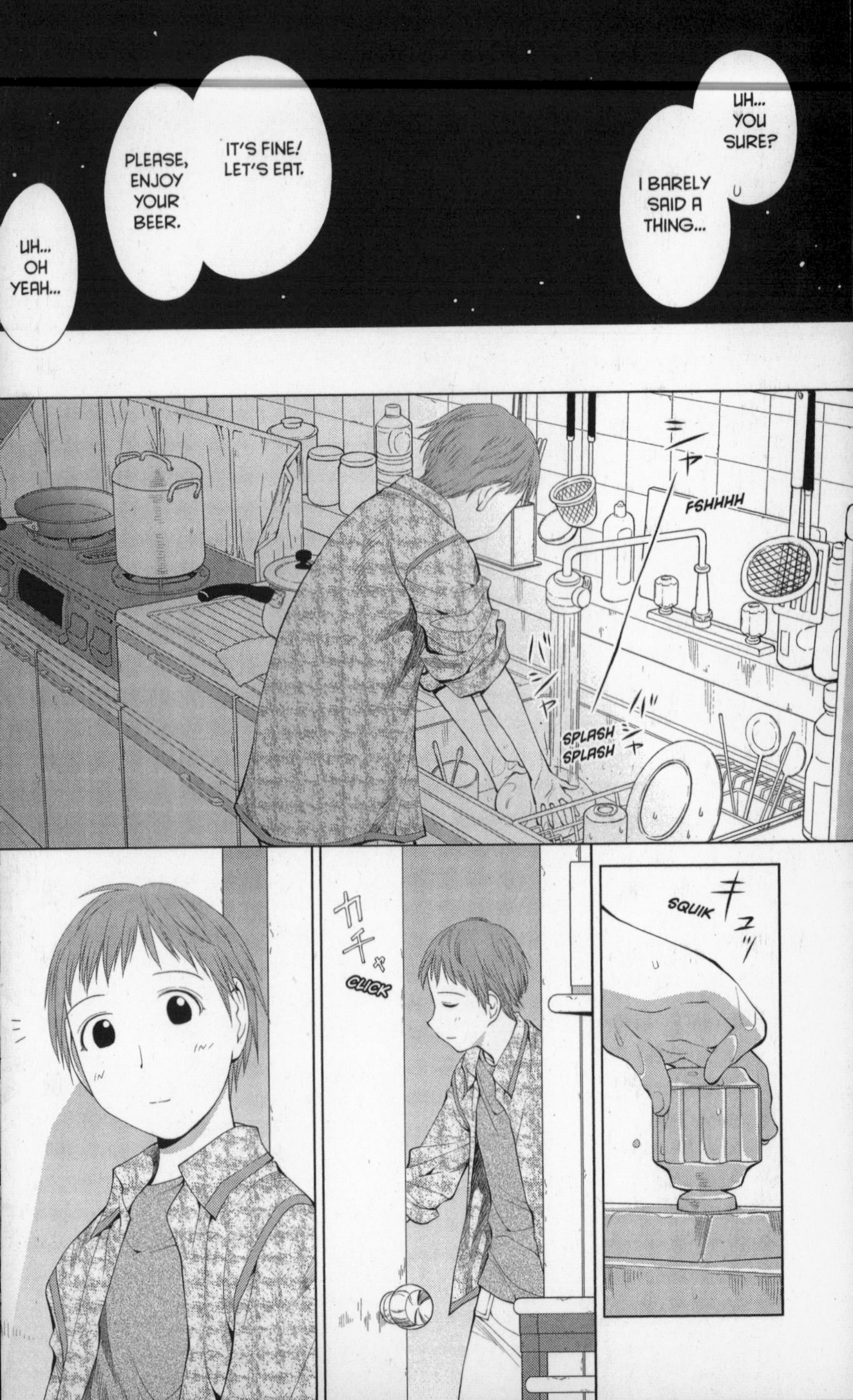
UH... YOU SURE?
I BARELY SAID A THING...
IT'S FINE! LET'S EAT.
PLEASE, ENJOY YOUR BEER.
UH... OH YEAH...
FSHHHH
SPLASH SPLASH
SQUIK
CLICK

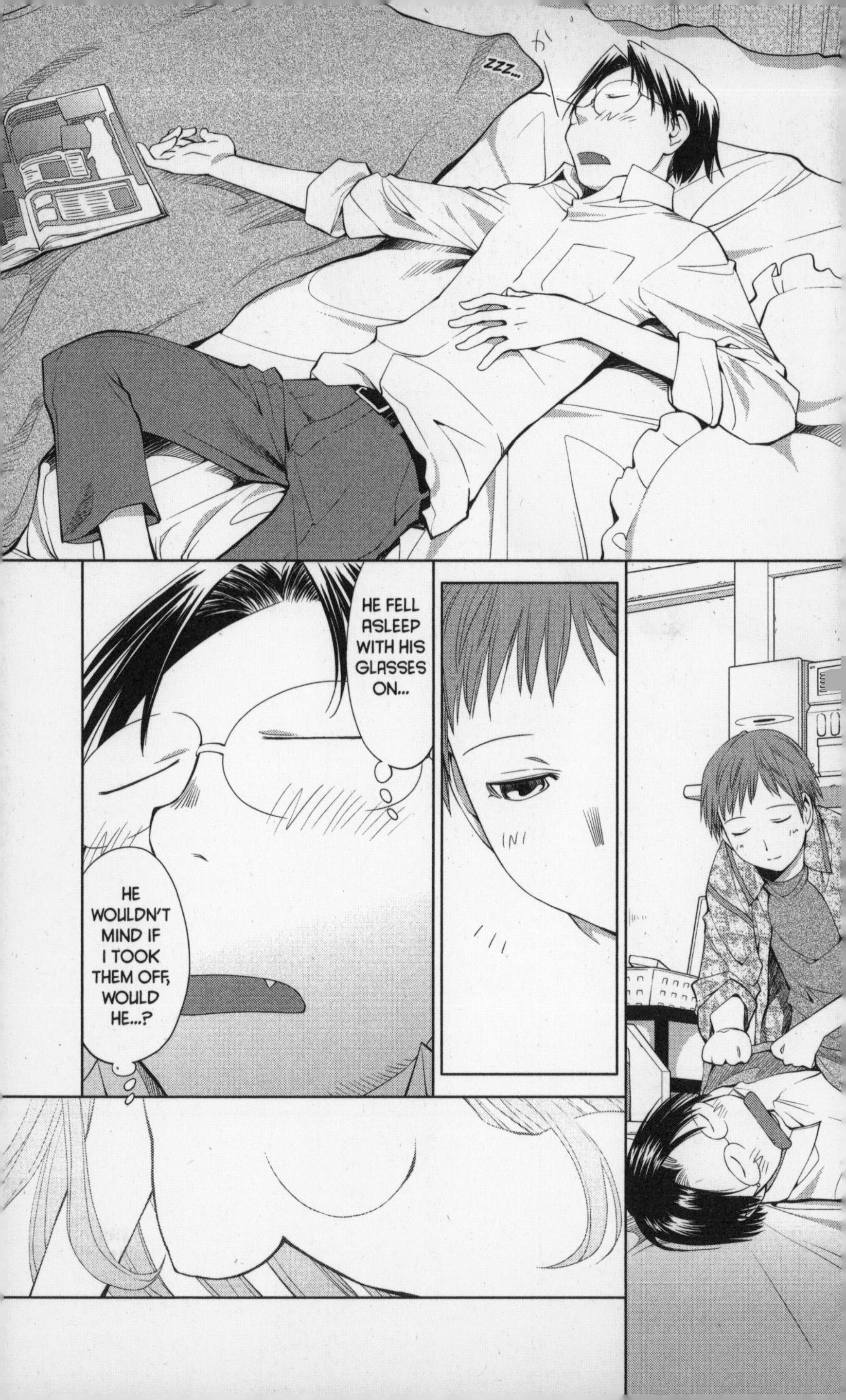
ZZZ...
HE FELL ASLEEP WITH HIS GLASSES ON...
HE WOULDN'T MIND IF I TOOK THEM OFF, WOULD HE...?

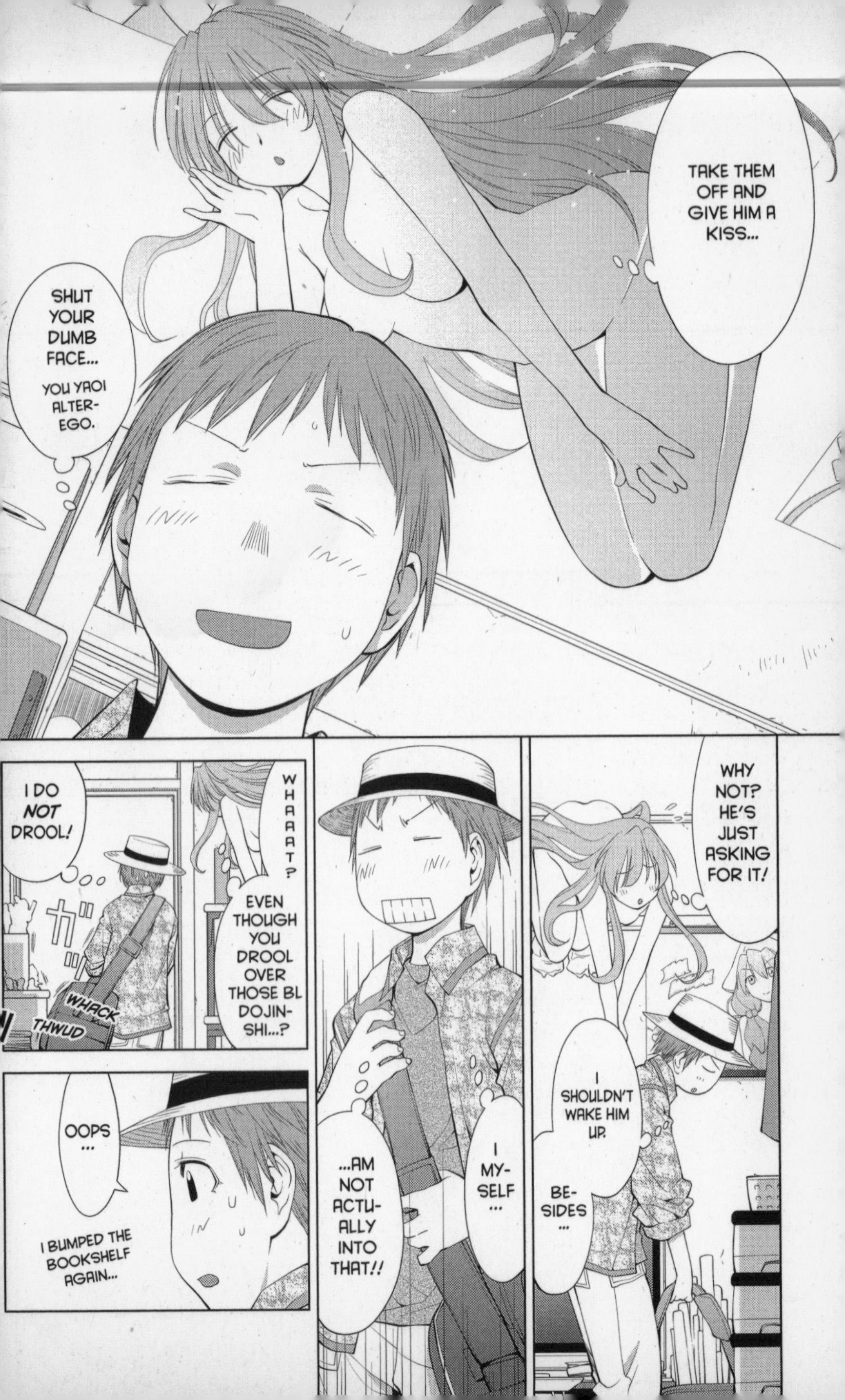
TAKE THEM OFF AND GIVE HIM A KISS...
SHUT YOUR DUMB FACE...
YOU YAOI ALTER-EGO.
WHY NOT? HE'S JUST ASKING FOR IT!
I SHOULDN'T WAKE HIM UP.
BE-SIDES...
I MY-SELF...
...AM NOT ACTU-ALLY INTO THAT!!
WHAAAAT?
EVEN THOUGH YOU DROOL OVER THOSE BL DOJIN-SHI...?
I DO *NOT* DROOL!
ガ
WHACK
THWUD
OOPS...
I BUMPED THE BOOKSHELF AGAIN...

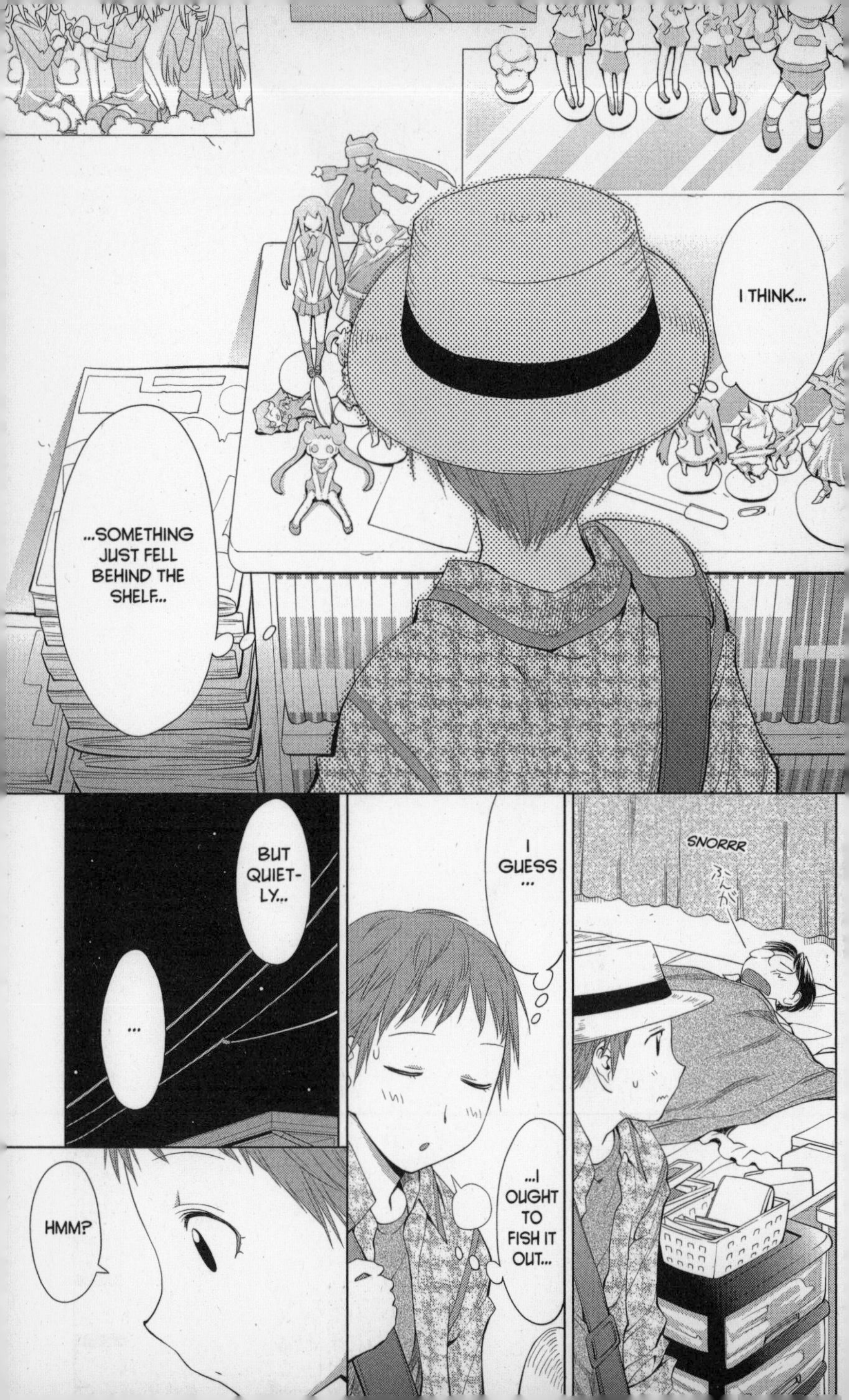
I THINK...
...SOMETHING JUST FELL BEHIND THE SHELF...
SNORRR
ふんが
I GUESS...
...I OUGHT TO FISH IT OUT...
BUT QUIET-LY...
...
HMM?

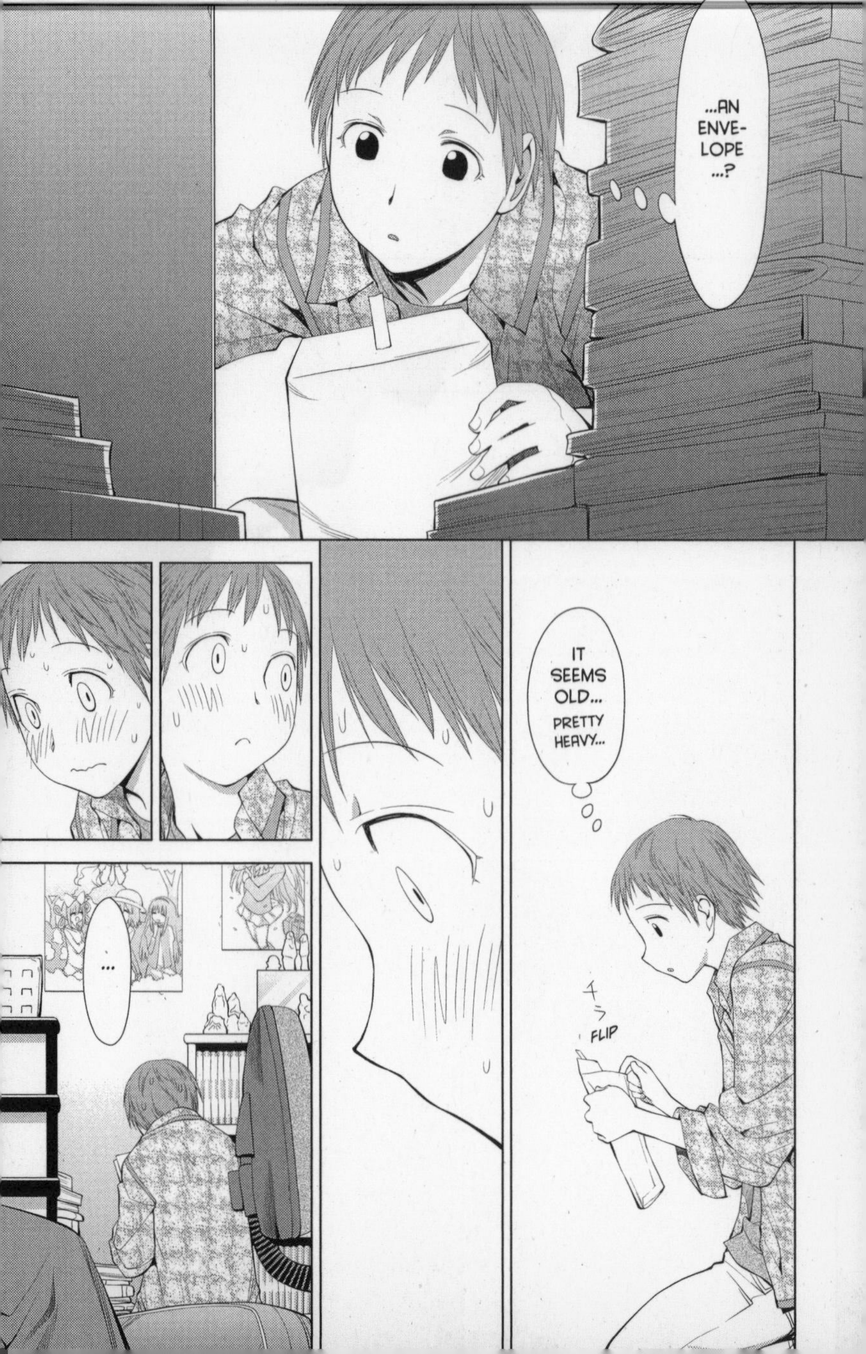
...AN ENVE-LOPE ...?
IT SEEMS OLD... PRETTY HEAVY...
チラ
FLIP
...

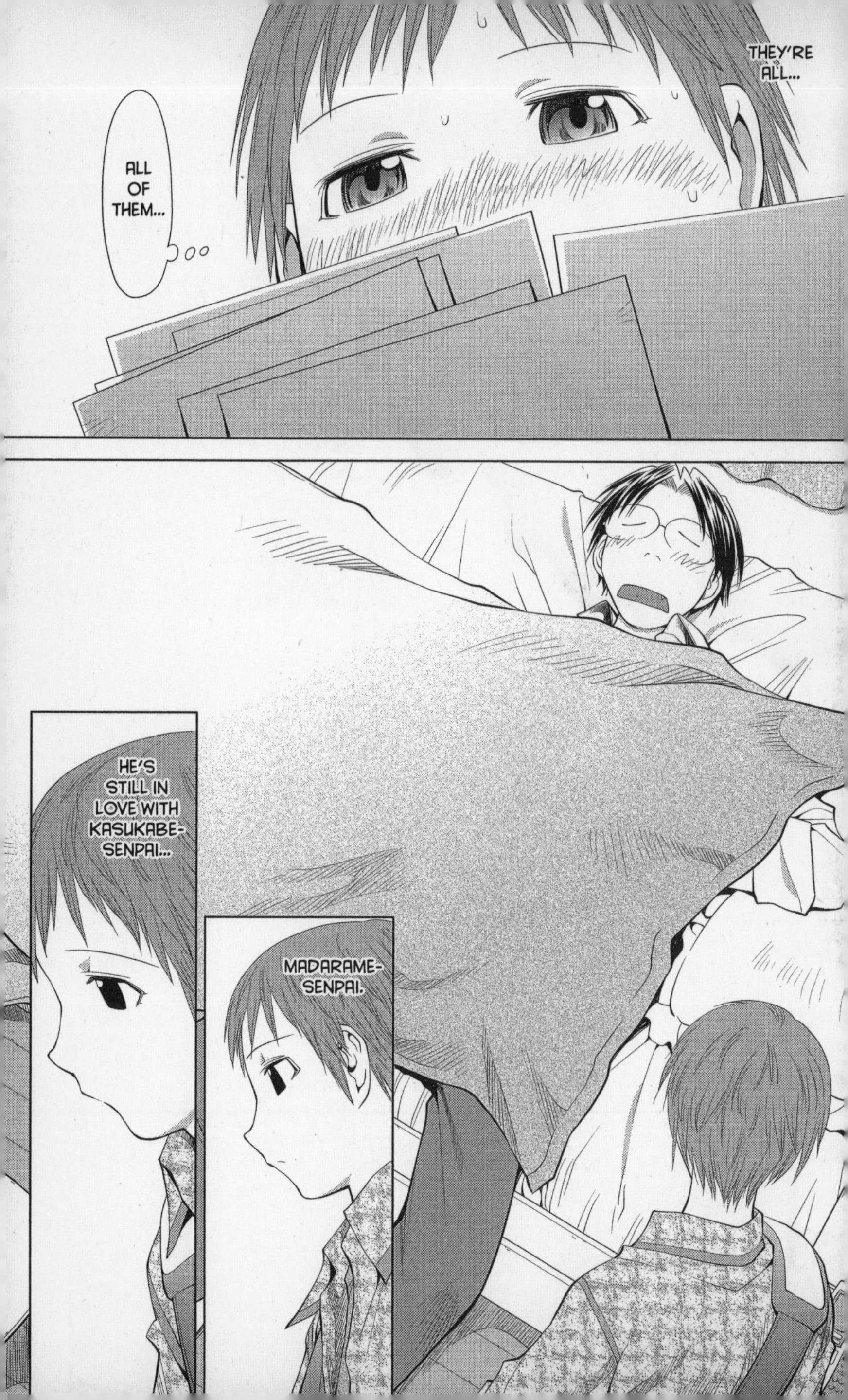
THEY'RE ALL...
ALL OF THEM...
MADARAME-SENPAI.
HE'S STILL IN LOVE WITH KASUKABE-SENPAI...

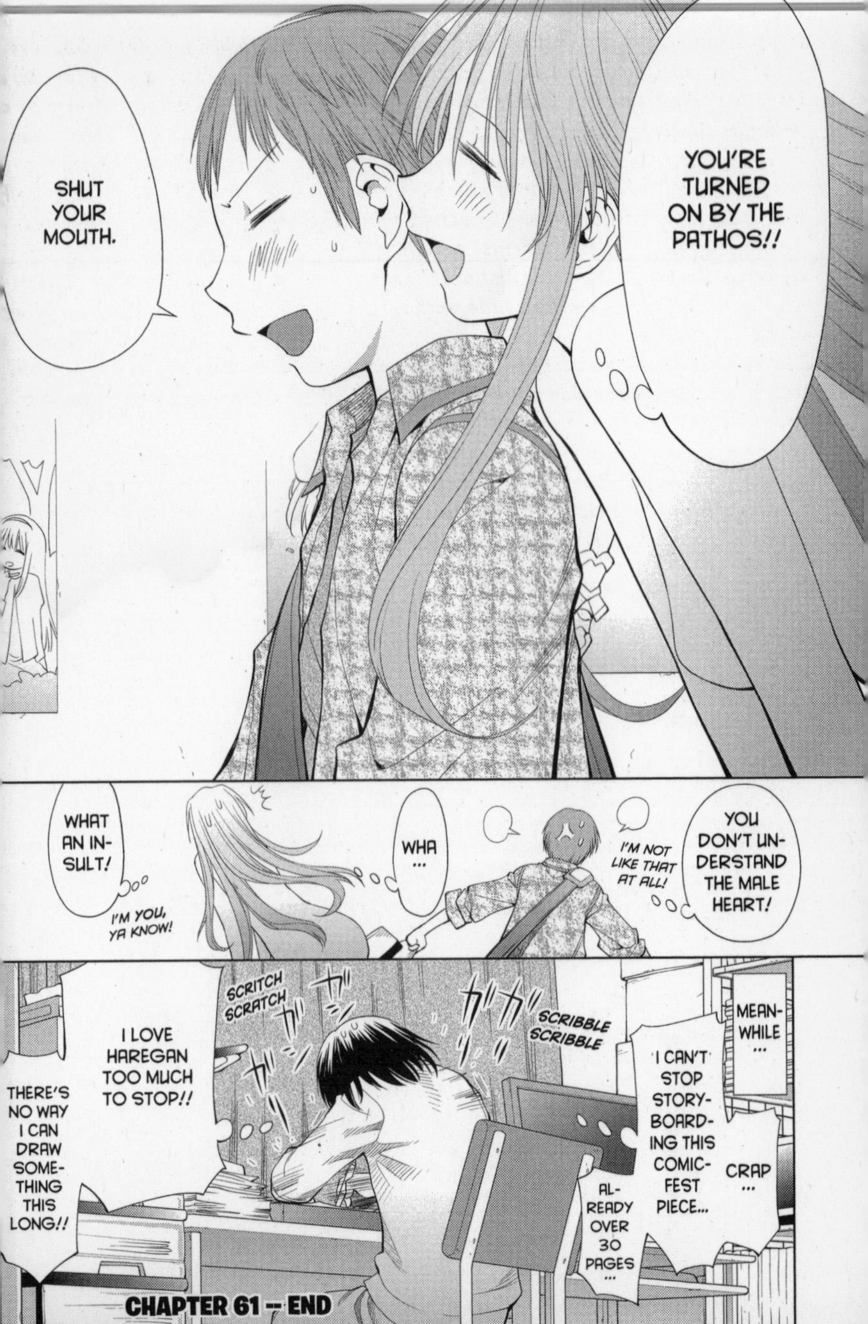
YOU'RE TURNED ON BY THE PATHOS!!
SHUT YOUR MOUTH.
YOU DON'T UNDERSTAND THE MALE HEART!
I'M NOT LIKE THAT AT ALL!
WHA...
WHAT AN INSULT!
I'M YOU, YA KNOW!
MEANWHILE...
CRAP...
I CAN'T STOP STORYBOARDING THIS COMIC-FEST PIECE...
ALREADY OVER 30 PAGES...
SCRIBBLE SCRIBBLE
SCRITCH SCRATCH
I LOVE HAREGAN TOO MUCH TO STOP!!
THERE'S NO WAY I CAN DRAW SOMETHING THIS LONG!!
CHAPTER 61 -- END

I spoke earlier about how the Sanada series needs to be given an anime or manga adaptation, so today I will be talking instead about a famous novel that harbors great potential for people with our "tastes." Tsuneo Tominaga's *Imataro Sugata*, a legendary judo novel. It's been turned into a live action film and even drawn by a veteran manga artist, but if you were to depict it in a particular way, it could be a very interesting story from our perspective! It's set in the Meiji era, featuring the great master and creator of judo! The protagonist is his brilliant student, both simple at heart but somehow menacing! The four Kodankan masters, connected by their bonds as fellow students! And the mighty foes that challenge our hero, one after the other! All these distinct characters, horsing around in their student clothes, then putting on their judo uniforms for the ritual slapping and grappling of flesh... ♡

Personally, the romance between master and student is all I need to begin with, but the protagonist is also popular with the ladies. There are two main heroines that both fall in love with him. The daughter of the noble family, and the humble town girl. And yet, cliché as it is, they both look identical at a glance. Honestly, Tominaga-sensei's novels are all about the characters. Also, the lady ninjas that show up in his *Chronicles of the Sanada War* are worth squee-ing over! Turn it into an anime! Turn it into a manga!!

Rika Yoshitake, signing off

KENJIRO HATO

Business Major, Freshman
Born in Niigata

FAVORITE WORKS
"Dwarara!!"
"Eviangelion Reboot"
"Hetalila"
"Winter Wars"
"Fuyume's Book of Friends"
"Sweets Basket"
"Love and Kyuso"
"Metro Dog"
"Suzuki-san and
Rokuhara-kun" series
"Fate/stop"
"When They Sob"

SHOWER

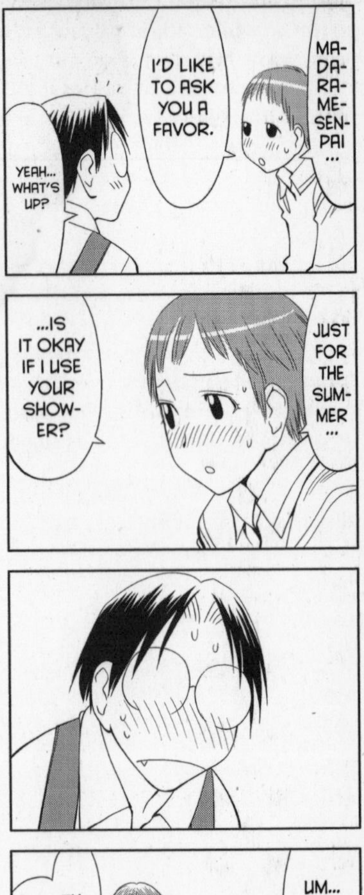
MADARAME-SENPAI...
I'D LIKE TO ASK YOU A FAVOR.
YEAH... WHAT'S UP?
JUST FOR THE SUMMER...
...IS IT OKAY IF I USE YOUR SHOWER?
UM... YEAH, I DON'T MIND.
TH...
THANK YOU SO MUCH!

THE YAOI-CHAN BEHIND ME

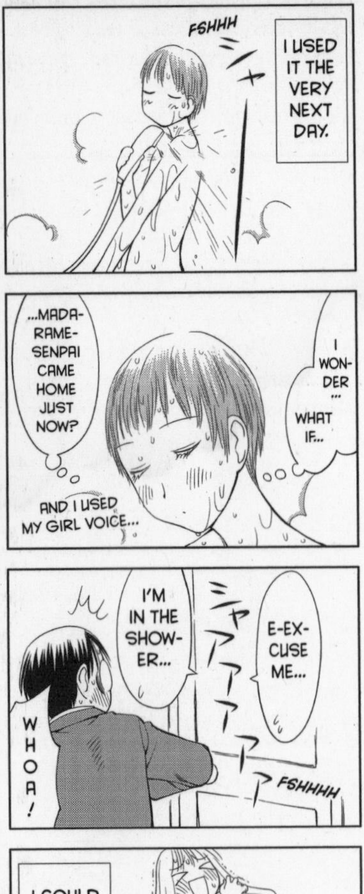
I USED IT THE VERY NEXT DAY.
FSHHH
I WONDER... WHAT IF...
...MADARAME-SENPAI CAME HOME JUST NOW?
AND I USED MY GIRL VOICE...
E-EXCUSE ME...
I'M IN THE SHOWER...
WHOA!
FSHHHH
I COULD FEEL HER DYING OF MOE RIGHT AROUND THE CEILING.

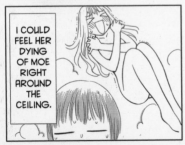

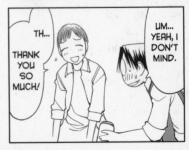

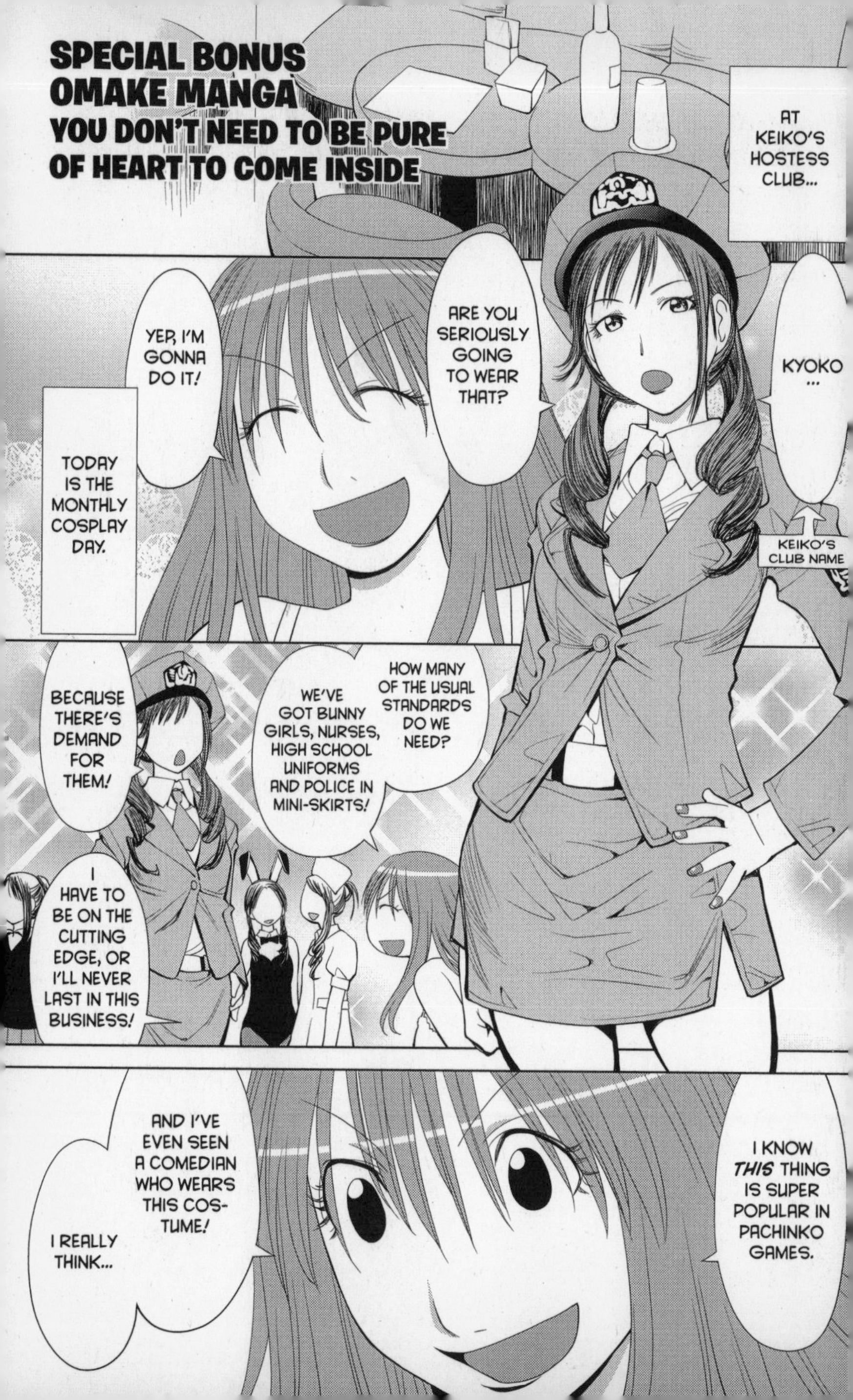
SPECIAL BONUS OMAKE MANGA
YOU DON'T NEED TO BE PURE OF HEART TO COME INSIDE
AT KEIKO'S HOSTESS CLUB...
KYOKO...
KEIKO'S CLUB NAME
ARE YOU SERIOUSLY GOING TO WEAR THAT?
YEP, I'M GONNA DO IT!
TODAY IS THE MONTHLY COSPLAY DAY.
HOW MANY OF THE USUAL STANDARDS DO WE NEED?
WE'VE GOT BUNNY GIRLS, NURSES, HIGH SCHOOL UNIFORMS AND POLICE IN MINI-SKIRTS!
BECAUSE THERE'S DEMAND FOR THEM!
I HAVE TO BE ON THE CUTTING EDGE, OR I'LL NEVER LAST IN THIS BUSINESS!
I KNOW *THIS* THING IS SUPER POPULAR IN PACHINKO GAMES.
AND I'VE EVEN SEEN A COMEDIAN WHO WEARS THIS COS-TUME!
I REALLY THINK...

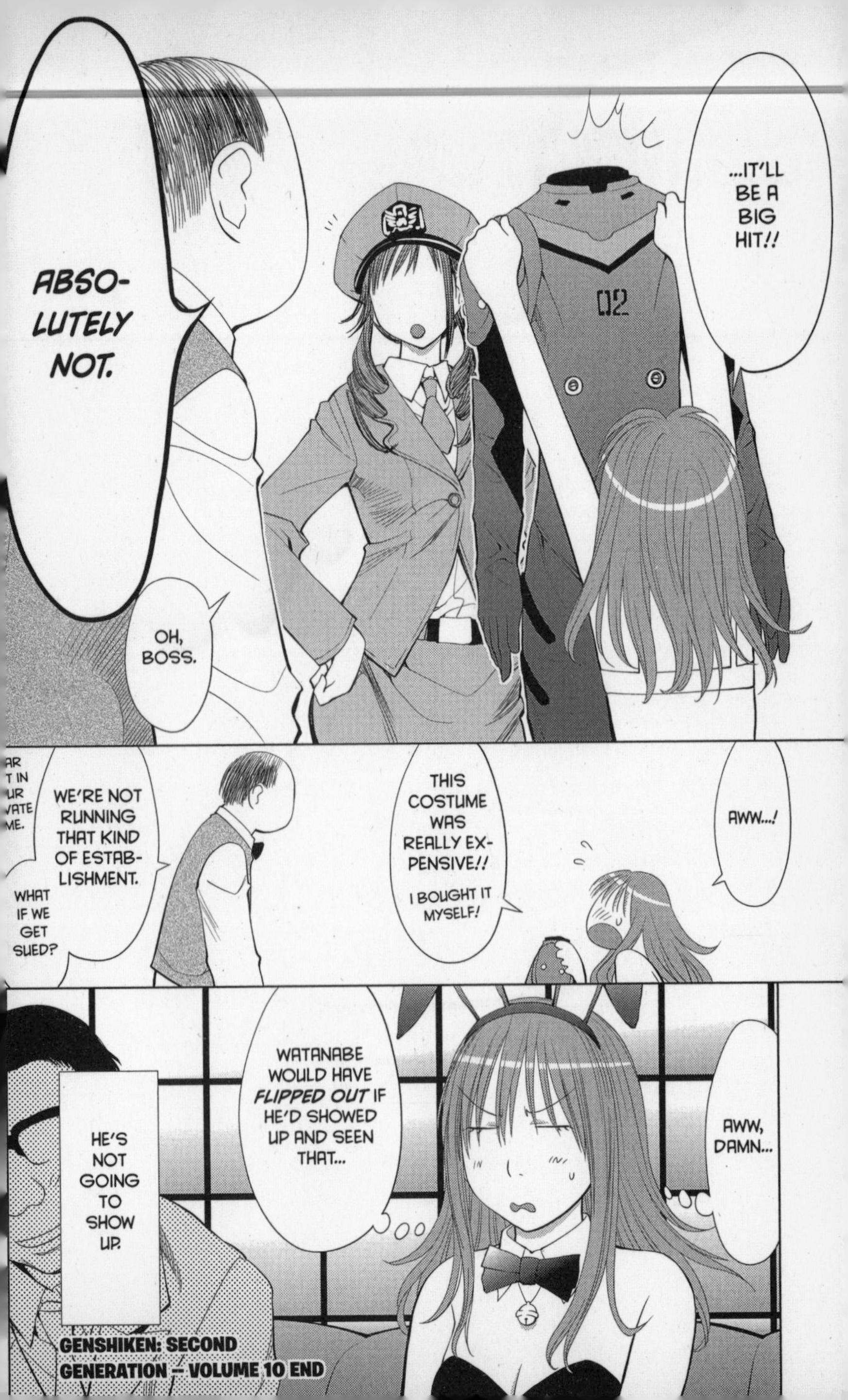
...IT'LL BE A BIG HIT!!
OH, BOSS.
ABSOLUTELY NOT.
AWW...!
THIS COSTUME WAS REALLY EXPENSIVE!!
I BOUGHT IT MYSELF!
WE'RE NOT RUNNING THAT KIND OF ESTABLISHMENT.
WHAT IF WE GET SUED?
AWW, DAMN...
WATANABE WOULD HAVE *FLIPPED OUT* IF HE'D SHOWED UP AND SEEN THAT...
HE'S NOT GOING TO SHOW UP.
GENSHIKEN: SECOND GENERATION -- VOLUME 10 END

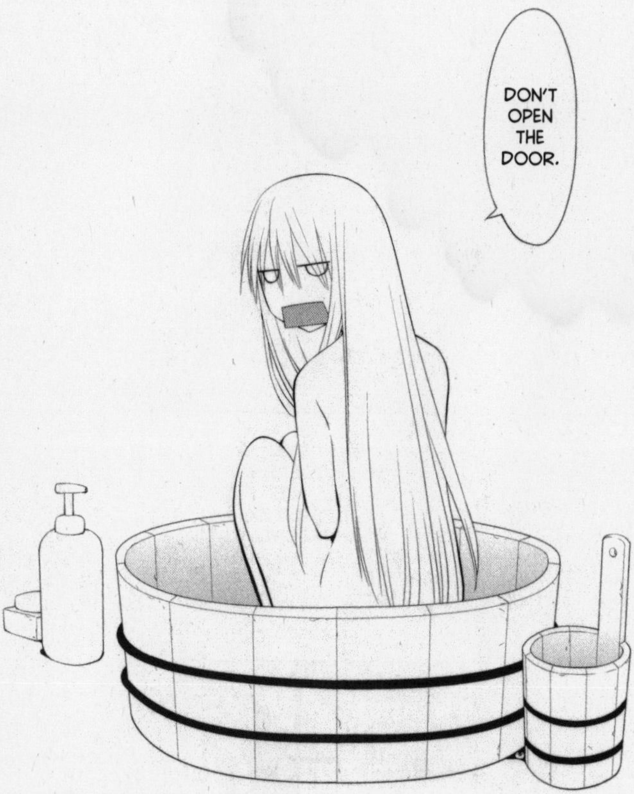
DON'T OPEN THE DOOR.

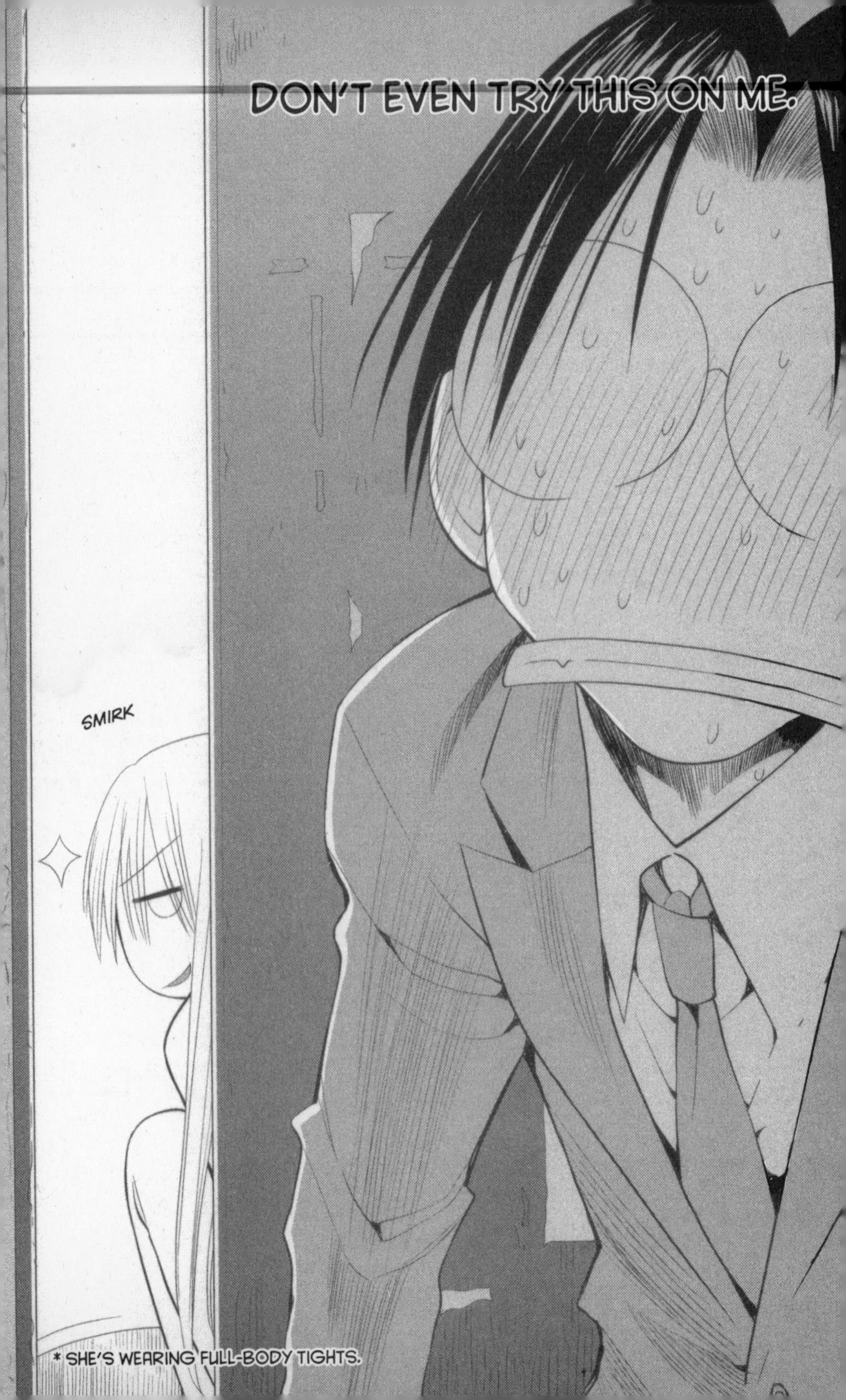
DON'T EVEN TRY THIS ON ME.
SMIRK
* SHE'S WEARING FULL-BODY TIGHTS.

Translation Notes

Japanese is a tricky language for most Westerners, and translation is often more art than science. For your edification and reading pleasure, here are notes on some of the places where we could have gone in a different direction with our translation of the work, or where a Japanese cultural reference is used.

Kinnikuman & Terryman, page 5

Sue's costume and her lines come from the classic 70s-80s manga and anime series from Shonen Jump, *Kinnikuman.* The series was briefly recognized in America in the 1980s when a line of toys were brought over under the name M.U.S.C.L.E. The series revolves around wrestling battles between Kinnikuman ("Muscle Man") and various Chojin (or "super men"), many based around the images of certain countries. In this scene, Sue is dressed as Terryman, Kinnikuman's American rival and friend (recognizable for the cowboy hat and hamburger). On page 6, Ohno is cosplaying as Kinnikuman himself, with his trademark "meat" character (niku) written on her forehead.

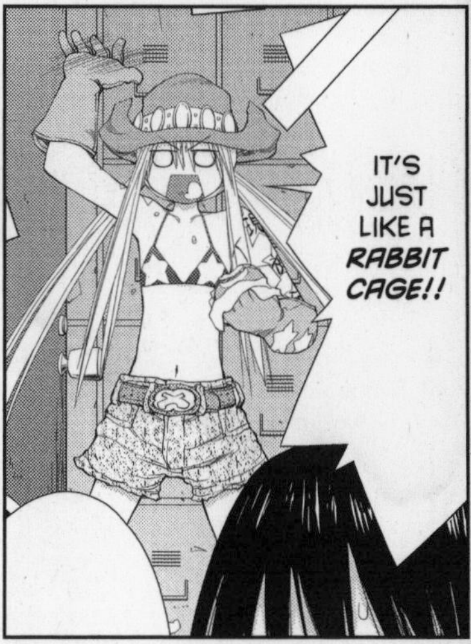
IT'S JUST LIKE A *RABBIT CAGE!!*

Dojinshi, page 9

Fan-made and distributed zines that can cover a wide variety of topics. Most are erotic in nature and feature a certain romantic pairing of characters from other anime, manga, novels or video games. *Dojinshi* are most often sold at fan events like the massive Comiket (Comic Market), a bi-annual convention held in Tokyo.

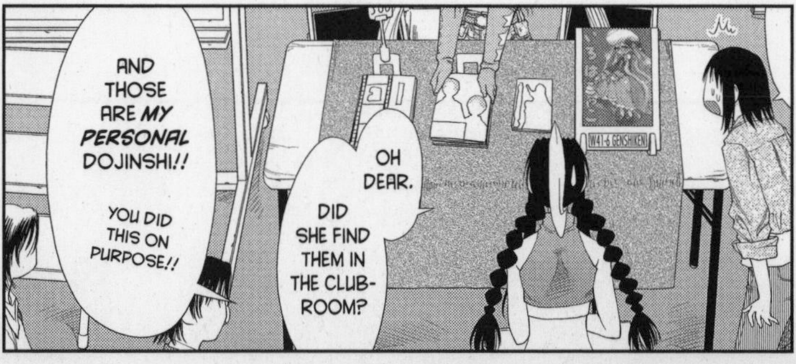
W41-6 GENSHIKEN
OH DEAR.
DID SHE FIND THEM IN THE CLUB-ROOM?
AND THOSE ARE *MY PERSONAL* DOJINSHI!!
YOU DID THIS ON PURPOSE!!

Ramen Angel Pretty Menma, page 13

A fictional series within the *Genshiken* universe. Like many series, it is described as starting from an adult computer game that subsequently spawns an anime series and other spinoffs. It actually received a real-life manga adaptation to go along with the second season of the *Genshiken* anime.

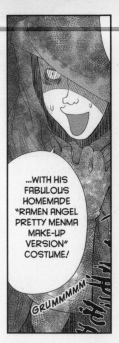

...WITH HIS FABULOUS HOMEMADE "RAMEN ANGEL PRETTY MENMA MAKE-UP VERSION" COSTUME!
GRUMMMMM

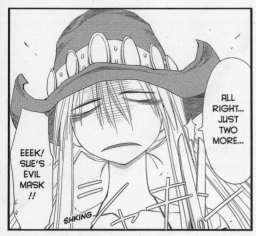

ALL RIGHT... JUST TWO MORE...
EEEK! SUE'S EVIL MASK !!
SHKING

Sue's evil mask, page 14

Another *Kinnikuman* reference, Sue is mimicking the expression of Asuraman, a wrestler with three faces and six arms, like the Buddhist *asura*. When Asuraman is driven into a rage, he switches to his "merciless mask," which signals a shift in personality to a much fiercer set of wrestling moves.

Sue's alchemy, page 15

A meta-reference of a quote from the heroine Hitagi of the *Bakemonogatari* anime series, which is itself a reference to the *Full Metal Alchemist* anime/manga. In FMA, attempts to alchemize the human body are described with a laundry list of minerals and ingredients, and the *Bakemonogatari* quote uses that same structure to describe the alchemical makeup of her insults, including "5 grams embarrassment and 97 kilograms of malice." Sue is quoting that one word for word.

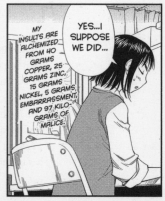

YES...I SUPPOSE WE DID...
MY INSULTS ARE ALCHEMIZED FROM 40 GRAMS COPPER, 25 GRAMS ZINC, 15 GRAMS NICKEL, 5 GRAMS EMBARRASSMENT, AND 97 KILO-GRAMS OF MALICE.

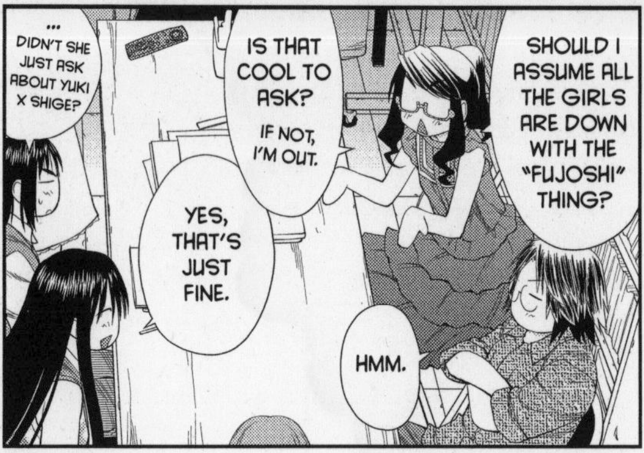
SHOULD I ASSUME ALL THE GIRLS ARE DOWN WITH THE "FUJOSHI" THING?
IS THAT COOL TO ASK?
IF NOT, I'M OUT.
... DIDN'T SHE JUST ASK ABOUT YUKI X SHIGE?
HMM.
YES, THAT'S JUST FINE.

Fujoshi, page 18

A term for female otaku with an interest in the BL (boys' love) or *yaoi* subculture, which features gay male romance, often between anime/ manga characters who are not openly gay. Within BL, characters are assigned either top (*seme*) or bottom (*uke*) roles based on their personalities, and character "pairings" or "couplings" are written in the style of "top x bottom."

The term *fujoshi* means "rotten lady," a reference to the supposedly "rotten" thoughts a fujoshi entertains. In the original Japanese, Yoshitake actually asks if the girls have the character for *fu* (rotten) written on their foreheads, which is a common joke reference to Kinnikuman's "meat" on the forehead. Fujoshi are sometimes depicted with *fu* written on their foreheads when they are imagining gay relationships between anime characters. The spinoff term *fudanshi* replaces the "female" character with "male," and refers to male fans of the same culture.

"I tuttered," page 27

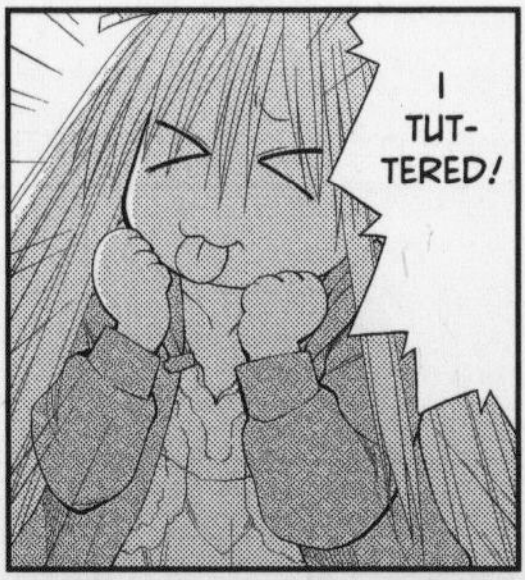
I TUT-TERED!

The entire interplay between Sue and Madarame in this scene comes from the *Bakemonogatari* anime, between protagonist Araragi (called "Rarararagi-san") and Mayoi Hachikuji, the spirit of a fifth-grade girl who was killed in a traffic accident. She often teases Araragi as he attempts to help her resolve her unfinished business.

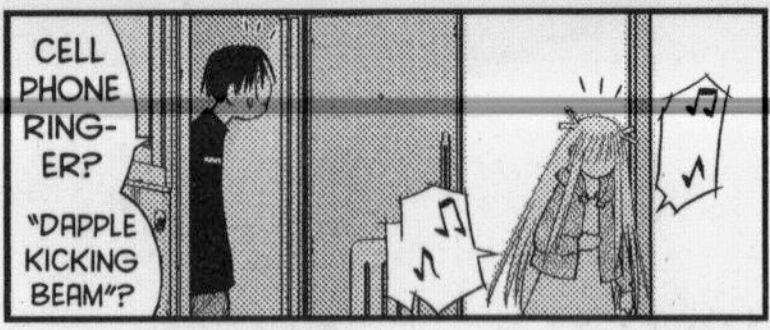
CELL PHONE RINGER-ER?
"DAPPLE KICKING BEAM"?

Dapple Kicking Beam, page 27

A parody of "Apple Picking Beam," a theme song from *Zan: Sayonara, Zetsubou-Sensei,* the third season of the *Sayonara, Zetsubou-Sensei* anime. The series is based on a popular satirical comedy manga of the same name, which features an extremely depressed and negative school teacher and his class full of students that represent various extreme archetypes and concepts. The manga is available in English from Kodansha Comics USA.

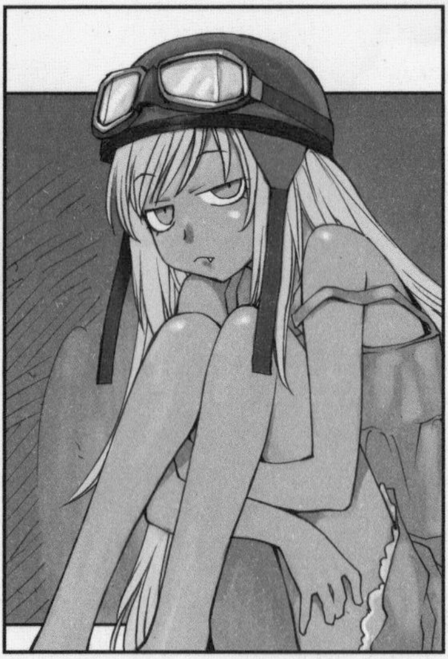

Shinobu, page 37

Sue's cosplay here is of Shinobu Oshino from *Bakemonogatari,* who is introduced sitting against a wall wearing an aviator cap. Shinobu takes the form of an eight-year-old girl, but is actually an ancient vampire. She isn't wearing any underwear beneath her dress, but has a band-aid strategically placed vertically over her crotch.

Across the Street, The Promised Place, page 38

A reference to Makoto Shinkai's anime feature film, *The Place Promised in Our Early Days,* which was originally titled *Beyond the Clouds, The Promised Place* in Japanese.

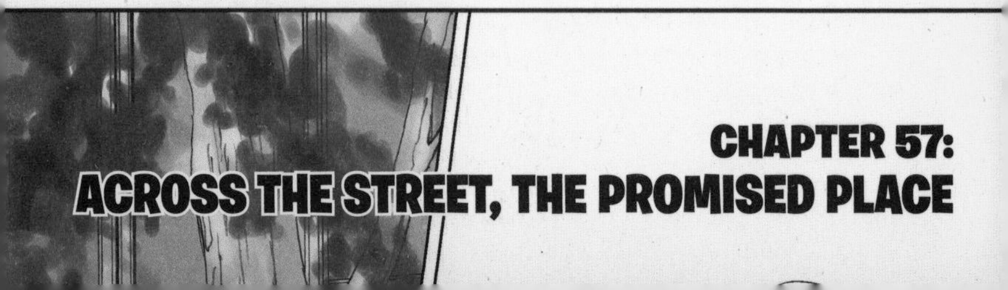
CHAPTER 57:
ACROSS THE STREET, THE PROMISED PLACE

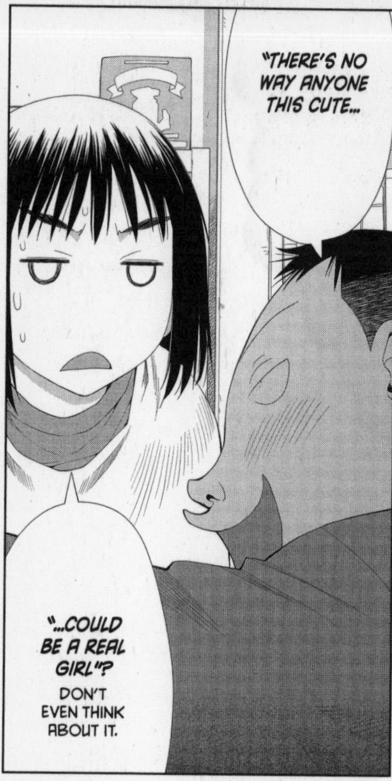
"THERE'S NO WAY ANYONE THIS CUTE...
"...COULD BE A REAL GIRL"? DON'T EVEN THINK ABOUT IT.

"There's no way anyone this cute could be a real girl," page 62

A popular Internet meme quote often applied to male characters (or of unspecified gender) with androgynous features. It has been quoted at times in other "self-aware" manga like Genshiken.

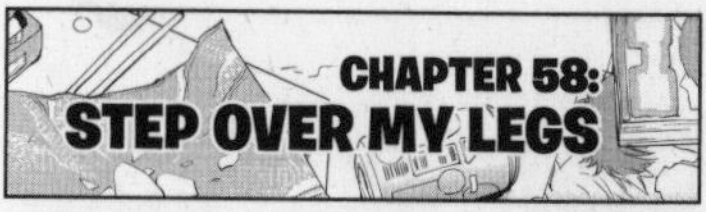
CHAPTER 58:
STEP OVER MY LEGS

Step Over My Legs, page 70

The title of this chapter is a parody of "Step Over My Dead Body" (*Ore no Shikabane wo Koete Yuke*) a 1999 Playstation RPG with a medieval Japanese setting.

"A neverending Ogiue," page 73

A parody of a military speech given in Volume 4 of the *Hellsing* manga by Kouta Hirano. In it, The Major (chief antagonist of the series) declares his intentions to start a wholehearted and neverending war.

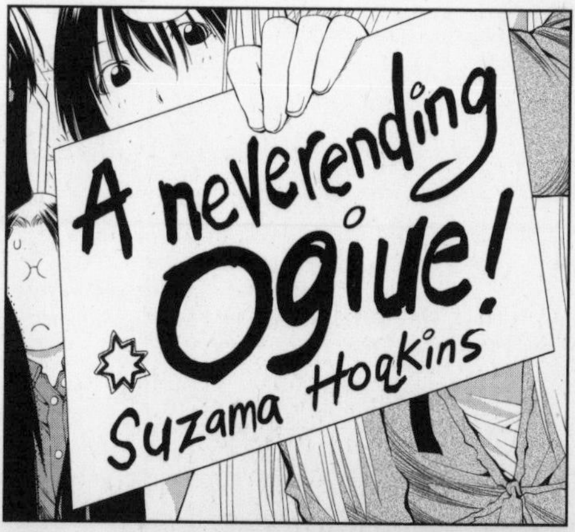
A neverending Ogiue!
Suzama Hoqkins

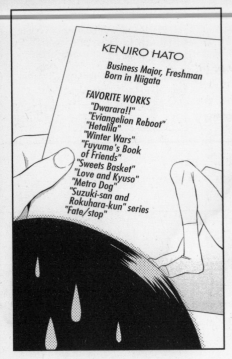

KENJIRO HATO

Business Major, Freshman
Born in Niigata

FAVORITE WORKS
"Dwarara!!"
"Eviangelion Reboot"
"Hetalila"
"Winter Wars"
"Fuyume's Book
of Friends"
"Sweets Basket"
"Love and Kyuso"
"Metro Dog"
"Suzuki-san and
Rokuhara-kun" series
"Fate/stop"

Hato's profile, page 96

All of the titles listed here are
parodies of existing anime/manga,
though some are very obscure.
"Dwarara!!" = *Durarara!!*
"Eviangelion Reboot" = *Reboot of
Evangelion*
"Hetalila" = *Hetalia*
"Winter Wars" = *Summer Wars*
"Fuyume's Book of Friends" =
Natsume's Book of Friends
"Sweets Basket" = *Fruits Basket*
"Fate/stop" = *Fate/stay*
"When They Sob" = *When They Cry*

Ogiue's profile, page 97

"Haregan" is a parody of
"Hagaren," the abbreviation of
Hagane no Renkinjutsushi,
known in English as *Full Metal
Alchemist.* "Kuji-Un" is, of
course, the abbreviation of
Genshiken's in-universe hit,
Kujibiki Unbalance. "Zennichi no
Kyojin" is a parody of *Shingeki no
Kyojin*, a dark fantasy manga set
in a world in which mankind must
fight off the assault of terrifying
man-eating giants.

CHIKA OGIUE

(NARUYUKI OGINO)

LIBERAL ARTS, JUNIOR
BORN IN YAMAGATA
MARCH 28TH, TYPE A

FAVORITE WORKS
"HAREGAN"
"KUJI-UN"
"ZENNICHI NO
KYOJIN"

Smooth-Smooth Fruit, page 98

A reference to the *One Piece* manga/ anime series, in which "Devil Fruit" give their eaters special powers.

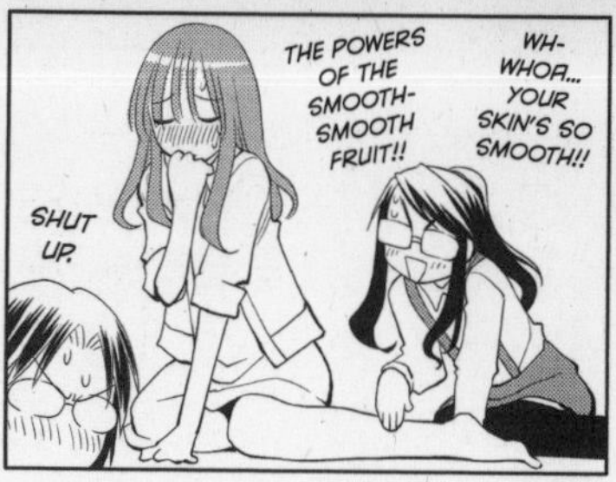
WH-WHOA... YOUR SKIN'S SO SMOOTH!!
THE POWERS OF THE SMOOTH-SMOOTH FRUIT!!
SHUT UP.

"I'm going to run to the store...", page 113

A quote from Tsukihi Araragi, the younger sister of Koyomi Araragi, protagonist of *Bakemonogatari*.

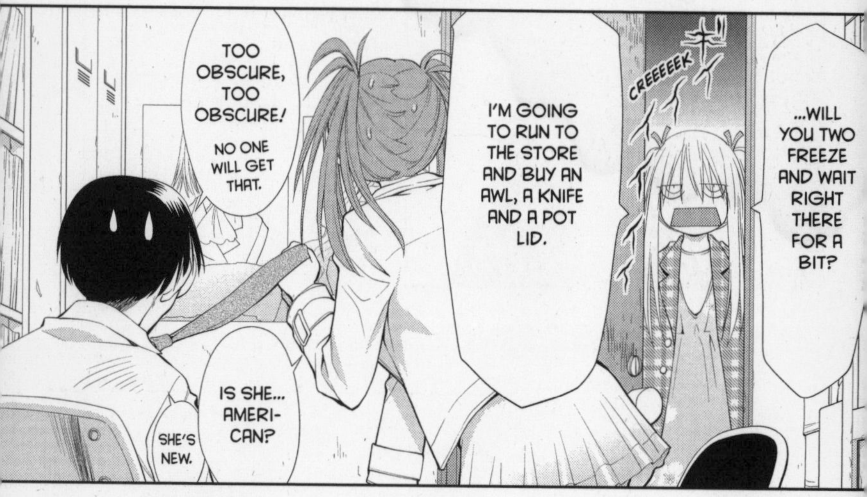
...WILL YOU TWO FREEZE AND WAIT RIGHT THERE FOR A BIT?
CREEEEEK
I'M GOING TO RUN TO THE STORE AND BUY AN AWL, A KNIFE AND A POT LID.
TOO OBSCURE, TOO OBSCURE!
NO ONE WILL GET THAT.
IS SHE... AMERI-CAN?
SHE'S NEW.

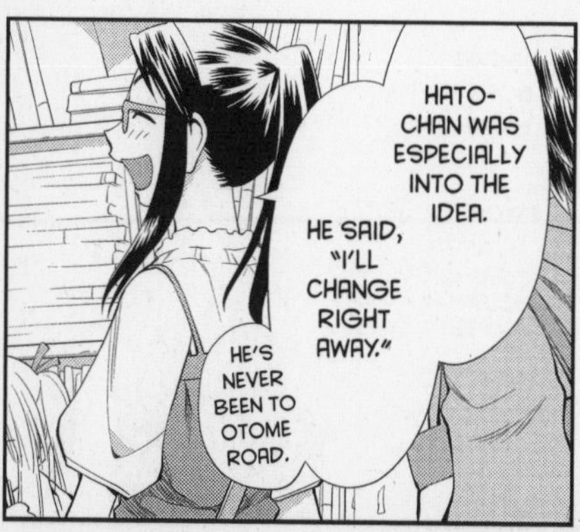
HATO-CHAN WAS ESPECIALLY INTO THE IDEA.
HE SAID, "I'LL CHANGE RIGHT AWAY."
HE'S NEVER BEEN TO OTOME ROAD.

Otome Road, page 117

An area in Ikebukuro populated with stores that specialize in yaoi/ BL merchandise. It's a landmark for fujoshi in the same way that Akihabara is for male-oriented otaku culture and tech geeks.

Yajima's profile, page 155

Yajima's profile is full of parodies of *Shonen Jump* hit series.

"Pakuman" = *Bakuman.*

"Kintama" = *Gintama*

"Ten Piece" = *One Piece*

"Menma" = *Naruto*

"Bear: Rise of the Monster Clan" = *Nura: Rise of the Yokai Clan*

MIREI YAJIMA
LIBERAL ARTS, FRESHMAN
BORN IN TOCHIGI
NOVEMBER 7TH, TYPE A
FAVORITE WORKS
"PAKUMAN"
"KINTAMA"
"TEN PIECE"
"MENMA"
"BUGBEAR: RISE OF THE MONSTER CLAN"

ALSO, THOSE FRESHMEN ARE MORE HELP THAN I'D HAVE THOUGHT.
YES, YES, YOU'RE A TSUNDERE.

Tsundere, page 159

A character archetype in otaku culture. *Tsundere* characters are identified by an initial nature that is off-putting or combative, but over time reveals itself or evolves into warmth and affection. The term is a combination of the words *tsuntsun* (pointed or hostile) and *deredere* (loving and sappy). Yabusaki's hostility and aggression masking her secret desire to be friends and creative partners with Ogiue is an example of *tsundere* behavior.

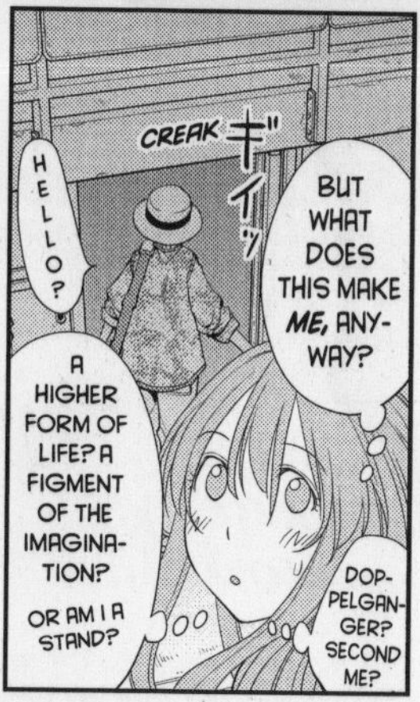
CREAK
ギイッ
BUT WHAT DOES THIS MAKE *ME*, ANYWAY?
HELLO?
DOPPELGANGER? SECOND ME?
A HIGHER FORM OF LIFE? A FIGMENT OF THE IMAGINATION?
OR AM I A STAND?

Stand, page 163

The primary form of power in the long-running *Jojo's Bizarre Adventure* series. Stands are supernatural powers that various characters in the series can wield, derived from various means such as genetics, willpower or training.

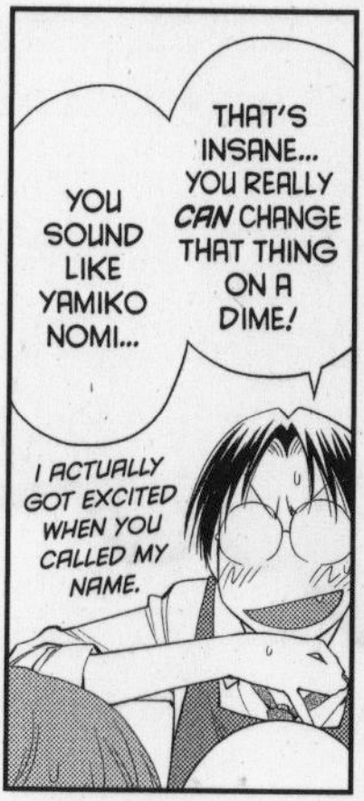
THAT'S INSANE... YOU REALLY *CAN* CHANGE THAT THING ON A DIME!
YOU SOUND LIKE YAMIKO NOMI...
I ACTUALLY GOT EXCITED WHEN YOU CALLED MY NAME.

Yamiko Nomi, page 173

A parody of famous voice actress Mamiko Noto, who is renowned for her soft, nasal voice and wide range. She is most famous for her roles in anime like *Sgt. Frog, Monster, Negima,* and *Clannad.*

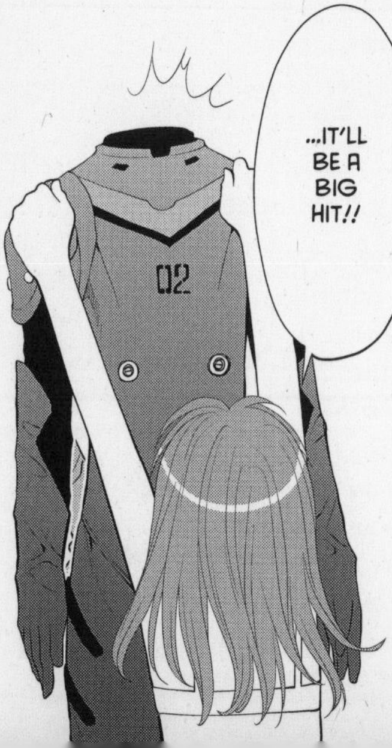
...IT'LL BE A BIG HIT!!

Keiko's costume, page 190

Keiko's attempted cosplay is Asuka's plug suit from *Neon Genesis Evangelion.* She recognizes it from its many pachinko tie-ins, which is a pinball-like game that is a Japanese form of gambling similar to a slot machine.

MARDOCK
マルドゥック・スクランブル
SCRAMBLE

Created by
Tow Ubukata

Manga by
Yoshitoki Oima

"I'd rather be dead."

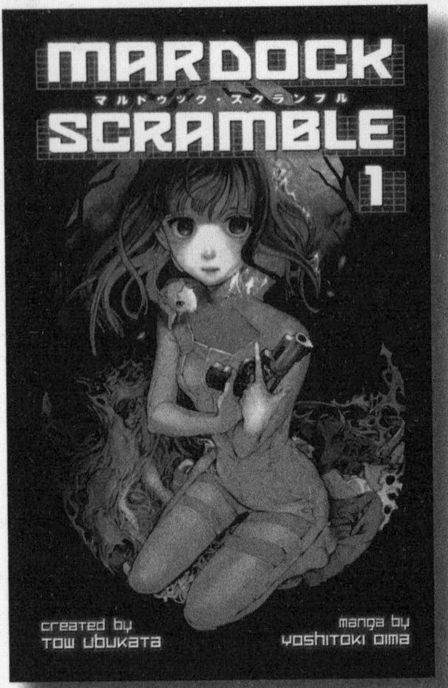
MARDOCK
マルドゥック・スクランブル
SCRAMBLE
1
created by
TOW UBUKATA
manga by
YOSHITOKI OIMA

Rune Balot was a lost girl with nothing to live for. A man named Shell took her in and cared for her...until he tried to murder her. Standing at the precipice of death Rune is saved by Dr. Easter, a private investigator, who uses an experimental procedure known as "Mardock Scramble 09." The procedure grants Balot extraordinary abilities. Now, Rune must decide whether to use her new powers to help Dr. Easter bring Shell to justice, or if she even has the will to keep living a life that's been broken so badly.

Ages: 16+

KC
KODANSHA COMICS

VISIT KODANSHACOMICS.COM TO:
- View release date calendars for upcoming volumes
- Find out the latest about upcoming Kodansha Comics series

Genshiken: Second Season volume 1 is a work of fiction. Names, characters, places, and incidents are the products of the author's imagination or are used fictitiously. Any resemblance to actual events, locales, or persons, living or dead, is entirely coincidental.

A Kodansha Comics Trade Paperback Original.

Published in the United States by Kodansha Comics, an imprint of Kodansha USA Publishing, LLC, New York.

Publication rights for this English edition arranged through Kodansha Ltd., Tokyo.

First published in Japan in 2011 by Kodansha Ltd., Tokyo, as *Genshiken Nidaime no ichi 10*.

ISBN 978-1-612622-37-8

Printed in the United States of America.

www.kodanshacomics.com

9 8 7 6 5 4 3 2 1

Translator: Stephen Paul
Lettering: Aaron Alexovich

TOMARE!
STOP

You're going the wrong way!

Manga is a completely different type of reading experience.

To start at the beginning,
Go to the end!

That's right! Authentic manga is read the traditional Japanese way—from right to left, exactly the opposite of how American books are read. It's easy to follow: Just go to the other end of the book and read each page—and each panel—from right side to left side, starting at the top right. Now you're experiencing manga as it was meant to be!